1991

third edition

SCIENCE AND BEHAVIOR

An Introduction to Methods of Research

JOHN M. NEALE
ROBERT M. LIEBERT
State University of New York at Stony Brook

PRENTICE-HALL, ENGLEWOOD CLIFFS, NEW JERSEY 07632

Library of Congress Cataloging-in-Publication Data
Neale, John M., (date)
Science and behavior.

(Prentice-Hall series in social learning theory)
Bibliography:
Includes indexes.
1. Social sciences—Research—Methodology.
2. Psychology—Research—Methodology. I. Liebert, Robert M., (date). II. Title. III. Series.
H62.N378 1986 300'.72 85-24445
ISBN 0-13-795139-6

Editorial/production supervision and interior design: **Barbara DeVries**
Cover design: **Lundgren Graphics, Ltd.**
Manufacturing buyer: **Barbara Kelly Kittle**

Prentice-Hall Series in Social Learning Theory
Albert Bandura, Editor

A Division of Simon & Schuster
Englewood Cliffs, New Jersey 07632

Printed in the United States of America

10 9 8 7 6 5

ISBN 0-13-795139-6 01

Prentice-Hall International (UK) Limited, *London*
Prentice-Hall of Australia Pty. Limited, *Sydney*
Prentice-Hall Canada Inc., *Toronto*
Prentice-Hall Hispanoamericana, S.A., *Mexico*
Prentice-Hall of India Private Limited, *New Delhi*
Prentice-Hall of Japan, Inc., *Tokyo*
Simon & Schuster Asia Pte. Ltd., *Singapore*
Editora Prentice-Hall do Brasil, Ltda., *Rio de Janeiro*

Contents

PREFACE x

chapter 1

OVERVIEW 1

THE BIRTH OF SOCIAL SCIENCE RESEARCH 2
THE NATURE OF SCIENCE 6
The Importance of Precision and Reliability 8
The Critical Attitude of Science 9
Language and Notations 10
RECURRING ISSUES 10
Prediction, Control, and the Search For Causal Relationships 10
The Relationship Between Theory and Research 13
Created Versus Natural Treatments 13
Laboratory Versus Field Settings 15
Basic and Applied Research 16
Individual Differences 16
ETHICAL ISSUES IN SOCIAL SCIENCE RESEARCH 17
PLAN OF THIS BOOK 23
FOR REVIEW AND DISCUSSION 23

chapter 2

OBSERVATION AND DESCRIPTION 24

OBSERVATIONS OF SINGLE SUBJECTS 25
Descriptive Uses 26
The Case History as Evidence 28
Generalization and the Case Study 30
POPULATIONS AND SAMPLES 31
The Goal of Representativeness 32
The Problem of Variability 33

DESCRIBING OBSERVATIONS 34
Scales of Measurement 34
Central Tendency and Variability 36
Reliability and Validity 37
Determining Reliability 38
The Concept of Validity 45
SURVEYING A POPULATION 49
Selecting a Sample 49
Techniques of Surveying 52
FOR REVIEW AND DISCUSSION 54

chapter 3
ASSOCIATION, CORRELATION, AND REGRESSION 56

CORRELATIONAL RESEARCH 58
Indexing a Relationship 58
Comparing r's: The Concept of Shared Variance 59
Statistical Significance 62
Sample Range and the Magnitude of the Correlation 63
Curvilinear Relationships 64
Correlations as Rank-Order Relationships 65
REGRESSION 67
TIME SERIES ANALYSIS 71
FOR REVIEW AND DISCUSSION 73

chapter 4
MULTIVARIATE ASSOCIATIONS 75

MULTIPLE CORRELATION 73
MULTIPLE REGRESSION 76
MULTIVARIATE RESEARCH 78
Factor Analysis 80
The Multitrait-Multimethod Matrix 85
FOR REVIEW AND DISCUSSION 87

chapter 5
IDENTIFYING CAUSAL RELATIONSHIPS: PROBLEMS AND THREATS 88

WHY CAUSAL INFERENCES CAN'T BE DRAWN FROM SIMPLE CORRELATIONS 89
The Third Variable Problem 90
The Directionality Problem 89
X AS A SUFFICIENT CAUSE OF Y: MILL'S CRITERIA 91

NULL HYPOTHESIS TESTING: TYPE I AND TYPE II ERRORS 92
The Problem of Accepting the Null Hypothesis 95
Effects of Sample Size on Hypothesis Testing 96
Statistical Versus Theoretical Hypothesis Testing: A Word of Caution 97
THREATS TO THE VALIDITY OF CAUSAL INFERENCES 98
THREATS TO STATISTICAL CONCLUSION VALIDITY 98
Low Statistical Power 98
Violated Assumptions of Statistical Tests 99
"Fishing" 99
Unreliable Measures 99
Unreliable Treatment Implementation or Settings 99
Heterogeneity of Subjects 100
INTERNAL VALIDITY 100
Plausible Rival Hypotheses 101
Within- vs. Between-Subjects Comparisons 101
THREATS TO THE INTERNAL VALIDITY OF WITHIN-SUBJECTS COMPARISONS 102
Maturation 102
Testing 103
Instrument Decay 103
Statistical Regression 104
History 105
THREATS TO THE INTERNAL VALIDITY OF BETWEEN-SUBJECTS COMPARISONS 105
Selection Bias 106
Differential Attrition 106
Diffusion 107
Compensatory Equalization 107
Compensatory Rivalry 107
Resentful Demoralization 108
IDENTIFYING AGE-RELATED CHANGES 108
Threats to the Internal Validity of Cross-Sectional Studies 108
Threats to the Internal Validity of Longitudinal Studies 109
Cross-Sequential Designs 110
Retrospective Versus Prospective Accounts 110
MULTIPLE THREATS TO INTERNAL VALIDITY 110
FOR REVIEW AND DISCUSSION 111

chapter 6

SUBJECT AND EXPERIMENTER BIASES 113

THE THREE ROLES IN THE RESEARCH ENTERPRISE 114
REACTIVITY: THE EFFECTS OF BEING OBSERVED 114
THE HAWTHORNE EFFECT 115
PRIVATELY HELD HYPOTHESES AND DEMAND CHARACTERISTICS 116
Problems in Assessing Situational Demands 118
Four Subject-Based Threats to Internal Validity 119

RESPONSE SETS AND THE TRUTHFULNESS OF SELF-REPORTS 119
REDUCING REACTIVITY: THE USE OF UNOBTRUSIVE MEASURES 121
Physical Traces 121
Archives 123
Unobtrusive Observation 124
SELF-FULFILLING PROPHECIES AND EXPERIMENTER BIAS 125
Bias Effects and the Adequacy of Research Observations 128
Low Interrater Reliability as a Threat to Validity 129
FOR REVIEW AND DISCUSSION 131

chapter 7

THE BASIC EXPERIMENT 133

CONCEPT OF THE TRUE EXPERIMENT 134
The Example of Experimentally Induced Compliance 134
The Rationale for Between-Subjects Comparisons 137
EXPERIMENTAL DESIGN 143
SELECTION OF SUBJECTS AND ASSIGNMENT TO GROUPS 144
The Necessity for Random Assignment 145
Free Random Assignment 145
Matched Random Assignment 146
EMPLOYING A CONTROL GROUP 147
PRETEST-POSTTEST CONTROL GROUP DESIGNS 147
THE POSTTEST ONLY CONTROL GROUP DESIGN 149
CHOOSING BETWEEN DESIGNS WITH AND WITHOUT A PRETEST 151
The Solomon Four-Group Design 153
FACTORS THAT INCREASE THE POWER OF AN EXPERIMENT 154
Maximizing Systematic Variance 154
Minimizing Error Variance 155
OPERATIONALIZING EXPERIMENTAL VARIABLES 157
Choosing an Independent Variable 157
Choosing a Dependent Variable 157
FOR REVIEW AND DISCUSSION 158

chapter 8

COMPLEX EXPERIMENTS 160

FACTORIAL DESIGNS 161
MULTIPLE CAUSATION: ADDITIVITY AND INTERACTIONS 163
Catalytic Interactions 165
Terminative Interactions 165
Antagonistic Interactions 167
Effects of Treatment Strength on Interactions 169
ANALYSIS OF VARIANCE (ANOVA) 170
Interpreting ANOVA Results 170
REPEATED MEASUREMENT (WITHIN-SUBJECTS COMPARISONS) IN THE

FACTORIAL EXPERIMENT 172
Carryover Effects and Counterbalancing 175
FOR REVIEW AND DISCUSSION 178

chapter 9

MIXED DESIGNS 180

DEFINITION OF MIXED DESIGNS 181
USES OF MIXED DESIGNS 183
Demonstrating the Generality of Experimental Effects 183
Identifying Limitations of an Experimental Effect 184
Identifying Antagonistic Interactions Between Classificatory and Manipulated Variables 189
INTERPRETING MIXED DESIGNS: FALLACIES IN CAUSAL INFERENCE 189
FOCUSING ON THE CLASSIFICATORY VARIABLE IN A MIXED DESIGN 191
SELECTING GROUPS FOR A MIXED DESIGN 193
FOR REVIEW AND DISCUSSION 197

chapter 10

QUASI-EXPERIMENTS 201

NONEQUIVALENT CONTROL GROUP DESIGNS 202
The Posttest Only Nonequivalent Peer Control Group Design 203
The Pretest-Posttest Nonequivalent Peer Control Group Design 204
The Simulated Posttest Only Design With a Cohort Control 206
The Simulated Pretest-Posttest Control Group Design 207
The Regression-Discontinuity Design 208
INTERRUPTED TIME SERIES DESIGNS 209
Simple Interrupted Time Series Designs 209
Interrupted Time Series With Reversal (A-B-A and A-B-A-B Designs) 213
Interrupted Time Series With Replication (The Multiple Baseline Design) 215
The Changing Criterion Design 217
Complex (Multiple Treatment) Interrupted Time Series Designs 217
Evaluating Single Subject Interrupted Time Series Designs 220
Limitations of the Single Subject Quasi-Experiment 225
FOR REVIEW AND DISCUSSION 226

chapter 11

CAUSAL ANALYSIS FROM PASSIVE OBSERVATION 227

A WORD OF CLARIFICATION 228
FORECASTING VS. CAUSAL INFERENCE 229

CORRELALTIONS WITHOUT CAUSAL ARROW AMBIGUITY: DIFFERENTIAL INCIDENCE 229
NATURALLY OCCURRING INTERRUPTED TIME SERIES DESIGNS 230
EX POST FACTO ANALYSIS 235
PARTIAL CORRELATION 238
Illusory Residual Correlations 239
A PARTIAL SOLUTION TO THE DIRECTIONALITY PROBLEM: TIME-LAGGED CORRELATIONS 240
ASSOCIATIVE NETWORK ANALYSIS 245
PATH ANALYSIS 249
FOR REVIEW AND DISCUSSION 252

chapter 12

EXTERNAL VALIDITY **254**

THE PROBLEM OF INDUCTION 255
Types of External Validity 255
POPULATION VALIDITY 256
Random Assignment Versus Random Selection 256
Generalizing to Versus Generalizing Across Populations 257
Threats to Population Validity 257
ECOLOGICAL VALIDITY 261
Generalizing Across Geographic Areas 261
Treatment by Setting Interactions 261
Temporal Validity 262
Generalizing Across Treatments 262
Generalizing From Unique Contexts 263
Generalizing Across Experimenters 263
HOW TO INCREASE EXTERNAL VALIDITY 264
Field Experiments 264
Broad Sampling 268
Meta-analysis 270
RELATIONSHIP AMONG TYPES OF VALIDITY 272
Relationship Between Internal Validity and External Validity 272
External Validity and Theoretical Validity 273
FOR REVIEW AND DISCUSSION 274

chapter 13

THEORETICAL (CONSTRUCT) VALIDITY AND PHILOSOPHICAL ISSUES **275**

THE PROBLEM OF INTERPRETATION 276
Operationism 277
The Multimethod Approach 278
The Manipulation Check 279
Further Empirical Analysis 279

THE PLACEBO EFFECT 282
Placebo Controls in Psychotherapy Research 282
INFORMED CONSENT AND THE INTERPRETATION OF EXPERIMENTAL FINDINGS 284
"Old" and "New" Research on the Effects of Environmental Stress: A Case Study 284
RECENT TRENDS ON THE PHILOSOPHY OF SCIENCE 287
Observation Is "Theory-laden" 288
Explanation Revisited 289
A Final Note on Science and Philosophy 289
THE SPECIAL POWER OF CONVERGING EVIDENCE 290
FOR REVIEW AND DISCUSSION 290

APPENDIX A: THE COMPUTER AS A TOOL 291

APPENDIX B: SCIENTIFIC REPORT WRITING 296

GLOSSARY OF TERMS 309

REFERENCES 314

NAME INDEX 320

SUBJECT INDEX 322

Preface

This book presents a broad general introduction to social science research methodolgy. Despite increased education, even today few people are prepared to evaluate claims made on the basis of social science research. I believe that underlying all social and behavioral research is the core logic of the scientific method itself; mastery and application of this logic is what is principally needed to discriminate between trustworthy and invalid scientific claims. The primary aim of this book is to explain the logic of science as applied to questions about behavior, especially human behavior.

I have assumed that readers do not have prior knowledge of the technical matters raised in the text. Thus each statistical concept is explained from scratch, every technical term is defined explicitly, and a verbal "translation" is provided for the few simple mathematical expressions that are introduced. Within the confines of this strategy, in this edition I have tried to present a reasonably complete survey of the concepts, methods, and issues that surround social and behavioral research.

This third edition is a major revision, with many additions and several important changes. The organization has been revised to follow the progression of scientific logic more closely than before. Chapter 1 presents an overview of the history and nature of behavioral science and of recurring issues in research design. It ends with a section on ethics in research involving human subjects, and includes the latest revision of the ethical principles for research adopted by the American Psychological Association.

Chapter 2 introduces the issues surrounding the collection of data, including a preliminary discussion of populations and samples, scales of measurement, reliability and validity, and variability, all of which are built on later. Chapter 3 addresses the question of detecting associations between variables, and goes on to a discussion of simple correlation and regression. Chapter 4 continues this discussion with the more advanced topics of multiple correlation, multiple regression, factor analysis, and the multitrait-multimethod matrix, all approached on a conceptual level that can be understood without prior experience with these techniques or the mathematics that underlie them.

Chapter 5 brings the reader to the basic issues involved in drawing inferences about causal relationships. Included are a new discussion of statistical conclusion validity, as well as an expanded discussion of internal validity that covers four new threats to internal validity recently identified by Cook and Campbell (diffusion, compensatory equalization, compensatory rivalry, and resentful demoralizaltion) and a discussion of the traditionally recognized threats. The chapter also has an extended section on problems in identifying and interpreting age-related associations, and includes a comparison of retrospective and prospective accounts. Chapter 6 extends this discussion by showing how subject and experimenter biases can lead to invalid causal inferences and explaining how these biases can be identified and overcome.

Chapter 7 introduces the true experiment, and Chapters 8 and 9 extend this discussion to complex experiments and mixed designs (i.e., those with both manipulated and classificatory variables). Chapter 10 is a new chapter on quasi-experiments, and explains each of the major types of nonequivalent control group and interrupted time series designs. Chapter 11 is also new, and deals with causal analysis from passive observation, including a basic discussion of the logic behind path analysis. Chapter 12, on external validity, has been considerably expanded, and is now conceptualized according to the two major issues with which external validity is concerned: ecological validity and population validity. A new discussion of meta-analysis is also included in this chapter.

Those familiar with earlier editions of *Science and Behavior* will note that this revision reflects a concerted effort to present the reader with the latest developments and thinking in application of the scientific method to the social and behavioral sciences, and endeavors to illuminate the goal of identifying or demonstrating causal relationships. Thus this edition focuses more attention on the relationship between research and theory throughout the presentation, culminating in the final chapter of the book, Chapter 13, which is devoted entirely to theoretical (construct) validity. This chapter includes a new discussion of questions about interpretation of all scientific data that have been raised recently by philosophers of science. In addition to a revised appendix on scientific report writing, drawn from the latest edition of the APA publication manual, there is a new appendix on the computer as a research tool. Finally, a glossary of terms has been added, as an aid to readers who are familiarizing themselves with the technical language of social science methodology.

Despite the changes, the beliefs and goals which led John Neale and me to first write *Science and Behavior* 16 years ago remain the same. I continue to believe that it is possible to introduce social science research in a way that is sensible to the novice, yet sufficiently accurate and precise for more advanced students and even practicing scientists. As in previous editions, the book emphasizes systematic repetition and usage of terms throughout, so that each major concept appears under several different, complementary lights. To present critical issues in concrete form, examples are drawn heavily from familiar or "real-life" situations. At the same time, several occasions are taken throughout to describe a piece of very basic research in the behavioral or even the physical sciences in order to illustrate a point or emphasize the logical continuity of the scientific approach, regardless of the domain to which it is applied.

In preparing this edition of *Science and Behavior* I was assisted greatly by students in my Fall 1984 undergraduate methodology course at Stony Brook; they provided feedback on new lecture material as it was woven into the previous edition of the book. I owe these students a considerable debt of thanks. I am also indebted to John Isley, Susan Willig, and Barbara DeVries at Prentice-Hall, who all provided encouragement and assistance as the revision developed. Finally, I owe a great debt to John Neale who, although unable to participate in this revision, made enormous contributions to the two earlier editions that continue to be reflected throughout the text.

Robert M. Liebert

1

Overview

THE BIRTH OF SOCIAL SCIENCE RESEARCH

THE NATURE OF SCIENCE

- The Importance of Precision and Reliability
- The Critical Attitude of Science
- Language and Notations

RECURRING ISSUES

- Prediction, Control, and the Search for Causal Relationships
  - levels of causal analysis
  - types of causal relationships
- The Relationship Between Research and Theory
- Created Versus Natural Treatments
  - manipulated variables: the experimental method
  - classificatory variables: the correlational method
- Laboratory Versus Field Settings
- Basic and Applied Research
- Individual Differences

ETHICAL ISSUES IN SOCIAL SCIENCE RESEARCH

PLAN OF THIS BOOK

FOR REVIEW AND DISCUSSION

No human activity is more fascinating than trying to predict, explain, and understand the thoughts and actions of others. We all want to know why people act as they do. This curiosity is not new. Our interest in ourselves and our fellow beings dates back virtually to the dawn of the species. One can find extensive discussions of the causes of human behavior in both theology and philosophy. The earliest historical records suggest that our remote ancestors were as preoccupied with questions about human nature and behavior as we are today, as rough drawings and other artifacts left from antiquity show (Kluckhohn & Stodtbeck, 1961).

How can we answer questions about human nature? How can we understand other people and ourselves? At least in a general way, there are two sources of knowledge that can help us understand any phenomenon. One source of knowledge is called the *rational* approach, and the other is called the *empirical* approach. The rational approach rests on the belief that people can understand through reason and intuition alone. The empirical approach begins with the assumption that direct observation and experience provide the only firm basis for understanding nature. (Of course, reason is always involved in interpreting observations.)

THE BIRTH OF SOCIAL SCIENCE RESEARCH

Many ancient peoples recognized that some types of knowledge could be obtained only empirically (that is, through observation). People using the empirical approach made enormous contributions to early science, as well as to the practice of medicine, architecture, and land cultivation. Empirical observations also played a central role in the writings of Leonardo, Copernicus, Galileo, and a legion of lesser-known scientists throughout the Renaissance. They gave birth to the sciences of physics, chemistry, and biology as we know them today.

The study of animals, plants, and inanimate nature has had a firm empirical base since pre-Christian times. However, most early conceptions of *human* nature was guided solely by philosophical or religious dogma. The reason for this disparity is not difficult to understand. Most human behavior is so much more complex than other natural events, at least at first glance, that a scientific analysis of human behavior appears a formidable task. The view of humans as a special phenomenon in the universe, whose actions are determined by free will, the will of God, or other essentially inscrutable forces makes the effort even more difficult.

What is more, Greek philosophy itself seemed to accept the notion that human nature was exempt from systematic empirical scrutiny. Protagoras' (480–410 B.C.) famous claim that "man is the measure of all things" implied that human nature is different from the rest of nature: it can be discerned from reason and intuition alone, and such reason and intuition, properly applied, invariably lead to wisdom. This rational approach to human nature flourished almost unchallenged until the late sixteenth century, when it fell under the scrutiny of Francis Bacon (1561–1626).

Bacon set himself the goal of systematizing an empirical approach to all knowledge. He established the groundwork for the scientific method of inquiry as we know it today. "Nothing is beneath science, nor above it," wrote Bacon. As Will Durant has pointed out:

> Despite his strong naturalistic bent [the scientist] feels the fascination of . . . problems; nothing human is alien to him. Who knows what unsuspected truth, what new science indeed, may grow out of these investigations as chemistry balked from alchemy: "Alchemy [says Bacon] may be compared to the man who told his sons he had left them gold buried somewhere in his vineyard; where they by digging found no gold but by turning up the mould about the roots of the vines, processed a plentiful vintage. So the search and endeavor to make gold have brought many useful inventions and instructive experiments to light." (Durant, 1954, pp. 122–123).

Although he acknowledged a debt to the Greek philosophers for giving the world its most important logical tools, Bacon took them to task for spending too much time on theory and too little on observation. Human reason alone, he said, will not always lead to truth, least of all when we try to analyze ourselves. Bacon issued the remarkably modern warning that "human understanding is no pure light . . . what a man had rather were true, he more readily believes" (Bacon, 1608, as cited by Durant, 1954, p. 130).

Bacon insisted that human judgment is not infallible, nor should it be accepted uncritically. Rather, human judgment and human behavior are natural phenomena that can be studied empirically. In the *Advancement of Learning* (1603), Bacon invented the idea of social science research and listed almost all the major factors in human conduct that social scientists study today. He wrote:

> Philosophers should adequately inquire into the powers and energy of custom, exercise, habit, education, example, imitation, emulation, company, friendship, praise, reproof, exhortation, reputation, laws, books, [and] studies [because] by these agents the mind is formed . . . (Bacon, 1603, as cited by Durant, 1954, p. 122).

In the centuries since Bacon wrote, the empirically based social and behavioral sciences he envisioned gradually took the place of purely rational views of human nature. One important landmark in the development of modern social science is the work of Gustav Theodor Fechner, professor of physics at the University of Leipzig in the mid-nineteenth century.

Having injured his eyes while looking at the sun through colored glasses, Fechner was obliged to resign from his chair in physics. After a protracted period of recovery, he turned to the study of philosophy. But his viewpoint remained that of a physicist, and thus he found much that was unsatisfactory in his newly adopted discipline. As E.G. Boring, a prominent historian, has noted:

> It was one thing to philosophize about mind and matter as two alternative ways of regarding everything in the universe and another thing to give the idea such concrete empirical form that it might carry weight . . . or even be satisfactory to Fechner, the one-time physicist . . . Philosophy, so Fechner thought, needed a solid scientific foundation (Boring, 1950, pp. 278–280).

Thus, Fechner the physicist, having turned his interest to the human mind, faced the problem of tying psychological phenomena to objective, physical events. He sought this firm ground in the relationship between measurable events, such as the sounding of a tone and the psychological sensations the tones give rise to. This effort to marry physical and psychological phenomena, referred to as *psychophysics,* appeared full-blown in Fechner's book, *Elemente der Psychophysik* (1860). This text purported to be "the exact science of the functional relations or relations of dependency between body and mind" (Boring, 1950, p. 281).

Fechner used a number of different methods in the investigations he reported in his book, but all had one feature in common. Physical stimulus events were systematically manipulated, and the subjects were obliged to give a report of their sensations, perceptions, and reactions. The relationships disclosed by this work were orderly, and Fechner went on to advance mathematical descriptions of the relationship between physical stimuli and their psychological effects. Thus, his work could have provided a major bridge between the physical and behavioral sciences. But it did not.

Instead, the Fechnerian technique led both his contemporaries and psychologists of the generation that immediately followed him to focus on that part of his method that was entirely psychological. Both in Germany and elsewhere the method of *introspection* pervaded psychology during the latter half of the nineteenth century. This method required subjects (usually well trained or at least practiced) to describe the contents of their own minds systematically. Thus, ironically, Fechner's efforts to merge the natural and behavioral sciences gave rise to efforts to drive a permanent wedge between the two in the name of psychophysics. This is indicated in the following statement of Wilhelm Wundt.

> [There are] two modes of treatment of experience. One is the mode of the *natural sciences,* which concern themselves with the *objects* of experience, which in turn is regarded as independent of the subject. The other is the mode of *psychology,* which investigates the whole content of experience in its relations to the subject and also in respect of the attributes that this content derives directly from the subject (Wundt, 1896, as reprinted in Herrnstein & Boring, 1966, pp. 595–596).

The method of introspection, although judged to be promising in its day, soon ran into great difficulties. Among the most dramatic was the argument of whether thought does or does not embody visual images. One laboratory said yes, one laboratory said no, and by the very nature of the evidence the dispute could not be resolved. Similarly, in the laboratory of Ivan Pavlov in Russia, it became increasingly clear that introspection would not give rise to definitive conclusions. Pavlov was not primarily interested in psychology, but, as a physiologist, he had discovered the conditional reflex in dogs. (When a "neutral" stimulus, such as a tone, was systematically paired with meat powder, Pavlov's dogs began to salivate on hearing the tone alone.) After Pavlov made his discovery, he first approached the problem by asking his research assistants to introspect—to try to reason out what the phenomenon must be like from the point of view of the dog. The assistants got into interminable and unresolvable arguments about the conditional reflex from the canine point of view, and Pavlov subsequently banished any use or even mention of this subjective approach from his laboratory (Hyman, 1964).

Instead, Pavlov insisted that the events that he had observed should be studied as *behavior,* and he began to manipulate systematically the environmental circumstances that gave rise to the phenomenon he had discovered. This strategy swiftly took a firm hold among individuals who were avowedly and completely psychologists. Of these, perhaps none was more explicit and outspoken in his acceptance of such a viewpoint than John Broadus Watson. Herrnstein and Boring (1966) describe Watson as "imbued with the functionalist outlook, a concern with the organism's adaptation to its environment, compared to which the analysis of consciousness into its elements seemed unimportant, uninteresting, and irrelevant" (p. 507). Watson himself put it this way:

> Psychology as the behaviorist views it is a purely objective experimental branch of natural science. Its theoretical goal is the prediction and control of behavior. Introspection forms no essential part of its methods, nor is the scientific value of its data dependent upon the readiness with which they lend themselves to interpretation in terms of consciousness (1913, p. 158).

Although Watson's views were in many ways radical, by the standards of either his day or ours, his insistence on studying human nature through objective methods is the cornerstone of all modern social and behavioral sciences.

Since the turn of the present century there has been a great deal of interest in and systematic exploration of behavior. From the rudimentary research beginnings of the nineteenth century, a whole host of disciplines devoted to behavioral research has emerged. These disciplines have subsequently become the social sciences of psychology, sociology, and education. The research practitioners in these disciplines have undertaken the arduous task of applying the scientific approach to their investigations. Endeavoring to disentangle their efforts and results from the preconceptions and prejudices of earlier times, these workers have made remarkable strides, often with substantial practical implications, toward understanding human nature and the various ways it can be brought under scientific scrutiny.

Because of their insistence on objectivity, the social sciences command a respect that philosophy and theology alone never did. Today the social sciences are flourishing as never before. Social science research is quoted, cited, and reported not only in professional journals but also in the popular press. Modern business executives and government officials increasingly rely on social scientists to answer a host of questions about education, race relations, voting patterns, the use of drugs, and attitudes toward the conservation of energy and natural resources, to name just a few.

This book provides a general introduction to the way social and behavioral science is, or should be, designed, interpreted, and evaluated. Our purpose is to describe and explain the research designs and related conceptual issues (and pitfalls) that face social scientists in their pursuit of reliable, factual information and coherent theories. These issues and problems are of concern not only in formal science. In a larger sense, they are also relevant to the way men and women pursue and evaluate knowledge in their private as well as in their public and professional lives, and about themselves as well as about each other.

We have tried to present the methods of social scientific research through basic explanations, followed by specific examples drawn from the research literature in psychology, sociology, and education. Because our primary purpose is to illustrate the advantages and limitations of the major research paradigms currently in use in the social sciences, we emphasize the application of each method to complex human behavior. However, we have also tried to draw the reader's attention to similar examples and problems in more basic research areas as well. We also provide a small number of parallel examples from the physical sciences and from the experiences of daily life to illustrate the logical continuity of scientific methods. Designed as a general introduction to behavioral research, this book does not require any special background (for example, in statistics) to be understood. We have, however, described some fundamental statistical concepts that readers must know. For the more advanced reader, this material may serve as a convenient review, or it can be passed over entirely.

THE NATURE OF SCIENCE

We have already mentioned the central role that the concept of science and the scientific method play in empirical social science research. Our discussion therefore begins with the question of what science is and what it is not.

Generally, *science* refers to the pursuit of objective knowledge gleaned from observation. Thus the term refers to a *method* (systematically acquiring and evaluating information) and a *goal* (identifying the nature of governing principles of what is being studied) rather than to any particular phenomena. Science is not restricted to the consideration of the inanimate physical universe or to test tubes, purified laboratories, or specific apparatus. In principle, it is possible to adopt a scientific approach to even the most complex aspects of human social behavior. What the specific approach does demand, as Bacon noted, is an empirical attitude and a commitment to the empirical approach. Empiricism dictates that one can settle questions about the nature of human thought and action by accepting only assertions and claims that can be probed by direct observation. Discussion, argument, and the opinions of various authorities (the rational approach) may give rise to important ideas, but proof always requires solid evidence.

Empirical research, the foundation of the scientific approach, refers to any activity that systematically attempts to gather evidence through observations and procedures that can be repeated and verified by others. The scientific approach requires that all claims be exposed to systematic probes. Statements, theories, and assertions, regardless of how plausible they seem, must be testable. The attitude of science is therefore an extremely doubting one. The apparently sensible statements that brushing one's teeth will reduce cavities, that cigarette smoking may be a health hazard, or that children will be psychologically better off if they are loved than if they are treated harshly are only propositions. They may be totally correct, totally incorrect, or correct under some circumstances. But in any case the basis of acceptance will be systematic, public exploration of each proposition rather than belief, good sense, or precedent. It is this demand for publicly observable evidence that hallmarks the objective nature of the empirical approach.

An interesting modern example of how an apparently sound rational belief can be dramatically shown wrong by an empirical scientific approach involves the baseball play known as the "sacrifice bunt." The sacrifice bunt is a purposeful attempt by the batter to hit the ball very gently into the infield; in fact, the bat is held in such a way that the ball is actually tapped or pushed rather than hit. Although the bunt will usually permit the opposing team to field the ball in time to put the batter out at first base, the successful bunt almost invariably permits a runner who is already on first base to advance safely to second or a runner who is already on second base to advance safely to third. The sacrifice bunt is a favorite tactic of baseball team managers when a runner is already on first or second base, the score is close, and there are no outs. The strategy behind the sacrifice bunt is to increase the chances of getting a run during the inning by sacrificing an out. The sacrifice bunt brings the player(s) already on base closer to home and thus increases the chances that a run can be scored.[1] On common sense rational grounds, the sacrifice bunt sounds like a good strategy, which is probably why it has been so widely used in American baseball.

However, as Hooke (1972) has shown, this faith in the sacrifice bunt is not borne out by the empirical evidence. The underlying assumption of the bunt, taken on faith by managers, has been that a team is more likely to score a run with one out and a player on second (the condition produced by a sacrifice bunt) than with a runner on first and no outs (that is, the condition that exists before

[1] A runner on first base will likely need either two singles or a double from subsequent batters to make it home, whereas a runner on second can often make it home on a subsequent batter's single. If a runner on second can be advanced to third through a sacrifice bunt (leading to one out), a run can subsequently be made if there is a hit, a long fly ball, an error, a wild pitch, a passed ball, a balk, or even a slow grounder.

the bunt is tried). What Hooke's empirical evidence shows is that this common-sense, "rational" assumption is wrong. As indicated in Table 1-1, an actual tally of past games reveals that the likelihood of scoring a run during an inning given a player on first and no outs is 0.396, whereas the likelihood of getting a run with a player on second and one out (as a result of a "successful" sacrifice bunt) is slightly *lower,* 0.390. Another analysis of the sacrifice bunt in Hooke's study involved determining the average number of runs scored by a team in an inning. Hooke found that with a runner on first and no outs, the average number is 0.813 runs per inning, whereas with one out and a runner on second the figure is 0.671. Thus, on the average, the *indiscriminate* use of the sacrifice bunt will *lose* 142 runs for every 1,000 times it is tried (0.813 − 0.671), contrary to the intuition and "common sense" of the managers.[2]

Table 1–1 Effectiveness of the Sacrifice Bunt

BASE OCCUPIED	*NUMBER OF OUTS*	*PROPORTION OF CASES WHEN AT LEAST ONE RUN IS SCORED*	*AVERAGE NUMBER OF RUNS PER INNING*
1st	0	0.396	0.813
2nd	1	0.390	0.671

Source: From data reported in Hooke, 1972

The Importance of Precision and Reliability

The requirement of science that all propositions be testable can be met only when propositions and ideas are expressed in a clear and precise way. Many common-sense notions are expressed in such a broad, vague, and nonspecific way that they are difficult to test adequately. It is for this reason that science is often (correctly) associated with the use of technical definitions and specialized terminology; in the social and behavioral sciences especially, one must have a high degree of precision of meaning to be able to conduct a thorough, critical test of an idea.

Closely related to the requirements of testability and precision is the demand that the observations that form a science or scientific body of knowledge be reliable. To be admitted as scientific knowledge, observations must occur under the prescribed cirumstances not once but repeatedly. And they must be seen or detected not just by a single individual or individuals within a given laboratory, community, or country but instead must be reproducible, under the circumstances stated, anywhere and any time. If they are not, qualifications must

[2] There are probably some special circumstances in which the sacrifice bunt can be used to advantage, as when a weak hitter is followed by a stronger one.

be added to our formal body of knowledge and to our statements of "principles." For example, a statement such as "Water boils at 212° F" is a reliable assertion (it can be demonstrated by anyone, anywhere) *only at sea level.* (The qualification is that at higher altitudes the boiling point is lower, and this qualification is also reliable regardless of who is doing the test.) The requirement of reliability, like the other requirements of science, is particularly demanding in the social sciences, but meeting it as closely as possible is the only road to useful knowledge.

The goal of scientific research, and of science itself, is to provide "hard" evidence about the universe. The scientific method was introduced as a way of understanding human nature because earlier efforts based on discussion, argument, the opinion of various authorities, and a general appeal to "reason" (that is, the rational approach) failed. The rational approach alone provided no universally accepted way of resolving differences of opinion. Resolving differences of opinion in a nonarbitrary way is the chief business of science. Properly designed scientific investigations provide a firm basis for either distinguishing among two or more alternatives or stating in explicit terms when one outcome, and when another, will occur. As a result, the scientific commitment involves a willingness to modify one's theories, opinions, and beliefs according to empirical findings. Science attempts to replace dogma with data.

The Critical Attitude of Science

The purpose of research in science is to bring a higher level of confidence and certainty to our understanding than is possible by belief, faith, or reason alone. Science therefore requires a highly critical attitude. The scientist must be a skeptic who has to be shown, a doubter who must be convinced, a cynic who believes that people may wittingly or unwittingly deceive or misunderstand one another. Research must be designed so that it is tight and its conclusions compelling. Conversely, if an investigation is flawed such that the results are open to plausible alternative interpretations, the findings cannot be admitted as evidence. It is the researcher's responsibility to eliminate or rule out all plausible alternative explanations and to recognize and point out when others have failed to be entirely convincing (rather than generously to overlook logical weaknesses because "they probably don't matter"). As we shall see, though, just how plausible an alternative explanation must be to be considered a serious threat can become a matter of heated debate. In addition:

> The scientific commitment also rests on a belief system that must be accepted on faith. This belief system assumes a reality consisting of objects and events anchored in a space-time continuum which relate to each other according to laws of cause and effect. It can be perceived correctly only by the waking, unintoxicated brain and is to be comprehended by the intellectual analysis of sensory data. According to this view, the ultimate test of the validity of any phenomenon is the ability to meet the criteria of scientific evidence, including replicability and the use of controls (Frank, 1977, pp. 555–556).

Thus, accepting the scientific approach is itself a decision.

Language and Notations

All social science research involves the empirical search for relationships between or among events. Such research requires, first of all, the ability to scale or measure the events of interest in such a way that a value can be assigned to each observation. As we shall see later, several different scales of measurement are used in social science research. For now, though, the important things to note are that social scientists assign numerical values to their observations and that the value assigned to one observation may vary from the value assigned to the next. Any class of events on which observations are made and potentially differing values are assigned is called a *variable*. The value assigned to each observation is its *score*.

When research is discussed abstractly (as is often done in this book) the phrase "any variable" is symbolized by X, the phrase "any other variable" is symbolized by Y, and the phrase "any third variable" is symbolized by Z.

If both X and Y scores are available for a particular person, place, or thing, we can ask whether X and Y are related; that is, whether some orderly relationship (regardless of its pattern) exists between X and Y. X—— Y symbolizes the situation in which there exists a relationship (or association) between X and Y. (And, by extension, X——Z and Y——Z symbolize the relationship between X and Z and Y and Z, respectively.) The critical problem for social science research is always one of determining the relationship among well-specified variables.

When the relationship between X and Y is such that a change in a person, place, or thing's X score will produce a change in its Y score, the relationship is symbolized $X \longrightarrow Y$. Conversely, if the relationship that exists is such that a change in Y will produce a change in X, the relationship $Y \longrightarrow X$ exists. These relationships are referred to as *causal relationships,* and we will have a great deal to say about them throughout this book.

RECURRING ISSUES

So far we have spoken as though there were only one type of scientific investigation. This is not so. There are several different methods of research, each with its strengths and weaknesses. Equally important, social science research must face a host of issues that have confronted scientists since Greek times. Social scientists must also face a number of other issues, problems, and recurring questions that are peculiar to doing research in the social sciences. Each of these major recurring issues is introduced in the sections that follow.

Prediction, Control, and the Search for Causal Relationships

It is often said that the social sciences deal with the prediction and control of behavior through the understanding of related physical and mental processes.

Prediction involves the accurate anticipation of future (or as yet unobserved) events. *Predictive efficiency* is often a measure by which two or more theories or ideas can be compared, and a good deal of social science research is aimed at comparing the relative predictive power of differing theoretical viewpoints.

Control in this context refers to the ability to influence or bring about change in a particular phenomenon, or the ability to state what the controlling factors are in a particular situation, or knowing what would have to be done to produce a certain outcome.

Both prediction and control (unless they occur accidentally) require an understanding of the underlying processes and relationships that govern a phenomenon. Understanding involves knowledge of the full set of causal relationships that underlie a phenomenon, including the ways in which various factors combine or interact to produce or alter it. Thus, the search for causes lies at the heart of the scientific enterprise.

The meanings of words like *cause* and *causality* have been the subject of philosophical debate for many centuries. Not only social scientists but all empirical scientists must partially skirt this debate rather than resolve it. In the social sciences, at least, causality is usually identified with the problem of specifying when (that is, under what circumstances) a relationship will change.

At first blush, the simplest way to identify causes would seem to be to look for covariations in nature. Francis Bacon suggested that a "Table of More or Less" is a good starting point in the search for causes. According to Bacon's scheme, the investigator simply tabulates all of his or her observations in such a way that he or she can identify qualities or conditions that increase and decrease together. Bacon himself applied the method to answer the question, What is heat? He looked for a factor that increased when heat increased, and decreased when heat decreased. After long and careful observation under many circumstances, Bacon satisfied himself that there was a nearly perfect correlation between heat and motion. Thus, using carefully classified observations, Bacon discovered that heat is a form of motion more than 350 years ago!

The search for causal relationships in nature is often not so straightforward, however. For one thing, there are a number of different types of causal relationships. Moreover, these different types can operate in various combinations to influence a given phenomenon.

Levels of Causal Analysis. Causal explanations vary in their specificity. What seems to be a single cause at one level of analysis may appear to leave an unresolved controversy between two or more possible causes at another level of analysis. For example, in his famous conformity experiments, Asch (1951) found that subjects were more likely to give incorrect judgments of the lengths of lines shown on a screen if the subjects were in a group in which everyone else gave an inaccurate judgment than they were if one other person in the group gave the correct judgment. Thus, at one level, we may say that exposure to one person who judged accurately caused the subject to break from conformity and respond accurately as well.

But what caused the presence of one accurate judge to have this conformity-releasing effect? Perhaps the mere fact that the accurate judge disagreed with the majority was the critical ingredient. Or perhaps the fact that his judgment agreed with the as yet unstated private judgment of the subject was the critical ingredient. Further research was needed to ask about causality at this level of analysis. (The evidence seems to suggest that both elements play a role in the causal chain. An extreme dissenter makes some contribution to breaking the subject's conformity when the judgments are objective [for example, line length], but a colleague who actually agrees with the subject is required to cause a break in conformity when subjective opinions rather than objective judgments are involved; see Allen & Levine, 1969).

Types of Causal Relationships. Regardless of the level of causal analysis involved, four broad types of causal relationships can be identified: necessary and sufficient relationships, necessary but not sufficient relationships, sufficient but not necessary relationships, and contributory relationships.

A *necessary and sufficient* relationship is one in which some factor or condition, *X*, is required to produce an effect and will invariably do so. A specific genetic anomaly is the necessary and sufficient condition for the appearance of certain hereditary diseases in the individual. In the social sciences it is rare to find important causal relationships that are both necessary and sufficient.

The world is filled with causal relationships in which some specifiable factor, *X*, is *necessary but not sufficient* for *Y* to occur. For example, a writing instrument is necessary but not sufficient to take written notes in class; the ability to read English is necessary but not sufficient to understand this book; possession of a loaded gun is necessary but not sufficient for a shooting to occur.

Sufficient but not necessary causal relationships are those in which *X* is one of many causes that can independently produce *Y*. For most people, the sight of an angry bear is a sufficient condition to stay out of a mountain cave. But the sight of the bear is not a necessary condition; a host of other factors will dissuade people from entering a dark cave, even if no bears are around to assert a territorial claim. Because most behavioral phenomena can be elicited by many different factors and circumstances, the most that can usually be done in social science is to identify sufficient but not necessary causes.

Contributory causal relationships are those in which *X* is neither necessary nor sufficient to cause *Y* but can nonetheless contribute to (that is, change the likelihood of) *Y*'s occurrence. Annoying experiences during the day are often contributory causes to the arguments that couples have during the evening. A "bad day at the office" may not cause a domestic scuffle or be necessary for one to begin, but if a person has had a bad day this factor may contribute to later getting into a fight at home.

Several more complicated varieties of causal relationship have been discussed in recent years. Our previous example of a contributory causal relationship implied that *X* (a bad day at the office) → *Y* (an argument at home). But an argument at home in the evening, particularly if it was not resolved, may contribute to having a bad day at the office the next day. So our causal model becomes complicated: $X \rightleftarrows Y$. X is still a cause of *Y*, but *Y* can now also be a contributory cause of *X*. The influence of *Y* on *X* is an example of what would be termed a *feedback loop*. Another recent concept is the *causal chain:* $X \longrightarrow Y \longrightarrow Z$ *Here, X* causes *Y* and *Y*, in turn, causes *Z*. For example, poor social skills (*X*) may cause a person to receive little social reinforcement (*Y*), which then leads to depression (*Z*). In this case, poor social skills (*X*) would be regarded as an indirect cause of depression (*Z*).

Because many different patterns of causal relationships might underlie and explain any phenomenon, the unguided empirical search for causes can be a clumsy or even an impossible strategy. For this reason, investigators in both the social and physical sciences almost invariably begin with some theoretical perspective. This permits them to structure and conceptualize the phenomenon of interest and its possible causes.

The Relationship Between Research and Theory

A theory is a coherent group of general propositions to explain a class of phenomena. The goal of any science is to advance theories to explain the phenomena it deals with. In science, competing theories must be evaluated through objective research. Thus, empirical research is a major tool through which theories can be evaluated.

Theory and research may also be said to bear a reciprocal relationship to one another. That is, research is used to evaluate theory, and theory is used to direct and guide research. Even a tentative theory or theoretical idea may, like a prospector's map, lead the investigator to a rich mine that might never be found by an unguided, hit-or-miss search alone.

It should also be pointed out that theories are not themselves directly proved or disproved by research. Rather, more specific propositions, referred to as *hypotheses*, are derived from the general propositions of a theory. These specific hypotheses may then be put to the empirical test through research. Technically speaking, even hypotheses cannot be proved or disproved absolutely. Rather, research may either *support* or *fail to support* a particular hypothesis derived from a theory. When research provides regular support for the hypotheses derived from a particular theory, scientists will tend to accept the theory as useful. On the other hand, theories that generate hypotheses that research consistently fails to support will tend to be discarded.

Created versus Natural Treatments

We have said that when an investigator hypothesizes the existence of a causal relationship, $X \rightarrow Y$, the implication is that a change in *X* will bring about a change in *Y*. To see if this is so, *X* must occur while observations of *Y* permit us to determine whether the expected change in *Y* has occurred.

It has long been recognized that such circumstances may either be created artificially or be found in the natural, ongoing course of events.

Manipulated Variables: The Experimental Method. Suppose a child psychologist wished to determine whether children will earn better grades in school if their parents praise them for good grades than if their parents do not. The psychologist might identify a group of children whose parents do not praise them for good school work and ask these parents to begin praising their children. If this manipulation of parents' responses (X) is followed by a change in the youngsters' grades (Y), we might take this observation as evidence for a causal relationship. Nonetheless, the evidence to this point is not entirely convincing. A critic could point out that the change in school performance might have occurred even if the parents' behavior had not changed. For this reason, properly designed experiments also include one or more *control groups,* which have received either a different manipulation or none at all.

Investigations in which the variable hypothesized to have a causal influence is manipulated by the investigator are said to employ *the experimental method.* When the experimental method is used, the manipulation of X is usually referred to as the *treatment,* and the Y scores become the *measure* (of the effect of the treatment).

Classificatory Variables: The Correlational Method. The alternative way of approaching causal relationships is to look for natural occurrences of X. This involves classifying people according to whether they have experienced the treatment of interest. For example, an investigator might identify a group of parents who praise their children for good school work and another group of parents who do not. The school grades of the children of the two groups of parents might then be compared. Presumably, if a causal relationship exists, children of parents who give praise will have better grades than children of parents who do not give praise. When an investigator examines relationships that are due to naturally occurring events by classifying rather than manipulating the experiences of subjects by providing differential treatments, the *correlational method* is being used.

Which of the two methods, experimental or correlational, is the superior tool for investigating social science phenomena? The question is a difficult one, and answers to it have divided researchers since social science research began in earnest over a century ago. Much of this book is devoted to explaining the particular strengths and weaknesses of each of these methods and to describing the major pitfalls that attend their use.

Briefly, the limitation of the experimental method lies in the problem that its treatments are often artificial and unlike the natural phenomena in which we are ultimately interested. The limitation of the correlational method lies in the uncertainty of inferring causal relationships from the data because the details of the supposed natural manipulation are uncertain. For example, the naturally existing relationship (or *correlation*) between parental praise and children's grades may result from the fact that children who do well in school elicit more praise from their parents ($Y \rightarrow X$) rather than because praise stimulates children to earn better grades ($X \rightarrow Y$).

These and other problems of the experimental and correlational methods are not insurmountable, but they do require a thorough understanding of how each method works, how each can be supplemented by additional observations, and how the two methods can be combined or used to complement one another in the search for understanding.

Laboratory versus Field Settings

Regardless of whether the correlational or experimental method is used, investigators must decide whether to make their observations in a laboratory or field setting.

A laboratory setting is any situation or facility that is visibly or apparently devoted to research. A field setting, in contrast, is an environment or situation that the subject perceives as occurring naturally, so that the variables of interest can be observed or manipulated in an apparently spontaneous way.

The advantage of administering treatments or making observations in the laboratory is that tight control over the situation can be maintained and extraneous factors and distractions can be eliminated or at least held in check.

The disadvantages of a laboratory setting are that research participants know they are in an investigation and that the environment itself is novel and artificial. As we will see, these factors can distort our observations. Further, some of the most interesting or socially important aspects of human behavior occur in circumstances where complete control is impossible. For example, serious acts of aggression simply would not or could not be permitted to occur under controlled laboratory conditions. Then, too, in some circumstances control may be possible, but placing people in an artificially controlled situation may have effects of its own. For example, measuring stress by strapping electrodes to a subject's arms or chest may give a more precise or objective measure than one would get if the subject's stress were simply rated by hidden observers. However, the electrodes and the experience of being "wired up" may also contribute to the subject's overall level of stress and thus alter the reaction the researcher is trying to measure.

It is therefore reasonable to wonder, at least in many circumstances, whether laboratory findings can be generalized to natural life situations. Also, as we will see, the distinction between laboratory and field settings may be thought of as a continuum from very laboratory-like to completely natural and unobtrusive. Many investigations represent a compromise between the extremes. Further, to demonstrate the operation of an important hypothesis convincingly, one must often show the operation of the hypothesis both in the controlled laboratory and in the natural field.

Basic and Applied Research

Applied research in the social sciences is guided by a focus on solving problems with some immediate practical importance. Would a newly designed instrument panel make it easier for an airplane pilot to tell at a glance whether any mechanism on a jumbo jet was malfunctioning? Does selecting graduate students on the basis of Graduate Record Examination scores make for a superior group of students? Is behavior therapy a better treatment for phobias than psychoanalysis? All these questions are within the realm of applied social science research. In each case, the research derives from a practical problem that requires a solution.

Basic research, in contrast, does not typically have an immediate practical payoff. Instead, basic research is oriented toward problems that are important within the context of a scientific discipline. Studies directed at understanding the way in which language is acquired would be an example of basic research. Very often, such research is guided by theory. That is, the investigator begins with a theory of language acquisition and then arranges to probe hypotheses derived from the theory by collecting data. But basic research is not always dependent on theory. Such nontheoretical questions as, "What happens to the frequency of a response when it is followed by a fixed-interval versus a fixed-ratio schedule of reinforcement?" are also part of basic research. Notice that in both examples, the research questions stem from what is regarded as important *within the scientific discipline.* But these basic research findings often can and do have practical implications. An understanding of language acquisition, for example, could serve as the basis for devising a treatment for children who have difficulty in learning to talk.

Individual Differences

It is obvious that people are not all alike. We differ not only in age, sex, education, and physical appearance but also in our reactions to personal and interpersonal situations. As a matter of fact, in a very real way each of us is a unique human being. In searching for the causes of behavior, social scientists must be mindful of these individual differences and make some allowance for them in their research strategies.

One way to deal with individual differences is to distribute subjects in research so that differences among the subjects are balanced out. This approach is often referred to as the *nomothetic approach* in social science research. The nomothetic approach calls for studying a wide variety of persons in a research investigation with the aim of identifying causal relationships that hold for people in general. The approach seeks to establish lawful relationships of great generality. (Nomothetic is derived from the Greek *nomos,* meaning law.)

It may also be argued that studying groups of people artificially masks the unique ways in which people respond. The *idiographic approach* calls for investigation of the behavior of individual persons. It often involves a considerably more exhaustive examination of each subject's behavior than does a nomothetic study. Although an investigator taking the idiographic approach will probably study the behavior of more than one person even within a given investigation or research project, the data from idiographic studies are always presented for individual subjects (rather than as group averages) so that each subject's unique response pattern is preserved.

ETHICAL ISSUES IN SOCIAL SCIENCE RESEARCH

Social scientists are trained to formulate questions and to design research that is best suited to answering them. But what of the impact of the research on the participants? Some research violates a subject's right to privacy, as happens when the subject is watched by hidden observers. In more extreme cases, participating in research may involve actual risk to the subject's health or psychological well-being. There is such a risk whenever dangerous drugs, frightening experiences, or stress-producing information is given to subjects. These issues lead us to ask about the ethics of social science research.

Until the end of World War II, individual investigators were expected and presumed to establish their own ethical standards and safeguards for their subjects. In the past few decades, professional organizations, government agencies, and scientists themselves have moved away from allowing the ethics of research to be determined solely by an individual researcher. In place of an individualistic system a number of formalized codes of research ethics have been developed. Reports of brutal experiments performed on prisoners in Nazi concentration camps were one important stimulus in this movement. (The Nuremberg Code of Ethics was formulated after the Nazi war crime trials.) But reports of gross scientific misconduct were not linked solely to the Third Reich. Beecher (1966), in a survey of medical research, found that in the United States human subjects were often placed at considerable risk through their participation in research. One such study compared penicillin versus a placebo (a compound with no specific pharmacological effect) as treatments to prevent rheumatic fever. Although it was already known that penicillin was an effective treatment for respiratory infections, which can sometimes lead to rheumatic fever, 109 servicemen with respiratory infections were given only the placebo.

Growing concern over research ethics led the Department of Health, Education and Welfare to create the National Commission for Protection of Human Subjects of Biomedical and Behavioral Research. This commission conducts hearings and recommends guidelines for safeguarding the rights and safety of research participants.

In the early 1970s, the American Psychological Association (APA) appointed a committee on ethical standards in psychological research to revise the APA's code of ethics. The committee first solicited information from members of the APA concerning research that posed ethical questions. Five thousand research descriptions were generated, and after reviewing these the committee wrote the first draft of a new set of ethical principles. This first draft was distributed throughout the profession and was published in the *APA Monitor,* a newspaper distributed to all members of the APA. Reactions to the first draft were then considered, and in 1973 a set of ten principles was adopted by the APA. The principles were revised again in 1982 to take into account issues and ambiguities raised by the 1973 version. The current principles are listed below.

> The decision to undertake research rests upon a considered judgment by the individual psychologist about how best to contribute to psychological science and human welfare. Having made the decision to conduct research, the psychologist considers alternative directions in which research energies and resources might be invested. On the basis of this consideration, the psychologist carries out the investigation with respect and concern for the dignity and welfare of the people who participate and with cognizance of federal and state regulations and professional standards governing the conduct of research with human participants.
>
> A. In planning a study, the investigator has the responsibility to make a careful evaluation of its ethical acceptability. To the extent that the weighing of scientific and human values suggests a compromise of any principle, the investigator incurs a correspondingly serious obligation to seek ethical advice and to observe stringent safeguards to protect the rights of human participants.
>
> B. Considering whether a participant in a planned study will be a "subject at risk" or a "subject at minimal risk," according to recognized standards, is of primary ethical concern to the investigator.
>
> C. The investigator always retains the responsibility for ensuring ethical practice in research. The investigator is also responsible for the ethical treatment of research participants by collaborators, assistants, students, and employees, all of whom, however, incur similar obligations.
>
> D. Except in minimal-risk research, the investigator establishes a clear and fair agreement with research participants, prior to their participation, that clarifies the obligations and responsibilities of each. The investigator has the obligation to honor all promises and commitments included in that agreement. The investigator informs the participants of all aspects of the research that might reasonably be expected to influence willingness to participate and explains all other aspects of the research about which the participants inquire. Failure to make full disclosure prior to obtaining informed consent requires additional safeguards to protect the welfare and dignity of the research participants. Research with children or with participants who have impairments that would limit understanding and/or communication requires special safeguarding procedures.
>
> E. Methodological requirements of a study may make the use of concealment or deception necessary. Before conducting such a study, the investigator has a special responsibility to (1) determine whether the use of such techniques is justified by the study's prospective scientific, educational, or applied value; (2) determine whether alternative procedures are available that do not use concealment or deception; and (3) ensure that the participants are provided with sufficient explanation as soon as possible.

F. The investigator respects the individual's freedom to decline to participate in or to withdraw from the research at any time. The obligation to protect this freedom requires careful thought and consideration when the investigator is in a position of authority or influence over the participant. Such positions of authority include, but are not limited to, situations in which research participation is required as part of employment or in which the participant is a student, client, or employee of the investigator.

G. The investigator protects the participant from physical and mental discomfort, harm, and danger that may arise from research procedures. If risks of such consequences exist, the investigator informs the participant of that fact. Research procedures likely to cause serious or lasting harm to a participant are not used unless the failure to use these procedures might expose the participant to risk of greater harm or unless the research has great potential benefit and fully informed and voluntary consent is obtained from each participant. The participant should be informed of procedures for contacting the investigator within a reasonable time period following participation should stress, potential harm, or related questions or concerns arise.

H. After the data are collected, the investigator provides the participant with information about the nature of the study and attempts to remove any misconceptions that may have arisen. Where scientific or humane values justify delaying or withholding this information, the investigator incurs a special responsibility to monitor the research and to ensure that there are no damaging consequences for the participant.

I. Where research procedures result in undesirable consequences for the individual participant, the investigator has the responsibility to detect and remove or correct these consequences, including long-term effects.

J. Information obtained about a research participant during the course of an investigation is confidential unless otherwise agreed upon in advance. When the possibility exists that others may obtain access to such information, this possibility, together with the plans for protecting confidentiality, is explained to the participant as part of the procedure for obtaining informed consent.

The preamble affirms the investigator's general responsibility to conduct research that will contribute to human welfare, and to adhere to all pertinent government regulations and professional standards. Principle A emphasizes the need for the individual researcher to evaluate the ethical acceptability of planned or proposed research and to seek advice whenever it appears that human welfare or participants' rights may be compromised in any way. Principle B elaborates on this requirement by calling on investigators to determine whether each proposed investigation involves anything more than negligible or minimal risk for participants.

Principle C establishes that investigators remain fully responsible for their work and extends the investigators' responsibilities to include not only their own actions but also those of their collaborators, research assistants, students, and others who, in practice, are often the ones who have face-to-face contact with participants.

Principle D requires an explicit agreement between the researcher and the participant concerning the responsibilities of each. The requirement is that the "contract" be fair; the participant must get something from the study that is commensurate with the demands made on him or her. Increased self-knowledge, awareness of having contributed to scientific knowledge, and monetary rewards are all possible compensations. Principle D also deals with what is called *informed consent.* Ideally, prospective subjects should be given full disclosure about all the details of the research so that they can make an informed decision concerning whether they choose to participate. Implementing this principle is sometimes difficult. Some potential subjects are infants, young children, or hospitalized mental patients who may not be competent to participate meaningfully in the informed consent procedure; in these cases, consent must also be obtained from parents or legal guardians.

Principle E deals with the difficult problem that some social science research requires that subjects *not* be fully informed about all the details of the study until after the critical observations have been made. The need for such deception is often claimed in studies examining honesty, sharing, and aggression, to name just a few. In these cases, providing complete information about the study in advance might easily bias or distort the way the subjects will respond. Deception has long been a thorny problem in psychological research. As one example, during the 1950s and 1960s hundreds of experimental studies were done on the effects of test anxiety. Typically this research involved selecting participants who had indicated earlier, through questionnaires, that they were very anxious in test taking situations. These individuals would be given a test, most often labeled an IQ test, and then deceived concerning their performance on the test. Very often the "false feedback" would indicate that the participant had failed badly. The effects of this failure experience would then be evaluated by giving the subject a second test. The critical, but hard to resolve, question in these studies is whether the value of the research can in some way justify the creation of anxiety, lowered self-esteem, and other negative effects in these participants. Principle E does, however, require that subjects be given complete information as soon as possible. Thus, subjects in a test anxiety study must be told that they have not really failed. The reasons for the deception must also be provided. The entire postexperimental explanation is referred to as *debriefing.*

Principle F deals with a participant's right to decline or discontinue participation, particularly in situations where the participant may feel constrained to go along with research because of the (presumed) power of the investigator. For example, there is a particular ethical concern when prisoners or mental patients are asked to participate in a study being conducted by someone on the staff of the institution in which they are confined. In these situations the participants may feel that failing to "volunteer" will bring some penalty or loss of favor. The researcher must therefore stress the right of the prospective participants to decline freely. He or she must assure the potential subjects that they will not be penalized in any way if they decline.

Another potential problem is raised by the "research requirement" associated with many undergraduate social science courses. This requirement generates a subject pool for faculty and graduate student research. Sometimes these courses require students to participate in a fixed number of hours of research, or students may be invited to participate in research for extra credit toward their course grade. In either case, one can question whether the system is truly voluntary. Thus, nowadays, most undergraduate courses provide alternative ways of meeting the research requirement or earning extra credit, such as reading and reporting on a fixed number of articles in professional journals instead of participating in the department's subject pool.

Principles G, H, and I all emphasize the researcher's obligation to protect subjects from harm, to inform them of any possible risks, and to minimize any stress that may be produced. The investigator must be able to detect and remove any negative after effects. A simple debriefing may not accomplish this. It may be necessary to follow up participants to be sure that the debriefing was effective. But researchers should also ask whether there are alternative means of answering a research question that would not induce stress in the participants. For example, test anxiety can be studied by observing students as they take actual, scheduled course examinations as part of their usual life experiences (for example, Liebert & Morris, 1967).

Principle J concerns confidentiality. Although assurances of confidentiality are routinely offered by social science researchers, the law does not recognize the contract between subject and researcher, nor does it consider the information provided by subjects as "privileged communication." The courts can, in fact, subpoena the investigator's data and records, in which case the researcher must choose between an ethical responsibility and a legal one.

Davison and Stuart (1975) have proposed a scheme that ties together some of the principles we have just presented (see Table 1-2). In determining how careful the researchers must be when obtaining informed consent, Davison and Stuart ask four questions:

1. *What is the level of risk?* Little harm is likely in a memory experiment, but greater risk is inherent in a study that requires a subject to withstand electric shock applied to the fingers.
2. *Is the research of potential benefit to the subject?* A subject might stand to gain a great deal from being in the study (for example, if the subject receives a potentially beneficial form of therapy), or the subject might gain nothing directly except the satisfaction of having helped science.
3. *Is the technique an established one whose risks and benefits are known, or is it new and experimental, so that the researcher is unable to indicate how beneficial, harmful, or discomfiting participation might be?*
4. *Is the subject realistically free to give consent or to refuse participation?* A college student has considerable freedom to refuse, but a prisoner would probably feel somewhat obliged or coerced to participate in a study when asked to do so.

Now that we have described the principles of research ethics held by social scientists today, we must ask how they are implemented. The APA guide-

Table 1–2 Guidelines for Protecting Subject's Right to Participate Only in Experiments of Own Choice (After Davison and Stuart, 1975)

LEVEL OF RISK	FREEDOM TO GIVE CONSENT	HIGH POTENTIAL BENEFIT TO SUBJECT		LOW POTENTIAL BENEFIT TO SUBJECT, HIGH POTENTIAL BENEFIT TO SOCIETY	
		Established Procedure	Experimental Procedure	Established Procedure	Experimental Procedure
LOW RISK	Great freedom	2–4*	4	2–4	4–5
	Feels some coercion	5	5	5–6	7
HIGH RISK	Great freedom	4	5	5–6	7
	Feels some coercion	6	6	7	8

*The numbers indicate the degree of care that should be exercised in obtaining consent.

1. *No consent by the subject is necessary.* The investigator assures protection of the subject's rights. The nonobtrusive observation of traffic flow in public places or other public behavior might fall into this category. This procedure and the next are permissible only when a review panel has determined that the potential risk of harm to the anonymously observed subjects is nil.

2. *Subject is simply asked to sign a consent form for participation in research as a subject of observations, with no explanation of the nature of the study.* One example would be observing the supermarket shopping of individuals; an explanation of the objectives of the study might change relevant behavior.

3. *Subject is asked to sign a consent form for participation in research, with "debriefing" following participation.* Such a study might examine interpersonal behavior in public places; prior disclosure of the hypotheses could change behavior. A panel of experts would have to determine that subjects risked little in participating, including minimal humiliation following debriefing.

4. *Subject is asked to sign a consent form for participation in a project, after full disclosure of the objectives and methods of the research.* This procedure would be applied in efforts to evaluate treatment by randomly assigning subjects to experimental, to placebo control, and to no treatment control groups. A review panel must judge that risk of harm to control subjects is equal to or less than it would be were there no experiment.

5. *Subject is asked to sign a consent form for participation in a project, after full disclosure of the objectives and methods of the research and in the presence of at least one witness who is not involved in the research.* This procedure would be appropriate any time a review panel senses that subjects may feel obliged to participate. Research with adjudicated offenders could fall into this category.

6. *Subject is asked to sign a consent form for participation in a project, after full disclosure of the objectives and methods of the research and in the presence of witnesses. The consent is reviewed by an independent human subjects committee within the institution.* This procedure might be applied in the experimental evaluation of a program carrying out an institutional objective, for example, vocational training in prisons and mental hospitals.

7. *Subject is asked to sign a consent form for participation in a project, after full disclosure of the objectives and methods of the research and in the presence of witnesses. The consent is reviewed by an independent human subjects committee within the institution and by a similar committee outside the institution.* The procedure could be applied when the research concerns behavior changes that are not strictly related to institutional objectives, for example, a study of the role of repetition when mental patients are taught phrases in a foreign language.

8. *No consent is possible because the rights of subjects cannot be protected.*

lines place the responsibility on the researcher in consultation with colleagues. But the safety of research participants is also protected by *human subjects committees,* usually composed of people from diverse disciplines (community citizens, clergy, lawyers), which are charged with evaluating research proposals on ethical grounds. Human subjects committees may require changes in or even turn down a proposal that places subjects at undue risk. In the United States, government funding for a research project is no longer possible unless the work has been approved by such a committee.

PLAN OF THIS BOOK

This book is an attempt to present an integrated view of social science research methodology. We believe that there is a natural progression from collecting descriptive data to detecting associations between events and then to attempting to determine whether these associations reflect cause-effect relationships. Once a cause-effect relationship has been demonstrated, its meaning becomes an important issue. Is it highly general or quite specific? How does it relate to theory? Throughout the rest of this book, we present the major social scientific research methods in a way that shows how they fit into the progression we have just described.

FOR REVIEW AND DISCUSSION

1. Discuss the major characteristics of science. Bearing these characteristics in mind, describe some of the difficulties facing a science of human behavior.
2. What is introspection? Evaluate it as a scientific method. Consider the requirements for a scientific method in your answer.
3. What is the relationship between theory and research in the social sciences?
4. What types of causal relationships are logically possible?
5. What is the major difference between the experimental and the correlational methods?
6. Distinguish between the nomothetic and idiographic approaches to social science research.
7. Discuss the role of ethics, including the idea of informed consent, in social science research.

2

Observation and Description

OBSERVATIONS OF SINGLE SUBJECTS
- Descriptive Uses
- The Case History as Evidence
- Generalization and the Case Study

POPULATIONS AND SAMPLES
- The Goal of Representativeness
  - biased samples
  - random samples
- The Problem of Variability

DESCRIBING OBSERVATIONS
- Scales of Measurement
- Central Tendency and Variability
  - central tendency
  - limitations of the mean
  - variability
- Reliability and Validity
- Determining Reliability
  - test-retest reliability
  - interitem reliability
  - interrater reliability
  - base-rate problems
  - item sampling
- The Concept of Validity
  - a first look at construct (theoretical) validity

SURVEYING A POPULATION
- Selecting a Sample
  - the *Literary Digest* debacle
  - the problem with quota sampling
  - stratified and free random sampling
  - choosing a sample size
  - advantages of stratification
- Techniques of Surveying
  - the distributed questionnaire
  - phone surveys
  - the total design method
  - systematic interviews

FOR REVIEW AND DISCUSSION

In the preceding chapter we emphasized the role of observation in all scientific endeavors. Now our discussion of observation will become more specific, as we turn to the questions, *What* and *Who* should be observed? and *How* should we describe our observations?

Our discussion begins with the most familiar and common method of making observations about others, namely, considering people one at a time as case studies. We will see that this method has many limitations, the most important being the question of whether any one case (or even a very small number of cases) can possibly be representative of the larger groups (for example, people in general) in which we are interested. This leads to the notions of populations and samples, which we discuss next. And finally, we turn to the way in which observations are formally described, by assigning numerical values (scores) to them.

OBSERVATIONS OF SINGLE SUBJECTS

The method of studying behavior most familiar to the lay person is the biography. Such a technique is used not only by novelists and film makers to illustrate various aspects of the human condition, but also by physicians in hospitals, by social workers in community service agencies, and in the practice of clinical psychology and psychiatry. In these contexts the procedure is typically referred to as a *case history* or *case study.*

The case study is an excellent method for examining the behavior of a single individual in great detail. Thus, it is useful in a clinical setting, where the focus of interest is ultimately on only one person. In both personality and clinical psychology, some investigators argue that the essence of psychological studies always lies in the unique attributes of the individual (see Allport, 1961). Believing that this uniqueness is the important element in behavioral research clearly calls for the intensive study of single cases. The method is therefore generally more appropriate for the *idiographic approach,* which emphasizes the uniqueness of the individual, than for the *nomothetic approach,* which insists that because science deals with general laws, behavior should be studied by observing a variety of people with the aim of formulating general laws of behavior (see Chapter 1). When researchers in the social sciences *are* interested in findings of greater generality, the case study is limited in usefulness.

Although simple descriptive accounts of behavior are often both unsystematic and uncontrolled, they have played some important roles in the scientific study of behavior. We can distinguish two broad ways in which the case history has been used: as a source of descriptive information and as evidence for or against theories.

Descriptive Uses

As description, the case history has been used in each of the following ways:

1. to illustrate some form of behavior by prototypical example
2. to demonstrate important methods or procedures
3. to provide a detailed account of a rare or unusual phenomenon, and
4. as a source of hypotheses

To illustrate several of these purposes, we will consider the famous case of a "multiple personality" reported by Thigpen and Cleckley in 1954. They described a patient, "Eve White," who displayed at various times three very distinct personalities. Eve White had been seen in psychotherapy for several months because she had severe headaches accompanied by blackouts. Her therapist described her as a retiring and gently conventional figure. However, one day during an interview she seemed to undergo a surprising and abrupt change:

> As if seized by sudden pain, she put both hands to her head. After a tense moment of silence, both hands dropped. There was a quick, reckless smile, and, in a bright voice that sparkled, she said "Hi there, doc!" The demure and constrained posture of Eve White had melted into buoyant repose. . . . This new and apparently carefree girl spoke casually of Eve White and her problems, always using *she* or *her* in every reference, always respecting the strict bounds of a separate identity. . . . When asked her name, she immediately replied "Oh, I'm Eve Black."[1] (1954, p. 137).

Following this rather startling observation, Eve saw her therapist over a period of fourteen months in a series of interviews that ran to almost 100 hours. During this time still a third personality, Jane, emerged. At first Jane appeared to be merely a composite of the two Eves, but later she became a well-integrated person.[2]

The case is a valuable classic in psychiatric literature because it is one of a very few detailed accounts of a rare phenomenon, a true multiple personality. In addition to illustrating the phenomenon itself, the investigators' original report provides valuable details of the interview procedures they used and many side-lights on how the behavior developed and the how problem was ultimately resolved.

The case study is also useful in demonstrating the application of various therapeutic techniques, and it is often the vehicle through which techniques are

[1] As is the case in most such reports, the names are pseudonyms.

[2] Many years later an autobiographical account appeared (Sizemore & Pittillo, 1977). Apparently Jane was not the final personality, and her problem was not resolved until she had experienced another twenty personalities.

introduced to other practitioners. One such incident arose in our own work (Neale & Liebert, 1969), when we were treating a mute psychotic woman through a combination of reinforcement and modeling procedures. The patient, whose pseudonym was Martha, had begun to produce simple sentences (for example, "May I have some bread, please?"). Her verbalizations were, however, quite low in volume. It was thus difficult at times for the therapist to be sure what Martha had said. Simple exhortations to speak more loudly did not work. Something else was apparently needed. We constructed a novel device to provide Martha with direct feedback about the audibility of her speech and thus facilitate her treatment. The device itself consisted of a microphone, an amplifier, and a neon light. We asked the patient to speak into the microphone and told her that only reponses of sufficient volume would turn on the light and produce a food reward. The volume necessary to turn on the light was controlled by a rheostat, which the therapist could adjust. The effect of the device was dramatic.

> Martha's volume increased markedly and this change was maintained throughout subsequent sessions. On Session 13, when the light was first introduced, Martha produced 47 responses which did not turn on the light. On Session 17, however, only three responses were produced which were not of sufficient volume (1969, p. 832).

A novel aspect of a treatment procedure, described in detail in a case report, can serve as a basis for its further application by others.

The case study often plays an important role because it is very exploratory in nature. Because circumstances are permitted to develop naturally, often new and perhaps important hypotheses are revealed that could not have been uncovered in a more controlled investigation. Lazarus and Davison have described how this may occur in a clinical setting.

> There is nothing mysterious about the fact that repeated exposure to any given set of conditions makes the recipient aware of subtle cues and contingencies in that setting which elude the scrutiny of those less familiar with the situation. Clinical experience enables a therapist to recognize problems and identify trends that are usually beyond the perception of novices, regardless of their general expertise. It is at this level that new ideas will come to the practitioner and often constitute breakthroughs that could not be derived from [other types of research] (Lazarus & Davison, 1971, p. 197).

The lack of control that characterizes case studies and permits circumstances to vary as they will also increases the method's potential for revealing new and perhaps important findings that might not otherwise appear. For example, prior to the investigations of Jean Piaget, the famous Swiss psychologist, many investigators had been interested in the intellectual capacities of preschool children. Their studies, which followed a formal design and focused on preselected measures, provided a descriptive account of the growth of children's abilities, but they led to relatively little understanding of the underlying processes.

In contrast, Piaget used an unstructured case study method with his own children as he presented a variety of problems to them. He gave little attention to control and permitted the situations to wander considerably in an effort to get the greatest possible grasp of the intellectual processes involved in the child's answers to various questions, as well as whether these responses were simply correct or not. As a result of Piaget's insights, many discoveries about children's thinking have been made, including a number of results that have subsequently been replicated and extended when groups of children served as subjects in more systematic research.

In one of Piaget's most famous single-subject explorations, a preschool child was presented with two short, wide glass beakers, each containing the same quantity of milk. The youngster was asked whether both beakers had an equal amount of fluid and agreed that they did. Then, while the child watched, the entire contents of one of these short, wide beakers was poured into a tall, thin one. When the child was then asked whether the beakers still had the same amount of milk in them, he replied that they did not! The taller beaker, according to the youngster, now had more milk. Adults, of course, would immediately point out that the two beakers must still have the same amount of milk, since they were equal to begin with and virtually no liquid was lost (or could possibly be gained) in the pouring operation.

Piaget interpreted the instance as showing that children below a certain age do not understand the principle of *conservation,* and he attempted to detail the logical operations that underlie appreciating that the amount of fluid cannot change (that is, is *conserved*) despite the pouring operation. The single-subject reports and the theorizing to which they gave rise were subsequently explored by others in a variety of correlational studies (for example, Elkind, 1961) and experimental tests (Flavell, 1963), which have generally confirmed both the finding and many, though not all, of Piaget's interpretations. Without Piaget's heavy reliance on the uncontrolled case study (and his own ingenuity and imagination) these discoveries might not have come to the fore.

The Case History as Evidence

Case studies are sometimes used to test broad hypotheses. In this regard, they have sometimes been offered as evidence in support of a theory. For reasons we will mention subsequently, the case study is seriously limited in its ability to contribute positive support to a theory. However, case studies can sometimes be extremely potent in *disconfirming* the implications of a theory. One powerful use of the single case occurs when the results from the case negate (that is, provide a negative instance of) an assumed universal relationship or law. Such a state of affairs logically must lead either to the rejection of the law or to the addition of special assumptions to handle the deviant event and therefore provides powerful evidence. In science the exception does not prove the rule and may disprove it.

As an example of such an instance, let us first consider a theory of speech perception that is generally termed the motor theory. The crux of this position is that the ability to decode the speech signals of others depends on the listener's ability to speak. An important and *universal* prediction of the theory is that if the subject is unable to speak, he or she will also be unable to perceive speech, that is, to understand what others are saying.

In 1962, Lenneberg presented a description of an eight-year-old boy who lacked the motor skills necessary for speaking. Despite this deficit, the lad could clearly understand the verbal communications of others. At least in this one case, there was a clear disjunction between the motor skills necessary for the *production* of speech and the skills required to decode and *understand* the speech of others. The existing motor theory had to be either discarded or substantially modified to handle the data presented by a single but extremely important case.

Even when theories do admit the possibility of some exceptions or non-applicable instances, a negative outcome in a case study still may cast suspicion on the usefulness of the theory for explaining the phenomenon in question. Moreover, a case study may suggest an alternative explanation that seems more plausible. Freud, for example, initially believed that his female patients' reports of sexual assaults by male relatives were accurate descriptions, but after careful analysis of a single case, he came to view them instead as fantasies.

Although it is a useful tool for discomfirming theories, the case history is weak as a source of evidence *for* a theory. In the presentation of a case such as that of Eve White, the requisite controls for ruling out alternative hypotheses (such as the possibility that she might be behaving according to the expectations of the investigator) are usually lacking. To illustrate this possibility, we can consider another case that received much public interest, the case of "Bridey Murphy." When hypnotized, a sedate American woman "regressed," apparently beyond her early childhood and into an earlier life in which she was Bridey Murphy, an Irish lass. Under hypnosis the woman was able to report many remarkable details of a town in Ireland that she had never visited and, in the course of doing so, took on a distinct Gaelic brogue. One competing hypothesis to the one that this case showed true reincarnation turned out to be viable.

The woman had been reared, in part, by an Irish maid who described most of the account that later appeared in hypnosis. The maid had also provided an excellent model for the brogue that the hypnotized subject was later to produce as convincingly as if it were her own. At least in this instance, it is apparent that the subject's particular life history may have played a heavy role in contaminating the evidence. It is virtually impossible to entirely eliminate contaminations of this sort from case studies.

Similarly, in the presentation of a successful psychotherapy case, the requisite controls for ruling out alternative hypotheses are entirely lacking. Suppose a clinician reports employing a particular treatment technique with an anxious patient, with the result that after six months of therapy the patient's tensions have markedly decreased. Such a result *may* be due to the treatment, but it may also be due to other factors. The patient's anxiety may have been caused by an increase in life stress, and these sources of tension may have decreased over the six months.

Generalization and the Case Study

Shontz (1965), maintaining that the case history is valuable as evidence, has argued:

> A chemist who wishes to study the properties of a compound or element need not concern himself with the number of samples of the substance on which his tests are run, as long as he is certain that he knows the identity of the particular material on which he is working and as long as his procedures are explicit and carefully followed. By the same token, a psychologist who wishes to study an important personality process, such as anxiety, need not concern himself greatly with the size of his sample, provided that his subject is appropriately selected and that he has procedures that enable him to recognize (that is, measure) anxiety when it occurs in the person he is investigating (p. 236).

Shontz's analogy is not entirely convincing, however. An inanimate compound may be completely defined in terms of its elements, but social scientists have no such complete definition of a person. Even if we were to agree that two individuals exhibited anxiety, these two people, unlike chemical reagents, might differ in important ways that would restrict generalizations.

But the problem of generalizing the results of an investigation employing only a single subject may not always be of paramount importance. This is especially true when a large measure of population generality can be assumed at the outset. In research on sensory processes the data of only a few subjects are often recorded because it is a plausible assumption that the sensory equipment of humans does not differ widely from person to person in ways that would invalidate any general laws that are discovered.

A classic example of such work may be seen in Heinemann's (1961) photographic study of retinal images. The lenses of the human eye focus light patterns on the retina, and Heinemann was able to measure the images thus produced using a specialized photographic technique. Because the human eye may be presumed to be roughly constant in its structure and function from one individual to another, the results of such a study should have rather wide generality even if they were based on a single case. In contrast, even casual observation shows that the manner in which humans handle frustration differs widely from individual to individual, and the study of one person's reactions could not be generalized.

Another problem with case studies, even as an illustration, lies in the "intuitive" nature of the selection process. That is, cases are *selected* to illustrate a particular point or even to confirm a theory. Rarely is any information presented on the representativeness of the case. Since the point being illustrated by the case is presumably a general one, it is necessary to establish that the results from the case presented can be extended to other similar cases. The fact that the cases selected for reporting purposes do not meet these criteria is apparent to professionals in many walks of life. Many physicians report that they have not, in their entire professional experience, found a single "textbook case" of this or that illness. Without a general description of the variations that occur in particular diseases (or, for that matter, particular social processes), the illustrative material of a single case might be more misleading than truly educational.

In summary, whether the disadvantages of the simple case study method outweigh its advantages or not inevitably depends on the purposes of the investigation at hand. For certain kinds of description it is invaluable. However, in the social sciences, the case study's value is primarily as a preliminary or adjunct research technique rather than as a workable method in its own right.

POPULATIONS AND SAMPLES

A major aim of science is to provide sound propositions about people in general or about specific groups of people (children, women, or minority group members, for example). Rarely, however, does a social scientist actually study or observe all the people he or she is interested in. More technically, we can express this same fact by saying that social science research typically tries to understand a segment of the world, a *population*, on the basis of observing a smaller segment, a *sample*. A population is thus the total collection of people, things, or events under consideration; it is whatever group the investigator wishes to make inferences about.

In social science, research populations are not defined by nature but by *rules of membership* that are chosen by the researcher. For example, all the college sophomores in the United States today make up a population. But all the nouns in the English language and all the restaurants in France that are open on Sunday are also populations. A population in social science research is very similar to the abstract concept of a *set* in mathematics, that is, "any well-defined collection of objects."

Because of the way populations are used in research, a population need not actually exist at any particular time; the only requirement is that it be well defined. In fact, many populations are defined in terms of *potential membership*. For example, all the males in the United States who might be given a new birth control pill constitute a population defined by potential membership.

A *sample* is some subset of a population. Samples can be any size and can be selected in a number of different ways. However, the alternatives are not all useful ones, and poor sampling procedures plague social science research as severely as any other methodological problem.

What constitutes an appropriate sample? To answer this question we must break it down into two component parts: *Which cases* should be sampled? and *How many* cases should be included in the sample? The answers lie in the concepts of representativeness and variability.

The Goal of Representativeness

If observations made on a sample will be used to characterize or draw inferences about a population, then the critical requirement for a sample is that it represents the characteristics of the population fairly and accurately. A *representative sample* thus tends to display variations among its members that are proportional to the variations that exist in the population. If 50 percent of all babies in the United States have spoken their first word by one year of age and the other 50 percent have not, we would obviously hope that a sample of babies used to determine the "normal" rate of infant language development should also contain one-year-olds who have and have not spoken their first words in the same proportion, about 50-50.

Biased Samples. A sample is said to be *biased* when it is not representative of the population to which the investigator wishes to generalize. A biased sample is *nonrepresentative* of the population of interest and thus invites inaccurate inferences. One of the major problems with case studies is that one cannot determine in what ways a single case is and is not representative of the population of interest. Johnson and Liebert (1977, p. 11) give this dramatized instance of the problem:

> Suppose, for example, that a team of scientists from another planet landed on Earth and met one man. They observed him carefully and noted he (1) had two eyes, (2) had ten fingers, (3) reported having one sister, and (4) could play the "Star-Spangled Banner" on a ukelele with his toes. *We* know (but our extraterrestrial guests would not) that this sample of one almost fully represents the population (of all people) on some characteristics (e.g., having two eyes), represents a fairly sizable portion on others (e.g., having one sister), and is almost unique in yet other characteristics, such as his musical ability. Without this knowledge, our imaginary research team might mistakenly guess that all humans can play the ukelele with their toes.

By the same reasoning, case studies are of greatest value when the one person being studied *is* the "population" in which one is interested. This is the case when studying the biography of a famous person, for example.

Random Samples. The procedure most likely to yield a sample that is representative of the population is *random sampling*. A sample is random when (1) every member of the population has an equal chance of being selected for the sample, and (2) the selection of any one member of the population does not influence the chances of any other member being selected. There are a number of different ways of obtaining a random sample. One way is to put the names or code numbers of all the members of a population into a hat, shake them up, and draw enough names for your sample without looking. This is the way Bingo numbers and winning lottery tickets are usually selected. Another way of accomplishing the same thing more efficiently is to use a random numbers table. A portion of one such table appears in Table 2-1.

The numbers in Table 2-1 were generated by a computer program that assures that every digit is as likely to appear as any other in a particular location. If you wished to select a sample of ten cases from a population of 600, you would enter the table at the upper left-hand corner (or any other arbitrary point you wished) and read three-digit numbers until you found ten numbers between 001 and 600. For example, using Table 2-1, our first three numbers would be: 528, 078, and 188. Note that 528 is the last three digits of the upper left-hand entry (39528), and that we skipped 616 and 767 entirely because they are larger than 600. This procedure, used in conjunction with a table such as this one (but typically a good deal longer), assures that the sample drawn is random.

Mathematically it can be shown that the random number selection procedure will tend to yield samples that mirror the population on all relevant characteristics; it yields a representative sample. Note, however, that we say *tend to* rather than *will,* because the mathematical proof is very much dependent on a large sample. Small samples, even when drawn randomly, may fail to mirror the populations they are intended to represent. This is an important fact, and we will return to it later.

The Problem of Variability

We have said that sampling is extremely important in social science research. Why? Simply, careful sampling is required because members of a population–almost any population–will differ or vary among themselves on many

Table 2-1 Portion of a Random Number Table

39528	72784	82474	25593	48545	35247
81616	18711	53342	44276	75122	11724
56078	16120	82641	22820	92904	13141
90767	04235	13574	17200	69902	63742
40188	28193	29593	88627	94972	11598
34414	82157	86887	55087	19152	00023
63439	75363	44989	16822	36024	00867
67049	09070	93399	45547	94458	74284
79495	04146	52162	90286	54158	34243
91704	30552	04737	21031	75051	93029
94015	46874	32444	48277	59820	96163
74108	88222	88570	74015	25704	91035
62880	87873	95160	59221	22304	90314
11748	12102	80580	41867	17710	59621
17944	05600	60478	03343	25852	58905

important characteristics. For any particular characteristic, the variability within the population may be small or large. When the variability is large, large samples are required to assure that the sample is reasonably representative of the population.

You can demonstrate the relationship between population variability and the sample size needed to characterize the population by turning to Table 2-2, which shows the hypothetical body weights of 105 ninth-grade boys. The variability in Table 2-2 is quite large; some boys weigh as little as 75 pounds, and others weigh as much as 180. Now suppose you try to characterize the body weight of the boys in this population empirically by selecting and weighing only one boy, selected randomly. Your characterization would never be right, and as often as not the boy selected would be quite different in weight from the average of all the boys. On the other hand, a random sample of fifty boys, drawn from the same population, will generally give an average that is close to the average of the population as a whole.

The converse principle also holds. When the variability of some characteristic is small within the population, a relatively small sample will tend to reflect the population accurately.

DESCRIBING OBSERVATIONS

Scientific observation usually involves coding observations as *values* or *scores* on the characteristic for each subject or event. How are such scores assigned? And once they are assigned, how can they be combined into a portrait of the sample as a whole? These are the questions to which we turn next.

Scales of Measurement

Most of the events or characteristics of interest to social scientists vary in magnitude. In some cases, we may be interested only in whether an event or characteristic was present or not; for example, was Robbie's temper tantrum preceded by frustration? But more often we are interested in being able to assess magnitude, not just presence or absence. We might want to be able to characterize

Table 2-2 Body Weights of 105 Ninth-Grade Boys

75	90	76	161	90	112	129	117	107	123	116	102	145	114	88
125	90	136	92	138	180	171	112	109	96	99	107	115	113	108
128	132	100	120	116	97	94	100	148	126	135	117	85	134	116
132	91	102	80	146	142	94	88	124	137	92	141	117	109	103
100	103	114	92	91	141	127	90	96	126	104	81	122	148	97
137	90	123	129	111	174	112	148	103	141	107	121	87	112	144
93	76	100	156	95	78	96	110	170	132	99	145	90	180	96

the degree or amount of frustration that Robbie experienced. Typically, then, we want to quantify the variation in events and characteristics. We do so by developing rules for assigning numbers to represent the different magnitudes of the events or characteristics in which we are interested.

Once we move to the realm of numbers, we must ask whether the events and numbers actually correspond. The real number system, for example, includes both the concepts of magnitude and additivity; 40 plus 40 equals 80. Do the events or characteristics to which we have assigned numbers also have this property of additivity? In some cases the answer is yes. Two 1-foot rulers have a combined length of 2 feet, and two 100-ohm resistors placed in series have a resistance of 200 ohms. But in much social scientific research, the numbers used to quantify events do not possess all the properties of the number system. Suppose we arranged for someone to listen to a 1,000 Hz tone of 40 decibels and rate, by assigning a number, the loudness he or she experiences. Now suppose that we simultaneously play two 40 decibel, 1,000 Hz tones. Is the experienced loudness the sum of the two tones? No. Although experienced loudness increases somewhat, the increase is not nearly as large as would be expected from the additivity of the real number system.

To describe the extent to which the numbers researchers assign to events actually match the properties of the real number system, Stevens (e.g., 1968) developed the concept of scales of measurement. The simplest type of scale is called *nominal.* Here the numbers are really only labels—for example, we may assign males the number 1 and females 2 or blacks 1 and whites 2. The magnitude of the numbers has no real significance.

The next type of scale, *ordinal,* allows the rank ordering of a set of events or characteristics. The dryness of champagnes, for example, can be rank ordered (from sweet to dry) from doux, demi-sec, dry, extra-dry, and brut. The numbers 1, 2, 3, 4, and 5 could be used to designate these five types of champagne—but so could any set of five numbers that preserve the ranking (for example, 3, 8, 22, 23, 38). There is no implication that a demi-sec (number 2) is twice as dry as a doux (number 1) or an extra-dry (number 4) twice as dry as a demi-sec (number 2). Indeed, a doux champagne typically contains about 10 percent sugar, a demi-sec 8 percent, a dry 4 percent, an extra-dry 3 percent, and a brut 1½ percent. Thus, with an ordinal scale many common mathematical operations (addition, multiplication) should not be performed, for they would produce misleading results.

With the *interval* scale, the researcher's numbers begin to match the number system more closely. Equal differences in the magnitude of events are now associated with equal intervals between the numbers they have been assigned. However, the scale still has no true zero point. Temperature is an example of an interval scale. The difference between 30°F and 40°F is the same as that between 50° and 60° or 80° and 90°; nonetheless, 0° is not the true zero point for the scale, and temperatures often dip below 0° in all but the tropical regions of the world.

Finally, with the *ratio* scale we have equal intervals and a meaningful zero point. Temperature does not have this property, and thus it is not meaningful to say such things as 40°F is twice as warm as 20°F. (In the Celsius system, these two temperatures would be 4.4°C and −6.7°C.) When a true zero point exists, all ratios are meaningful, and we can properly speak of one magnitude as twice as much as another. Many scales of physical characteristics have a true zero point and thus have more than interval properties. For example, the length of a line or the weight of an object can both be scaled with real numbers so that 0 scores truly mean the absolute absence of the property being measured, that is, a true zero point. Ten pounds of anything *is* twice as much as 5 pounds of the same substance, and 40 pounds of anything is 4 times as much as 10 pounds of it. This characteristic is what we have in mind when we speak of a ratio scale.

Being aware of the type of measurement scale being used is very important for a researcher. The type of scale has important implications for the way data are mathematically treated. Some statistical procedures are inappropriate for certain kinds of data. For example, two common procedures, the *F*-test and the *t*-test, may produce misleading results if they are applied to data that do not have at least interval properties.

Scales of measurement do not usually reside intrinsically within the phenomena we wish to measure. Rather, social scientists often impose a particular scale of measurement on a phenomenon by their choice of a rule for assigning scores. The scores assigned to observations by a researcher must also reflect the phenomena of underlying theoretical interest. This requirement often limits the choice of a scale of measurement. Psychological constructs such as aggressiveness, intelligence, generosity, and stress, to name just a few, tend to refer to one's relative status and cannot be readily conceptualized as having meaningful absolute zero points (not, at least, in a living organism). Thus, efforts to measure complex behavioral phenomena are usually on interval, ordinal, or nominal scales.

Central Tendency and Variability

When observations have been made and scores assigned according to some scale, it will usually be necessary or desirable to describe the set of observations numerically. Any set of observations can be characterized through the use of two descriptive statistics, one measuring central tendency and the other measuring variability.

Central Tendency. By *central tendency* we mean a number representing the most "typical" score in a set of scores. Several different measures of central tendency are used in social science research. The *mode* is that score that occurs most frequently in a sample. The *median* is that score above and below which 50 percent of the scores in the sample fall. The *mean* is the arithmetic average of the scores in the sample, obtained by summing the scores and dividing by the number of scores in the sample (or, as it is sometimes called, *N*). The mode can be computed with a nominal scale; the median requires an ordinal scale; and the mean requires at least an interval scale to be meaningful.

Limitations of the Mean. Most often the mean is used as the measure of central tendency in social science research. The mean can be deceptive, however, even when a ratio scale is involved. This is especially true when the set of observations includes unusual outlying scores. Suppose we had the following set of eleven scores: 1, 7, 3, 4, 6, 5, 2, 7, 11, 259, 7. Although the mean of the set is 28.36, that number hardly reflects the typical score in the set. Here the mode (7) or the median (6) is more representative.

Variability. The *variability* of a set of scores is the typical degree of spread among the scores, or the degree to which they are scattered rather than tightly packed around some value. In social science research, the two most commonly reported measures of variability are the range and the variance (or the square root of the variance, the standard deviation).

The *range* is simply the difference between the largest and the smallest scores in a set. The range alone is rarely an acceptable measure of variability because it is dramatically influenced by a single outlying score. For example, the range of the scores 3, 4, 1, 2, 1, 3, 1, 4, 40 is a whopping 39, hardly a good estimate of the typical variability, or scatter, among the nine scores in the set.

The *variance* is derived from an interest in measuring the average distance of the scores from the mean of the set in which they appear. The variance is computed by obtaining the mean of the set, subtracting each score from the mean to yield its so-called "deviation score," squaring each deviation score, summing these squares, and dividing by the number of scores in the set, N. The *standard deviation* of a set of scores is simply the square root of the set's variance.

The variance and the standard deviation are the most widely accepted measures of variability in social science research (though ranges are often provided as supplementary information). As we shall see, the concept of variability and an understanding of the factors that influence it play a major role in the methodological decisions and judgments made in the social sciences.

Reliability and Validity

We mentioned in Chapter 1 that the value of any scientific observation depends in part on its repeatability, or replicability. An observation that cannot be replicated is unreliable and should not be admitted as scientific evidence. *Reliability*, as applied to social science measurement, refers to the degree that a particular observation has yielded a "true" score. A score is unreliable to the degree that it contains *measurement error*, that is, to the extent to which it has been influenced by irrelevant, chance factors.

To understand the concept of reliability, it is best to begin with the notion of a test. A *test* is any systematic procedure for making and scoring observations.[3]

[3] At a congressional hearing on psychological testing, the American Psychological Association stated that, "Psychological tests are nothing more than careful observations of actual performance under standard conditions" (APA, 1958).

An important historical event in the psychological testing movement occurred when the Paris school board asked Alfred Binet to construct an assessment device to allow the selection of children who might profit most from education. The test Binet developed was successful in predicting educational success, and a subsequent modification of it, the Stanford-Binet, became the first widely used test of intelligence. The field of psychological testing grew out of this early effort to measure intelligence. We now have tests that try to measure vocational interests, brain damage, personality, and abnormal behavior. Each psychological test attempts to gather information about a person using some standardized procedure. The actual procedures can vary tremendously. For example, personality assessment runs the gamut from a person answering true or false to a series of questions (as is done on the Minnesota Multiphasic Personality Inventory or MMPI) to telling an examiner what he or she "sees" in an inkblot (as in the Rorschach). College examinations, the most familiar tests to many students, are procedures used by instructors to observe and quantify how much students have learned. But many of the tests used by social scientists are not of this type. In *situational tests,* for example, the "test" consists of an experimentally controlled but apparently natural situation, such as a subject being asked for help by a person in distress, when the person is in fact an experimental confederate. Both college and situational tests share the essential characteristics of being systematic procedures that will yield scores. (In the case of the situational test, scores might be the number of seconds or minutes it took before the subject responded to the distressed person.)

Regardless of this variation, all tests must meet two criteria. They must be reliable and valid.

Determining Reliability

Consider the following example. A student attending an introductory class in psychology knows that the class is scheduled to begin at 10:10 on Monday, Wednesday, and Friday mornings. A bell, controlled by a university-wide electronic clock system, signals the start of class. When it rings on Monday, the student looks at his watch, which reads 10:05. The watch continues to run for the next two days but, when the bell rings on Wednesday, the student notices that his watch reads 10:20. Finally, on Friday, the watch reads 9:45 when the bell rings. In this circumstance, assuming that the college clock itself is substantially accurate, the student would have little or no confidence in his watch, despite the fact that it continues to run without stopping. He cannot trust, or *rely on,* the watch. Measured against the university clock and bell system, which he has every reason to presume is accurate, the watch does not provide stable information. The time reading changes *in an arbitrary or random fashion* against a criterion that he knows remains constant. In behavioral research, the same problem may be every bit as important but less apparent.

A more formal definition of reliability requires that we again note that most measurements contain some error. Whatever variable is being measured, a person will have an obtained score, *X obtained,* which is composed of two parts: a stable or systematic component and an unaccounted-for random component. These components, in terms of the variability of scores, may be considered as follows:

$$\text{variance obtained} = \text{systematic variance} + \text{random variance}$$

The random component represents the unreliability of the measure. Thus, as is shown below, reliability can be defined as the proportion of systematic variance to the total obtained variance in the test.

$$\text{reliability} = \frac{\text{systematic variance}}{\text{systematic variance} + \text{random variance}}$$

The greater the random or unaccounted-for variance, the larger will be the total variance and hence the *smaller* the ratio; that is, the measure becomes less reliable with increments in unaccounted-for variance.

An examination of two different methods for measuring a person's height provides a good illustration of these concepts. In a physician's office, height is usually measured using an extendable precision ruler, which is permanently fitted in the vertical column of an instrument specially designed to measure height. Use of the device involves a specific and well-defined set of procedures (having the person stand barefoot straight up on a fixed platform while the ruler is extended until its height corresponds to the top of the person's head). If a person's height is measured on five occasions over the period of a week by five different individuals who all follow the same instructions, very likely the person's five height scores will be almost identical. More important, if a second person's height were measured in the same way, and the second person were, in fact, one-half inch taller than the first, the measurements would probably allow us to discriminate between the height scores of the two people. Now suppose that the heights of the same two people had each been measured five times by five different individuals using a twelve-inch plastic ruler instead of a physician's measuring platform. In this second case it is a good bet that the five height scores obtained for each person would be less consistent because of the imprecision involved in using the plastic ruler. As a result, the systematic variation that actually exists in the height of the two persons (one is one-half inch taller than the other) may be masked by the random variation found in the less reliable method of measurement. Hypothetical data illustrating this point are shown in Table 2-3. In this table, case I measurements would correspond to those taken in the doctor's office, and case II measurements would be obtained by using a plastic ruler. The less precise procedure, case II, yields random variation that masks the systematic variation (the true difference) in the heights of persons *A* and *B.* (In both cases the mean difference between *A* and *B,* the systematic variation, is equal.)

The need for determining the reliability of one's measuring instruments and procedures is very acute in the social and behavioral sciences. The great

Table 2-3 Hypothetical Data Illustrating the Relationship of Systematic to Random Variation in Determining the Reliability of a Measurement Procedure*

CASE I		CASE II	
A	B	A	B
66.0	66.5	66.4	66.4
66.0	66.6	65.7	66.3
66.1	66.5	65.9	66.9
65.8	66.5	66.6	66.6
66.0	66.4	65.5	66.5

* The difference between A and B is the systematic variation, whereas the differences among measurements within *A* or *B* is the random variation.

majority of educated people throughout the world will take some sort of personality, intelligence, or ability test in their lifetimes; many people's personal fates will depend on the outcome of these test results. Plainly, then, before using the information gathered from psychological tests to assign people to jobs, educational programs, or categories of any kind, we want to be sure that their scores provide an accurate index of what we wish to measure. To the extent that test scores are influenced by random variation and thus possess *measurement error*, they do not satisfactorally or *reliably* represent the phenomenon the test purports to measure. The problem, of course, is to find techniques that permit us to evaluate the degree to which a particular instrument, test, or evaluating procedure possesses or is free of measurement error. Several techniques for assessing reliabilities are available.

Test-Retest Reliability. One way to evaluate any test is to give a group of people the test and then to give them the same test again later. Let us suppose that such a procedure is carried out and the two scores obtained for each person correspond closely (are highly correlated).[4] The instrument would be said to possess high test-retest reliability. The question is, how much confidence may we now have in the instrument? To answer, note that the test-retest reliability could be high only if an individual's relative position (to the other individuals who were tested) remained very nearly the same from test 1 to test 2. (The reason why this is so will be explained in Chapter 3.) Since this is the case, high test-retest reliability permits us to conclude that the scores obtained with this instrument are positionally stable. What, exactly, does this imply? High test-retest reliability implies that a test is measuring systematic variation among people and contains relatively little error variance. That is, the test will tend to order a sample

[4] We will describe the way in which such correlations are actually obtained in Chapter 3 but the details need not concern us at this point.

of people in the same way regardless of whether they have all taken the test previously or whether they are all naive (have not taken the test).

Nonetheless, high test-retest reliability does *not* mean that a person's first and second test scores are interchangeable, and it is in fact a serious error to view high test-retest reliability this way. High test-retest reliability implies relative stability but not absolute stability of test scores over administrations. In fact, a test in which scores always rise markedly from a first to a second administration may have perfect test-retest reliability, and thus is not discriminable on this measure from a test in which the scores are both relatively and absolutely stable. These points are illustrated in Figure 2-1.

Another important fact to keep in mind when interpreting test-retest reliability has to do with the meaning of low test-retest reliability. High test-retest reliability permits an investigator to conclude that an instrument is free of certain measurement errors, but it is not necessarily the case that low test-retest reliability permits a researcher to conclude that the test possesses a high degree of measurement error.

There are two possible reasons for low test-retest reliability. One is that the actual condition or state that the investigator is endeavoring to measure remains constant, but the measuring instrument is at fault or contains error. The other is that the actual state or condition of the person or thing being measured has changed from the first test to the second. In such an instance, low reliability would simply reflect correct and accurate measurement of these changes rather than a fault in the instrument. Such a circumstance is exemplified in the situation

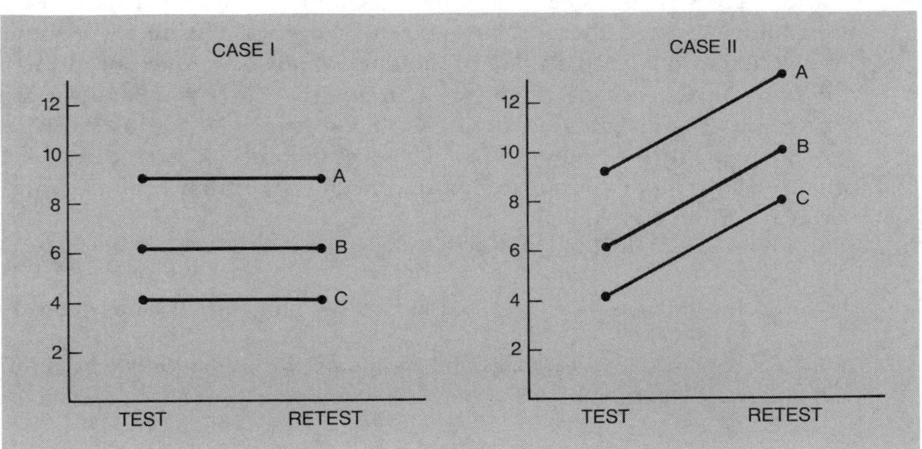

Figure 2–1 Hypothetical data for two possible sets of test-retest scores. In case I, persons *A*, *B*, and *C* each obtain the same scores on the retest as on the original test. In case II, persons *A*, *B*, and *C* each show a marked gain on the retest relative to the original test. Yet because test-retest reliability measures only the degree to which a person's score is relatively (or positionally) stable across readministrations, the test-retest reliability is the same for case I and case II. In fact, in both cases the test-retest reliability would be "perfect."

in which psychiatric patients are evaluated for the severity of their behavioral disorder on admission to the hospital and then reassessed several weeks later. If the most disturbed persons show the greatest degree of change in the first few weeks, low reliability would result not from measurement error but from actual changes in the condition of the individuals being assessed.

Interitem Reliability. A second technique commonly used for assessing the reliability of a particular measurement instrument involves correlating scores on two or more subsets of items on a test. This is referred to as a *split-half* procedure. According to some rule, the items in the test are divided into halves, and the items in each half are correlated with those in the other. For example, individuals' scores on the first half of the items on a particular test can be correlated with the scores on the second half of the items. Similarly, scores on the *even* items of a thirty-item test can be correlated with scores on the *odd* items. There is even a procedure that calculates the average of all possible split-half correlations. Supposing that these correlations are high, what can the investigator conclude?

The investigator may reasonably conclude that the items on the test reflect or measure the same thing or have similar content. Another way of describing high interitem correlations is to say that the items are *internally consistent.* Demonstrating the presence of interitem reliability may or may not be important, depending on theoretical considerations about the purpose of the measurement. On a psychiatric instrument designed to measure the presence or absence of various sorts of problem behavior, it is unimportant to demonstrate interitem reliability, because there is little or no theoretical reason for assuming that an individual who is high on one of the dimensions being measured will necessarily be high on the others. In this case, items reflecting problems such as anxiety, drug abuse, hallucinations, depression, and delusions are not expected to intercorrelate highly. In contrast, consider a test designed to measure a child's achievement in arithmetic. Suppose, for simplicity's sake, that the following two items appear on the test:

1. If a boy has 4 oranges and his mother gives him 9 more oranges, how many oranges will he have?
2. If a boy has 3 baseballs and his mother buys 6 more baseballs for him at the store, how many baseballs will he have?

If it can be shown that children do not tend to answer both item 1 and item 2 correctly or both incorrectly, there is reason to doubt whether the instrument is a consistent measure of the child's arithmetic ability. Instead, we might suspect that the test is unintentionally measuring the child's interest in baseballs versus oranges. Such a finding would suggest that we are indeed measuring *something,* but the "something" is not arithmetic competence per se.

Interrater Reliability. Yet another form of reliability involves having the same individual rated, examined, or observed by two or more individuals. The scores assigned to the examinee by these multiple raters may then be correlated. To the extent that the correlations are high, the investigator may conclude with some confidence that the measurements obtained with the procedure are reasonably independent of who did the testing, examining, or measuring. When several scores on a test have been collected by several examiners, we can hope that the examiner differences did not introduce unaccounted-for variance. Again, however, the important point is that such a reliability estimate relates only to the *relative* position of individual scores. If two different examiners give a standard test of intelligence and one examiner regularly obtains scores ten points higher than another, the interrater reliability is just as high as it would be if the two examiners obtained the same scores for each child. Such a possibility is often overlooked in assessments of interrater reliability and in conclusions drawn when such reliability is found to be high.

Base-Rate Problems. The reliability of raters is often assessed by calculating the percent agreement between them. A ratio is formed of the number of agreements to the total number of judgments. Consider, for example, two raters making psychiatric diagnoses. Each patient is interviewed by both raters, and each of the raters subsequently decides whether the patient is schizophrenic, neurotic, or psychopathic. Let us assume there are 100 cases and that the raters were in agreement on 70 of them, so that the percent agreement would be 70 percent (70/100).

At first blush, 70 percent seems to represent a relatively high level of agreement, given the difficulty of categorizing deviant behavior. However, consider another two raters who assign diagnoses to 100 patients in a random fashion, that is, with no reference to their behavior. Assume that each rater used each of the possible diagnostic categories with the following frequencies:

	RATER A	RATER B
	%	%
Schizophrenic	85	80
Neurotic	10	10
Psychopathic	5	10

By chance alone these two raters would agree 69.5 percent of the time. The reasoning behind this calculation is as follows.

The probability of the joint occurrence of two independent events equals the product of their separate probabilities. Since the diagnoses provided by the two raters are independent, we can determine the overall probability of agreement by multiplying the probabilities of each of the diagnoses and summing $[(.85 \times .80) + (.10 \times .10) + (.05 \times .10) = .695 = 69.5\%]$.

A related problem arises when raters must make a dichotomous judgment between the occurrence and nonoccurrence of some event whenever one of these categories has a much lower actual frequency of occurrence than the other. For example, if two raters are asked to independently watch a two-hour television movie and note, every two minutes, whether or not a sexually explicit act has occurred, we would expect that for most segments raters would find that no such event had occurred. (Overt sexual acts on television are in fact quite rare. See Franzblau et al., 1977.) As a result, simple percent agreement would be very high even when the raters never agree on the occurrence of any sexual act. To see how this might be so, imagine a program divided into fifty two-minute segments, that is, a 100-minute program. Suppose that rater A noted four segments with an explicit sexual act and that rater B also recorded four such segments—but that in fact they were not the same four segments. In this case there is virtually complete disagreement about when (or if) sex occurred, yet the simple percentage of agreement appears to be quite high:

$$\frac{\text{agreements}}{\text{agreements} + \text{disagreements}} = \frac{42}{50} = 84\% \text{ agreement}$$

A much more accurate computational procedure is to ignore agreement on nonoccurrence:

$$\frac{\text{agreed occurrences}}{\text{agreed occurrences} + \text{disagreed occurrences}} = \frac{0}{0 + 8} = 0\% \text{ agreement}$$

Thus, without additional information it is difficult to evaluate a simple percent agreement figure. If few categories are available to the raters and if one of these categories is used frequently, a high level of agreement could be due to chance rather than to actual agreement among the raters. Techniques are available to correct for the influence of chance in calculating agreement between raters, by subtracting the probability of agreeing by chance (Cohen, 1960).

Item Sampling. One of the most critical determinants of the reliability of any assessment procedure is the number of items that are taken from or sampled from the population of items or events of interest. For example, in a seven-game World Series, there is a percentage of cases in which the first game is won by the team that later loses four straight games and hence the series, yet nobody doubts that the team that won four out of five is the better team. But if the series were based on a single game—the first—a conclusion exactly opposite to the accepted one would have been incorrectly drawn. *Reliability tends to increase as the number of items in the sample increases toward the total set of items in the population of interest.* To illustrate, we shall consider the familiar problem of classroom examinations.

In a high school history course, it is likely that the students will be exposed to (or be asked to read) a very large number of facts during a term. The instructor is obliged to determine the degree to which the students have learned the material. How can this be done? Clearly, it will not be feasible to ask each and every possible question that should be answerable on the basis of all the material that has been covered during the semester. The full set of potential questions, not all of which can be asked, represents the *population* of items of interest in this instance. Since all cannot be asked, the instructor must *sample* from this population a set of items that will permit drawing an inference about the degree to which the population has been learned. The problem is: how large shall that sample be?

The instructor may elect to give one multiple-choice question. It is possible that the single fact represented by that question would be remembered by a number of students who were fortunate enough to have studied it although they learned, absorbed, and remembered very little else from the course. In contrast, quite good students who had mastered most of the material in the course might by misfortune have not noted or not be able to recall this item. Such a one-item test would likely be highly unreliable. We would not feel confident in saying that individuals who answered this item correctly would have a high probability of being able to answer some other single item correctly, or some other small set of items correctly, or the entire population (if it were feasible to give such a large test) correctly. Thus, although the entire population of items is clearly too large, a single item test is too small. A compromise must be struck.

In general it can be shown that a moderately large number of items will provide quite good reliability and that the addition of items thereafter will contribute little to reliability.[5]

We have said that a one-item, multiple-choice test is unreliable. Such a test will not reliably predict performance on other sets of items drawn from the population of interest (all the materials presented in the course). It is likely, however, that performance on a one-item test would show high test-retest reliability. It would, in other words, serve as an excellent prediction of whether students who once answered that particular question correctly would be likely or unlikely to do so hours or days later (unless some or all students subsequently had an opportunity to look up the answer). This striking contrast between reliability of prediction to a population and test-retest reliability of a particular item or small set of items suggests an important principle of research. *Adequate measurement requires a definition of the phenomenon that the investigator is trying to measure that is independent of the issue of reliability.* This leads us to the concept of validity.

The Concept of Validity

Social scientists are rarely interested merely in the observations and scores derived from their test procedures. Instead, they are interested in what the test score presumably reflects. For example, most IQ tests require examinees to do such things as solve problems, dilemmas, or riddles put to them by the examiner, but a measure of puzzle solving per se is not the aim of these tests. Rather, they

[5]Although somewhat beyond the intended scope of this book, a mathematical description of this relationship will relate two aspects of the test: 1) the reliability of a test of a given item size and 2) the number of items that are added to the initial test.

are designed to measure an abstract, hypothetical characteristic of the examinee—intelligence. This an IQ test may or may not actually do.

Broadly speaking, two types of validity are discussed in the behavioral sciences. One type has to do with the validity of tests or measures used in research, and the other type has to do with the validity of the inferences (for example, causal inferences) that the investigator draws from his or her research findings. Our discussion here is limited to the validity of tests and measurements. We will consider the problem of valid inference in detail in Chapter 12.

A test is valid to the degree that it measures what it purports to measure (or what the investigator believes it to measure). All measures of validity involve determining the relationship between test scores and other independent observations about the subject's past, present, or future behavior. Broadly, three types of validity are recognized in social science research: content validity, criterion validity, and construct validity.

Content validity is the property of containing content that is directly and representatively sampled from the domain of interest. A college examination possesses content validity as a measure of academic learning to the extent that it samples fairly from the reading assignments and lectures given during the course. In the same way, a behavioral test of sharing possesses content validity to the degree that it actually simulates the life situations in which the investigator is ultimately interested.

Many tests could not substantiate their worth on the grounds of content validity alone. Such tests, of which the IQ test is one, rely heavily on demonstrations of their criterion validity.

Criterion validity is the degree to which the test scores predict or are associated with an individual's behavior in situations to which they should predict if the test is measuring what it purports to measure. Academic achievement is often used as a criterion for validating IQ tests. IQ tests *should be* predictors of how well people will do in school; otherwise, they wouldn't be IQ tests. Conversely, a test that does predict school performance enjoys some validation as an IQ test.

A First Look at Construct (Theoretical) Validity. The third type of validity, *construct validity,* refers to the extent to which a test measures a particular theoretical construct (that is, an entity with no actual existence that is nonetheless hypothesized to operate in the causal chain of real events). The construct validation procedure usually involves examining the relationship between test scores and a network of other observations made on the person. In a definitive statement, the American Psychological Association put it this way:

> Construct validity is ordinarily studied when the tester has no definite criterion measure of the quality with which he is concerned, and must use indirect measures. Here the trait or quality underlying the test is of central importance, rather than either the test behavior or the scores on the criteria (APA, 1954, p. 14).

Many of the phenomena studied by social and behavioral scientists fall into the category of not having a single, definite criterion measure or operational definition with which they can be equated. Thus, when the idea of construct validity was introduced to the behavioral sciences, it seemed to provide a legitimate way of getting at complex phenomena that defied measurement by any one procedure, method, or instrument. It appeared that by using a construct validation approach, one could define a complex psychological phenomenon by showing that its meaning lay in a network of relationships among directly measurable variables. Measurements of the construct of "anxiety," for example, might be validated by showing that anxiety can be produced by such varied experiences as taking an examination, expecting to receive an electric shock, or fighting with a friend. At the same time, one can show that each of these provocations produces a symptom we would expect to be associated with anxiety, such as the person's subjective report of discomfort, or psychophysiological changes, or a visible hand tremor.

Assuming that these various measures of anxiety are reliable, how can we tell if the construct is valid? The answer lies in examining a network of relationships between measures of the construct and measures of other variables or processes. This network is referred to as a *nomological net* (Cronbach & Meehl, 1955). If we find that anxiety is related in predicted ways to a variety of other behaviors (for example, to poor performance on a college exam, avoidance of potentially stressful situations, or the use of particular defense mechanisms) the construct is said to be valid. It is the network of relationships that exists among variables, rather than any one measure, that constitutes the construct validation of anxiety. The whole idea is represented graphically in Figure 2-2.

The construct validation approach is not without its problems, however. Early discussions of construct validity were followed by some stinging criticisms

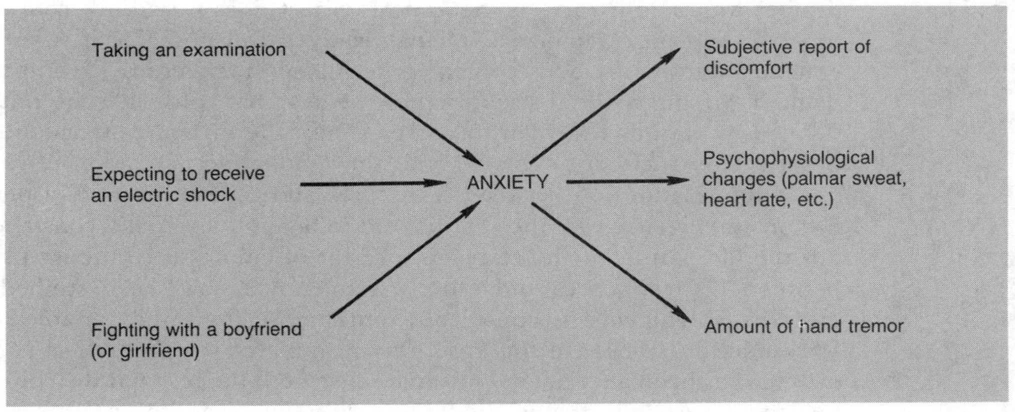

Figure 2–2 A simplified nomological net, in which the theoretical construct anxiety is defined by a network of relationships that serve to support or validate the construct, rather than by a single measure.

of the notion, because it seemed that the whole idea of construct validation was somewhat circular. Bechtoldt, in one of the best-known critiques, gives this example of the use of the theoretical construct, "overcompensated inferiority complex."

> If a person has an overcompensated inferiority complex, he blusters, is aggressive, domineering, and dogmatic; this man blusters, is aggressive, domineering and dogmatic; therefore, he has an inferiority complex (Bechtoldt, 1959, p. 627).

This reasoning, Bechtoldt points out, is quite wrong logically because it confuses *sufficient* with *necessary and sufficient* (see our earlier discussion, p. 12). Bechtoldt dramatizes his point by showing that the reasoning behind the inferiority complex example produces inferences that are obviously absurd when applied to less exotic matters. For example:

> If "Old Dog Tray" was run through a large and powerful sausage-grinder, he is dead; he is dead, therefore, he was sausaged (Bechtoldt, 1959, p. 627, citing Johnson, 1954).

In the last analysis, Bechtoldt's criticisms apply to the use of any theoretical constructs. His objection is that in defining a term (for example, a theoretical construct) in terms of many partial relationships (for example, IQ should be related to academic achievement but it is not the same as academic achievement; IQ should be related to creativity but it is not the same as creativity; and so on), no really explicit definition is provided at all.

Many social scientists do not take Bechtoldt's objection seriously. If a completely explicit definition can be offered, they point out, we are no longer dealing with a construct, or theoretical term. Genes were once constructs used to try to explain resemblance among relatives. But now that it is known that a gene is an array of DNA, the gene is no longer a construct. It can be explicitly defined. So, many social scientists now believe that constructs are only partially defined by various tests and measures. Thus, the meaning attached to the theoretical constructs does change with the gradual accumulation of information about the relationship between test scores and other aspects of a person's behavior. Intelligence was once considered to be quite fixed and constant throughout the lifespan. Now, however, as a result of empirical relationships observed between IQ test scores and other variables that have been studied developmentally, intelligence is considered much more fluid and variable (Liebert & Wicks-Nelson, 1981). In this case, the meaning of the theoretical construct *intelligence* has been altered, and in some sense both the test and the construct have become more valid—that is, the IQ tests of today come closer to measuring what they purport to measure than did the IQ tests of thirty years ago, when the underlying conception of intelligence was different.

SURVEYING A POPULATION

A fundamental question social scientists ask refers to the frequency of an event or characteristic in the population at large. Research directed in this way is usually referred to as survey research. Manufacturers conduct surveys to determine the percentage of people who may buy a new product; television networks survey people to determine the popularity of shows so they can fix the price of advertising time; and people's attitudes toward political figures and significant social or political issues are under continual scrutiny by the survey researcher.

A key issue in survey research is that it would be uneconomical and impractical to survey everyone. In predicting whether a particular political candidate will win next November's election, one might wish to determine the percentage of voters who would favor his or her candidacy now. This question could be asked directly by inquiring into the preferences of the entire voter population. However, such a strategy is not usually feasible; the population is simply too large to be studied economically.

To determine the frequency of some characteristic in the population, social scientists will typically draw a sample systematically from it. After determining the frequency of the characteristic in the sample, the investigator will wish to generalize back to the parent population. Such generalizations must be made with some caution. They involve an *inference* and can only be made according to a series of assumptions and rules that tend to assure their legitimacy within certain bounds. Many of the issues will parallel those in our earlier consideration of sampling (pp. 32–34).

Selecting a Sample

The interpretation of the results of any survey hinges on the method of sampling that was used in gathering the data. A fairly common practice in some television commercials has been to display the results of an apparent survey. A good example is an ad depicting a series of taste comparisons between Coke and Pepsi. Although the four people shown claim to be Coke drinkers, they select Pepsi as the better-tasting beverage. As evidence, this information is totally worthless. Because we do not know how many people were tested, we have no way of evaluating the information provided. Did four of four Coke drinkers prefer Pepsi, or were the figures four of eight—or even four of 100? Somewhat better but still inadequate are claims such as, "Four out of five dentists surveyed recommend Brand X gum for their patients who chew gum." Here we know that four of five made the recommendation, but we do not know how many dentists actually participated in the survey or how they were sampled.

The broadest sampling decision facing the survey researcher is between *probability* and *nonprobability sampling.* Probability sampling refers to any procedure in which each population element has a specifiable likelihood, or probability, of being included in the sample. Nonprobability sampling refers to procedures into which the foregoing restriction is not built.

Nonprobability sampling can occur in any number of ways. One might select the first 100 people one meets in the street (as is typically done in many newspaper surveys) or the first 50, 100, or 500 people whose names appear in the telephone book. A second, and more sophisticated, form of nonprobability sampling is the so-called *quota sampling procedure.* In such a procedure, the sample is selected so that it is a "replica" of the population along certain dimensions. If the population at large contains approximately 20 percent black individuals, then the sample would be selected in such a fashion that it, too, contains a 20 percent black representation. Samples are sometimes drawn so that they replicate the population in respect to race, ethnic background, age, geographic location, and so on.

The difficulty with both forms of nonprobability sampling is that any inferences drawn to the population at large are questionable because they are unlikely to produce a representative sample. It is easy to see why this is so in the case of accidental sampling procedures, since the first 100 people one meets on the street might very well differ from the population at large simply because of their presence on a particular street corner at a particular time of day. Selecting individuals from the phone book presents several difficulties. The very wealthy and the very poor are somewhat less likely to appear than are middle-class persons. Single women may be somewhat less likely than families to have listed phone numbers. Sampling errors due to using the phone book or similar directories as a source of potential respondents can be quite serious and extremely embarrassing, as the publishers of a once-famous magazine learned more than 50 years ago.

The Literary Digest Debacle. In 1936 pollsters for the *Literary Digest* (which was then a widely known and highly respected periodical) predicted that Republican Alf Landon would defeat Democrat incumbent Franklin Delano Roosevelt by a landslide. The outcome was indeed a landslide, but favoring Roosevelt rather than Landon! The mistake the pollsters made was in using telephone directories as a source for identifying respondents. In 1936 only 35% of all households had telephones (and these tended to be the more affluent families who have always disproportionately favored the Republicans).

The Problem With Quota Sampling. Potential biases in the quota sampling procedure are somewhat more difficult to see intuitively, but they are present. The problem lies in the relationship between the *sampled* subpopulation and its parent subpopulation in the overall population at large. Including black people as 20 percent of our sample (when the population at large is 20 percent black) will not ensure that the characteristics of black persons in our sample will correspond to characteristics of black people in the population. We could include blacks who are, on the average, substantially wealthier or poorer than would be true of the population at large. Thus, although nonprobability sampling procedures are easy to employ, they are generally not to be recommended for drawing inferences to the population at large. To do so confidently, the investigator is advised to turn to a probability sampling procedure.

Stratified and Free Random Sampling. The critical aspect of any probability sampling procedure is that each element in the population has some *specifiable* probability of inclusion in the sample. This is not to say, however, that the probability of each element being represented must be equal to that of other elements. In *simple random sampling,* each element has an equal probability of being included in the sample. In contrast, *stratified random sampling* involves dividing the population into two, three, or more strata (for example, by socioeconomic background) and then *randomly sampling from each stratum.*

Regardless of the actual sampling procedure undertaken, the first step in any type of research is to define the population of interest. This definition will typically involve some exclusions. In surveys that are pertinent to national elections, one would systematically exclude all individuals who are not yet of voting age. Or, in the case of certain market surveys, individuals below (or above) a certain economic level might well be excluded from a survey designed to determine the probable marketability of some new product or service.

The major advantage of random probability sampling is that the investigator can draw explicit inferences regarding the frequency of certain characteristics in the population in which he or she is interested. For example, with a probability sample of about 800 homes, in which it is found that 98 percent have television sets, the investigator can specify with a particular certainty level (for example, 19 chances in 20) that somewhere between 97 percent and 99 percent of all American homes are equipped with televisions.

Choosing a Sample Size. When probability sampling is employed, the question arises, How large a sample should be drawn? Clearly, a variety of economic considerations must be brought to bear on this question. *As a general rule, the larger the sample the more precise will be the estimate of the characteristic in the population.* This is especially true in the lowest ranges of sample size, say below 100.

Advantages of Stratification. A stratified sampling procedure has several related advantages over a simple random one. Two are particularly important. When the investigator is employing a small sample, a simple random procedure is fairly likely to exclude characteristics of the population that have a low frequency of occurrence. A stratified random sampling procedure will ensure that they have some representation, and thus it will increase the efficiency of the population estimate.

Likewise, stratified sampling secures a major advantage for the investigator when the basis for stratification does, in fact, relate to the characteristics being measured. Sex of the respondent may matter little and age a lot on certain political issues. In the latter case, estimates to the population will be markedly more efficient if stratified random sampling according to age is employed. Because few investigators will be able to stratify on all the conceivable dimensions, some sort of *a priori* judgment of which characteristics are likely to matter will be required. Typically the outcome of earlier research will serve the investigator in good stead when making such decisions.

Techniques of Surveying

There are three major techniques in survey research: the distributed questionnaire, the phone survey, and the systematic interview. The first two are typically chosen for the sake of economy. Whether the economic gain outweighs the cost introduced by other problems is often doubtful, however, as we shall see.

The Distributed Questionnaire. The distributed questionnaire is employed whenever individuals are mailed written materials to be completed or invited to respond to a series of items about some product in movie theaters, restaurants, and the like. The major disadvantage of this approach is that even if a stratified random sampling procedure is employed in the distribution of the materials, there is a fairly high likelihood of self-selection bias among the respondents.

Consider the situation in which audience ratings of a particular film are gathered. All members of the audience might be distributed a questionnaire to complete, with a return rate of 50 percent. Suppose that *among the returned questionnaires,* the response to the film is overwhelmingly favorable. What can be concluded about the population? In this circumstance it is very likely that the investigator will obtain an inflated estimate of the potential popularity of the film. Individuals who liked the film will be more likely to complete and return the questionnaire than will those who did not. The same problem should also be apparent in those restaurants which invite their customers to fill out a response card evaluating the food and service, or in mail political surveys. A disproportionately large number of extremely *negative* views can also be picked up through mail research. Clearly, in this situation, a "silent majority" of neutral persons is left out. Advertisements indicating that "four out of five doctors" have recommended a particular product are particularly susceptible to an overwhelming positive bias about physicians' approval of the product. Those who did not like it may not have responded at all.

Phone Surveys. Fewer persons will fail to reply to a phone questionnaire than to a distributed questionnaire, but the telephone survey still involves systematic bias regarding a failure to answer particular questions. It is likwise very difficult to make an immediate distinction between accurate and inaccurate replies on the telephone. It has been shown, for example, that individuals will provide evaluations (sometimes quite strong ones) of nonexistent television programs when asked to do so over the telephone (Greenberg, 1971, personal communication).

The Total Design Method. Dillman (1978) has developed an approach to mail and telephone surveys referred to as "the total design method." The basic idea behind the method is that the survey researcher must give close attention to every detail of a proposed survey that might affect responses. For example, among the factors that might increase response to a mail survey are:

1. Advance notification by letter or phone that a questionnaire is being sent
2. Use of certified mail for delivery
3. Personalization of correspondence
4. Offering or enclosing incentives for completing the questionnaire
5. Emphasis in the cover letter on the social importance of the survey
6. Well-timed, repeated follow-ups to nonresponders.

Dillman also urges a close analysis of the type of information being sought. This is especially important because people may be especially sensitive to any preferences implicit in the wording of the questions. Suggesting that the status quo is "about right," for example, may bias respondents in the direction of approval. For example, Schuman and Duncan (1974) reported markedly different outcomes of an attempt to measure U.S. attitudes toward the Vietnam War in 1969, depending on the way the survey question was worded. Here are the two versions and the results:

I President Nixon has ordered the withdrawal of 25,000 troops from Vietnam in the next three months. How do you feel about this—do you think troops should be withdrawn at a faster rate or slower rate?
- 42% faster
- 20% same as now (not mentioned as an alternative, but accepted if offered)
- 16% slower
- 13% no opinion

II In general do you feel the pace at which the president is withdrawing troops is too fast, too slow, or about right?
- 28% too slow
- 49% about right
- 6% too fast
- 18% no opinion

(as quoted in Dillman, 1978, p. 85)

Systematic Interviews. Surveying by systematic personal interview may be an effective survey technique for reducing some of the biases we have mentioned. Nonetheless, the investigator must still be wary of a variety of biases.

Personal interviews that follow a systematic sampling plan are likely to provide adequate data, but a large number of checks will be necessary to assure that the plan is carried out. If not constrained formally, interviewers will tend to meet their own quotas by sampling friends, concentrate on areas where there are large numbers of people, and favor making home visits when some potential respondents are more likely to be at home than others. Finally, interviewers will tend to avoid upper stories and dilapidated buildings (Selltiz, Jahoda, Deutsch, & Cook, 1959). These problems are all compounded by the usual procedure in which interviewers are paid by the unit, that is, for each interview secured.

But these disadvantages can be largely overcome, and the personal interview is the preferred technique for gathering survey data. It is possible to arrange systematic "call-backs" to obtain information from potential respondents who are not available for a first interview. It is also possible to obtain a reliability estimate of the information gathered by systematically reinterviewing a subsample of persons. In this event the investigator will get at least some feel for the degree to which the information obtained is reliable from one interview to the other.

In addition to securing reliability data, personal interviews that involve the cooperation of the respondents may also permit obtaining data on the *validity* of the information gathered. Bechtel, Achelpohl, and Akers (1972) were able to compare information obtained from interview and diary data with actual monitoring of the television-watching behavior of a number of respondents. (Interestingly, although Bechtel found rather good agreement between direct observations and interview data, he did find a tendency for persons to overestimate the amount of time they spent watching television.) As LoSciuto (1972) has noted, the quality of interview data may also be improved by following these recommendations:

1. Provide detailed training and explicit instructions concerning the way in which respondents are recruited and the way in which the interview is to be conducted.
2. Ensure means of checking samples of the interviewers' work.
3. Provide incentives for respondents if a good deal of work is required of them, for example, keeping a weekly diary of TV viewing.

FOR REVIEW AND DISCUSSION

1. Of what value is the case study approach to hypothesis testing?
2. One of the most important features of behavioral research is control (over all relevant variables). How does the researcher using the case study approach deal with this problem?
3. What factors would you consider before making inferences about the population on the basis of a case study?
4. On one Friday morning, every fifth person who entered a certain grocery store in the suburbs was asked to take part in a poll assessing political candidates. Would you say that the result from this sample could be generalized to the relevant population? What is the relevant population?

5. What factors make the use of probability sampling more desirable than nonprobability sampling?
6. List three phenomena that are usually measured on ordinal scales, and devise an alternative procedure for converting measurement of these phenomena to an interval or ratio scale.
7. Under what circumstances will the median, mode, and mean of a set of scores all tend to assume the same value?
8. What differences exist between psychological tests (for example, of intelligence or various aspects of personality) and other types of measures used in social and behavioral research?
9. Under what circumstances would you expect test-retest reliability to be low even though interitem and interrater reliability are both high?
10. What would be the disadvantages of equating every theoretical construct with a single, explicit measuring procedure?
11. What is meant by the term *scales of measurement?* Explain the different properties of nominal, ordinal, interval, and ratio scales.
12. Explain the concept of variance.

3

Association, Correlation, and Regression

CORRELATIONAL RESEARCH
- Indexing a Relationship
- Comparing r's: The Concept of Shared Variance
- Statistical Significance
- Sample Range and the Magnitude of the Correlation
- Curvilinear Relationships
- Correlations as Rank-Order Relationships

REGRESSION

TIME SERIES ANALYSIS

FOR REVIEW AND DISCUSSION

In our everyday lives we often notice that two events are related or associated; when one occurs, so does the other. Sometimes, the relationship is a universal one, as when we perceive that ice forms (one event) only on days when the temperature is below 32°F (the other event). Other times, though, the association is less strong; it tends to rain on some, but not all, cloudy days. Here rain and clouds are associated, but the degree or strength of association is less than that between the freezing of a liquid and temperature.

In the previous chapter, we examined several means by which behavioral scientists collect descriptive information. In the course of doing this or conducting other research, scientists are also likely to notice associations between events. Indeed, noticing these associations is often the beginning of a scientific discovery. While performing his Nobel prize-winning research on digestion, Ivan Pavlov noticed that after several days of experimentation his dogs began to salivate when they were approached by the person who fed them. Two events—the approach of the familiar laboratory assistant and the dog's salivation—were associated. The subsequent pursuit of this association gave rise to discovering the phenomenon we now know as classical conditioning.

Although these chance happenings have played an important role in all sciences, the bulk of scientific research is directed at a more systematic examination of associations. Sometimes a researcher will wonder whether two or more variables might be associated. For example, is the occurrence of schizophrenia related to socioeconomic status? Or, are grades related to the frequency with which students attend class? In other instances the scientist may be testing or evaluating a theory. Because theories specify that certain variables should be associated, determining whether a predicted association is present becomes a way of evaluating the theory. To take a simple example, we can consider a theory that proposes that schizophrenia, one of the most severe psychological disorders, is genetically transmitted. One way of evaluating the theory is to identify a sample of schizophrenics and then carefully assess various members of their families (siblings, parents, uncles, aunts) to see how many of the family members are also schizophrenic. The genetic theory predicts that the greater the genetic similarity between a family member and a schizophrenic, the more likely it is that the family member will also be schizophrenic. Among the schizophrenic's siblings, who are on the average 50 percent similar to him or her genetically, we should find more instances of schizophrenia than in a schizophrenic's grandparents, who are on the average only 25 percent genetically similar to him or her. The association we are seeking, then, is between the extent to which genetic background is shared and the likelihood of co-occuring schizophrenia.

In this chapter we will examine several ways in which associations are evaluated by social scientists, beginning with a discussion of correlational research.

CORRELATIONAL RESEARCH

Correlation, as the term suggests, refers to the co- or joint relationship between (or among) two or more variables. Correlational techniques can answer questions like, Do variable X and variable Y go together or vary together? In other words, are the two variables associated? Correlations between tests or parts of tests are involved in assessing reliability, as we saw in Chapter 2.

The first step in doing correlational research involves obtaining pairs of observations on a group of subjects. For example, we may obtain the IQ scores of ten children and the IQ scores of one of each child's parents. Then we might arrange the information in tabular form, as in Table 3-1. We would then wish to ask two questions: How can we index the degree of relationship shown in the data? How can we determine whether such a relationship also holds in the population from which our sample has been drawn?

Indexing a Relationship

In the late nineteenth century, Karl Pearson, building upon the foundation laid by Sir Francis Galton, devised the most prevalent means of indexing a relationship between two variables. Referred to as the *Pearson product moment correlation coefficient,* it is often abbreviated r.[1] This statistic may take values between -1.00 and $+1.00$ and involves the assumption that the underlying relationship between the variables is *rectilinear* that is, can be represented by a straight line. (Curvilinear relationships are discussed later in this chapter). Both the *magnitude* and the *direction* of a relationship are reflected in the correlation coefficient. The higher the *absolute value* of r, the larger or stronger is the relationship between the two variables. An r of either $+1.00$ or -1.00 designates a perfect (and thus equally strong) relationship between two variables, whereas an r of 0.00 indicates that the variables are unrelated. When we have a correlation of either $+1.00$ or -1.00 between two variables, we are able to predict one variable from the other without making any errors. In contrast, with an r of 0.00, we can make no accurate predictions. The variables are not associated. Intermediate values of r (either plus or minus) mean that the variables are associated to some degree. But because the relationship is not perfect, attempts to predict one variable from the other will be somewhat in error. An example of such an intermediate correlation is the association of height and weight. In general, the taller people are, the heavier they tend to be. But this relationship is not perfect. Some people tend to be underweight and others overweight for their height.

If the sign of r is positive, the two variables are said to be *positively related.* As scores on variable X increase, scores on variable Y tend to increase also. Income, for example, is positively related to the purchase of luxuries. The more

[1] There are several correlation coefficients, of which r is only one. Our comments on correlational research apply to the others as well.

Table 3-1 Pairs of Observations (Child's and Mother's IQ Scores) for Ten Pairs of Individuals

CHILD	CHILD'S IQ	MOTHER'S IQ
1	97	90
2	104	96
3	86	111
4	120	150
5	101	98
6	115	110
7	112	100
8	136	124
9	90	82
10	99	107

money people have, the more likely they are to buy luxuries. If the sign of r is negative, the variables are said to be *inversely related:* High scores on one variable are related to (or go together with) low scores on the other. The frequency of schizophrenia, for example, is inversely related to socioeconomic status. Higher social class is associated with lower frequencies of schizophrenia.

To see the particular relationship that has been obtained between two variables, social scientists often find it helpful to plot the relationship as a *scatter diagram.* Examining these scatter diagrams is even more important now that most analyses are performed by a computer so that the researcher has little direct contact with the data. Figure 3-1 presents diagrams of several of the possible forms of relationships, as well as the specific example presented in Table 3-1.

Note that in Figure 3-1 each entry point corresponds to the two scores of a given subject (that is, a score for variable X and a score for variable Y). In the case of perfect relationships (positive or negative, that is, $+1.00$ or -1.00), all the points fall on a single straight line. For these subjects, if we knew an individual's score on only one of the variables (and it would not matter which one), we could determine with certainty the score that he or she had on the other. When there is a perfect correlational relationship, regardless of direction, the corresponding graphic presentation will show no "scatter," or deviation, from the perfect line of correlation. Likewise, as Figure 3-1 shows, in the case of relatively large correlations, there is only a small degree of scatter about the line of perfect correlation. As the correlations become lower, the scores tend to increasingly scatter and become dispersed. Finally, when the correlation equals 0.00, there is so much scatter that the scores tend to look like a circle.

Comparing r's: The Concept of Shared Variance

Often, investigators will want to compare the relative magnitude of two or more r's. For example, we may wish to know how much stronger the relationship between X and Y is when $r = 0.80$ than it is when $r = 0.40$. The first

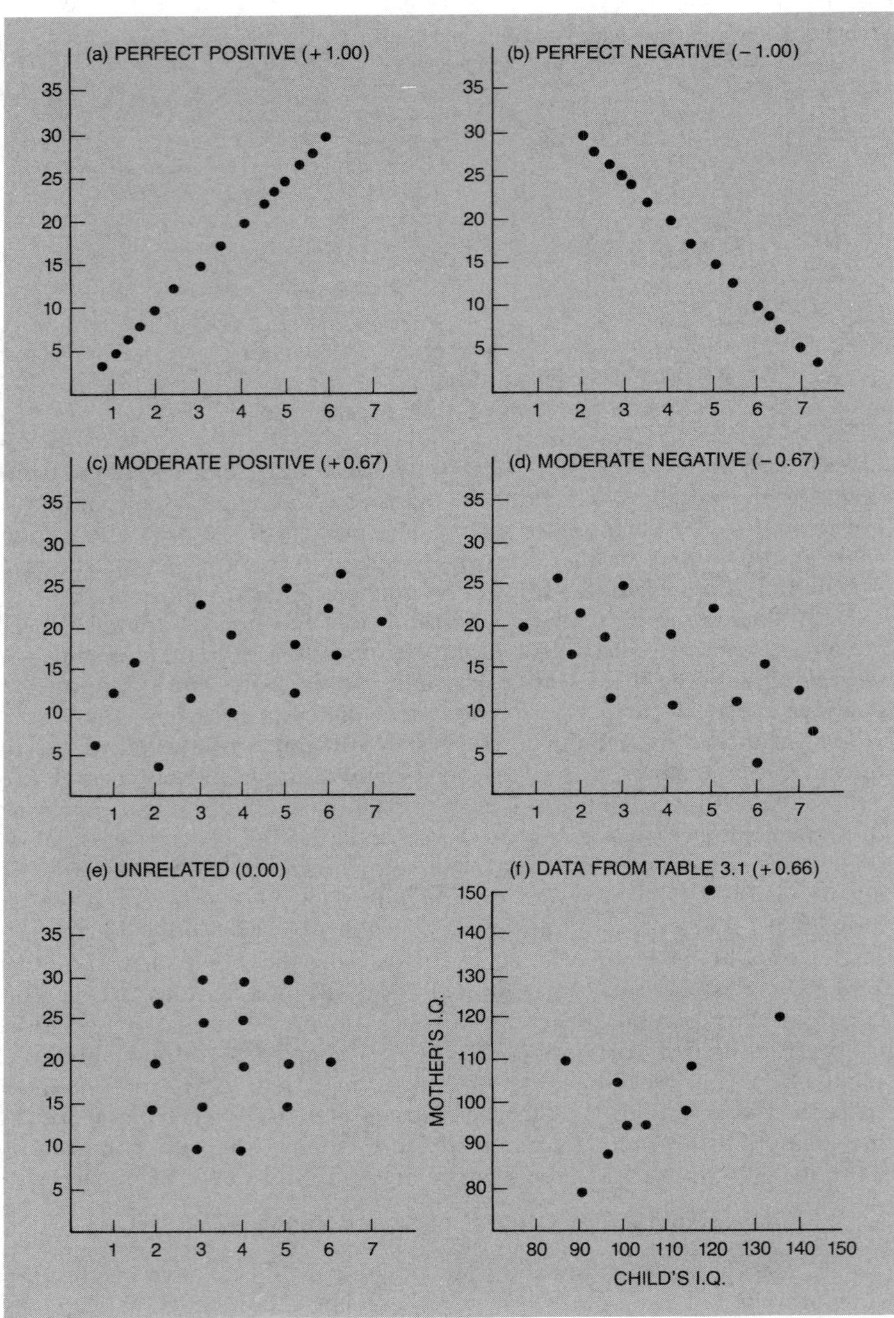

Figure 3-1 Scatter diagrams showing various degrees of relationships.

point to note is that because of their mathematical derivation, r values form only an ordinal scale (see p. 35). Thus the r's of 0.10, 0.20, 0.30, and 0.40 do *not* reflect equal increments in the magnitude of the associations they represent, and an r of 0.80 does *not* represent a degree of relationship twice as large as an r of 0.40.

To determine the relative strength of two or more r's, one must square r, thus forming a new measure, r^2, which can be treated as a proportion and compared with other r^2s. (This is another way of saying that values of r^2 form a ratio scale.)

What, though, does r^2 actually represent? It is a measure of the amount of variance in Y scores that can be accounted for by variance in X scores. When all the variance in Y scores is accounted for by variance in X, there is no unaccounted-for variability and no "scatter" about the line formed in a scatter diagram of the relationship (see Figure 3-1). Another way of expressing the same idea is to think of r^2 as the proportion of "shared variance" between X and Y. When $r^2 = \pm 1.00$, all the variance in X is shared with Y and vice versa. When $r^2 = \pm 0.50$, half the variance in Y scores is accounted for or shared with X scores, but the remaining half of the variance in each set of scores is unaccounted for by the other. The concept of shared variance can also be displayed visually, through the use of Venn diagrams. These represent the degree of overlap (the strength of association) between X and Y. Figure 3-2 shows the relationships that exist when $r = 0.00, 0.20, 0.40, 0.60, 0.80$, and 1.00. (Note that the corresponding r^2s are 0.00, 0.04, 0.16, 0.36, 0.64, and 1.00.)

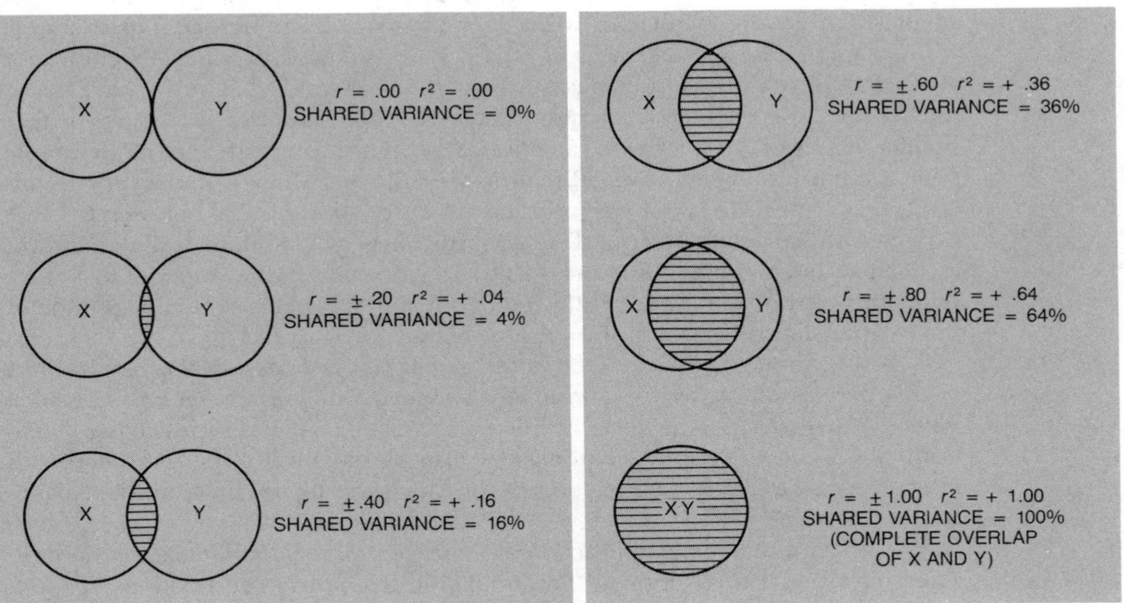

Figure 3-2 Correlation as shared variance.

Statistical Significance

After the researcher has obtained a particular correlational relationship in a sample, he or she will want to determine whether it also holds in the population. In other words, the researcher wants to know whether the relationship is "real" or whether it could have simply been a chance occurrence. *Statistical significance* is the concept used in evaluating this question. A statistically significant result is one that has a low probability of occurring by chance alone.

Traditionally in behavioral research, a result is considered statistically significant if the likelihood is 5 in 100 or fewer that it is a chance finding. This level of significance is called the 0.05 level (commonly written "$p < .05$" and understood to mean "probability less than 5 percent"). The greater the likelihood that the result is not due to chance alone, the more confidence a researcher will usually place in the results. If all other things are equal, a scientist will have even greater confidence in the results if it is shown that they would have occurred by chance only one time in a hundred ($p < .01$) than if the outcome simply reached the customary "0.05" level. Given the former (lower) probability, the researcher can be more confident that a similar relationship would be found in future research.

The larger the value of the correlation coefficient, the more likely it is to be statistically significant. For example, with 30 cases an r of 0.35 or above will be significant; those below 0.35 will not. Correlational studies can also vary in their *power* for detecting statistically significant relationships. The size of the sample plays an important role in determining power. With larger sample sizes, smaller correlation coefficients will achieve statistical significance. For example, with a sample of 100 cases an r of only 0.19 is required to achieve significance at the 0.05 level, but with 20 cases an r of 0.42 is required. Thus, with a larger sample the test for statistical significance is more powerful in the sense that smaller values of r will achieve statistical significance. But with very large sample sizes, we encounter the problem that very small r's, although statistically significant, may have little *practical* significance. A correlation of 0.19 between College Board exam scores and later performance in college will be statistically significant if the sample contained 100 cases. But such a small relationship would not be of much practical use for selecting successful students because the magnitude of the relationship reflected by $r = 0.19$ is almost trivial (see Figure 3-2).

The important point to be noted is that *the size or magnitude of a relationship and the question of whether the relationship will be statistically significant are independent features of any set of sample data.* This is true not only of studies involving classificatory variables (e.g., correlations) but also of statistical tests associated with manipulated variables (e.g., experiments), which will be discussed in later chapters.

In sum, statistical significance is a measure of the confidence we can have when inferring relationships in the population from observed relationships in a sample. Obviously, though, inferences drawn from biased or nonrepresentative samples cannot be trusted regardless of the outcome of tests of statistical significance.

Sample Range and the Magnitude of the Correlation

For an accurate estimate of a correlation, the sample must approximate as closely as possible the full range of scores that are expected in further research. This is another instance of the concept of representative samples, which was introduced in Chapter 2. If an adequate sample range is not used and a somewhat *truncated range* is employed, then the obtained correlation will be artificially depressed. This nonintuitive point can be seen through a simple example using the scatter diagram technique.

Suppose we are interested in the relationship between the number of children in a classroom and the degree to which they engage in disruptive behavior. If the full range of such possibilities were represented in the sample used, we might obtain a distribution or scatter diagram between the scores reflecting amount of disruptive behavior and the number of children in the class. The scatter diagram would look something like that presented in Figure 3-3A.

Note that the relationship is high and positive, with a correlation coefficient of 0.67. Now consider the small or restricted range of that scatter plot in the boxed area of Figure 3-3A. In Figure 3-3B, without changing any of the scores, the boxed area has been blown up to represent a scatter plot of its own. In contrast to the clear positive relationship seen in Figure 3-3A, note that the data represented in Figure 3-3B show a quite weak relationship. This appearance is confirmed by the obtained correlation for these data, which yields an r of only 0.25. Likewise, the reader can demonstrate that by selecting a similarly restricted sample from the low range of scores, or even a restricted sample from the middle range of scores, the obtained relationship will again be depressed. Inflated confidence in the size of a correlation may also result from using a more extensive range in the sample than is actually of interest. Thus, *a fundamental rule for obtaining samples for correlational research is to represent adequately the range of scores in the population of interest.*

The concept of truncated range also helps to explain why one predictive relationship is stronger than another, even when the same conceptual question seems to be involved in both cases. Weizmann (1971) offers as an example of this point the fact that IQ scores predict college grades rather well but do not predict graduate school grades at all. He observes:

> Intelligence quotient scores . . . predict academic success relatively well overall. They do not, however, predict success in graduate school with any great degree of accuracy, because graduate school applicants tend to cluster around the high end of the IQ distribution. Thus, although an obtained correlation accurately describes the relationships between two variables for a given sample, if the range of sample scores is truncated, that relationship will not generalize to more representative samples containing a wider range of variation (p. 589).

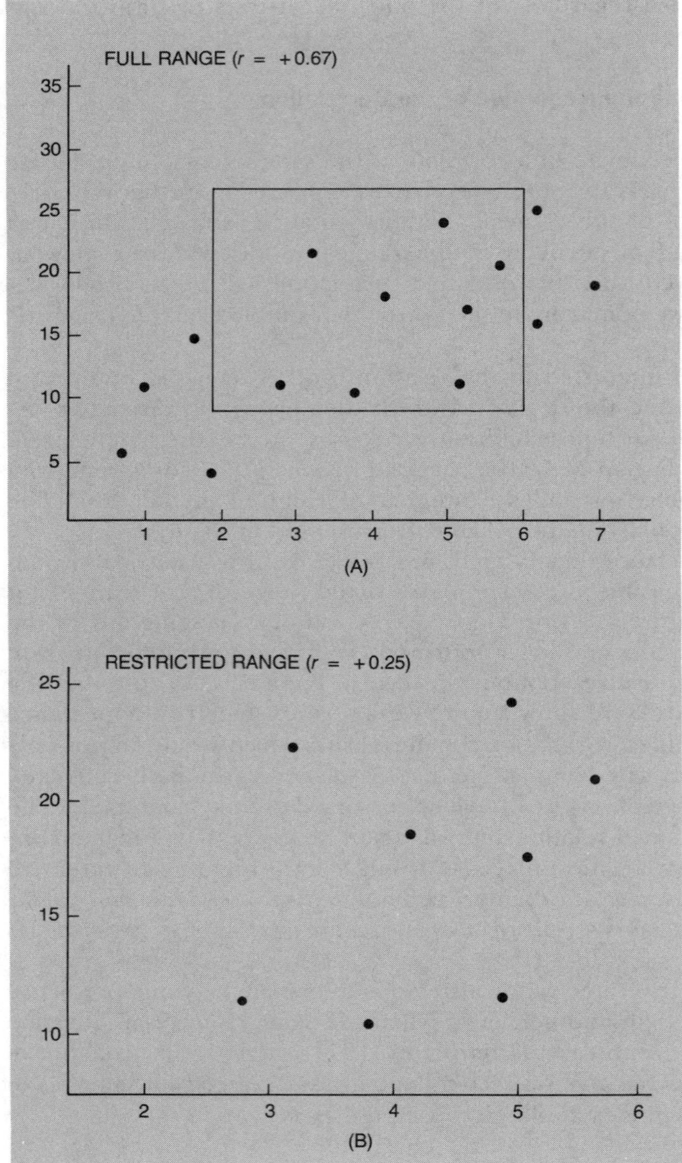

Figure 3-3 The magnitude of relationships can vary as a function of the range of scores employed. In this case, the truncated range lowers the correlation.

Curvilinear Relationships

Thus far we have focused on correlation as a measure of the degree of *rectilinear* relationship between two variables. As we have said, perfect relationships are indicated by all the points falling on a single straight line. For *curvilinear*

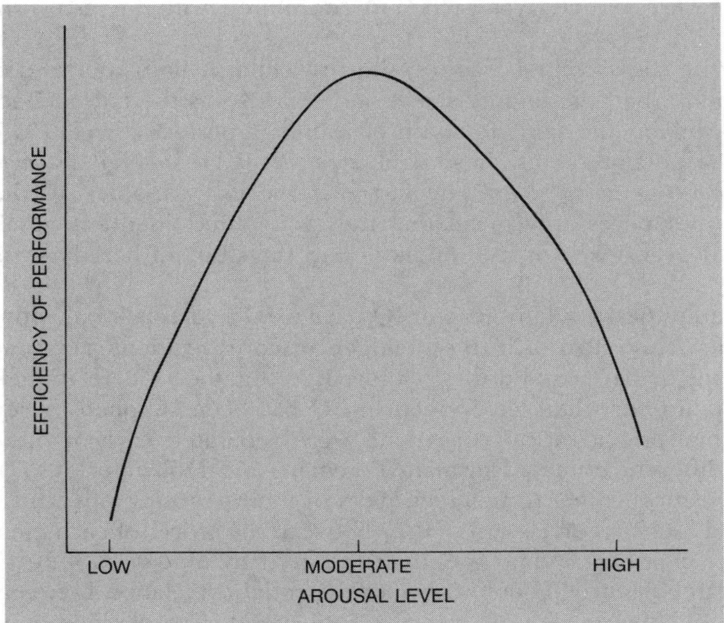

Figure 3-4 Hypothesized relationship between performance efficiency and level of arousal, illustrating a curvilinear relationship.

relationships, special correlational statistics sensitive to them must be employed (for example, see Nunnally, 1967).

As an example of a curvilinear relationship, consider the correlation between efficiency of performance and an individual's level of physiological arousal. Some theorists (for example, Malmo, 1959) have suggested that performance will be best at moderate levels of physiological arousal and that performance will be poorer when arousal levels are either too high or too low. This hypothetical relationship, depicted in Figure 3-4, has often been described as an *inverted U.* If the usual correlational procedures (for example, Pearson's r) are applied to these data, it will be found that the correlation coefficient is low. This is because the relationship between the two variables in question is not rectilinear, rather than because the relationship is weak. The potential presence of curvilinear relationships is another important reason for inspecting scatter diagrams so that the researcher can determine whether special correlational procedures would be required to index the observed pattern accurately.

Correlations as Rank-Order Relationships

The statistic for indexing the correlation between two variables primarily reflects the similarity of their rank orders (see our discussion of test-retest reliability in Chapter 2). To take a simple example, let us suppose that we had obtained two measures of height on each of three children, with the results shown in Table 3-2.

As may be seen, child 1 was the shortest child at both four and eight years of age, child 2 had the middle score, and child 3 was the tallest. Because the rank order remains the same for both measures, a perfect correlation ($r = +1.00$) would be obtained from these data, *even though the scores at age eight are always higher than those at age four.* The fact that the two variables are highly correlated does not necessarily mean that they will reflect identical numbers. This fact is often overlooked or misunderstood in the study of hereditary influences on IQ.

Most studies of the inheritance of IQ have used a correlational approach to determine the degree to which the intelligence scores of identical or monozygotic (MZ) twins or parents and their children go together. Correlational evidence suggesting an hereditary component in IQ has been supplied by several major studies involving identical twins who were separated early in life and brought up in different homes. Newman, Freeman, and Holzinger (1937) administered the Stanford-Binet to nineteen pairs of monozygotic twins who were reared apart, and found a correlation of 0.77 between the scores of each member of a pair. A corroborative finding was then reported by Shields (1962) with a different test of intelligence. There is also a substantial correlation between the IQs of parents and their children, typically about 0.50. Correlations between adopted children's IQ scores and those of their adoptive parents are a good deal lower, ranging between 0 and 0.20 (Honzik, 1957).

Because the effect of heredity seems so powerful, these data may give the mistaken impression that IQ cannot be raised by special training programs or other environmental influences: Such an impression is erroneous because the latter possibility is a different question, based on the magnitude of individuals' scores rather than whether they go together or are associated with other scores.

To illustrate this point concretely, consider the data in Table 3-3. On the left side of the table (column I), hypothetical data from seven MZ male twin pairs are shown, along with the correlation coefficient (r) and the mean, or average, score. Note that r is quite high, that the overall means of the pairs of twins are quite similar, and that each twin has nearly the same IQ as his mate.

Table 3-2 Heights of Three Children at Ages Four and Eight, Illustrating that Correlations are Sensitive to Ranks Rather than Mean Differences

CHILD	*HEIGHT AT 4 (IN INCHES)*	*HEIGHT AT 8 (IN INCHES)*
1	37	48
2	40	51
3	42	53

Table 3-3 Hypothetical Means and IQ Scores of a Set of MZ Twin Boys Before and After a Special Training Program: An Illustration of the Difference Between Means and Correlations

I (BEFORE)			*II (AFTER)*	
			[TRAINING]	*[NO TRAINING]*
Twin A	*Twin B*		*Twin A*	*Twin B*
80	82		90	82
103	100		112	100
94	94		107	94
105	109		115	109
97	95		108	95
121	116		140	116
68	77		85	77
95.4	96.1	Means	108.0	96.1
$r = 0.98$		Correlations	$r = 0.96$	

Let us assume that only one member of each pair is now given a special and intensive training program for increasing intellectual ability. If the program worked in raising IQ (and the IQ scores of the control twins remained unchanged), a comparison would be similar to that shown in the right side of Table 3-3 (column II). Now the overall means are quite different, and most twin pairs are not very similar in their scores. The environmental intervention has worked, and the means show this effect. But what about the correlation between twins *after* the environmental manipulation? It has, in this example, remained virtually unchanged and still shows an impressively high relationship. This is the case because the scores of the twins in each pair still "go together" in the sense that if twin A in column II has a relatively high score (compared to the other individuals in column II-A), his twin will have a relatively high score compared to the other individuals *in column II-B.* It is precisely such a phenomenon that is tapped by the correlational approach, and not necessarily the similarity between parent and child or twin and twin per se. To ask whether the environmental intervention was effective, we must inspect means rather than correlations.

REGRESSION

Regression is a way of using the association between variables as a method of prediction. When we considered correlation in terms of shared variance, it did not matter whether we began with X or Y. The correlation coefficient is a symmetrical measure of the relationship between two variables. In regression, however, one variable is specified as the *predictor* and the other as the *criterion* (the variable to be predicted). Regression begins with data just like those in the correlational examples we presented earlier. We have a sample of subjects and have collected two measures on each (for example, frequency of class attendance and grades). Using regression, our aim would be to predict grades from classroom attendance. Suppose, for example, that we simply tried to guess about a student's grades. If we had no other information but the distribution of grades in the student's class, our best guess would likely be that the student's grades fall at the mean of the distribution. Now suppose that we tried to improve our prediction by using attendance as a predictor. To simplify, let us assume there are only six people in the class. Their scores on each of the two variables are shown in Table 3-4. In this case classroom attendance does *not* help our prediction. The reason is that there is no relationship between attendance and grades. The average grade of people attending class for 40, 50, or 60 days is 2.0.

Now consider the data shown in Table 3-5. Here a knowledge of attendance matters, for different grade point averages are associated with different numbers of days attended. The mean grade point averages of students who attended 40, 50, or 60 days are, respectively, 1.0, 2.0, and 3.0. Using attendance as a predictor, we can improve our prediction of the criterion measure, grades.

The formal regression technique seeks a rectilinear relationship that will allow us to predict one variable from another. Such a rule can be written as:

$$Y' = bX + a$$

where Y' is the predicted score on variable Y (grades), X is the score on variable X (attendance), and b and a are constants.

The constants b and a are chosen to provide the best prediction of Y; b is called the *regression coefficient* for estimating Y from X, and a is the *regression constant.* The regression constant is used to adjust for differences between the means of Y and X. "Best" is the rule that minimizes the average squared error of prediction (that is, the average of the square of the differences between the real and predicted scores on Y). The regression coefficient, b, represents the rate of change in Y units per X unit. When a line is actually drawn to depict the regression function, b indicates the *slope* (or steepness) of this line. The larger

Table 3-4 Hypothetical Data for Predicting Grades from Class Attendance

	DAYS ATTENDED	GRADE POINT AVERAGE
	40	1.0
	40	3.0
	50	1.0
	50	3.0
	60	1.0
	60	3.0
Mean	50	2.0

Table 3-5 Hypothetical Data for Predicting Grades from Class Attendance

	DAYS ATTENDED	GRADE POINT AVERAGE
	40	0.0
	40	2.0
	50	1.0
	50	3.0
	60	2.0
	60	4.0
Mean	50	2.0

the regression coefficient, the better our prediction rule will be. When predicting *Y* from *X*, the regression constant, *a*, equals the value of *Y* that corresponds to an *X* value of zero. Thus, the regression constant is the point at which the regression line crosses the *Y* axis. Figure 3-5 displays two regression lines for the data shown in Table 3-6. Note that the regression lines for predicting *Y* from *X* and *X* from *Y* are different. This is because each regression line is trying to minimize different errors. In predicting *Y* from *X*, we want to minimize the vertical distance between a data point and the regression line. In predicting *X* from *Y*,

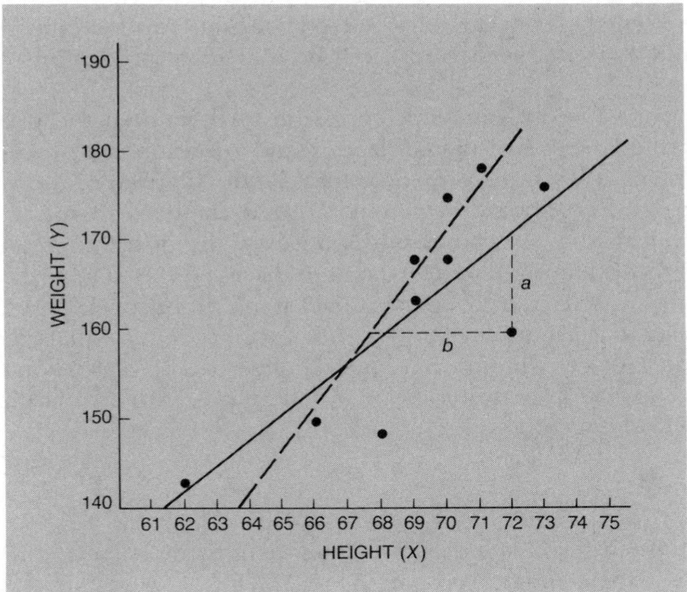

Figure 3-5 Regression line for data shown in Table 3-6. The solid line is for predicting *Y* from *X*; the broken line is for predicting *X* from *Y*. The distance *a* is an error in predicting *Y* from *X*; the distance *b* is an error in predicting *X* from *Y*.

Table 3-6 Sample Data for a Regression Problem*

	X	Y
Subject	*Height (in.)*	*Weight*
1	70	175
2	72	160
3	68	148
4	66	150
5	71	178
6	69	164
7	73	176
8	62	143
9	70	168
10	69	167

* After Welkowitz, Ewen, and Cohen, 1971.

we are trying to minimize the horizontal distance from data points to the regression line.

The regression coefficient for predicting weight (Y) from height (X) is 0.65. Thus, the regression line does not fit all the data points exactly, but all the points are relatively close to the regression line, a reflection of the strong association between the two variables. Of course, the stronger the relationship between X and Y, the more accurate will be individual predictions of Y scores from X scores.

It is instructive to examine regression further when the predictor and criterion variable have been standardized. Standardization is a process whereby data are mathematically transformed so that the distribution of scores will have a mean of zero and a standard deviation of 1.0. A standard score (or Z-score) is obtained by subtracting a score from the mean of the distribution and dividing by the standard deviation. A more complete discussion of standard scores may be found in most basic statistics texts (for example, Johnson & Liebert, 1977).

With standardized scores, the regression constant, a, equals zero because both the X and Y scores will now have means of zero. The regression coefficient, b, equals the correlation between X and Y. Therefore, with standardized scores, our prediction rule becomes:

$$Z'_y = r_{xy} Zx$$

where Z'_y is the predicted standard score on Y, r_{xy} is the correlation between X and Y, and Zx is the standard score of x.

As was true of the correlation coefficient, regression coefficients are typically evaluated for their statistical significance. The factors that affect the correlation coefficient (for example, sample range) are also relevant to regression. Moreover, as with correlations, the assumption is that the underlying relationship between X and Y is rectilinear and thus predictions made using regression are accurate only to the extent that the variables are rectilinearly related.

TIME SERIES ANALYSIS

Time series analysis is a technique for examining a special kind of relationship, the relationship between behavior and time. The technique is applicable to those situations in which measurements of behavior are made either continuously or at regular intervals along the time axis. Time series analysis is used to determine how long it takes for a behavior to repeat itself. (The technical name for the frequency with which any behavior repeats itself is that behavior's *period*.)

Time series analysis accomplishes *spectral decomposition,* a procedure involving mathematical formulas which need not concern us here.[2] Conceptually, spectral decomposition can be likened to what happens when rays of sunlight are passed through a prism to produce a rainbow-like spectrum, which reveals the basic colors which compose sunlight, although the colors are not at all visible when we look at sunlight with our naked eyes. (Sound waves can also be decomposed in much the same way.)

Gottman (1981) has described the many potential applications of time series analysis in the behavioral sciences. One is *forecasting,* which employs time series analysis to predict the behavior of individuals or groups of people in the future by analyzing the temporal patterns that underlie their previously observed behavior. Another application is in identifying what Gottman calls the "hidden changes" that result from various kinds of medical and psychological treatments. By hidden changes Gottman means changes that would not be visible from a normal frequency analysis but which can be revealed by application of an appropriate (mathematically complex) spectral density analysis. Gottman offers the example of a schizophrenic patient who was given a word association test over 120 days, first in a placebo and then in a drug condition. (The drug, chlorpromazine, is a powerful tranquilizer.) A "simple" graph of the patient's association revealed no apparent drug effect (see Figure 3-6a), but the spectral density functions of the patient's word associations under the two conditions revealed that the patient's associations had become more erratic and less smooth under the drug, that is, he had shifted from a 10-day to a 5-day cycle, as seen in Figures 3-6b and 3-6c. (Such a shift may be "bad" or "good." As Gottman notes, the point is that it was there, and could only be identified by the application of these advanced time-analytic techniques.)

[2] A thorough explanation of time series designs and the mathematics which underlie them can be found in Gottman (1981).

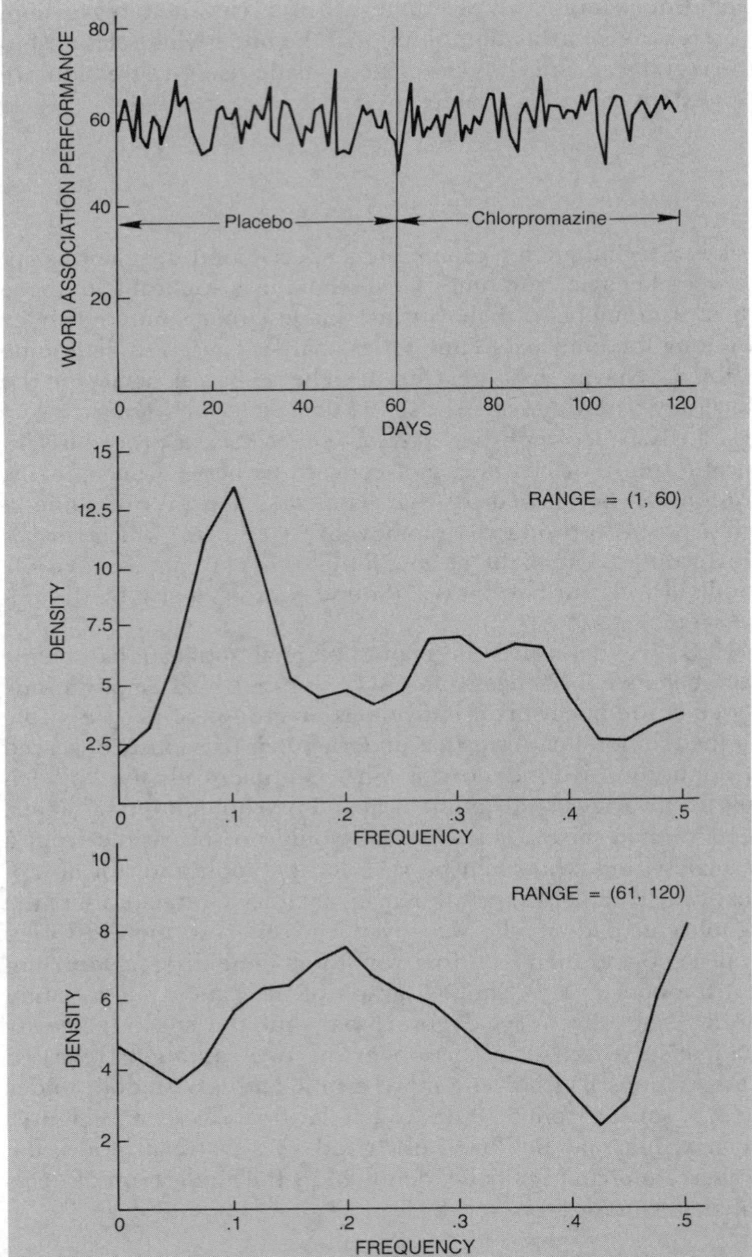

Figure 3-6(a) Simple graph showing performance under both conditions.

Figure 3-6(b) Spectral density function in the placebo condition, showing a 10-day cycle.

Figure 3-6(c) Spectral density function in the chlorpromazine condition, showing a 5-day cycle.

Source: From Gottman (1981), pp. 8-10.

Figure 3-6 Word association test scores of a schizophrenic patient under two drug conditions, showing how a spectral density analysis can identify differences not visible in a simple graphic presentation.

FOR REVIEW AND DISCUSSION

1. State in words the hypothetical relationships between the following variables, as indexed by *r*. What is the amount of variance accounted for by each relationship?
   (a) $r = -0.67$ between quality of prenatal nutrition and care, and mental retardation.
   (b) $r = 0.33$ between scores on a hyperactivity scale and an aggression scale.
   (c) $r = 0.15$ between grades in college and number of dates.
2. Plot the following scores, which were obtained from ten subjects on variables *A* and *B*. Does the resultant scatter diagram indicate no correlation, a moderate correlation, or a high correlation? Is the correlation, if any, positive or negative?

(a)

Subject	A	B
1	3	2
2	4	9
3	5	8
4	6	1
5	7	3
6	5	5
7	8	7
8	2	8
9	9	7
10	2	4

(b)

Subject	A	B
1	4	5
2	3	5
3	2	3
4	6	5
5	7	9
6	3	3
7	8	8
8	1	1
9	5	7
10	9	10

3. Compare and contrast the regression and correlational approaches to assessing associations.
4. Discuss the concept of statistical significance.
5. Discuss the factors that influence the magnitude of the correlation coefficient.
6. Why is it important sometimes to consider r^2 rather than r?
7. Explain the basic concept behind time series analysis.

4

Multivariate Associations

MULTIPLE CORRELATION
MULTIPLE REGRESSION
MULTIVARIATE RESEARCH
Factor Analysis
factor analysis: a geometric representation
uses and abuses of factor analysis
The Multitrait-Multimethod Matrix
FOR REVIEW AND DISCUSSION

In Chapter 3 we dealt only with *bivariate* associations, that is, relationships between two variables. However in many investigations in the social and behavioral sciences three, four, five, or sometimes even dozens of variables are simultaneously of interest. In such cases we speak of *multivariate* associations. The nature, use, and analysis of such relationships is the focus of the present chapter.

MULTIPLE CORRELATION

In attempting to predict a particular behavior, we often suspect that more than one variable is important. When several variables all are related to the criterion variable, a best prediction of the criterion can often be made by combining the predictor variables through the use of the *multiple correlation technique*.

Suppose a research team is interested in predicting grades in college. They may decide to obtain measurements on several variables (rather than just one) in a large sample of high school seniors and then correlate each of these measures with the students' first semester grade point averages. For example, the following two might have been chosen: (1) academic average in high school, and (2) college board examination scores. The (hypothetical) results of obtaining individual correlations with each of these two predictor variables are presented in Table 4-1. The correlations between high school grades and college grades, and between college board scores and college grades, are relatively high. It appears that either might provide a fairly good prediction.

Because both a student's academic average in high school and his or her college board examination scores appear to be associated with college grades, the investigator must select one of the two or both. If the latter choice is made, the question arises as to how the two variables can be combined to produce an even better prediction.

This can be accomplished with the multiple correlation technique. Conceptually, this technique makes it possible to generate an improved prediction from two or more variables (both fairly good predictors), which tap somewhat different dimensions of the criterion we are trying to predict. In all cases, the multiple correlation will tend to be high if any of the variables included have high correlations with the criterion. The multiple correlation cannot be less than the highest correlation found between a single predictor and the criterion. However, the combination of variables will offer improved prediction of the criterion

Table 4-1 Correlations of College Board Scores and High School Grades with College Grades

	COLLEGE GRADES
College Board Scores	0.70
High School Grades	0.68

only to the extent that the predictor variables do not correlate highly with each other. When the correlations between (or among) the predictor variables are high, redundant information is being provided, and the combined variables will offer no great advantage in prediction. Suppose one attempted to predict the success of a baseball team from two variables, players' salaries and measures of the preceding years' performance of the team's pitchers and hitters. Each measure would likely be a relatively good predictor. But taking both together might not improve our ability to forecast success. The reason is the redundancy, or overlap, of our predictors. Because the salaries of the players are likely to reflect their previous success (or lack of it), the two variables provide redundant information. In other words, when predictors share variance, taking both together may not improve our ability to predict.

Returning to our example of predicting grades, we would expect that the multiple correlation would differ only slightly from 0.70 (the higher of the two correlations between a predictor and a criterion) if the simple correlation between high school grades and college board scores, the predictors, was high. Conversely, if the two predictor variables are not highly related, we would expect the multiple correlation to offer a better prediction than either alone can. In this instance, the combination of the variables might correlate 0.85 with the criterion. And, it will be recalled, this is an improvement in prediction of almost 50 percent (the two correlations, 0.70 and 0.85, must be squared before a direct comparison is made).

Multiple correlations can also be represented graphically by Venn diagrams, which provide another way of showing how they work. Figure 4-1 shows that when X and Z are both perfectly correlated (case 1), Z adds nothing to our ability to account for variance in Y; all the variance in Z overlaps with the variance already explained (or "covered") by X. When X and Z are moderately correlated (case II), a multiple r including Z can account for that portion of the variance in Y that Z shares with Y but not with X. Finally, when Z and X are uncorrelated ($r = 0.00$; case III), Z's contribution to a multiple r is greatest.

MULTIPLE REGRESSION

Another way of combining several variables for prediction is multiple regression. Let us first consider the simple case of trying to predict one variable, Y, from two others, X and Z. Two regression coefficients could be chosen to combine the information in our predictors, X and Z, providing the prediction rule that will minimize errors. Now, if our predictors were unrelated, we could develop our prediction equation simply using the regression coefficients for predicting Y from X and Z, and we would have the same result as in multiple correlation. But predictors are often correlated, as we have shown. To eliminate this redundant information, a multiple regression equation uses what are termed *partial regression coefficients*. With standardized variables, the first regression coefficient becomes

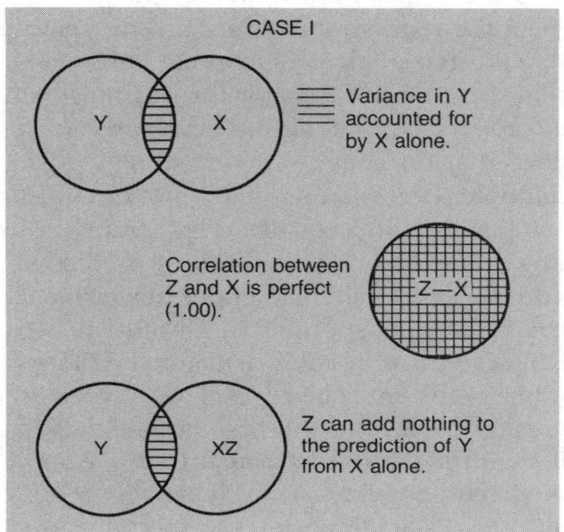

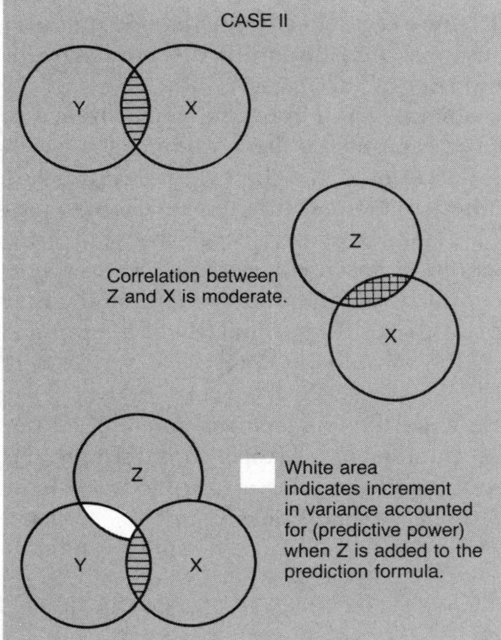

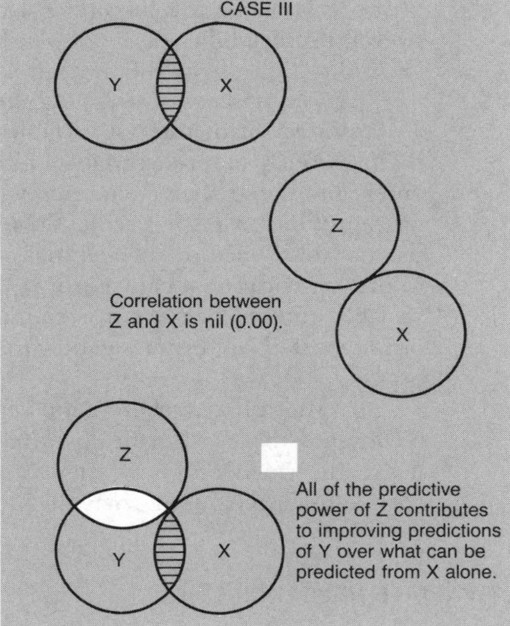

Figure 4-1 Increments in predictive power resulting from adding Z to the prediction of Y from X. Correlation between Z and X is perfect (Case I), moderate (Case II), and nil (Case III). Note that lower correlations between Z and X result in higher contributions by Z.

the correlation between Y and X, after Z has been "partialled." Similarly, the second is equal to the correlation between variables Y and Z, with X removed or partialled. Once the regression coefficients are selected, we may ask several questions. How well can a single course grade (Y) be predicted from attendance (X) and time spent studying (Z)? What is the relationship between a course grade and either attendance or study time, holding constant (partialling) the variable not being considered at the time?

In the multiple regression procedure we have just described, all variables are treated simultaneously and equally. This strategy is useful when the investigator is focusing simply on finding the best prediction rule or has no causal model in mind. But there are other situations in which a *hierarchical regression model* is used. Here the researcher specifies in advance the order in which variables will be entered. The regression coefficient for the first variable to be entered is a simple regression coefficient. The regression coefficient for the second variable is a partial regression coefficent; the first variable has been partialled out. The regression coefficient for the third variable is also a partial coefficient; variables one and two have been partialled. As each variable is added to the equation, the investigator conducts a statistical test to determine whether the newly added variable increases the predictability of Y beyond what has already been accomplished. Thus, in the hierarchical model the researcher evaluates not only the overall predictability of Y but also the unique contribution to the prediction of each of a logically or theoretically ordered set of variables.

The process of ordering the variables is very important. The variance in Y accounted for by the last variable entered can only be the Y variance for which the previously entered variables have not accounted. To the extent that this last entered variable shares variance with other predictors, it is not as likely to significantly increase the predictability of Y. The researcher usually tries to order the variables on some conceptual or theoretical basis. For example, when trying to predict vocational choice from gender and attitudes, gender would be the first variable entered because it is causally prior to attitudes. Similarly, if a temporal order existed among a set of variables, they would be entered to reflect this order.

Multiple correlation and regression are the logical forerunners of all the techniques that systematically combine a number of variables to determine the degree to which, and how, they form regular patterns, clusters, or factors. These correlational techniques may all be called *multivariate research strategies*.

MULTIVARIATE RESEARCH

Often, a social scientist will want to deal not with two or three variables but with many more. Suppose that we were interested in assessing the social adjustment of elementary school children from the perspective of their peers. We might begin by constructing a large number of descriptive statements: "Is well liked," "Doesn't pay attention to the teacher," "Is easily upset," and so on. After some pretesting, we would construct a final version of an assessment instrument and then administer it to a large group of school children. The resulting data are often depicted in what is called a *correlation matrix*, in which the rows and columns list the variables, and the entries provide the correlations between each possible pair of variables.

One purpose of generating a correlation matrix is to see how the variables relate to one another. Do the variables fall into groups or clusters? Let us first consider a simple case of a six-item assessment of classroom behavior. A hypothetical correlation matrix is presented in Table 4-2. The items clearly form two clusters. Items 1, 2, and 3 are positively related to one another but are either negatively (inversely) or minimally related to items 4, 5, and 6. Similarly, items 4, 5, and 6 are positively related to one another. From evidence such as this, an investigator might conclude that the six items seem to tap two dimensions of classroom behavior. The first dimension, reflected by items 1, 2, and 3, might be given such a label as "aggressive-disruptiveness." The second dimension, composed of items 4, 5, and 6, might be called "competence-popularity." An investigator could conclude that from the viewpoint of other children there seem to be two important dimensions of classroom behavior.

In actual research practice, many more than six variables would typically be included in a study of classroom behavior of this type. A six-item test could hardly be expected to cover the domain, or range, of what children do. Instead of a six-item correlation matrix, a researcher is often confronted with one based on thirty, fifty, or even more variables. When a correlation matrix reaches this size, it is no longer possible to simply inspect it. A number of mathematical techniques, however, are available to systematically explore the interrelationships among a large set of variables. One of the most frequently used is called *factor analysis*.

Table 4-2 Correlation Matrix for Six Items Reflecting Classroom Behavior

ITEM	*IS MEAN AND CRUEL TO OTHER CHILDREN* 1	*DISTURBS OTHERS WHEN THEY ARE TRYING TO WORK* 2	*IS DISRESPECTFUL TO THE TEACHER* 3	*IS WELL LIKED* 4	*DOES GOOD WORK* 5	*HELPS OTHERS* 6
1	1.0	0.62	0.75	−0.40	0.06	−0.32
2		1.00	0.71	−0.19	0.14	−0.41
3			1.00	−0.11	−0.02	−0.14
4				1.00	0.63	0.79
5					1.00	0.63
6						1.00

Factor Analysis

Factor analysis is often used to explore the interrelationships among a large number of variables. The hope is to find a smaller set of dimensions, *factors*, that can account for the entire array of intercorrelations. In addition to this process of exploration, factor analysis can also be used with a more theoretical intent. When a particular construct, such as "anxiety," becomes central in a large number of research investigations, one problem that emerges almost immediately is that investigators do not agree on the referent behaviors or events that will be interpreted as reflecting it. A method that allowed investigators to interrelate various research findings and simultaneously examine a number of different measures of a particular construct would enable them to solve—or at least manage—the problem.

Let us consider a simple example of factor analysis using this latter emphasis. Suppose an investigator was interested in the concept of creativity and had administered six tests, supposedly measuring creativity, to a large sample of undergraduates. An initial look at the data might be accomplished by constructing a correlation matrix, such as the hypothetical one in Table 4-3. It contains the correlations of each of the six measures with every other measure; for example, the matrix tells us that there is a relatively high relationship between measures 1 and 2 ($r = 0.55$) and a much lower relationship between 2 and 4 ($r = 0.25$).

In our example the investigator is interested in the construct of "creativity" and has assumed, on an *a priori* basis, that it can be tapped by each of the measures listed in the rows and columns of the table. The correlations among measures 1, 2, and 3 tend to be rather high (ranging from 0.43 to 0.55) and thus go together. A similar pattern emerges for the relationships among measures 4, 5, and 6. In contrast, the relationships between any one of the first three measures and any one of the second three tend to be lower (with correlations ranging from 0.25 to 0.39). Thus, there is some tendency for two different groupings of relationships, rather than one consistent level of association, to be present in the matrix. The question becomes one of determining the degree to which a single factor or unit, versus two or more such factors, will be most efficient in describing

Table 4-3 Correlations Among Six Measures of Creativity

MEASURE	*1*	*2*	*3*	*4*	*5*	*6*
1	1.00	.55	.43	.32	.28	.36
2		1.00	.50	.25	.31	.32
3			1.00	.39	.25	.33
4				1.00	.43	.49
5					1.00	.44
6						1.00

the data represented in the matrix. It is precisely at this point that the computational procedures of factor analysis enter the picture.

To appreciate the nature of these mathematical operations, we should note that even the modest evidence for two groupings of correlations in the matrix in Table 4-3 is somewhat more clear-cut than is often found when real data are employed. Moreover, although our hypothetical example has only six measures, it is not uncommon for dozens or even hundreds of measures to be correlated with each other in some studies. The complexity of such data and the time needed to summarize and interpret them in words should be apparent.

One of the major functions of factor analysis is to reduce such large sets of data to more manageable and comprehensible units. By means of fairly complex mathematical formulas, factor analysis reduces the data to the smallest number of reasonably homogeneous dimensions—the factors—that adequately account for the relationships or correlations among all the measures. A detailed explanation of these factor-analytic procedures is beyond the scope of this book, but we will discuss some of the major terms and considerations that underlie the technique, as well as the actual factor-analytic results obtained in our example.

The mathematics of factor analysis involves the sequential extraction of factors from the data. Each factor is a linear combination of the variables. Usually, the researcher selects weights for this linear combination to maximize the variance the factor accounts for. One way of approaching the maximization of the variance a factor accounts for is to select weights so that the sum of the squared correlations between the variables and the factor is maximized. Once a first factor is identified, the variance it accounts for is statistically removed (partialled) from the data. Then a second factor, also a linear combination of variables, is formed; again, the weights are selected so that it accounts for a maximal amount of the remaining variance in the data.[1] This second factor is partialled from the data, and the process continues until there is so little variance left that the extraction of further factors would be meaningless.

Table 4-4 presents the results of a factor analysis of the correlation matrix in Table 4-3. Two factors (*A* and *B*) were obtained in this analysis. The values in the columns labeled *A* and *B* are the correlations of each measure with each of the factors, commonly referred to as the *loadings* of the measures on the factors. Table 4–4 shows that all the measures load substantially on factor *A*. The investigator has obtained some support for the hypothesis that they all are related to creativity. However, an inspection of the loadings on factor *B* shows that differences among the measures are also present. Measures 1 through 3 load positively on the factor *B*, whereas measures 4 through 6 load negatively.

A summary of the main steps of factor analysis is presented in Figure 4-2.

[1] This process assures that the factors are statistically independent (orthogonal). However, this statistical independence is forced by the mathematics of the procedure; it does not indicate that the factors are truly independent.

Table 4-4 Matrix of Factor Loadings

MEASURE	*FACTOR*	
	A	*B*
1	0.71	0.40
2	0.70	0.46
3	0.70	0.37
4	0.69	−0.41
5	0.65	−0.43
6	0.71	−0.39

Factor Analysis: A Geometric Representation. Figure 4-3 shows the manner in which factor analysis does, in fact, identify concise and meaningful groupings for the six measures in the original matrix. The number corresponding to each measure finds a unique place on the two coordinates representing the factors, *A* and *B*, as a function of the actual factor loadings taken from Table 4-4. Thus, all six measures are located in similar positions with reference to the vertical axis

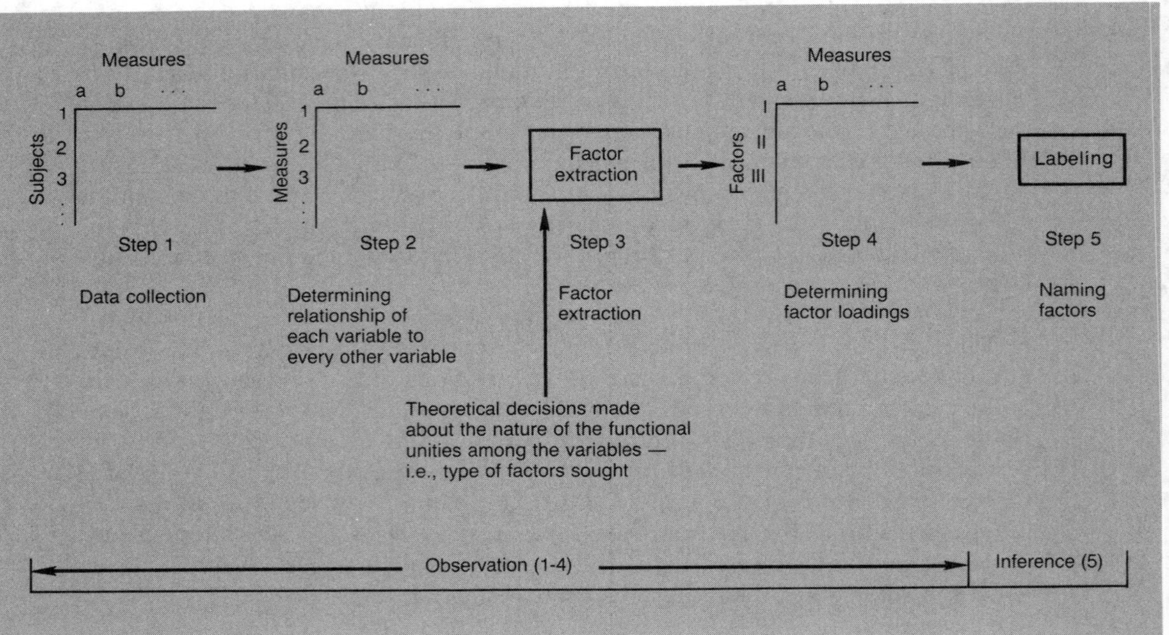

Figure 4-2 The five steps involved in factor analysis. The purposes of the procedure are to reduce the information available about a large number of measures (variables) to a manageable size and to interpret the pattern that emerges.

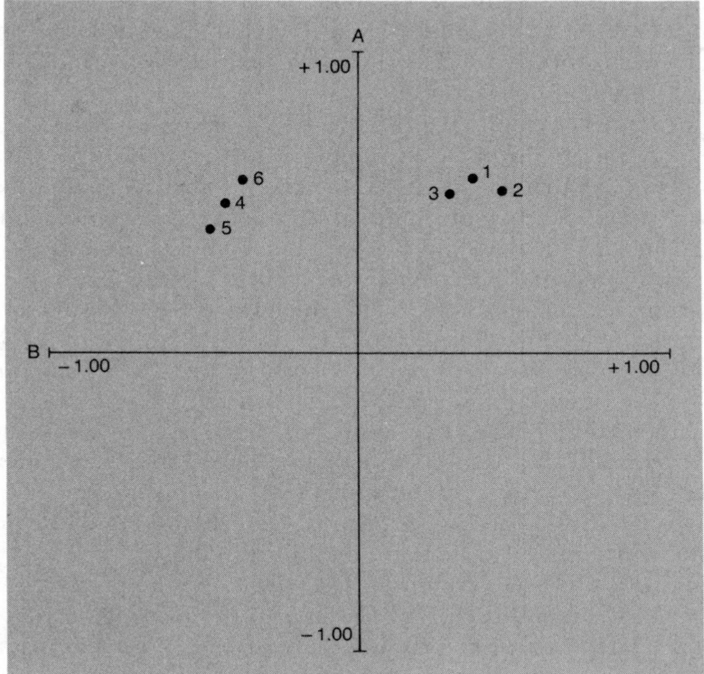

Figure 4-3 Geometric representation of the factor loadings shown in Table 4-4. All six measures load positively on factor A, but 1, 2, and 3 load positively on B, while 4, 5, and 6 load negatively.

(factor *A*), but two clearly different groups emerge when we consider their positions relative to the horizontal axis (factor *B*).

In our example the two factors, *A* and *B*, are said to be *orthogonal*, because they are completely independent of one another. However, this independence of the factors (implying that they involve two quite separate and unrelated dimensions) does not necessarily reflect independence of the relationship in the original correlation matrix. To illustrate, a factor analysis can be conducted based on measurements of the physical size of people. Two orthogonal dimensions can be found, height and weight. Although the two dimensions are independent as they emerge from the factor analysis, the heights and weights of humans are clearly related. People who are taller tend to weigh more, and people who are shorter tend to weight less.[2]

Uses and Abuses of Factor Analysis. We have seen that factor analysis can be extremely useful as a method for summarizing and integrating large arrays of data into manageable units. Nonetheless, at least part of both the appeal and the awe of factor analysis is that it involves mathematical computations that are highly

[2]Other forms of factor analysis are specifically designed to identify factors that are not orthogonal but rather *oblique* (related to one another). A detailed discussion of the relative uses and merits of orthogonal and oblique factor analysis can be found in Nunnally (1967).

sophisticated. But complex mathematics alone does not make any particular investigation any more or less scientific than one that does not rely on such sophisticated statistical procedures. Therefore, we will suggest several cautions in the use and interpretation of factor analysis.

At various stages in employing factor analysis, one must make decisions concerning the appropriate formulas to employ (for example, the particular method of factor analysis that will be used and the number of factors that will be sought). There are a number of guidelines for making such decisions (see Nunnally, 1967), but they involve opinions and are therefore subjective.

A particularly important step in factor-analytic research is replication. Because of the complex mathematics, factor analyses do not always produce results that are repeatable. Therefore, replication is essential before the results can be confidently accepted. Similarly, when a particular result is *statistically* significant, it may not be practically, socially, or theoretically significant. Likewise, a factor that is mathematically pure or accounts for a large portion of the variance in a particular correlation matrix may nonetheless have little "real" meaning. This point has been illustrated in a rather remarkable demonstration analysis by Overall (1964), which had as its ostensible purpose the "discovery" of the primary physical dimensions, or factors, of books from a library shelf.

Beginning with what are commonly accepted to be the primary physical dimensions of books—height, width, and thickness—the investigator devised a number of equations into which he could enter the actual measurements of various books. Three of the equations were merely the actual primary dimensions of books; the remaining nine consisted of various combinations of these dimensions (that is, differential weights were assigned to the three dimensions following the usual factor-analytic procedure). After measuring 100 books and computing a score for each on all of the variables, Overall factor analyzed the resulting 12 × 12 correlation matrix. Three factors emerged—but instead of being the familiar dimensions of books, these dimensions appeared to be best labeled size, obesity, and squareness! Thus, in this one demonstration, there were obviously no grounds for the common assumption that the factors identified in such an analysis are the "actual" or true primary factors of the objects or persons under investigation. The problem is obvious because we knew ahead of time the actual dimensions of library volumes. In contrast, and as the point of the demonstration, Overall notes that *"when we do not know beforehand what the primary dimensions are, it is difficult to justify the belief that factor analysis will somehow magically point them out to us"* (1964, p. 273).

However, and this point is equally important, Overall goes on to emphasize:

> Does all this mean that factor analysis is a false and worthless methodology? Certainly not. It promises to be one of the most useful research tools in social science and will realize that promise more surely if we strip it of myths and embellishments (1964, p. 275).

Overall's point is that factor analysis does allow us to talk about factors and the extent to which they account for variance in a data matrix. But factors, although useful in accounting for variance, may not represent the "true, underlying structure" of the domain of interest.

The Multitrait-Multimethod Matrix

In the previous section, we noted that factor analysis is often used to determine whether a group of variables "go together." When several measures are indeed found to load on a common factor or to correlate highly with each other, it is often concluded that all of them tap the same construct or variable. For example, if an investigator had developed several questionnaire measures of anxiety, he or she would want to validate these measures by correlating them with already accepted indicants of anxiety. This process is referred to as *convergent validity* and is based on the notion that two measures of the same thing should correlate highly (Campbell & Fiske, 1959). *Discriminant validity* is also required. The new test must be found *not* to correlate too highly with tests purported to measure different processes. An investigator must be able to specify both what a particular test does measure and what it does not measure.

At first blush, it appears that it ought to be a fairly easy matter to establish convergent and discriminant validity merely by examining a correlation matrix that includes variables that should and should not correlate highly. However, such a correlation matrix contains an important confound. Each test in the matrix may be thought of as containing two types of variance—the variance due to the process being measured and variance due to the method of measurement. A process cannot be measured independently of some method, because the systematic variance of any test is a combination of variance due to the content of the test and variance due to the method (questionnaire, interview, behavioral analysis) employed. Returning to our hypothetical correlation matrix, the correlations obtained could have resulted from correlations among the underlying processes being measured, the methods employed to measure them, or any combination of these two factors.

The fact that two measures of "anxiety" are highly related may reflect only that they were both obtained via questionnaire. Research (for example, Edwards, 1953) suggests that an individual may respond affirmatively or negatively to a questionnaire item largely on the basis of whether his answer would be "socially desirable" rather than on the basis of whether the content actually pertains to his own behavior. But if social desirability did account for questionnaire responses, we would expect a poor relationship between anxiety as measured by questionnaire data and anxiety as measured through techniques (such as behavior ratings) in which the social desirability hypothesis would not be applicable. How can such a check be performed? Campbell & Fiske (1959) proposed a validation process, a *multitrait-multimethod matrix,* in which at least two processes are measured by at least two different methods. As an illustration of the technique, we will consider a hypothetical example of two processes—anxiety and hostility—each measured by both verbal report and direct behavioral observation in a structured situation. The results, presented in Table 4-5, show four major components.

1. Reliabilities indexing the degree of relationship between each variable that has been measured in the same way on different occasions (for example, r_{A1A1} = 0.89) are included, presented in the parentheses of the table. The reliabilities of both methods of measuring both processes are adequate, ranging from 0.88 to 0.93.
2. Validity correlations representing the degree of relationship between the same process measured by two different methods (for example, r_{A1A2} = 0.57) are included, shown as the coefficients enclosed by brackets in the table.
3. The remaining values in the upper left and lower right quadrants of the matrix (0.39 and 0.32) reflect the degree of relationship between two different processes when they have been assessed employing the same method, that is, method variance.
4. The remaining values (0.20 and 0.22), in the lower left quadrant, reflect the degree of relationship between measures of different processes obtained by different methods.

Convergent validity is obtained when the values of the correlations between two different methods of assessing the same process are high. In the example, correlations between $A1$ and $A2$ (0.57) and between $B1$ and $B2$ (0.67) are significantly different from zero, and they are high enough to lend some confidence to the assertion that the measures of both anxiety and hostility do share common variance after the possible biasing contribution of method variance is removed.

Discriminant validity is evaluated through two considerations. First, the validity coefficient for a measure should be higher than the correlation between that measure and any other having neither method nor process in common. This requirement is met for both anxiety and hostility, that is, r_{A1A2} (0.57) is greater

Table 4-5 Example of a Multitrait-Multimethod Matrix

	METHOD 1 VERBAL REPORT		*METHOD 2 BEHAVIORAL OBSERVATION*	
Processes	*A1*	*B1*	*A2*	*B2*
METHOD 1				
Verbal Report				
Anxiety (*A*1)	(0.89)			
Hostility (*B*1)	0.39	(0.93)		
METHOD 2				
Behavioral Observation				
Anxiety (*A*2)	[0.57]	0.20	(0.88)	
Hostility (*B*2)	0.22	[0.67]	0.32	(0.90)

than r_{A1B2} (0.22) and r_{B1B2} (0.67) is greater than r_{B1A2} (0.20). Second, different measures of the same process should correlate more highly than measurements of different processes obtained by the same method. Again, the data in Table 4-5 meet this requirement, since r_{A1A2} (0.57) and r_{B1B2} (0.67) both are significantly larger than r_{A1B1} (0.39) and r_{A2B2} (0.32).

FOR REVIEW AND DISCUSSION

1. Suppose that the future status of the national economy is predicted by the amount of installment buying ($r = 0.65$). In this case you would be interested in improving your predictive powers, since you cannot account for approximately 60 percent of the variance. You also know that the price of stocks on the New York Stock Exchange correlates 0.50 with future economy. How would you improve your predictions using this additional data? What factors should you consider before implementing this procedure?
2. Interpret the following multivariable-multitrait matrix, in which the concepts of (*A*) intelligence and (*B*) artistic ability are evaluated. Are the measures reliable? Do the concepts have convergent and discriminant validity? Why?

		I PEER RATINGS		*II* COURSE GRADES		*III* PSYCHOLOGICAL TESTS	
		A1	*B1*	*A2*	*B2*	*A3*	*B3*
I	*A1*	(0.83)					
	B1	0.51	(0.94)				
II	*A2*	[0.63]	0.54	(0.87)			
	B2	0.49	[0.26]	0.58	(0.91)		
III	*A3*	[0.57]	0.50	[0.54]	0.52	(0.92)	
	B3	0.56	[0.43]	0.48	[0.31]	0.39	(0.86)

3. Interpret the results of the following factor analysis. Label the factors and discuss how the pattern of loadings supports your interpretation.

MEASURE	*FACTOR 1*	*FACTOR 2*
Geometry Skills	0.73	0.13
Word Knowledge	0.04	0.86
Conceptual Ability	0.11	0.74
Algebra Skills	0.66	0.08
Calculus Skill	0.71	0.10
Reading Skill	0.08	0.73

4. Compare multiple correlation and multiple regression. What features do they share? How do the techniques differ?

5

Identifying Causal Relationships: Problems and Threats

WHY CAUSAL INFERENCES CAN'T BE DRAWN FROM SIMPLE CORRELATIONS
- The Third Variable Problem
- The Directionality Problem

X AS A SUFFICIENT CAUSE OF Y: MILL'S CRITERIA

NULL HYPOTHESIS TESTING: TYPE I AND TYPE II ERRORS
- The Problem of Accepting the Null Hypothesis
- Effects of Sample Size on Hypothesis Testing
- Statistical versus Theoretical Hypothesis Testing: A Word of Caution

THREATS TO THE VALIDITY OF CAUSAL INFERENCES

THREATS TO STATISTICAL CONCLUSION VALIDITY
- Low Statistical Power
- Violated Assumptions of Statistical Tests
- "Fishing"
- Unreliable Measures
- Unreliable Treatment Implementation and Settings
- Heterogeneity of Subjects

INTERNAL VALIDITY
- Plausible Rival Hypotheses
- Within- versus Between-Subjects Comparisons

THREATS TO THE INTERNAL VALIDITY OF WITHIN-SUBJECTS COMPARISONS
- Maturation
- Testing
- Instrument Decay
- Statistical Regression
- History

THREATS TO THE INTERNAL VALIDITY OF BETWEEN-SUBJECTS COMPARISONS
- Selection Bias
- Differential Attrition
- Diffusion
- Compensatory Equalization
- Compensatory Rivalry
- Resentful Demoralization

IDENTIFYING AGE-RELATED CHANGES
- Threats to the Internal Validity of Cross-Sectional Studies
- Threats to the Internal Validity of Longitudinal Studies
- Cross-Sequential Designs
- Retrospective versus Prospective Accounts

MULTIPLE THREATS TO INTERNAL VALIDITY

FOR REVIEW AND DISCUSSION

The scientific practices described thus far have been oriented toward describing and measuring variables and observing and indexing associations between or among variables. We have explained how a social scientist would go about drawing a sample from a population, and we indicated the importance of describing a sample in terms of its central tendency and variability. We have also introduced certain technical issues of measurement, such as reliability and validity. Finally, we have explained how one goes about determining the pattern of relationships that exist among variables, a technique that lends considerable predictive power to the social scientific enterprise. But despite the wide range in these activities, they all have one characteristic in common: They are activities aimed at describing events or relationships in a sample or inferring they exist in a population. As we emphasized in Chapter 1, science is intended to go beyond description and into the realm of explanation. The scientist wants to know not only *that* a given percentage of the population is aggressive or conservative or has an IQ of over 120; he or she also wants to know *why* these relationships occur. Answers to "why?" questions involve bridging the gap between observed associations and correlations on the one hand and inferences about cause and effect on the other. Such inferences must be made very carefully. There are many serious pitfalls for unwary social scientists who too readily read a causal relationship in their data. In this chapter we will introduce the basic issues involved in identifying causal relationships and explain the major conceptual problems that attend this process.

WHY CAUSAL INFERENCES CAN'T BE DRAWN FROM SIMPLE CORRELATIONS

When a social scientist observes a naturally occurring correlation between two variables, X—— Y it is often tempting simply to assume that the relationship is causal in nature, that is, $X \longrightarrow Y$ This assumption is unsound whenever the observed relationship can reasonably be explained in a different way. That is, causal inferences require research designs that can control for plausible rival hypotheses. When X—— Y there are two major rival hypotheses to the inference that $X \longrightarrow Y$ (1) that instead $Y \longrightarrow X$ and (2) that some third variable (arbitrarily called Z) is the joint cause of both X and Y. These rival hypotheses are referred to as the directionality problem and the third variable problem, respectively.

The Directionality Problem

A simple correlation between two variables tells us only that they are related or tend to covary, but it does not tell us whether one is caused by the other. For example, a correlation can be found between grades and attendance in class. One possible interpretation of this relationship is that greater attendance in class increases the amount learned and thus causes higher grades. A second and equally plausible hypothesis is that good grades lead students who obtain them to attend class more frequently. Hence the oft-cited dictum: "Correlation does not imply causation." But the directionality of the relationship is not always impossible to determine. Some relationships can be conceptualized only in one direction. For example, a manufacturer of certain exotic foods might determine the relationship between the frequency with which these foods are purchased and the income of the purchasers. Suppose a positive relationship between these two variables is found (the wealthier a person is, the more likely he or she is to buy the product). It is extremely unlikely that buying or eating the particular food will make an individual rich, but possession of wealth may cause a person to buy something. Here, the causal relationship might lead the manufacturer to predict the circumstances (for example, a booming or a troubled economy) in which sales can be expected to increase or decrease.

Although simple passive correlations do not often allow statements about causation, they may contribute to the disconfirmation of certain causal hypotheses. *Causation usually implies correlation.* Let us suppose that an investigator has asserted that cigarette smoking causes lung cancer. This causal relationship implies that lung cancer and cigarette smoking will be positively related. If a correlation between smoking and lung cancer were *not* obtained, our confidence in the hypothesis should be reduced.[1] The presence of a correlation between smoking and lung cancer still does not allow the causal inference to be drawn, because the nature of the relationship has not been specified. Specifically, the relationship could be due to a third variable.

The Third Variable Problem

The third variable problem refers to the possibility that neither of the two variables involved in a correlation produces the other. Rather, some unspecified variable or process has produced the relationship. For example, there is a high positive correlation between the number of churches in a city and the number of crimes committed in that city. The more churches a city has, the more crimes are committed in it. Does this mean that religion fosters crime or that crime fosters religion? It means neither. The relationship is due to a third variable—population. The higher the population of a community, the greater are (1) the number of churches and (2) the frequency of criminal activities. As a second example, consider the high positive correlation between the number of drownings on a particular day and the consumption of ice cream on that day.

[1]There are certain exceptions to this general proposition. For example, smoking might adversely influence only a small segment of the population so that its effects would not show up in a study that included all smokers. Likewise, smoking might cause cancer in some individuals and reduce its likelihood in others, thus "washing out" the overall effect to zero. But in most circumstances such cumbersome arguments are poor rivals for the proposition, "Causation implies correlation."

The drownings do not cause depressed people to comfort themselves by consuming large amounts of ice cream, nor does eating ice cream lead to drowning. Instead, temperature causes both. The warmer the weather, the more people are likely to be swimming (which is directly related to the frequency of drowning). And more ice cream is sold and eaten on warm days.

The fact that we cannot infer causation from simple passive correlations does not necessarily mean that a cause and effect relationship does not exist. It merely means that it is often impossible to obtain enough information to be sure of the specific nature and direction of this causal relationship.

The examples we have presented are intuitively fairly obvious. It is easy (1) to see that a third variable may be causally responsible for the relationship and (2) to identify the third variable readily. Often, it is not possible to determine whether or not a third variable is operating—or, if it is, what the variable is.

X AS A SUFFICIENT CAUSE OF Y: MILL'S CRITERIA

We have seen that a passively observed simple correlation alone is not grounds to claim that *X* is a sufficient cause of *Y*. Under what circumstances, then, can one logically conclude that *X* is a sufficient cause of *Y*? The answer to this question can be found in the writings of John Stuart Mill (1806–1873).

Mill proposed that if *X* is a sufficient cause of *Y*, when *X* occurs, *Y* should also occur. Mill called the procedure of demonstrating the conditional relationship, *if X, then Y*, the "method of agreement." But, as Mill realized, the method of agreement alone does not prove that *X* causes *Y*. *Y* may have occurred even if *X* had not, in which case the relationship would be spurious. Because the method of agreement is not sensitive to this possibility, Mill propounded a second method, the "method of differences." The method of differences, like the method of agreement, states a conditional relationship between events: *if not X, then not Y*. Mill concluded that *on an abstract, logical level, causality can be inferred if it can be shown that (with everything else equal) Y occurs when X occurs and does not occur when X does not occur.*

At first glance this formulation may seem to imply that *X* is necessary (and not merely sufficient) for *Y* to occur. Such an impression is wrong, because other possible sufficient causes have not been logically excluded by the model. To see that this is so, consider a set of observations made about an electric light switch on the wall. An observer first notes that the light in the adjacent hall is on (*Y*) when the light switch is "on." Later, the observer notes that the light is not on when the switch is "off." Finally, a practical experimental test shows that throwing the switch "on" turns the light on, whereas throwing the switch "off" turns the light off. Mill's criteria are amply satisfied. When all other things are equal, throwing the switch "on" (*X*) has been shown to be a sufficient cause of turning the light on (*Y*). But the "on" switch may not be *necessary* to turn the light on, and in fact other sufficient causes can readily be imagined. (Suppose, for example, that the switch is "three-way" wired so that another switch at the other end of the hall can also turn the light on and off.) Likewise, *X* may fail to cause *Y* when some other set of conditions prevails, as would be the case when the bulb itself is burned out. For these reasons, the Millian model (and most social science research) is limited to showing empirically that *X* can be *a* cause of *Y* but not that *X* is *the* cause of *Y*.

The central aim of most social science research is therefore to provide data that allow a comparison between responses (*Y*) that have and have not been preceded by a hypothesized cause (*X*). The problem for scientists is to translate the requirements of Mill's proposition into concrete terms, including the difficult problem of being sure that everything else but the critical element in a comparison has been kept as equal as possible.[2]

Much of the rest of this book is devoted to evaluating the strengths and weaknesses of various research designs for achieving a demonstration of causality that satisfies Mill's abstract requirements. As will soon be evident, social science research designs are riddled with traps for the unwary. Taking into account the practical limitations and ethical constraints actually faced by social scientists, it should not be surprising that causality is often very difficult to establish when probing for explanations of behavior.

NULL HYPOTHESIS TESTING: TYPE I AND TYPE II ERRORS

The suggestion or possibility that changes in one variable (X) cause changes in another variable (Y) may be considered a hypothesis. Hypotheses may be derived from many sources, including formal and informal theories, informal observation, or even hunches. It is useful to think of the search for causal relationships as hypothesis testing.

Hypothesis testing involves formulating an explicit claim about the relationship between two (or more) variables, choosing a design or plan for making relevant observations or gathering relevant data, and then analyzing the data to see if they support or fail to support the hypothesis. The goal of the researcher is always to reach a valid ("true" or "correct") conclusion from the data. The problem, therefore, is to avoid erroneous or unjustified conclusions. Our attention now turns to the multitude of issues involved in avoiding such errors. We begin with a central idea in the logic of research design and interpretation: null hypothesis testing.

Concerned with the problem of logical causal inference, Sir Ronald Fisher developed the procedure called *null hypothesis testing*. First, samples of data are taken (for example, the means from two groups, only one of which received a particular treatment). The null hypothesis, set up artificially for logical purposes, would be that the means of the two groups would *not* differ if the experiment

[2]The Latin phrase *ceteris paribus* ("other things being equal") is often used in science, philosophy, and the law to refer to this same idea.

were repeated an infinite number of times. If the sample means differ enough from each other, the null hypothesis can be rejected. Logically, this is equivalent to the conclusion that the *population* means (for example, of potential treated and untreated children at other schools) also differ and thus that the observed experimental effect is reliable. Within the Fisher model, one has only two choices: (1) to reject the null hypothesis, and (2) to draw no conclusion—to neither reject nor accept the null hypothesis.

We have already seen that the question of how much the means must differ for the null hypothesis to be rejected involves the question of variability and thus leads to a further consideration of the concept of statistical significance. As noted previously, we are dealing with samples but wish to make inferences about populations. We want to be confident that observed sample differences, if obtained, actually reflect differences in the population. The critical notion here is determining the likelihood that a given result will occur by chance if the null hypothesis is correct. In other words, given the null hypothesis that the two population means are equal and that a discrepancy between the two sample means was in fact observed, we ask, What the probability is of obtaining such a result. (Recall that results that occur rarely or with a low probability by chance are likely to result from real treatment effects; they may be said to be statistically significant.)

The reasoning underlying null hypothesis testing can be understood through a concrete nonexperimental example. Suppose we knew the distribution of mean temperatures in Jacksonville, Florida, on January 1 of every year for 100 years (1850–1949) and plotted these data as in Figure 5-1. We now have a distribution of samples that closely approximates the theoretical population of temperatures that have occurred (or will occur) on this day in Jacksonville. The mean of the distribution is equal to 50°. Of greater importance is the bell-shaped

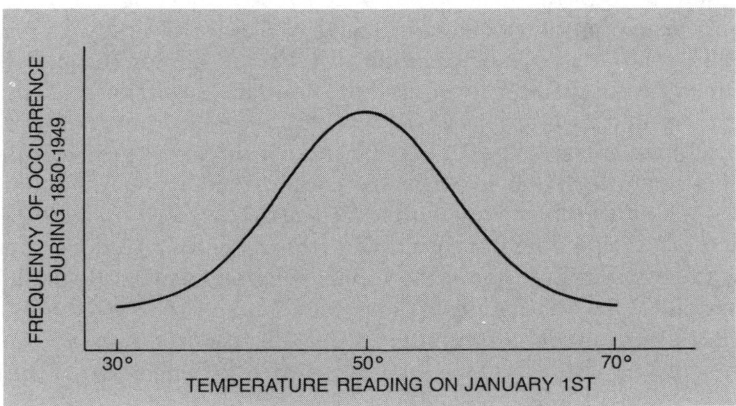

Figure 5-1 A hypothetical distribution of sample temperature means on January 1st in Jacksonville, Florida. The figure illustrates the problem of inferring that a sample has not been drawn from a given population. It is easy to see why a temperature reading of 18° probably was not taken in this city in any January between 1960 and 1969.

(or "normal" curve) form of the distribution, so that some of the means (those with values below 30 or above 70) have had a relatively low frequency of occurrence; we would therefore expect that, in the future, they will only rarely be found for this city. Thus, if we were given ten temperature samples from a given January 1 in some city for the years 1960 to 1969 and these samples had a mean of 18°, we could be virtually certain that the new readings were not taken from the theoretical population (that is, temperature readings in Jacksonville) shown in Figure 5-1.

The statistical inference problem is that most often only one sample, rather than ten or more, is drawn. Further, on the basis of that single sample, we must decide whether the observed mean differences depart enough from the expected value in order to claim statistical significance, that is, that our sample was *not* drawn from that population. As may be seen from Figure 5-1, only those relatively infrequent results on the tails of the curve would be sufficient evidence to lead to the rejection of the null hypothesis. Such results occur with relatively low probability, and therefore the likelihood of incorrectly rejecting the null hypothesis is minimized if these values are obtained.

But the experimenter must decide upon the particular probability of incorrectly rejecting the null hypothesis (concluding that there is a difference when in fact there is not) that he or she is willing to tolerate. In practice, researchers often set this probability at a value of .01 or .05 (see p. 62). The probability of incorrectly rejecting the null hypothesis is therefore (1) under the experimenter's control and (2) set at a low value, either one in 100 or five in 100 times. The sample result must be sufficiently rare in the population to have a likelihood of occurrence of only five or one in 100 times if the null hypothesis were true. Thus the only consideration involved in setting up statistical hypotheses is the minimization of the likelihood of incorrectly rejecting the null hypothesis. Such errors are commonly referred to as *Type I errors.*

Why, within the Fisher school, can we not accept the null hypothesis? The problem, in its general form, is that there are a host of reasons for failing to obtain a significant effect in any given experiment, other than the possibility that the null hypothesis is true. To illustrate, consider the nine-year-old boy who has lost his homework and looks in his room for it. If he finds the homework there after his first look, we know that (at least this time) it was there all along. But if a first inspection does not turn up the missing work, that does not necessarily show that the homework is not in the room. Weighing against this null hypothesis is the possibility that the youngster may have looked too quickly, looked in the wrong place, and so on. Only after repeated searches (or, of course, if the documents turn up elsewhere) would it be prudent to conclude that the homework is not in the child's room.

An investigator may fail to reject the null hypothesis when it is, in fact, false. Such an outcome has been labeled a *Type II error.* The distinction between Type I and Type II errors is shown in Table 5-1. Two hypotheses are considered: H_1 that cigarette smoking is dangerous to health, and its obverse, the null hypothesis H_0, that cigarette smoking is not harmful. The question is whether H_0

Table 5-1 Experimental Decisions and Types of Errors, Considering the Example of Cigarette Smoking and Health

H_0: Cigarette smoking is not harmful to one's health.
H_1: Cigarette smoking is harmful to one's health.

DECISION	*POPULATION*	
	H_0 *(true)*	H_1 *(true)*
Reject H_0	Type I	No Error
Do not Reject H_0	No Error	Type II

or H_1 is true in the population. On the basis of the observed data from a single experiment, the researcher must decide to reject or not reject H_0. To reject H_0 is to implicitly accept H_1. Thus, there are two circumstances in which no error is made. First, H_0 may be correctly rejected; that is, if H_1 (that cigarette smoking causes lung cancer) is true for the population and we correctly *reject* the hypothesis (H_0) that it does not cause lung cancer. Second, we may fail to reject H_0 when H_0 is in fact true for the population.

There are also two circumstances in which an error is made. The error with which Fisher was most concerned is indicated in the upper left quadrant of Table 5-1 (a Type I error), the error of rejecting H_0 when it is in fact true in the population. The probability of a Type I error is under the direct control of the investigator, through the selection of a level of significance.

The error of failing to reject H_0 (the null hypothesis) when it is in fact false in the population (the Type II error) is shown in the lower right quadrant of the table. How is a Type II error to be avoided? Type II errors have a determinable relationship to certain properties of the research. First, they decrease in probability as the number of subjects in an investigation is increased. Second, the probability of a Type II error is related to the level of statistical significance chosen by the investigator. The higher the level of statistical significance (for example, .01 instead of .05), the larger the probability of a Type II error.

The Problem of Accepting the Null Hypothesis

The possibility of a Type II error raises further complexities in the logic of null hypothesis testing. One of these is accepting the null hypothesis. As we have seen earlier, it would be easy to do so by conducting a poor experiment. In order not to reject the null hypothesis one need only design an experiment that is insensitive, for example, by employing very few subjects or a very weak manipulation.

Because acceptance of the null hypothesis violates strict logic, the possible reasons for accepting it should be mentioned. Consider the discovery of a new drug that is known to have many positive effects but that might also have negative side effects that should prevent it from being used. In such a situation the null hypothesis states that the drug has no such ill effects and is pitted against the experimental hypothesis that such effects are present. If continuous comparisons of patients who have and have not been given the drug are made and no ill effects are observed, it is not logically valid to accept the null hypothesis. But it will be accepted, and that is often a reasonable decision. If powerfully designed experiments with a wide range of subjects repeatedly fail to display a particular effect, it may be prudent to violate stringent logic and tentatively accept the null hypothesis from experimental data (Greenwald, 1975). Nonetheless, acceptance of the null hypothesis should never be considered more than a provisional decision. Further, as Cook and his associates have pointed out, even provisional acceptance should not be considered until the corresponding experimental hypothesis has been tested fully and fairly (Cook, Gruder, Hennigan, & Flay, 1978).

Effects of Sample Size on Hypothesis Testing

The issues we have just discussed lead us again to a consideration of sample size in research design. First, any two sample means, though close if the null hypothesis is correct, will not be identical. Small differences are a likely occurrence and with very large samples may lead to the incorrect rejection of the null hypothesis for the population (see Meehl, 1967).

Second, since one way of increasing the sensitivity of an investigation is to increase the sample size, very large samples may lead to rejection of the null hypothesis based on quite small differences. With a sufficiently large number of subjects, virtually any difference (even a trivial difference from a practical or theoretical viewpoint) could be detected as statistically significant. This fact is essentially a corollary of the effects of increasing sample size on reducing error variance, which we discussed on page 51.

There appears to be some confusion among readers of behavioral research literature concerning the interpretation of the level of significance of results as a function of sample size. This point may be illustrated through the consideration of an investigation conducted by Rosenthal and Gaito (1963). These investigators surveyed graduate students and faculty at the University of North Dakota. Each subject in the research completed a questionnaire in which he or she indicated their degree of confidence in pairs of research findings. For each pair of findings, the subjects were given the level of significance and the number of subjects. Within the pairs, the level of statistical significance was identical; however, the number of subjects was different. Virtually unanimous agreement was found among the respondents in choosing as favored results those that had been obtained with larger numbers of subjects.

In fact, confidence in social science research should depend solely on level of statistical significance and *not* on sample size. Thus Rosenthal and Gaito's subjects should have had equal confidence in the two sets of results. Moreover, if one's criteria were practical importance, results obtained with a smaller sample require a larger treatment effect and thus become a *more* impressive result from a practical point of view. This is because a difference of a given magnitude between two group means will be easier to detect, the larger the sample size. Conversely, the smaller the sample, the larger will be the mean difference required to reach significance. For *a given significance* level, *one ought to place at least as much confidence in results obtained from a small as from a large number of subjects.* And for some purposes, significant differences obtained with small samples may be more important theoretically and/or practically.

Statistical versus Theoretical Hypothesis Testing: A Word of Caution

Our discussion thus far has focused exclusively on tests of hypotheses that are set up in a formal, statistical model. However, the underlying interest of most investigators is usually not in the statistical hypothesis per se but in the theoretical hypothesis from which it was derived. As Meehl (1967) has noted, failure to see this distinction may lead to the following:

> . . . the investigator, upon finding an observed difference which has an extremely small probability of occurring on the null hypothesis, gleefully records the tiny probability number "$p < .001$," and there is a tendency to feel that the extreme smallness of this probability of a Type I error is somehow transferable to a small probability of "making a theoretical mistake." It is as if, when the observed statistical result would be expected to arise only once in a thousand times through a Type I statistical error given H_0, therefore one's substantive theory *T*, which entails the alternative H_1, has received some sort of direct quantitative support of magnitude around .999 [$=1 - .001$] (p. 106).

This is faulty logic and, as Meehl notes, it leads to conclusions that are patently wrong. The difference between a theoretical and a statistical hypothesis may be seen clearly through the problem of *placebo effects* in drug studies. Suppose an experimenter hypothesizes that a newly developed pharmacological agent will impede certain types of neural transmission and thus have a relaxing effect on psychiatric patients. To test this hypothesis, the investigator randomly assigns a large sample of appropriate patients to an experimental (drug) or a control (no drug) group. Suppose also that because the drug is expected to have its effect within a half hour of administration, a variety of behavioral measures related to a "calm-irritable" dimension is reliably obtained during this period. When these measures are analyzed, the hypothesis that drug subjects will display greater calm than control subjects receives clear statistical support (perhaps $p < 0.001$). What can the investigator conclude?

The investigator can state that the statistical hypothesis as set up received support (or, more correctly, that the statistical *null* hypothesis can be rejected with a particular and impressive degree of confidence). The investigator *cannot* state that the theoretical proposition on which the study was based (that the drug influences neural transmission, which, in turn, influences behavior) received an equivalent degree of support. It has been shown in many earlier drug studies that a *placebo,* or substance known to be pharmacologically inert, can often produce powerful, if temporary, changes in behavior. Thus, in the present experiment, there exists a rival explanation for the theoretical hypothesis being tested but not for the statistical hypothesis that is being evaluated formally. Such problems occur often in social science research. We shall consider them in detail in Chapter 13. For now, though, there is more to say about basic problems associated with causal inference.

THREATS TO THE VALIDITY OF CAUSAL INFERENCES

Determining whether a legitimate (valid) inference can be drawn involves two distinct steps. First, the investigator must show that there is a statistically significant association between the presumed cause and the presumed effect. Second, the investigator must be able to argue that the way in which the data were produced, that is, the design of the data collection process, warrants the claim that the observed association is, in fact, interpretable as a cause and effect relationship. This second step requires showing that one, and only one, causal explanation of the observed association is plausible. Our discussion begins with the first step, correctly deciding whether the presumed cause and the presumed effect are associated. This issue has been referred to by Cook and Campbell (1979) as *statistical conclusion validity.*

THREATS TO STATISTICAL CONCLUSION VALIDITY

As we explained in Chapter 3, most social science research is evaluated by statistical tests to determine whether a relationship observed in a sample is statistically significant and can therefore be taken to reflect a real relationship in the population. Therefore, the first question about a hypothesized causal relationship is whether the presumed cause and the presumed effect are in fact associated, using conventional statistical tests. In deciding whether such an association is present in the population, our conclusion may be threatened by either Type I or Type II errors, depending on the size of our sample and the tests, measures, and procedure used in our investigation. All of these issues fall under the heading of statistical conclusion validity.

Low Statistical Power

The possibility of making a Type II error (i.e., failing to identify associations that are, in fact, present) arises whenever statistical power is low. As we mentioned in Chapter 3, small samples lower the power of statistical tests so that with very small samples even a large population effect will not be statistically significant in the sample.

Violated Assumptions of Statistical Tests

Statistical tests employ mathematically derived estimates of chance occurrence (i.e., "*p* values") by making a set of assumptions about populations of numbers. For example, many commonly used statistical tests assume that the variances of the sets of scores being related or compared are roughly the same (i.e., "homogeneity of variance"). Violation of these assumptions in an actual set of data may invalidate the statistical conclusions reached, potentially increasing the likelihood of either a Type I or a Type II error. To be sure, many statistical tests are "robust," and provide reasonably accurate *p* values even when their underlying assumptions are moderately violated. But this is not true of all statistical tests. The suitability of any particular test for a given set of data is thus an important consideration in determining statistical conclusion validity.

"Fishing"

Many investigations are designed so that large numbers of different statistical comparisons among various groups or conditions can be made. If an investigator "fishes through" all possible comparisons one or two are almost certain to appear significant merely by chance. Fishing is therefore an invalid use of statistics that can greatly increase the probability of Type I errors unless specially designed, appropriately conservative tests are used for the purpose.

Unreliable Measures

In Chapter 2 we explained the importance of employing reliable measures, i.e., measures containing as little random error as possible. When measures are unreliable they may make it difficult or impossible to detect real effects, thus increasing the likelihood of making a Type II error.

Unreliable Treatment Implementation or Settings

In studies involving explicit manipulations or treatments it is essential that the treatments given to the participants in each group be fully comparable. If the treatment implementation or the setting in which the treatments are given is poorly controlled and varies from participant to participant within the same group or condition, this is likely to increase variability on the response measures and thus increase the likelihood of Type II errors.

Heterogeneity of Subjects

If participants vary among themselves on factors relevant to the measure of the presumed effect (for example, in age, experience, or abilities) then these variations will also produce uncontrolled variance, which decreases the ability to identify true effects and thus increases the likelihood of Type II errors.

INTERNAL VALIDITY

A businessman wished to determine whether taking two aspirin on returning home from the office would relax him during the evening. To test this hypothesis, he took aspirin on some evenings but not on others and hoped to assess the differential effects of the treatment (aspirin) and control (no aspirin) situations. However, he usually "washed down" the aspirin with a glass of beer, and he discontinued the beverage along with the aspirin on control days. Thus, an important competing hypothesis for the conclusion that aspirin can cause relaxation would be that the *beverage* was responsible for the observed difference, invalidating the businessman's study and conclusions. This example illustrates the basic question of when a causal inference can be described as internally valid.[3] *Causal inferences are internally valid only when the observed change or difference can be attributed confidently to a specific variable that has been identified or isolated by the investigator.* Internal *in*validity results when a difference has been observed between two groups or conditions that are unlike on some dimension other than (or in addition to) the variable of primary interest to the investigator. This was the case in our aspirin and beer example. To establish internal validity for a causal inference, one must (among other things) demonstrate that the groups or conditions being compared were equivalent except for the treatment or event that is being subjected to causal analysis. If the critical treatment cannot be isolated, the investigation is internally *invalid,* and thus it does not provide a legitimate basis for drawing inferences about causal processes.

[3]The technically minded reader should note that our use of the term internal validity is different in two important ways from Campbell and Stanley's (1966) original usage. First, Campbell and Stanley used *internal validity* to refer to the validity of attributing causal power to manipulated variables (that is, in experiments), whereas we wish to emphasize that precisely the same problems are involved in drawing causal inferences regardless of whether one is dealing with manipulated variables in experiments or classificatory variables in correlational studies. Second, Campbell and Stanley used *internal validity* to refer to a property of various research designs. Internal validity as we define it is not a property of research design; rather, it is a property of inferences that are drawn from research and can be based on the convergence of evidence from several different studies using more than one design. This last point is extremely important, for it is the integrating philosophy that lies behind this entire book.

Plausible Rival Hypotheses

The general point underlying the concept of internal validity is that a causal inference is valid only if the research design used has effectively eliminated all *plausible rival hypotheses,* so that the inference $X \longrightarrow Y$ is secure. The burden of proof is thus on the investigator to show that the claimed effect is due to X. However, it is also important to emphasize the word *plausible.* In practice, almost any comparison that can be made in social science research will be open to some remotely conceivable rival hypothesis. For example, in comparing groups of children who do and do not receive reward for doing their homework, it would be almost impossible to be sure that the groups were exactly identical in height. Thus, technically, height differences might rival the use of reward as an explanation for an observed difference in the quality of the two groups' homework. But generally, height would not be considered a plausible rival hypothesis in this comparison, and thus it would not greatly threaten the inference that reward affects homework. (Of course, depending on the details of the study, some other factors might operate as plausible rival hypotheses and threaten the internal validity of the causal inference.) Often, then, a decision as to whether a rival hypothesis is plausible enough to threaten a causal inference comes from our existing knowledge.

Investigators may differ as to whether an uncontrolled rival hypothesis is viewed as plausible enough to threaten a causal inference. Many would insist that it is never possible to cover all the plausible alternatives. But research data can be treated cumulatively (a point to which we shall return in Chapter 13); and it is possible to show that one has just about eliminated all plausible rival hypotheses by drawing upon a number of different types of studies that can bring converging data to bear on the same causal hypothesis.

In addition to the considerations already discussed, a number of threats to the validity of causal inferences must always be guarded against. Some of these threats arise only for particular designs, whereas others are more generally pervasive.

Within- versus Between-Subjects Comparisons

The joint use of the method of agreement and the method of differences always implies a comparison between Y scores obtained when X has occurred and Y scores obtained under otherwise identical conditions when X has not occurred. In practice, such comparison can be made either "within-subjects" or "between-subjects."

Within-subjects comparisons are those in which the comparison is made between Y scores obtained before X has occurred and Y scores obtained for the same subjects after X has occurred. For example, an investigator might try to determine whether rewarding children for doing their homework improves homework performance by comparing the homework of a group of children before they were given reward for homework with the efforts of the same children after a reward-for-homework policy had been instituted. The comparison is made within the performance record of each subject (before versus after); hence the term, "within-subjects comparison."

Between-subjects comparisons are those in which the comparison made is between the *Y* scores of two separate groups that differ in whether or not they have experienced *X*. For example, an investigator might try to determine whether rewarding children for doing their homework improves homework performance by comparing children who do and who do not receive reward for their homework efforts. The comparison is called "between-subjects" because it is made between the scores of one group of subjects and the scores of another.

THREATS TO THE INTERNAL VALIDITY OF WITHIN-SUBJECTS COMPARISONS

We will discuss five general threats to the internal validity of any within-subjects comparison: maturation, testing, instrument decay, statistical regression, and history (cf. Campbell and Stanley, 1966). All of these may be considered potential third variables that can invalidate inferences of the type $X \longrightarrow Y$ from within-subjects comparisons.

Maturation

The term *maturation* refers to those processes that produce changes in a subject over time that are *not* related to the variable of interest. This definition of maturation is more general than the usual dictionary definition, inasmuch as it includes phenomena such as becoming tired, growing hungry, and the like. Thus, *maturation refers to any or all systematic changes in an organism's biological or psychological condition over time.*

Consider the following study of the effects of tutoring on poor readers. At the beginning of the term all the children in a classroom are given a reading test, and a special tutoring program is initiated for everyone. At the end of the program (six months later) all subjects are retested, and it is found that their reading scores have risen markedly. Though it is tempting to conclude that the tutoring program produced this effect, the improved reading scores could be due to maturation: in this case, changes produced by experience and the passage of time. For these reasons, the children might have shown an equally impressive gain if they had simply remained in their regular classrooms. This latter explanation is not necessarily the correct one, of course. Rather, maturation competes with the suggestion that the tutorial program caused the effect and, in the study we presented, there is no satisfactory way to discriminate between the two hypotheses.

Testing

Testing as a source of causal ambiguity *refers to the possible effects of having already taken a test on an individual's score when the individual takes the test a second time.* In general, it is known that taking a test in itself affects performance on the same test or a quite similar (parallel) form. For example, on IQ tests there is typically an increase in IQ from the first to the second testing (Anastasi, 1968). On personality tests, an individual typically appears to be better adjusted when taking the test for a second time. Clearly, people are unlikely to actually become either brighter or better adjusted as a function of taking a test. It is merely their scores on these instruments that are affected by administering them twice.

In the case of children given tutoring in reading, we presumed that all the children were given an initial test and then retested after the special program had been completed. If so, it is possible that their increase in reading scores was attributable, or partly attributable, to repeated testing.

Instrument Decay

Instrument decay occurs when a measurement device changes in certain of its characteristics over time. Physical measurements are, of course, subject to minimal problems in instrumentation. The calibration of a ruler will typically show only minor changes under normal use in usual conditions. The situation is quite different when we consider measurement in social scientific research. An interviewer (who is, in the special sense in which we are using the term here, an instrument) may easily become more skilled over time and thus collect more complete information from interviewees.

Similarly, observers are frequently used to assess the effects of various therapy techniques in psychiatric facilities. Consider a study in which researchers undertake an initial observation period of psychiatric patients in a hospital to determine the frequency of deviant behavior. A treatment is then introduced to reduce the occurrence of such activities. After the program has been put into effect, the observers again record the frequency of deviant behavior. Unless special precautions are taken, the observers may show a systematic change in their recording of behavior from time 1 to time 2. They may be less likely to record minor events on the second occasion, as a result of having observed some very high levels of deviant behavior during their first observation period. On the other hand, the first experience in observation may have "sensitized" the observers to instances of abnormal behavior so that scores are systematically increased from the first to the second test. It would not be easy to discriminate between these two possibilities. The critical point, in either case, is that the causal effect of the treatment (if any) is virtually impossible to determine.

Or consider the individual who begins an exercise program using an inexpensive rubber stretch cable (sometimes referred to as a "pocket gym") to build arm and chest muscles. One possible way of determining whether the exercise is in fact building strength is to see if the cable becomes easier to pull over time. However, the cable might become easier to pull either because the individual is getting stronger through exercise or because the rubber is stretching and hence becoming easier to pull over time. In this case, the possibility of instrument decay is easy to see and, as in our previous examples, it stands as a clear rival hypothesis to the claim that exercise has caused a real improvement.

Statistical Regression

Statistical regression refers to the fact that the extreme scores in a particular distribution will tend to move (that is, regress) *toward the mean of the distribution as a function of repeated testing.* Regression is an important source of causal ambiguity when subjects are selected for a study based on their initial extreme scores on some variable. Suppose subjects are selected for the treatment of test anxiety based on their initially high scores on a paper-and-pencil anxiety questionnaire. The treatment is applied and the subjects are retested. The anxiety scores on the second test are considerably lower than those on the first test. The result could be entirely due to statistical regression rather than to the treatment.

Statistical regression is different from maturation or the simple effects of repeated testing. Such regression results from the imperfect relationship between the first and the second tests and therefore from a certain kind of measurement error (see Chapter 2). Because measurement error is a random process, extremely high scores will decrease somewhat and extremely low scores will increase somewhat simply as a function of random variations.

An example of how statistical regression can become a significant rival hypothesis to a causal inference can be found in analyses of the effects of the television series, *Sesame Street.* Bogatz and Ball (1972) found that among viewers of the show, children with the lowest initial scores on a variety of preschool academic skills (such as recognizing letters of the alphabet) gained more than other children over a season of viewing. That is, there was a negative correlation between the child's initial scores and the amount he or she gained. Does this mean that the more disadvantaged a child is, the more the child will gain from *Sesame Street?* Presumably, this is what the creators of the series hoped. But the evidence is ambiguous because of the possibility that mere statistical regression accounts for the unusually large gains of the children with the lowest initial scores. That is, both the children's initial obtained scores and their final obtained scores contain (1) a *true score* and (2) *measurement error* (see pp. 38-40). Measurement error, caused by transient random factors (such as having had an unusually tiring day prior to taking the test), is almost certainly one reason why some of the initially low scorers did as poorly as they did on the first test. These same chance factors will probably not befall these same youngsters again when they take the test at the end of the television season. Thus, the scores of this group will tend to regress upward regardless of the true effects of *Sesame Street* (Cook et al., 1975; Liebert, 1976).

Regression may also be considered, from a more mathematical point of view, as an inevitable result of the social scientist's particular mode of prediction. Recall from our discussion of regression that with standardized scores, the best prediction of Y from X can be expressed as the correlation of X and Y times the standardized X-score (predicted $Y = r_{xy}Zx$). In this instance, when predicting test score number 2 from number 1, our equation would be: predicted score on test number 2 $= r_{(\text{test } 1 \times \text{test } 2)} Z_{\text{test } 1}$. Now whenever the correlation between the two tests is less than 1.0, the scores on the second test will always be smaller than those on the first. A distribution of standardized scores has a mean of 0; scores above the mean take positive values and scores below negative ones. Thus, when these scores are multiplied by a correlation coefficient less than 1, they shrink (for example, $+2.0 \times 0.80 = 1.6$; $-3.4 \times 0.7 = -2.38$). The scores, then, have regressed toward the mean.

History

In the context of exploring sources of causal ambiguity, *history refers to those environmental events other than the treatment or experience of interest that occur between a first and second testing.* Suppose a social scientist has developed a group training technique to reduce the racial prejudices of individuals who are initially highly prejudiced against blacks. A group of such individuals is brought together and tested to determine the extent of their prejudicial attitudes. The group meets for ten sessions and is then retested. The investigator finds that on this retest, the participants' prejudices have decreased markedly and concludes that the technique was quite successful. Such a conclusion would be cast into serious doubt if any major historical events occurred in the intervening period that could also account for the change. Suppose that during the treatment period a major black political leader had been shot. This shocking incident itself might result in a temporary reduction of prejudice. History, like maturation, becomes an increasingly plausible rival hypothesis as longer intervals of time (with correspondingly greater opportunity for maturation or historical events to occur) pass between the first and the second testing.

THREATS TO THE INTERNAL VALIDITY OF BETWEEN-SUBJECTS COMPARISONS

We will discuss six major threats to the internal validity of between-subjects comparisons: selection bias, differential attrition, diffusion, compensatory equalization, compensatory rivalry, and resentful demoralization.

Selection Bias

Selection bias refers to any systematic differences other than those caused by experiencing the treatment that are present when subjects are selected for comparison groups. Suppose, for example, that ten high school mathematics teachers are told about a new method of teaching math. If five volunteers were solicited from this group to try the new program, the progress of their students might be compared with the progress of a group of comparable students who are taught mathematics in the traditional way by the five teachers who did not volunteer for the new program. Inasmuch as the volunteers may be generally more enthusiastic or more skilled than the nonvolunteers, differences in the progress made by their students could result from differences among the teachers. Thus, the new instructional technique might in fact be no better than the old one even though the students exposed to it seemed to do better than those studying the established curriculum.

In other cases, selection bias is introduced when subjects have been formed into groups for reasons other than participating in a research study. For example, an investigator might pursue the question of the effects of psychotherapy on bizarre behavior by administering the treatment in one mental hospital ward and comparing it with a "control" ward, perhaps supervised by different personnel. When the investigator compares the frequency of bizarre behavior of these two groups, he or she will want to attribute any differences between them to the presence or absence of therapy. However, this inference would not be internally valid. Perhaps the ward that received the therapy manipulation was already producing less bizarre behavior than the no-therapy ward. It is possible that the patients were assigned by hospital authorities to the two different wards as a function of some systematic characteristics. If the patients were grouped with respect to their symptoms or previous histories or almost any other variable that could bear on their behavior, such grouping could render the results of the study causally ambiguous.

Differential Attrition

Attrition refers to the loss of subjects from one or more groups of a study. *Differential attrition refers to differences in the number of subjects that are lost as a function of which group is being considered.* Suppose that an investigator wishes to explore the influence of a treatment for reducing smoking. The investigator forms two groups that are approximately equal in the number of cigarettes per day that they smoke; one of the groups is given treatment, the other (control) group is not. During the study, many subjects drop out of the treatment group but few drop out of the control group. Thus, when the second measurement of the frequency of smoking is obtained, the groups may no longer be as similar as the logic of causal inference requires, owing to the differential dropout rate. If in the treatment group the heaviest smokers, or those with the longest smoking history, dropped out of the treatment because it was clear to them that improvement was unlikely, the mean frequency of smoking score for the treated group would now be lower than that of the control group—but not necessarily as a result of the treatment.

Diffusion

Diffusion refers to the spread of treatment effects from the treated to the untreated groups. It is an important problem when the treatment involves giving information to some individuals or groups but not to others. For example, if some college students in a memory experiment are told that they will be tested on material a week later while other students are not told of the subsequent test, the investigator must be sure that knowledge of the later test does not spread to all participants (e.g., by discussion of the experiment among friends or classmates before all the participants have completed the testing). Diffusion may mask or wipe out the true effects of treatment.

Compensatory Equalization

Compensatory equalization refers to the situation in which untreated individuals or groups learn of the treatment received by others and demand the same treatment or something "equally good" for themselves. For example, in comparing the effects of violent and nonviolent television on boys in a residential facility, one team of investigators faced the problem that boys in the nonviolent TV group learned that those in the violent TV group were allowed to watch the series *Batman* (which had just made its television premiere), and demanded the right to watch *Batman* too. A similar problem has arisen in testing many large-scale educational enrichment programs; parents, teachers, and local school administrators in areas not receiving the enrichment may hear of the special program and demand that their children receive something of equal value. As with diffusion, compensatory equalization can obscure real treatment effects that might otherwise be demonstrated.

Compensatory Rivalry

Compensatory rivalry occurs whenever an untreated group learns of the treatment received by others (such as special new tools) *and works extra hard to see to it that the expected superiority of the treatment group is not demonstrated.* Compensatory rivalry has been called the "John Henry effect" after the famous steel driver who learned that his performance was being compared to a steam drill and drove himself to outperform his inanimate competitor—only to die of overexertion as a result (Saretsky, 1972).

Resentful Demoralization

Resentful demoralization may be considered the flip side of compensatory rivalry. It *involves the situation in which individuals in an untreated or control group learn that others are receiving special treatment and become less productive, efficient, or motivated than they would have been because of feelings of resentment.* Resentful demoralization may occur even when the special treatment given to the other group is in fact of no benefit; in such cases resentful demoralization can create the appearance of an advantage for the treated group when the treatment itself actually has no beneficial effect.

IDENTIFYING AGE-RELATED CHANGES

People change throughout their lives. There are age-related changes in cognitive abilities, motor skills, and most aspects of social behavior. Some of these changes (often called *developmental trends*) result from maturational processes within the body, and some result from learning and experience; most age-related changes of interest to social and behavioral scientists involve both maturational and experiential factors.

Often, however, what appear to be age-related changes are spurious in the sense that some difference other than age or age-related processes may be responsible for an observed difference among groups of various ages. Thus the conclusion that there are *changes* over age in any aspect of functioning requires an inference that may or may not be internally valid. Moreover, as with other questions about behavior, the comparisons on which such inferences are based may be made between-subjects or within-subjects. Between-subjects age comparisons are referred to as cross-sectional studies; within-subjects age comparisons are referred to as longitudinal studies. Each has strengths and weaknesses.

Threats to the Internal Validity of Cross-Sectional Studies

In cross-sectional studies, people of different ages are observed at approximately the same calendar time. For example, a study of age-related changes in vocabulary could sample 3, 7, 11, 15, and 19-year-olds and assess each group on a test of word knowledge. The average score of each group could be compared in a between-subjects fashion. At first it appears that the cross-sectional strategy has a clear economic benefit—a 16-year span of development (ages 3 to 19) has apparently been assessed with an outlay of only several weeks of work. But there is a rub. The subjects in a cross-sectional study may differ on variables in addition to age.

Let us examine our vocabulary example more closely. Suppose our observations revealed that the average vocabulary score of each of the groups was as follows: 3-year-olds: 18, 7-year-olds: 2500, 11-year-olds: 10,000, 15-year-olds: 15,000, and 19-year-olds: 15,000. (The numbers are hypothetical and do not reflect the actual vocabularies of people of different ages.) From these data we might conclude that there is no vocabulary change between ages 15 and 19. But we must remember that we have assessed different people in each of these groups. The 15-year-olds whose mean score was 15,000 in our study might show further growth in vocabulary over the next four years; thus at age 19 they might have larger vocabularies than our present 19-year-old sample. Likewise, there is no guarantee that our sample of 19-year-olds didn't know fewer words at 15 than they know at present. In either case our inference that there are no changes in vocabulary between age 15 and age 19 would be wrong.

More technically, the age groups in a between-subjects study of change are referred to as *cohorts,* and *cohort differences* always constitute a rival hypothesis to the inference that an observed between-subjects (cross-sectional) difference among age groups reflects a true age-related change. For example, in our vocabulary study the 15-year-old and 19-year-old cohorts may have differed in their educational backgrounds because of possible changes in public educational philosophy (vocabulary may be emphasized more now than it used to be).

Threats to the Internal Validity of Longitudinal Studies

The preceding example was extreme; researchers interested in developmental trends are usually quite sensitive to cohort differences that could contaminate their studies. But the possibility always remains that the groups differ on some overlooked variable that has an important impact on the results. The only solution is to perform a truly longitudinal study, in which the same people are observed at different points in their lives. Thus, a longitudinal study involves within-subjects comparisons of measures taken repeatedly over time. A longitudinal study of vocabulary development might start with a sample of 3-year-olds and periodically reassess them. Using the within-subjects longitudinal approach, we can both measure growth directly and also answer questions pertaining to the stability of various aspects of behavior.

Although the longitudinal method has a major advantage, it is a difficult research strategy to employ. Longitudinal studies are time-consuming and expensive. Furthermore, there is an ever-present danger of losing participants as the years pass. People may relocate or become unwilling to continue participation. In both these cases the researcher may, at the end of the study, be left with a biased sample. Nonetheless, longitudinal data are indispensible for studying age-related changes and many developmental processes.

Cross-Sequential Designs

Because the cross-sectional and longitudinal approaches to studying age-related changes have complementary strengths and weaknesses, some investigators have combined them using so-called *cross-sequential designs*. These designs employ several different cohorts, as in cross-sectional studies, but follow them longitudinally rather than relying on "one-shot" observations. Returning to our vocabulary example, we might obtain vocabulary scores for 7, 11 and 15-year-olds and retest everyone four years later. Such a design permits the investigator to observe vocabulary growth in three cohorts cross-sectionally at two different times and to examine an age span of 12 years (7 to 19) in a study that requires only four years to complete. When analyzed with appropriate statistical techniques, such a design allows one to partially disentangle developmental trends and cohort effects.

Retrospective versus Prospective Accounts

Longitudinal data may be gathered either retrospectively or prospectively. Retrospective studies involve asking subjects or their friends, relatives, or associates to "look back" and recall what was said or done at various earlier times. Prospective studies, on the other hand, set out to follow subjects forward in time, so that each important event or circumstance can be noted and recorded as it occurs. Obviously, retrospective accounts are considerably less expensive to obtain than prospective accounts because they do not require a substantial time commitment from the investigator. Unfortunately, however, retrospective accounts have been shown to be easily biased, and respondents often claim to have high confidence in what has turned out (from access to hard data such as archival records) to be quite wrong. Thus, in general, retrospective data have dubious value and are no substitute for the more demanding but much more credible prospective approach.

MULTIPLE THREATS TO INTERNAL VALIDITY

The threats to rigorous causal inference that we have described individually may appear together in a single study. This produces a situation that is literally fraught with ambiguity. Consider a study that attempts to determine the efficacy of a type of counseling therapy in improving persons' self-concepts. One group of persons whose self-concepts are very unfavorable is selected, and a control group of individuals with more favorable self-concepts is also employed. After the treatment, which lasts approximately six months, the treatment and control groups are both retested, the latter to assess the degree to which self-concepts simply

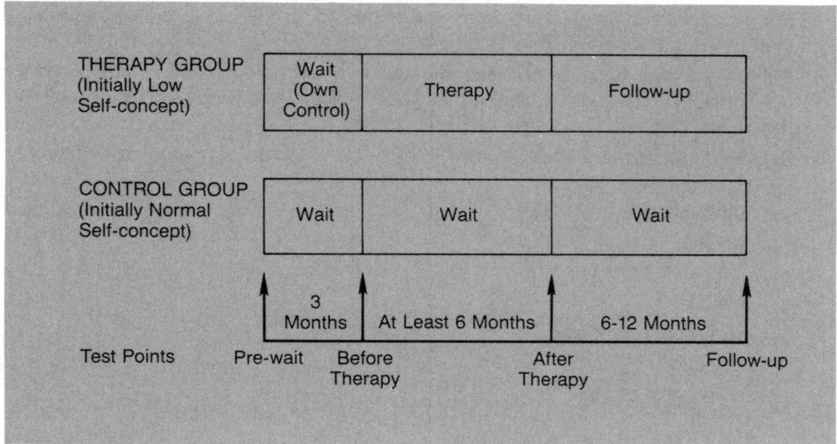

Figure 5-2 A portion of the design of Rogers and Dymond's 1954 study. Despite the "Own Control" period and the normal control group, the investigation suffers from multiple sources of causal ambiguity and is virtually impossible to interpret.

change with the passage of time. The design of such a study, which was actually conducted (Rogers & Dymond, 1954), appears in Figure 5-2.

Note that the study depicted in Figure 5-2 invites at least two rival hypotheses that threaten the internal validity of the hypothesis in which the investigators are interested (namely, that therapy brings about improvement in those who receive it). First, because of selection bias, the two groups are not comparable at the outset of the study. It is quite possible that individuals with initially poor self-concepts may change in a favorable direction, but one would not expect development of more favorable self-images in individuals who are not troubled in the first place. Additionally, the fact that the "own-control," or wait period, in the therapy group is only three months whereas the treatment period is at least six months introduces the problem of differential maturation in making comparisons within this group. It may be that time increases the possibility that individuals' self-concepts will improve. If those that receive therapy show improved self-images, the improvement may be an instance of so-called *spontaneous remission* (a clinical term for improvement with the mere passage of time), which in this case could be specific to individuals with initially low self-concepts. The results of such a study do not allow us to reach any conclusions about causality.

FOR REVIEW AND DISCUSSION

1. Explain how Mill's "method of agreement" and "method of differences" can be used to show that *X* is a sufficient cause of *Y*.
2. In what ways do between- and within-subjects comparisons differ?

3. Discuss the third variable problem as it relates to sample selection and equivalence of groups in correlational research.
4. If there is a high *negative* correlation between grades in high school and number of dates, can we conclude that people who make good grades are socially unattractive? What is a rival hypothesis?
5. Explain each term and indicate how it might be a source of internal invalidity:

    maturation
    testing
    instrument decay
    history
    statistical regression
    selection
    differential attrition

6. One of the most controversial areas of social science involves the relationship between race and intelligence. A number of studies have compared the IQs of blacks and whites. These studies, using one variable that has many values (IQ)and one variable with only two values (race, as defined in this country) are correlational; neither variables can be experimentally manipulated. The general procedure is to compare the mean IQ of whites to the mean IQ of blacks; very often the mean IQ of whites is higher. Can we conclude that blacks are therefore genetically inferior to whites on the dimension of intelligence? Why or why not?
7. Diffusion, compensatory equalization, compensatory rivalry, and resentful demoralization are only threats to internal validity when subjects who do not receive a treatment know that others are receiving one. Under what circumstances are subjects most likely to obtain this knowledge? How can these threats be avoided?
8. In the text it is pointed out that almost any differences between groups can reach significance when the sample size is large enough. What value can there be, then, in placing so much emphasis on the "significance level" if the results may be trivial? In other words, why use statistical tests at all?
9. Explain the difference between a retrospective and a prospective account of changes over time.

6

Subject and Experimenter Biases

THE THREE ROLES IN THE RESEARCH ENTERPRISE
REACTIVITY: THE EFFECTS OF BEING OBSERVED
THE HAWTHORNE EFFECT
PRIVATELY HELD HYPOTHESES AND DEMAND CHARACTERISTICS
Problems in Assessing Situational Demands
Four Subject-Based Threats to Internal Validity
RESPONSE SETS AND THE TRUTHFULNESS OF SELF-REPORTS
REDUCING REACTIVITY: THE USE OF UNOBTRUSIVE MEASURES
Physical Traces
Archives
Unobtrusive Observation
SELF-FULFILLING PROPHECIES AND EXPERIMENTER BIAS
Bias Effects and the Adequacy of Research Observations
Low Interrater Reliability as a Threat to Validity
FOR REVIEW AND DISCUSSION

In the preceding chapter we discussed threats to the validity of research results that arise from problems in the statistical analysis or design of research. In this chapter we turn to another type of threat to the validity of research conclusions, namely, those that arise from the participants themselves.

THE THREE ROLES IN THE RESEARCH ENTERPRISE

Broadly speaking, three roles are involved in any behavioral research enterprise: the subject, the experimenter, and the investigator.

The *subject role* is held by the persons (or animals) whose behavior is actually being studied.

The *experimenter role* is held by those who actually make contact with the subjects, including the administration of treatments (if any), testing and/or observing subjects' responses, and scoring and recording the data gathered from tests or observations. (Note that we are using the term experimenter in a broad sense, to include research personnel in any study, regardless of whether an experimental manipulation of treatments is involved.)

The *investigator role* is filled by those who design, analyze, interpret, and report the results of research. In any given study the role of investigator may be played by a single individual or by several individuals working in collaboration. Note, too, that the investigator and experimenter roles can be filled by the same individuals, although in practice senior individuals typically play the investigator role while research assistants administer the treatments and carry out the data collection.

Earlier in this century social scientists took a relatively credulous view of the research enterprise, assuming that research data were always pure. Beginning in the 1930s, however, evidence suggesting that both subjects and experimenters can systematically distort or bias research data began to accumulate. Today it is widely acknowledged that both subjects and experimenters can bias research results, sometimes in quite subtle ways, and that well-designed research must include safeguards against these potential biases. Our discussion begins with a consideration of subject biases.

REACTIVITY: THE EFFECTS OF BEING OBSERVED

In most human behavioral research, the participants know that they are serving as subjects in an investigation.

The act of observation may produce changes in the phenomenon under investigation, a problem not unique to social scientific research. In physics, the celebrated Heisenberg principle of uncertainty makes a similar point. In a "thought experiment," Heisenberg (1958) notes:

> One could argue that it should be at least possible to observe the electron in its orbit. One should simply look at the atom through a microscope with a very high resolving power; then one would see the electron moving in its orbit. Such a high resolving power could to be sure not be obtained using ordinary light, since the inaccuracy of the measurement of the position can never be smaller than the wave length of the light. But a microscope using gamma rays with a wave length smaller than the size of the atom would do. . . . The position of the electron will be known with an accuracy given by the wave length of the gamma ray. The electron may have been practically at rest before the observation. But *in the act of observation* at least one light quantum of the gamma ray must have passed the microscope and must first have been deflected by the electron. Therefore, the electron has been pushed by the light quantum, it has changed its momentum and velocity, and one can show that the uncertainty of this change is just big enough to guarantee the validity of the uncertainty relations (p. 47).

In social scientific research, the problem caused by knowing that one is in the role of "subject" may be particularly acute. The presence (or possible presence) of such reactions may make the obtained results unrepresentative of the natural situation in which the investigator is ultimately interested. When observations or test scores are influenced by the act of measurement, they are said to be *reactive.* In the following sections we provide an overview of the problem of reactivity in behavioral observation and describe several nonreactive methods of observation.

THE HAWTHORNE EFFECT

Some years ago, a group of investigators at the Hawthorne plant of the Western Electric Company began a study of factors related to worker productivity. The general design of their studies was to select a group of workers, introduce a treatment (for example, changes in work hours, temperature, and the like), and then assess the production rate. Surprisingly, a series of investigations revealed that *every treatment the investigators tried produced increases in worker productivity.*

Could the investigators therefore conclude that all the various manipulations they tried should in fact be recommended as treatments to be implemented in other plants so as to effect an increase in productivity? No. The workers' heightened output was due to their awareness of being specially treated rather than to any specific aspects of the treatments employed. The increase in performance due to knowledge that one is being observed subsequently came to be known as the *Hawthorne effect.* The experiments themselves would be invalid in terms of generalizing to other plants and employees. In implementing the techniques tested in this study, future plants would presumably not treat the workers as participants in a special project. In the absence of this situation (which may have led the individuals under study to believe that since they were under scrutiny, they should work harder), some or all of the manipulations would not have been successful.[1]

PRIVATELY HELD HYPOTHESES AND DEMAND CHARACTERISTICS

Subjects entering a test situation are not merely passive recipients of the manipulations or instructions provided by the investigator. Rather, they will undoubtedly develop their own hypotheses about the nature and purposes of the investigation. These hypotheses, together with the subjects' "reading" and interpretation of the circumstances in which they are placed, constitute the *demand characteristics of the situation.* Thus, the concept of demand characteristics, introduced into the methodological literature by Martin Orne (1962), recognizes the fact that subjects often care about the outcome of the investigation and/or try to show the investigator that they are sophisticated individuals or shrewd problem solvers.

A subject's *role behavior* is behavior that is elicited by the demand characteristics of the situation. When subjects respond according to what they judge to be an appropriate role in the situation rather than as naive or credulous individuals, the study's findings may be misleading or worthless.

An interesting example of how demand characteristics may operate is found in a study by Orne and Scheibe (1964). Prior to this study, a number of investigations of the effects of sensory deprivation had been conducted. In these studies, subjects were put in isolation rooms to reduce external stimulation as much as possible (for example, by having them wear translucent goggles and cardboard "gloves" and by restricting movement). Dramatic effects, apparently due entirely to sensory deprivation, were typically produced: hallucinations, disorientation, and deterioration in intellectual and emotional behavior. However, Orne and Scheibe's work demonstrates the possibility that some of these effects are due, in part, to demand characteristics.

They asked how much of the bizarre behavior of subjects in sensory deprivation experiments was caused by cues that communicated the expectancy of bizarre behavior. Two groups of subjects were randomly assigned to one of two conditions. In the first condition, an attempt was made to maximize demands for bizarre behavior; in the second, the demands were minimized. In the first situation, the study was conducted in a psychiatric hospital by an experimenter who wore a white coat. A medical history was taken and a tray of drugs and medical instruments, labeled the "emergency tray," was in full view. During the

[1] One interpretation that has been put on the Hawthorne experiments is that improving working conditions does no more for productivity than minimally consulting with workers. This interpretation is *not* justified, as has been pointed out repeatedly (Bramel & Friend, 1978; Carey, 1967; Sykes, 1965).

instructions it was stressed that the subjects should report any unusual experiences. Finally they were shown a red button marked "Emergency Alarm," which they could press if they could stand the situation no longer. In the second condition, subjects were told that they were a control group for a sensory deprivation study and were not exposed to suggestive cues such as the panic button, emergency tray, medical interview, and so on.

Afterward all subjects were treated identically, spending three hours in an isolation room. Results indicated that the demand characteristic group showed more sensory deprivation symptoms than the controls, including such bizarre reports as that "the walls of the room are starting to waver."

Other investigations that seem to suggest the importance of subjects' cognizance of the nature and purposes of experimental treatments may be found in various studies of verbal conditioning. Early investigations of this type sought to show that a person's conversation could be modified by an experimenter's systematic use of certain verbal rewards (such as "good" or "mm-hmm"). It was thought that the effects of these rewards were automatic, so that the subject would show changes in the frequency of using particular words (for example, naming more plural nouns or men's proper names or the like) regardless of whether he or she was *aware* of the contingency. More recent experiments have, however, suggested that the effects of verbal conditioning experiments may depend on the subject's both being aware of and *deciding to go along with* the probable intent of the experimenter (Hamilton, Thompson, & White, 1970).

One possible means of reducing the potential effects of demand characteristics is to manipulate the variable of interest so that the subject does not even think that the critical events are connected to the experiment. The subject is not informed of the true purpose of the research. For example, the manipulation may be made to appear as an accident. In a classic experimental study of fear (Ax, 1953), the subject, after being connected to an electrical apparatus, "accidentally" received a shock. Or deception can be implemented through the use of a confederate who appears to be a naive participant. Such deceptions have been widely used. As Kelman noted:

> Deception has been turned into a game, often played with great skill and virtuosity. A considerable amount of the creativity and ingenuity of social psychologists is invested in the development of increasingly elaborate deception situations. . . . One well-known experiment, . . . for example, involved a whole progression of deceptions. After the subjects had gone through an experimental test, the investigator made it clear—through word and gesture—that the experiment was over and he would now "like to explain what this had been all about so you'll have some idea of why you were doing this. . . ." This explanation was false, however, and was designed to serve as a basis for the true experimental manipulation (1967, p. 1).

In addition to the ethical problems associated with such deceptions (see Chapter 1) the fact that social scientists often deceive their subjects has become increasingly widely known. Many college student subjects may come to the lab with the expectation that they will in some way be tricked. This "set" undoubtedly leads subjects to treat the research situation as one in which they are attempting to solve a problem—to determine the "true" purpose of the investigation. Thus, rather than reducing demand characteristics, subjects' knowledge about the widespread use of deception might increase such influences. Fortunately, the years that have passed since Kelman's article appeared have witnessed a decline in the frequency with which deception is used in psychological research.

Problems in Assessing Situational Demands

It is relatively difficult to determine adequately the degree to which demand characteristics constitute a serious challenge to the validity of a particular result. One possible way of making such an assessment is through a detailed interview with subjects, after the fact, to determine whether they have adduced certain of the experimental hypotheses and thus "played along" so as to assist the experimenter in obtaining the desired results. However, as Orne (1969) has observed, this strategy has its own pitfalls. He noted:

> The greatest danger is the "pact of ignorance" . . . which all too commonly characterizes the postexperimental discussion. The subject knows that if he has "caught on" to some apparent deception and has an excess of information about the experimental procedure he may be disqualified from participation and thus have wasted his time. The experimenter is aware that the subject who knows too much or has "caught on" to his deception will have to be disqualified; disqualification means running yet another subject, still further delaying completion of his study. . . . Hence, neither party to the inquiry wants to dig very deeply (1969, p. 153).

If an investigator wishes to reduce or eliminate the effect of demand characteristics, the general solution should take the form of disguising the fact that research is being done. For example, the research might be conducted in a "naturalistic environment" so that from the subject's point of view, he or she is not participating in a scientific investigation, but rather merely engaging in day-to-day activities. Unfortunately, many research problems are difficult to examine in a naturalistic environment.

Four Subject-Based Threats to Internal Validity

Four of the threats to internal validity discussed in Chapter 5—diffusion, compensatory equalization, compensatory rivalry, and resentful demoralization—are subject-based in the sense that they occur because of subjects' perceptions, motivation, or role behavior.

Diffusion is often a threat to laboratory-type experiments done with student populations, especially when one of the manipulated treatments involves giving more (or different) information to subjects, depending on the group to which they have been assigned. It is easy to see how such information could travel rapidly through a classroom or dormitory, especially when the subjects are run one at a time and the treatment has a "trick" to it, such as an unexpected test of memory. Moreover, because of the pact-of-ignorance problem mentioned above, investigators are unlikely to detect that diffusion has occurred through ordinary post-experimental interviews.

Compensatory equalization is most likely to be a problem in applied studies, such as investigations involving treatments that may be beneficial to those who receive them. Unlike diffusion, compensatory equalization is relatively easy to detect because the demand for equal treatment must be openly expressed before it can be satisfied. Unfortunately, when the demand for compensatory equalization is not met, compensatory rivalry or resentful demoralization may occur as a result.

Compensatory rivalry and *resentful demoralization* can also occur even in the absence of prior demands for equal treatment. They are especially likely to pose a threat when the behavior of interest has a strong motivational component; that is, when performance depends on the amount of time or energy expended to produce it.

RESPONSE SETS AND THE TRUTHFULNESS OF SELF-REPORTS

One important assumption often made by behavioral scientists who use self-reports in gathering data is that an individual's response to any particular question reflects his or her disposition toward the *content* of that item. To the extent that this assumption is not correct, research using such measures may be misleading.

Suppose a man is presented with the statement: "I attend a party at least once a week." If he answers "Yes," or "True," or otherwise indicates that the statement applies to him, can we assume that he *does* attend social gatherings frequently? Often the answer appears to be no, since it has been found that people with certain test-taking or questionnaire "sets" may not respond to this type of item in terms of its manifest content. Several types of *response sets,* as these orientations are called, have been identified.

Response acquiescence, or "yea-saying," is the tendency to agree with statements regardless of their content. *Response deviation* is the tendency to answer items in an uncommon direction regardless of their content. *Social desirability* is a response set characterized by answering questions in the direction that is most socially accepted regardless of whether such an answer is actually correct for the respondent. For instance, in the example above, a man who abhors (and avoids) parties might say that he attends them at least once a week because he feels that such a response is likely to be considered "right" or appropriate.

To illustrate the problem and some possible solutions, we shall consider the pioneering work of Edwards (1953, 1957) with social desirability. He began with an investigation designed to assess the relationship between the likelihood that an item would be endorsed and the social desirability of the item as measured independently. First, a large number of subjects were asked to judge 140 different self-descriptions on a 9-point scale, in terms of ". . . the degree of desirability or undesirability of these traits in people. . ." (1957). Some of the items are listed below:

1. To like to punish your enemies.
2. To like to read psychological novels.
3. To like to make excuses for friends.
4. To like to go out with your friends.

In the next phase of the study, Edwards presented the same 140 items to a different sample of undergraduates who were asked to respond *yes* if the particular item was characteristic of their own behavior and *no* if it was not. The percentage of subjects responding *yes* to each of the items was computed and then correlated with the judged social desirability of the response. An impressively high correlation was obtained, leading Edwards to conclude that if we know where a statement lies on the social desirability-undesirability dimension, ". . . we can then predict, with a high degree of accuracy, the proportion of individuals who will say, in self-description, that the statement does describe them" (1957, p. 3). The effect does not appear to be reduced when respondents are led to believe that they will remain anonymous.[2] Thus, several other methods have been devised for controlling its influence.

One is to measure the respondent's tendency to give socially desirable answers and then to adjust his or her other responses in a manner that will take this tendency into account. Unfortunately, some very complicated assumptions would have to be met to make such a technique completely legitimate. For example, one would have to show that the tendency to give socially desirable responses is highly general across different content items. Alternatively, a *forced-choice inventory* may be used, in which items of differing content are equated in terms of their (independently determined) social desirability. Edwards himself used this latter technique in constructing his *Personal Preferences Schedule.* The manner in which it forces respondents to choose between equally desirable (or

[2]There is more than one possible interpretation of these data. For example, if behaviors that are judged as most desirable in a particular culture are also those that are most common, then social desirability and probability of endorsement would "go together" even if subjects were not misrepresenting themselves. But the evidence does not favor this view.

undesirable) alternatives and thus to make a content-related response can be seen from the two alternatives that appear below:

Choose A or B

I.
A: I like to tell amusing stories and jokes at parties.
B: I would like to write a great novel or play.

II.
A: I feel like blaming others when things go wrong for me.
B: I feel that I am inferior to others in most respects.

Another attempt to reduce the problem of response sets in self-reports involves the use of so-called *behavioroid measures* (Aronson & Carlsmith, 1968). Such measures require subjects to commit themselves to a particular action, without actually ever having to perform it later. For example, Marlowe, Frager, and Nuttall (1965) asked subjects to agree (after various treatments) to spend a great deal of time escorting some visiting blacks around campus. Although only a verbal statement was elicited, it is quite different from a yes-no response to a question such as "I like blacks."

REDUCING REACTIVITY: THE USE OF UNOBTRUSIVE MEASURES

Several partial solutions to the problem of reactivity have been mentioned in previous sections. One, *unobtrusive measures* (those that do not intrude upon, and therefore cannot interfere or interact with, the observations being made), appears particularly promising. Three broad classes of unobtrusive measures have been recommended in an excellent and extensive treatment of this topic by Webb, Campbell, Schwartz, and Sechrest (1966). These are *physical traces, archives,* and *unobtrusive observation.*

Physical Traces

The term *physical traces* refers to those measurement procedures that look to the durable residue of earlier events as evidence for the occurrence of particular actions or processes. Four types of physical traces may be employed.

Erosion measures involve inspection of the relative "wear and tear" of various objects and facilities as an index of their degree of use. For example, inspection of library books acquired at approximately the same time may serve as a useful index of the reading preferences of library users. This measure might be markedly more accurate than others, such as questionnaires. Respondents to a questionnaire might indicate a strong preference for intellectually oriented or other high-status volumes, but an inspection of the books themselves might reveal that these erudite pieces are rarely checked out and their pages almost never turned. In contrast, although novels featuring excitement, adventure, or sex might rarely appear on the respondents' questionnaire listings of their favorites, the books' dog-eared pages might attest to their actual popularity. Even more exotic techniques for erosion measurements have been offered. Webb et al., (1966) have suggested that the relative frequency with which persons visit exhibits at a museum could be indexed by the frequency with which the floor tiles must be waxed or the handrails and doorknobs leading to various corridors require polishing.

Natural accretion refers to the measurement procedure of examining remnants of past behavior that have been laid down naturally, without the investigator's intervention. Under some circumstances, it can indeed be both a powerful and durable source of evidence. Sawyer (1961) estimated liquor consumption in a supposedly dry town by examining trash containers and counting the number of empty liquor bottles that were found. (Not surprisingly, very few dry towns are really dry.) Natural accretion is also used in modern police techniques. Webb and his colleagues (1966) note that criminal investigations often employ complex analyses of such natural accretions as soil from shoes and clothing to demonstrate that a suspect was likely to have been at the scene of a crime. Impressively, the murder of Napoleon, which apparently occurred in 1821, was discovered 140 years later (1961) on the basis of arsenic traces found in the remains of his hair.

A third type of physical trace, *controlled erosion,* involves a predetermined plan to measure some form of erosion that would index a relevant type of behavior. For example, researchers have measured children's activity level by having them wear self-winding wristwatches that were adapted to record body movement. It has also been suggested that activity level might be measured by the rate at which shoes are worn out. With imagination and perseverence, one could devise many such measures for a variety of purposes.

Finally, related to the controlled erosion measure are measures of *controlled accretion.* For example, Politz (1958) devised a "glue-seal record" in which a pair of magazine pages are bound together by a small spot of glue that does not readhere after the seal has been broken. It is then possible to determine the popularity of particular magazines by counting the number of broken seals in samples of a particular issue. The method was devised because earlier attempts with questionnaire responses had suggested that individuals would claim falsely that they had read or looked at particular advertisements when they had not. Again with imagination, the possibilities are almost limitless. Here is a particularly clever example:

> The relative popularity of exhibits with glass fronts could be compared by examining the number of noseprints deposited on the glass each day (or on some

> sample of time, day, months, and so forth). This requires that the glass be dusted for noseprints each night and then wiped clean for the next day's viewers to smudge. The noseprint measure has fewer content restrictions than most of the trace techniques, for the age of viewers can be estimated as well as the total number of prints on each exhibit. Age is determined by plotting a frequency distribution of the heights of the smudges from the floor and relating these data to the normative heights by age (minus, of course, the nose to top of head correction) (Webb et al. 1966, pp. 45–46).

Archives

Archives are the ongoing and continuing records of society. Archival records of birth, marriage, and death may be used to test various hypotheses in an unobtrusive and unbiased manner. For example, investigators who posited that people can extend their lives for at least short periods of time by "will power" alone have related dates of death in public records to birth dates, religious holidays, and the like. People are less likely than would be expected by chance to die shortly before their own birthdays or shortly before holidays related to their own religious beliefs. In a somewhat earlier use of archival records, Galton (1872) used longevity data to measure the efficacy of prayer, reasoning that if prayers were effective in preserving life, then members of royal houses (who were probably among the most prayed-for individuals, witness the British anthem "God save the Queen") should know greater longevity than other groups with comparable medical attention. Interestingly, and contrary to the "efficacy of prayer" hypothesis, Galton found that members of royal families had, on the average, shorter life spans (64.04 years) than men of literature and science (67.55 years).

Political and judicial records, weather reports, moon phases, items appearing in the mass media, and a variety of other sources may also be related to meaningful hypotheses in the behavioral sciences. McClelland (1961) has even used children's stories of an earlier era to "predict" the economic progress of various countries.

The major problem that arises in using archival records as a source of evidence is that they are produced *by* someone else and *for* someone else. The investigator must be wary of selectivity in both the material that is deposited and the material that survives, particularly when looking at records over a long span of time. If, for example, a full set of newspaper issues is not available for a given journal, the ones that remain may not adequately characterize the time from which they are taken. Decisions made by some unknown clerk, at an unknown time, as to what was "worth saving" and what was not may bias our knowledge of the period.

Not all archival records are in the public domain. Some of the more private ones may also be useful for testing certain hypotheses. The sales records of particular products, commodities, or even companies might be systematically related to a variety of changes in the customers they serve. Likewise, hypotheses relating to such phenomena as apprehension about flying in aircraft might be detected through relating the amount of flight insurance sold to the frequency of recent crashes as reported in newspapers. Similar techniques might be employed to relate seasonal changes, congressional votes, and economic fluctuations in the country to the incidence of shoplifting in department stores.

Unobtrusive Observation

Simple observational techniques may also be used unobtrusively. At least since Polonius advised Laertes that "the clothes oft proclaim the man," many people have tried to relate individuals' physical appearance, mode of dress, or other characteristics to aspects of their behavior. Some of these findings, such as the fact that more delinquents than nondelinquents wear tattoos, appear to be intuitively sensible. Others are more difficult to assimilate into existing viewpoints. For example, it has been reported that a bullfighter's beard is often longer on the day he fights than on other days. One possible explanation is that the matador's anxiety can be indexed by beard length. But a quivering hand is not the only possible explanation for the phenomenon. Webb et al. note, "Maybe it wasn't the anxiety at all. Perhaps the bullfighter stands farther away from the razor on the morning of the fight, or he may not have shaved that morning at all (like baseball pitchers and boxers)" (1966, p. 116).

Sometimes, research efforts using unobtrusive observations have been lighthearted. Here is an example that is only half serious.

> . . . It was discovered that there is a strong association between the methodological disposition of psychologists and the length of their hair. The authors observed the hair length of psychologists attending professional meetings and coded the meetings by the probable appeal to those with different methodological inclinations. Thus, in one example, the length of hair was compared between those who attended an experimental set of papers and those who attended a series on ego-identity formation. The results are clear-cut. The "tough-minded" psychologists have shorter hair. . . . Symptomatic interpretations, psychoanalytic inquiries as to what is cut about the clean-cut young man are not the only possibilities. The causal ambiguity of the correlation was clarified when the "dehydration hypothesis" (that is, that lack of insulation caused the hard-headedness) was rejected by the "bald-head" control, that is, examining the distribution of bald-headed persons who by the dehydration hypothesis should be most hard-headed of all (Webb et al. 1966, pp. 116–117).

It will not always be possible to observe subjects unobtrusively, and obviously there are practical constraints in using nonreactive measures. But it is remarkable what one can think of with a bit of imagination. And certainly, social scientists must continually be aware of the possibility that self-reports and laboratory behavioral measures are both subject to reactivity.

SELF-FULFILLING PROPHECIES AND EXPERIMENTER BIAS

People tend to see and even to bring about what they expect, a phenomenon referred to as the *self-fulfilling prophecy* (Darley & Fazio, 1980). The tendency to judge matters according to our expectations is, in fact, quite pervasive. For example, in the United States it has been shown repeatedly that voters overwhelmingly tend to believe that their preferred candidate will win the election unless their candidate is the extreme underdog. Thus, in a careful poll before the 1980 U. S. presidential election 87 percent of those intending to vote Democratic expected Jimmy Carter to win whereas slightly more than 80 percent of those intending to vote Republican expected Ronald Reagan to win.

In recent years there has been a growing interest in the possibility of a general threat to the validity of behavioral research—the so-called *experimenter bias effect* (Rosenthal & Rosnow, 1984). Robert Rosenthal and his colleagues have performed many studies to demonstrate that the investigator's expectations regarding the outcome of a particular investigation may influence the data collected. Most studies done by social scientists are designed with clear expectations about the likely or predicted outcome. If it can be shown that these expectations do make the data collected more favorable to the investigator's hypotheses or biases, research in the social sciences may be faced with a serious problem.

Let us consider two experiments that apparently demonstrate this phenomenon. In a study by Rosenthal and Fode (1963a), undergraduate students served as experimenters in a simple maze problem with rats as subjects. Half of these student experimenters were randomly assigned to a group that was told that their rats were bright and should therefore learn quickly; the remaining half were told that their rats were dull and should show "little evidence of learning." In fact, the rats assigned to both groups of students were drawn randomly from a relatively homogeneous population of rodents. The only systematically manipulated difference between the groups was that half of the student experimenters expected their animals to do well, the others expected them to do poorly. Thus, this study appears to provide a direct probe of the possibility that the expectancies themselves may influence the data. The results indicated that the expectancy manipulation did produce a marked difference in the data reported. Students working with the presumably "bright" animals presented data suggesting that their rats performed approximately 50 percent better than did the animals who were presumed to be "dull."

In a second experiment (Rosenthal & Fode, 1963b), a person-perception task was employed. A subject was shown a series of faces and rated each on a scale from -10 to $+10$ according to whether he thought that the individual had been experiencing failure (extreme failure was rated -10) or success (extreme success was rated $+10$). Although the same photographs were employed in both conditions, one group of student experimenters was told that the overall average ratings for the photographs should average about -5, and a second group was told that the average rating of their photographs should be approximately $+5$.

In addition, the experimenters were offered a monetary inducement to obtain the desired results. If the data collected followed the expected pattern, they would be paid $2.00 an hour, but if the data did not conform to these expectations they would be paid only $1.00 an hour. These incentives were sufficient to produce significantly higher ratings of the photographs from student experimenters led to expect an average of +5 than those led to expect an average of −5.

It is now a well-documented fact that at least under some circumstances the expectancies of an investigator may appreciably influence the data he or she collects. Nonetheless, the question of the degree to which this phenomenon actually pervades scientific research remains. Studies of these effects have employed as subjects individuals who have not been extensively trained in the importance of careful and unbiased observation. Moreover, as Barber and Silver (1968) have argued, there are other reasons for believing that the experimenter bias effect is not as general a phenomenon as Rosenthal and his associates have suggested.

The core of Barber and Silver's argument involves the specific manner in which the experimenter bias effect operates. These writers have explained the problem of identifying the underlying process in studies like those of Rosenthal and Fode as follows:

> There are at least eleven possible ways that an experimenter's expectancies and desires can influence the results of his research: (a) The experimenter may unintentionally influence his subjects to give expected-desired responses through unintentional paralinguistic cues, for example, by variations in his tone of voice. (b) The experimenter may influence his subjects to give expected-desired responses by means of unintentional kinesic cues, for example, by changes in his posture or by changes in his facial expression. (c) The experimenter may influence his results by unintentionally reinforcing his subjects verbally when they give expected-desired responses. (d) The experimenter may unintentionally misjudge his subjects' responses. (e) The experimenter may unintentionally misrecord the subject's responses (p. 18).

Each of these five possible unintentional sources of experimenter bias could also result from the experimenter's *intentionally* engaging in one of these activities. The eleventh possibility is that the experimenter may simply fabricate all of his or her data.

Identifying which of these possibilities or combination of them is operating in any given study would have a decided influence on the way the bias might be eliminated or dealt with. We must assume that the majority of behavioral scientists do not intentionally try to alter the outcomes of their experiments or simply fabricate their data. This assumption is not based merely on the presumed integrity of professional investigators. Data and results collected by professional scientists will also be made public. If intentional biases have influenced these results, other investigators will detect it when they are unable to replicate the reported findings. This sort of double-check is particularly viable when investigators who do not share the same theoretical viewpoints, expectancies, and biases successfully replicate each others' results. Clearly, systematic replication of any major scientific finding is important. Unfortunately, the social sciences, in which the bias effect might be especially likely to operate, have been extremely delinquent in this regard. Simple replication, or even a study that introduces minor variations in an earlier report, is unlikely to be acceptable to major professional journals. Thus, failures to replicate may be effectively suppressed because an investigator or a journal editor judges that they are "not worth reporting."

More serious for social scientific research are those cases in which investigators unintentionally influence their results. Demonstrating that such unintentional influences are in fact operative has proved to be quite difficult (Barber & Silver, 1968). In the Rosenthal and Fode (1963a) study of "bright" and "dull" rats, some of the student experimenters were observed to literally prod their allegedly bright animals down the maze—hardly an unintentional influence. It is extremely unlikely that any well-trained investigator would engage in such an activity by virtue of his or her training, from fear of public disapprobation, or from personal integrity.

Further, in considering the Rosenthal and Fode manipulations, we must keep in mind the important distinction between merely expecting to obtain particular results (as may well be the case in most scientific investigations) and being explicitly told to obtain particular results (as in the case of the Rosenthal and Fode studies). The latter would, presumably, be a much more potent biasing condition than the former and, in fact, may seem to the student experimenters to justify some intentional forms of bias. In the Rosenthal and Fode studies, the experimenters were directly told what results to obtain and in one were given more money if they did obtain them. But other, more recent studies have manipulated observer expectancies and found that observers may record biased observations even without a strong incentive to do so (Kent, O'Leary, Diament, & Dietz, 1974; O'Leary, Kent, & Janowitz, 1975).

To determine more conclusively whether self-fulfilling prophecy effects influence ordinary data collection, Rosenthal (1978) reviewed data from 21 studies involving more than 300 observers and 140,000 separate observations, looking for recording errors in the data. He found that there was a marked tendency for even quite simple recording tasks to lead to errors which favored the hypothesis held by the observers. Thus, investigators must be continuously on guard to prevent any form of bias from affecting their results and research reports, and the larger scientific community must continually be sensitive to the variety of possible interpretations that may be placed on a particular pattern of results.

There are a number of specific ways to handle the problem of experimenter bias. First, principal investigators may employ research assistants or data collectors who are *blind to*, (that is, unaware of) the hypothesis being tested. Second, the degree of contact between experimenter and subject can be minimized, for example, by means of tape-recorded instructions, automated data collection procedures, and the like. Third, experimenters may be led to believe that their behavior will be carefully monitored. Finally, Rosenthal has suggested that the potential effects of expectancy may be *assessed* by employing two groups of experimenters who have been led to have opposite expectancies about the outcome of the research. The evidence collected so far suggests that these precautions are advisable. In our judgment, however, experimenter bias does not discredit the great majority of substantive findings reported in the social science literature.

Bias Effects and the Adequacy of Research Observations

How can one determine whether bias effects have undermined the adequacy of observations made in a particular investigation? Perhaps the best way of determining the empirical worth of observations is to assess the degree to which two or more observers witnessing the same events would agree about their description. *In any study in which the data might be subject to interpretation or misperception, it is the responsibility of the investigator to demonstrate that independent observers would agree on the observations being reported.*

Usually such demonstrations involve assessing interrater reliability (see Chapter 2). However, high interrater reliability is not good evidence of agreement unless the check is carried out very carefully. In many studies that claim to have checked interrater reliability, two observers were present only for some portion of the period of observation. If it is found that they are in substantial agreement for this portion of the data, it is assumed that they would also have been in agreement for the remainder of the data collection period. From a sampling point of view, this is a reasonable assumption. But one also assumes that the presence of a second observer (or knowing that a second observer is to be used) does not influence the accuracy of observation. There is evidence to suggest that this second assumption is *not* viable.

Reid (1970) recruited seven undergraduate women to assist in the coding of mother-child interactions from videotapes. The women were informed that some of the tape content had been precoded so that their progress could be assessed; this condition is referred to as *overt assessment.* They were also told that after they had reached a certain criterion their scoring would never be checked either by the experimenter or by anyone else and that the tapes involved would be immediately erased; this condition is referred to as *covert assessment.* The findings have been concisely summarized by the experimenter:

> The results of the present investigation do not lend support to the hypothesis that overt reliability estimates accurately describe data collected by unmonitored observers. In the present situation, the estimates consistently exaggerated the reliability of [observers] in the covert-assessment condition by about 25 percent. The drop observed in observer performance was not gradual, but occurred suddenly as [the observer] made the transition from overt to covert assessment. . . . It is quite possible that other strategies for the collection and assessment of

> observation data are immune to the effect observed in this study. However, this would seem to be a question that could be better answered on an empirical rather than a priori basis (pp. 1149–1150).

The finding that reliability of observations is significantly higher when observers know reliability is being checked than when they believe they are the sole observers was later confirmed by another team of investigators (Romanczyk, Kent, Diament, & O'Leary, 1973). We therefore conclude that *it is always desirable to employ two independent observers when the recording of ongoing behavior is the goal*. Or, if employing two or more independent observers is not possible, observers should be least believe that their data can be checked in some way. The necessity for independent reliability checks is especially important when the observations to be made involve judgments that are difficult or open to ambiguity. In investigations particularly sensitive to bias, it is also desirable to employ observers who are blind to the treatments that individual subjects have received.

Low Interrater Reliability as a Threat to Validity

In some circumstances the major effect of employing measures on which there is poor interrater reliability is to reduce the likelihood of finding evidence for a causal relationship. Here the cost of low interrater reliability is paid by the investigator. Under other circumstances, however, low interrater reliability may be cited by critics and used to challenge the empirical validity of a causal inference that has been drawn.

To illustrate, consider a study involving twenty raters, each of whom independently observes the behavior of two groups of youngsters. One of the groups has been exposed to a "diet" of highly aggressive television programs; the other group has been exposed to a diet of nonaggresive television programs. The task for the raters is to evaluate the degree to which the subjects behave aggressively toward one another and toward authority figures at school. The investigator may take the mean scores provided by each rater for both the experimental and control groups and determine the difference between the two. If the raters are all providing evaluations based exclusively or predominantly on the objective data (the degree to which the children are behaving aggressively), then we would expect the differences between the obtained means for the raters to produce a normal distribution, such as that shown in Figure 6-1a. If, under these circumstances, interrater reliability were relatively low, the difficulty of obtaining a significant effect would be increased. Suppose, in contrast, that a large subset of the raters entertains the hypothesis that children who observe aggressive programs will become less aggressive because these entertainment offerings tend to "drain off" aggressive impulses. Let us further suppose that the actual behavior of the youngsters, if objectively recorded, would not support such reasoning. In this instance, we would expect to observe a difference between experimental and control group evaluations only for one subset of raters, those

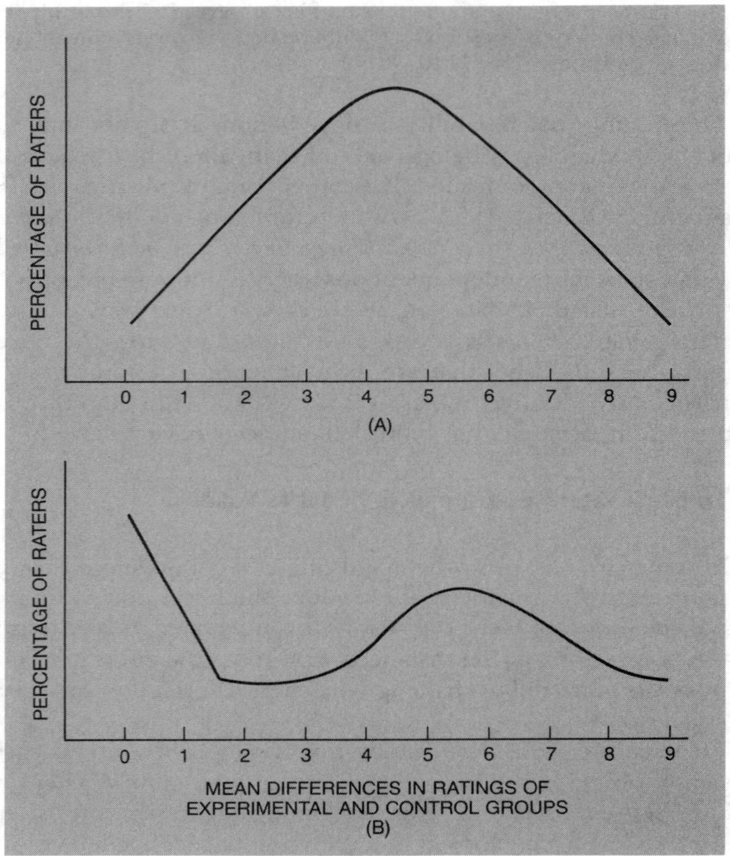

Figure 6-1 Normal and bimodal distributions of differences in the ratings of two groups. Case *B*, showing the bimodal distribution, suggests the presence of rater bias because many of the raters did not observe a difference at all.

who entertained the biasing hypothesis. We could tell whether this is so by plotting the mean differences of each rater. If such a bias were present, the obtained results might look something like those shown in Figure 6-1b. Note that the distribution in this case is not normal but *bimodal*. The so-called "overall" effect clearly results from the striking differences in evaluation provided by some of the raters, but not by others who were also witness to the same behavior. In this case, the consequences of low interrater reliability would not necessarily reduce the possibility of obtaining a statistically significant effect. Rather, the differences in rated scores clearly implies that the two subsets of raters differed in some way other than in the information to which they were exposed. In this circumstance, low interrater reliability may not exact a price from the experimenter, but it will introduce invalid conclusions into the body of scientific knowledge.

Providing multiple observers or raters when observations require difficult judgments is clearly an important feature of sound empirical research. Additionally, data provided when multiple raters are available may provide hints as to one possible reason for failing to obtain significant effects and may also provide evidence, even when such effects are obtained, to cast doubt on the validity of a causal inference.

There is a competing explanation for the one we have just offered. The investigator might be tempted to say that the bimodal distribution occurs because those raters who do not perceive a difference are not sufficiently attentive, experienced, or competent to detect it. However, upon careful consideration, this argument can be seen to be insufficient.

One major and important rule throughout all scientific research is that a single datum (such as obtaining a bimodal distribution among raters) cannot be permitted more than one explanation. If two antagonistic explanations for a finding are pointed out and the scientist can provide no logically convincing basis for discriminating between them, he or she is pressed to admit "no contest" and begin the research afresh. The obligation of the critic is merely to show the *plausibility* of some rival hypothesis, not that the rival hypothesis is itself necessarily valid. In contrast, the investigator making the original causal claim must be able to show that his or her causal inference *is* empirically valid. This can only be done if the investigator has used a research design that effectively rules out or discredits all plausible competing explanations. In the next three chapters, we will consider in detail how this important task can be accomplished.

FOR REVIEW AND DISCUSSION

1. Suppose an investigator is interested in the effects of viewing "all white" television and "integrated" television on the attitudes of twelve-year-old whites toward blacks. The measure involves showing subjects pictures of black children and of white children and then asking if they think the children in the pictures are smart and whether they like them.
   a. What are possible sources of reactivity? How could they have influenced the results?
   b. Redesign the study to eliminate those sources of reactivity; indicate alternative methods of measurement.
2. One possible measure of people's attitudes toward some newsworthy event (like the energy crisis) would be examination of the letters to the editor in major newspapers. What is this type of measure called? In what ways is it or is it not a good measure?
3. There is a high incidence of psychosis in the lower social classes. The indication of psychosis is often based on a "yes" response by the subject to questions such as, "I sometimes feel that everyone is out to get me." Discuss how different types of response sets might conspire to produce the relationship.

4. A business woman is building a new drive-in theatre. She wants to determine her customers' parking preferences so that she can design the drive-in to satisfy their desires—location of the concession stand, exits, playground, and so forth. Using unobtrusive measures, how would you go about providing the needed information?
5. In many ways, compensatory rivalry and resentful demoralization seem to be opposite effects; that is, one suggests an increase in the performance of subjects who do not receive a special treatment, whereas the other suggests a decline in performance. Under what circumstances is compensatory equalization more likely? Under what circumstances is resentful demoralization more likely? Why?
6. Explain how the roles of investigator and experimenter are different. What problems exist when the two roles are played by the same person?
7. In each of the following research designs, specify sources of internal invalidity and explain how they could have produced the results.
   (a) The experimenter is interested in the effects of rate of presentation on the ability to learn a paired-associate list. She uses forty students from her introductory psychology class as subjects. Twenty students in the first three rows form group *A*, which sees each word for ten seconds; twenty students in the last three rows form group *B*, which sees each word for five seconds. Group *A* takes fewer trials to learn the list than group *B*.
   (b) An experimenter is interested in the effects of drug X on pre-school children's ability to learn a list of words. She takes forty pupils and randomly assigns them to either group *A* or group *B*. Subjects in group *A* are administered the drug, and those in group *B* were not given the drug. Group *A* is tested in the morning and group *B* in the afternoon. Group *A* learns the list more rapidly than group *B*.
   (c) An experimenter wishes to test the long-term effectiveness of a particular form of therapy. Students who apply to the university mental health-clinic are assigned to the treatment groups, and students selected at random from the university student directory serve as controls. At the beginning of the study, all subjects are assessed during an interview. Through the entire study the experimenter serves as both interviewer and therapist. At the end of three months of therapy, all subjects are reassessed and then assessed again after five years. Those subjects who have received other psychological help besides that offered in the study are included in the results. Students who received therapy improved most as measured by the interviews. Enough information has not been provided to evaluate some of the possible sources of internal invalidity. Which ones?
   (d) The experimenter in problem 7(c) recognizes errors in his study and does it over. This time, students applying to the clinic are divided into two groups—treatment and no treatment. They are all interviewed at the beginning of the study, after three months, and after five years. The experimenter again serves as both interviewer and therapist. Only subjects who have not received other psychological help are included in the results. Once again students who received therapy improve most. Our experimenter repeated some mistakes and made new ones. What are they? What possible sources can you not evaluate on the basis of the information given above?

7

The Basic Experiment

CONCEPT OF THE TRUE EXPERIMENT
- The Example of Experimentally Induced Compliance
- The Rationale for Between-Subjects Comparisons

EXPERIMENTAL DESIGN

SELECTION OF SUBJECTS AND ASSIGNMENT TO GROUPS
- The Necessity for Random Assignment
- Free Random Assignment
- Matched Random Assignment

EMPLOYING A CONTROL GROUP

PRETEST-POSTTEST CONTROL GROUP DESIGNS

THE POSTTEST-ONLY CONTROL GROUP DESIGN

CHOOSING BETWEEN DESIGNS WITH AND WITHOUT A PRETEST
- The Solomon Four-Group Design

FACTORS THAT INCREASE THE POWER OF AN EXPERIMENT
- Maximizing Systematic Variance
- Minimizing Error Variance
    - minimizing error variance by experimental control
    - minimizing error variance by reliable measurement
    - minimizing error variance by aggregation
    - minimizing error variance by using homogeneous groups of subjects
    - minimizing error variance by increasing sample size

OPERATIONALIZING EXPERIMENTAL VARIABLES
- Choosing an Independent Variable
- Choosing a Dependent Variable

FOR REVIEW AND DISCUSSION

So far in our discussion we have emphasized the difficulties encountered in drawing causal inferences. We now turn to a simple and logically compelling way of drawing causal inferences: the true experiment.

CONCEPT OF THE TRUE EXPERIMENT

The hallmark of the experimental method is that variables of interest (as causes) are manipulated directly. Often one will hear lay persons (and even some social and behavioral scientists) refer to a correlational study involving only classificatory variables as an "experiment"; however, from a technical point of view this is an incorrect usage and can be misleading. In addition to the manipulation of relevant variables, the proper use of the experimental method involves two features: random assignment and the use of control groups or conditions to eliminate the effects of third variables. Thus in our discussion we will speak of the *true experiment* as one in which causal inference is made on the basis of random assignment, manipulation of relevant variables, and direct control over irrelevant variables.

In the true experiment, the investigator administers or manipulates the hypothesized cause as a *treatment* and thus can directly observe its effects. Properly executed and controlled, the true experiment can eliminate the third variable and directionality problems completely. What is more, the logical requirements of Mill's criteria are completely satisfied.

The Example of Experimentally Induced Compliance

To introduce the basic concepts and terminology associated with the true experiment, we shall begin with a well-known experiment in social psychology reported by Freedman, Wallington, and Bless (1967). This experiment involved only between-subjects comparisons, which is the more common type of experimental design in social science research. In Chapter 8 we will discuss several issues connected with within-subjects comparisons in the true experiment, but the basic logic of experimentation and all of the major concepts will remain the same.

Freedman et al. were interested in the question, How can people be induced to do something they would not otherwise do? As we already know and as Freedman and his associates noted:

> One kind of answer to this question involves increasing the pressure on the individual until he is forced to comply. If a person is subjected to enough social pressure, offered enough reward, threatened with enough pain, or given enough convincing reasons, he will, under most circumstances, eventually yield and perform the required act. Inducement through pressure of this kind is one very effective means of producing compliance (1967, p. 117).

But there are many circumstances in which it is not possible or would be unethical to employ the amount of pressure required to produce compliance.

In these instances it is important, both theoretically and practically, to identify other factors that may increase another person's willingness to accede to a request. One of these, which was the focus of the Freedman research, is guilt. The investigators suggested:

> Presumably when someone feels that he has done something wrong there will be a tendency for him to make up for his wrongful deed. He can do this by subjecting himself to punishment or by doing something good to balance the bad. Either of these processes might lead to increased compliance if the request is appropriate. Given the opportunity to engage in some extremely unpleasant behavior, the guilty person should be more likely to agree than the nonguilty since the former can use this as a form of self-punishment. Similarly, if he is asked to do someone a favor, pleasant or otherwise, the guilty person should be more likely to agree than the nonguilty because the former can view it as a good deed for the day, which will make up for the bad deed about which he feels guilty (pp. 117–118).

This argument forms the basis for a single, testable *experimental hypothesis,* namely that "guilt will lead to greater compliance [than nonguilt] in a wide variety of situations" (p. 118). At this point in the argument the hypothesis is still untested. It is no more than an idea or possibility, but it has been sufficiently formulated to be tested subsequently in a *controlled experimental situation.*

The controlled experimental situation must meet all the conceptual demands of the basic hypothesis but systematically eliminate factors not supposed to be relevant. What are the demands of the hypothesis of Freedman and his associates? First, a situation must be created in which some subjects can be made to feel guilty while others are not. Second, all subjects must be exposed to a relatively demanding request to which they can accede or not as they choose. Finally, measurement of the *variable of interest* (in this case, compliance with the request) must be possible. To meet these requirements, Freedman and his associates performed a series of three experiments, all of which dealt with the effects of guilt on compliance according to these specifications. The first of these investigations will be considered in some detail.

The principal experimental manipulation in this study was to induce some subjects, but not others, to tell a deliberate lie. Telling such a lie was presumed to induce guilt and, in turn, to increase their willingness to comply with a subsequent request. In order to accomplish this, the researchers told male high school students that the experiment for which they had been recruited would require a few minutes of preparation time. They were then left in a waiting room for five minutes with another individual, who was ostensibly the previous subject but was, in fact, an experimental confederate.

The manipulation that took place during this period was extremely simple. As the subject and the confederate chatted, the confederate described to a randomly selected half of the subjects (those in the *lie condition*) the test they were going to take. Included in this disclosure were examples of the items used and some of the previous subject's ostensible theories about the purpose of the test and how to do well on it. Because this informant was, in fact, a confederate, his statements could be controlled precisely. To the remaining subjects (those in the *nonlie* condition), no mention was made of the details of the test. Thus, the *independent variable, the condition or stimulus the experimenters manipulated or had under their control,* was whether or not the subject received advance information about the test he was about to take.

Subsequently, the experimenter returned to the waiting room, announced that she was ready to begin, and added, "This is a Remote Associates Test. . . . Since we are testing a slightly different hypothesis, *we must make sure that you have not taken this test before or heard about it from friends*" (italics added). With a single exception, all subjects (including those who had heard a great deal about the test from the confederate just moments ago) stated that they had not heard about the test before. Freedman and his associates assumed that those who lied were feeling guilty about it.

A *dependent variable is that aspect of a subject's behavior that is measured after the manipulation of the independent variable.* One can remember the term by noting that it is expected to *depend on,* or be controlled by, the conditions set up or manipulated by the experimenter. In our example, the dependent variable was straightforward. After taking the Remote Associates Test, the experimenter added that another member of the psychology department was doing a study for which he had no grant support. The subject was asked whether he was willing to participate in this "other study" without pay. After he answered, the experiment was terminated. The subject's reply, compliance or noncompliance, was the dependent variable. The results themselves are shown in Table 7-1, from which it can be seen that the experimental hypothesis received clear support. Subjects who received the lie treatment were considerably more likely to comply than those in the control (nonlie) condition, as the experimenters had predicted.

To summarize briefly, in a true experiment subjects are assigned randomly to conditions in which they receive different treatments (the independent variable is manipulated) and then scores on one or more measures (the dependent variable or variables) are obtained. Experiments may simply involve two groups (for example, an "experimental" or treatment group and a control group, as in the Freedman et al. study), or they may be considerably more complex, as we shall see. In any event, the researcher must plan in detail any experiment so as

Table 7-1 Percentage of Subjects Complying According to Experimentally Manipulated Guilt

	EXPERIMENTAL (LIE)	*CONTROL (NONLIE)*
Complied	64.5%	35.5%
Did Not Comply	35.5	64.5

Source: Data from Freedman, Wallington, and Bless (1967)

to maximize the likelihood that he or she will be able to detect differences produced by differences in treatment and thus infer a cause and effect relationship between the independent variable and the dependent variable.

The Rationale for Between-Subjects Comparisons

To get a closer look at the rationale behind a true between-subjects experiment, consider a hypothetical experiment designed to determine the effects of praise on children's classroom performance. Suppose that a particular teacher has twenty-eight children in her classroom. She is asked to arbitrarily select fourteen of these children (for example, by drawing their names out of a hat) and to praise them for every instance of classroom participation. In contrast, she is instructed not to praise the other fourteen children when they participate in discussion. Underlying this procedure for deciding which children will receive praise and which will not is the practice of *random assignment.* Specifically, each child had an equal chance of being assigned to either the praise or the no-praise group. The advantage of such a procedure over, for example, permitting the teacher to decide on the basis of her opinion which of the children should receive praise and which should not, is that differences between the two groups initially, or with respect to the likelihood that praise would "work," are lessened.

Once the children have been assigned randomly to one of these two groups, all children (those in both groups) must be dealt with in exactly the same way except for the administration of the independent variable. Thus, the only difference between the two groups in this example would be in the presence or absence of the experimental treatment, that is, the administration of praise contingent on each instance of classroom participation.

Subsequently, another teacher[1] might be asked to take over the classroom for a day and systematically record the frequency with which each child participated in discussion. A tabulation of these frequencies, providing a single score for each (the number of times he or she participated during the *test* period), would then be prepared according to whether the children had received the praise or no-praise treatment. A hypothetical example of how this tabulation might appear is presented in Table 7-2.

In considering Table 7-2, note that *on the average* children who received praise for their classroom performance from the first teacher were more likely to participate in class with the second teacher than were those who did not. When an experiment is conducted with groups of subjects, individual performances are combined to produce some measure of the overall performance of the groups and provide the basis for determining whether or not satisfactory evidence for a cause and effect relationship has been found.[2] To the extent that the two treatment groups differ or *vary* systematically, we may speak of having obtained an *experi-*

[1] There are several advantages to using a second teacher. For example, the second individual could be kept from knowing (that is, would be *blind* to) which children had received which treatment, and thus her own expectations would not influence the obtained results.

[2] Such estimates may involve *means, ranks,* or *percentages,* depending on the nature of the data.

Table 7-2 Hypothetical Example of an Experiment to Evaluate the Effects of Praise on Classroom Performance

NUMBER OF RESPONSES IN CLASS	
Group I (No Praise)	*Group II (Praise)*
4	6
4	7
3	7
1	4
6	5
8	3
6	6
5	6
5	8
3	9
4	8
5	4
7	10
2	5
Σ* = 63	Σ = 88
M† = 4.5	M = 6.3

* The sum of the scores in a group is customarily identified with the Greek letter Sigma (Σ).
† The average, or mean, of the scores in a group is customarily labeled *M*.

mental effect. Having found a difference with this one sample, the researcher further wishes to know whether or not he or she can infer that a similar difference would be produced by other teachers in other classrooms (the population in which the researcher is ultimately interested) as a function of their introducing praise for pupil participation in classroom discussion. How can such a determination be made?

One answer is provided by another concept we have mentioned before, variance. We have already noted that the scores vary systematically between the groups. The difference(s) between (or among) the groups in an experiment is referred to as *systematic variance.* But it is also the case that *within* each of the two groups (see the respective scores in Column I and then in Column II in Table 7-2), not all of the entries are the same. Regardless of whether the children received or did not receive social praise, it is clear that some children spoke up in class more frequently than others. This unaccounted-for variability is usually referred to as *error variance.* Error variance includes both random errors of measurement, which occur in all social science research (see p. 37), and systematic differences among subjects on factors not manipulated in the experiment or on which subjects differed from one another at the outset.

In our hypothetical experiment, a substantial amount of participation (eight responses) was evidenced by a child who did not receive social praise for his earlier participation. For this reason, one might easily wonder whether or not the average difference between the two groups occurred by chance, rather than as a function of the praise itself. Perhaps the more talkative children "just happened" to be the ones who received praise, and the praise itself did not produce the difference. It is through a systematic examination of the variability (the average difference) *between* the two groups relative to the degree to which the scores differ *within* each group that we find an answer.

The reasoning is as follows. The average difference between the two groups in an experiment will almost never be zero, even if the treatment given to one of them is totally ineffective. This is because not all the scores, even *within* one of the groups, will be the same. *Any two randomly selected groups will differ to some extent.* The degree to which individual scores differ, simply by chance, provides a basis for estimating whether the difference obtained between the groups is actually larger than would have been expected by chance alone. It is only through this type of analysis that we can be confident that our effects are reliable.

We must find a way of estimating how much difference we might expect by chance. The source of this information is the degree to which the scores within the groups vary among themselves. The procedure involves measuring the variance within groups, that is, the degree to which each score is different from, or deviates from, the group's average. A particular statistic, the *variance statistic* (S^2), provides an index of this variability or dispersion. (Detailed instructions for calculating S^2 may be found in any standard statistics text, but they do not concern us here.)

The variance statistic is extremely important in calculating the actual effect of the manipulation of the independent variable on the dependent variable. In our example (Table 7-2), we see that the group that received praise produced (on the average) 1.8 more instances of classroom participation than did the group in which no such praise was provided. Is this difference large enough to warrant the conclusion that praise encourages performance?

To evaluate this question, researchers employ the now familiar concept of statistical significance, which refers to the likelihood or probability that relationships observed in a particular sample were due to chance. It is usually assessed by comparing the accounted-for and unaccounted-for variability among the scores in an experiment. In the most widely used of modern statistical tests, the F-test, the systematic variance due to treatments is evaluated, as a ratio, against the amount of variance due to unknown sources (that is, the error variance). Conceptually, the formula for the F-test is straightforward:[3]

$$F = S^2 \text{ systematic}/S^2 \text{ error}$$

[3]The actual formulas may be found in Hays (1963).

In this formula, the systematic variance is an index of the difference between or among treatment conditions (that is, the variance in the dependent measure produced by the experimental manipulation), and the error variance is the remaining variance in scores on the dependent measure. Thus, everything else equal, as the F ratio becomes larger, the probability that experimental results were due to chance becomes less. That is, the results become increasingly significant, statistically. In reporting the results of research, the phrase *significant difference* between treatment groups is often employed. Recall that a so-called statistically significant difference is one that has a low probability of occurring by chance alone and thus reflects a difference that could be reliably expected in other samples, that is, a "real" difference. The greater the likelihood that a difference is not due to chance alone, the more confidence an experimenter will usually place in his or her results. If all other things are equal, an experimenter will have even greater confidence in results that would occur by chance only one time in 100 ("$p < 0.01$") than if the outcome simply reached the customary "0.05" level. Given the former (lower) probability that the results were due to chance, the experimenter can place more confidence in the belief that the manipulated variables will successfully produce the same results in the future. In our example, $p < 0.05$.[4]

To illustrate further the importance of relative variability rather than mean differences alone in experimental research, consider a second hypothetical study. Suppose that this second investigation, conducted in a different classroom, employed material rewards, such as tokens, rather than verbal praise, and that the results were those shown in Table 7-3. Particularly note that in this second case the average difference between the groups is relatively small. It may be tempting to *wrongly* conclude that we can have more confidence in the results of the first experiment than of the second. That is, in comparing the average differences between the two groups in each of the experiments we have discussed, if we were to consider these means alone, it appears that praise was more effective than tokens. The average (mean) difference between the groups is almost two points in our first example; the children who were praised performed in class about 40 percent more often than those who were not. In contrast, the material rewards in our second example appear to have produced a difference of only one point.

Ironically, for purposes of deciding whether the obtained experimental effect can be generalized, there is an important sense in which we can have at least as much confidence in the effects of material reward as in praise on the basis of these two experiments.

Comparing our examples, we may first examine the total distribution of scores across both groups in each experiment. These are presented graphically in Figure 7-1 (based on the data shown in Tables 7-2 and 7-3). As can be seen,

[4]Our $F = 5.78$. Statistics other than F may be employed in making such comparisons, but the underlying logic is the same.

Table 7-3 Hypothetical Example of an Experiment to Evaluate the Effects of Material Reward on Classroom Performance

NUMBER OF RESPONSES IN CLASS	
Group I (Not Rewarded)	*Group II (Rewarded)*
5	7
5	8
5	4
6	6
6	6
5	7
4	6
4	6
4	7
5	4
6	5
6	7
5	6
4	5
$\Sigma = 70$	$\Sigma = 84$
$M = 5.00$	$M = 6.00$

there is much spread in the representation of the data from the first experiment, whereas the data from the second experiment form a considerably "tighter" pattern. (That is, there is much greater variability in the data from experiment 1 than from experiment 2.) If either social praise or material reward produced no effect on classroom participation, the form of the distribution displayed in Figure 7-1 would *not* be expected to change if we plotted each of them separately. Instead, the two distributions of curves within each experiment would be highly similar; that is, they would overlap almost completely.

In contrast, if the experimental manipulations did make a difference, the distributions would look more like those shown in Figure 7-2. As can be seen, the groups' scores depart from the distribution of the combined scores (Figure 7-1). The overlap, represented by the shaded areas, is far from complete in either experiment. Moreover, the ratio of the nonoverlapping to overlapping areas is about the same in the experiment involving material rewards as in the social praise experiment. Consequently, although the mean difference between the groups is less in the experiment involving material reward, there is a sense in which we can have at least as much confidence in these results as in those from the social praise study. For the second study $p < 0.05$.

Thus, the less *variance overlap* between two groups, the more likely it is that a difference will be present reliably in the remaining population and thus

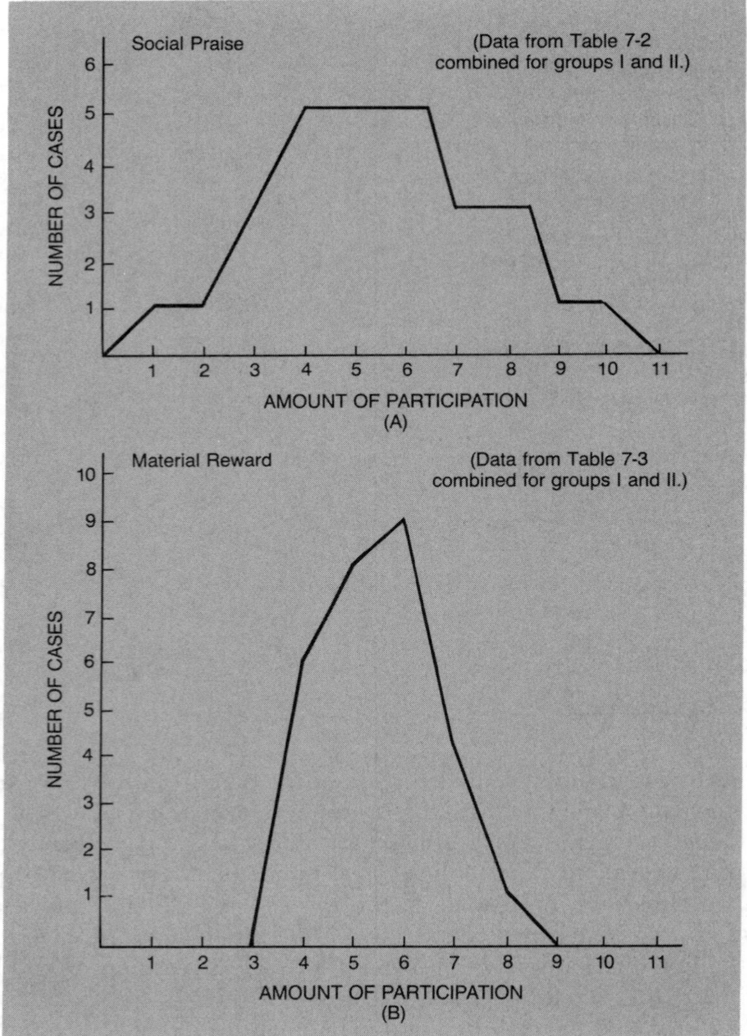

Figure 7-1 Distributions of the data shown in Tables 7-2 and 7-3 (combined over groups) illustrating the differences in *variability* between A (large) and B (small).

the more statistically confident we can be that a real effect has occurred. Note, too, that the concept of variance overlap as used here carries the same basic meaning that it did in our discussion of variance and correlations in Chapter 3.

We have seen that the probability of a given mean difference occurring by chance is a function of both the size of that difference and the variability of all the scores within the experiment. In the two examples used, material reward appears to have produced a smaller effect than social praise when we look at the means alone, but the scores in the former experiment were also more tightly

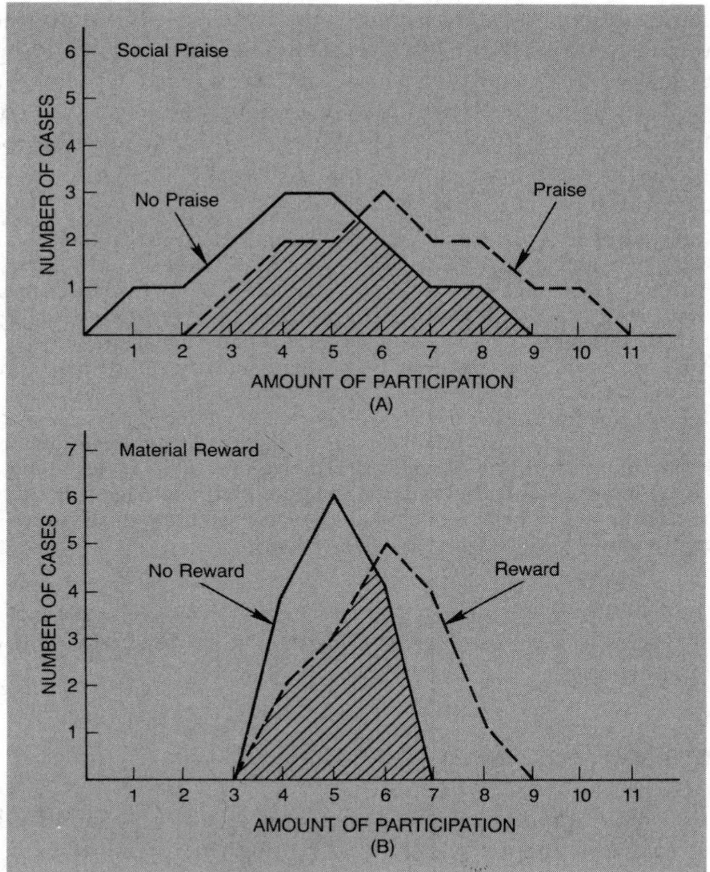

Figure 7-2 Distributions of responding in class for two hypothetical experiments, illustrating the relationship between *variability* and *statistical significance*. The mean difference is smaller in B than in A, but because the *variability* is also smaller we detect a significant difference in both cases.

packed (less variable). Thus two factors—*systematic variance* and *error variance*—are involved in detecting a reliable effect. Both have important implications for designing experimental research.

EXPERIMENTAL DESIGN

In the preceding section we introduced the concept of the true experiment and described its underlying logic. Now we discuss in greater detail the design of such experiments. As we shall see, the investigators must design or construct experiments with an eye to fitting together the hypotheses being tested and the alternative methods available for testing them. The process of experimental design involves many choices and decisions. In a very real way, experiments can and should be tailored to the questions they are intended to ask and constructed with a methodical, critical attitude. B. J. Winer, in the introduction to his book *Statistical Principles in Experimental Design,* put it this way:

> The design of an experiment may be compared to an architect's plans for a structure, whether it be a giant skyscraper or a modest home. The basic requirements for the structure are given to the architect by the prospective owner. It is the architect's task to fill these basic requirements; yet the architect has ample room for exercising . . . ingenuity. Several different plans may be drawn up to meet all the basic requirements. Some plans may be more costly than others; given two plans having the same cost, one may offer potential advantages that the second does not. . . . The individual best qualified to design an experiment is the one who is (1) most familiar with the nature of the experimental material, (2) most familiar with the possible alternative methods for designing the experiment, (3) most capable of evaluating the potential advantages and disadvantages of the alternatives. When an individual possesses all these qualifications, the roles of experimenter and designer are one (1962, p. 1).

We will describe the major options available at each stage of planning experimental research and point out and explain the advantages and disadvantages of each alternative.

SELECTION OF SUBJECTS AND ASSIGNMENT TO GROUPS

No decision is more important in experimental research than selecting one's subjects and assigning them to treatment groups. In the ideal experiment, a sample of subjects would be selected randomly from the population in which the investigator is interested, and then subjects in this randomly chosen sample would be assigned randomly to treatment groups within the experiment. We say "in the ideal experiment" because the first criterion, random selection of a sample, is rarely if ever achieved in social science research. In essence, selecting a random sample entails all the problems involved in accurately surveying a population (see Chapter 2) and is considered too costly for most experiments.

Consider, for example, the psychologist interested in experimentally demonstrating some cause and effect relationship in the behavior of preschool children, say, that they will benefit from a special form of preschool education. The psychologist will probably not draw a truly random sample of preschoolers in the United States (still less in the world); rather, the children will likely be drawn from one or more local populations (for example, children in the county). Moreover, only those children whose parents consent to their participation will be sampled. Such a sampling procedure obviously is not random; all members of the population of interest do *not* have an equal chance of being selected, and some have no chance at all. Can one generalize from samples chosen in this way?

We will take up this question in detail in Chapter 12, when we consider the problem of the external validity of causal inferences. For the moment, it is sufficient to note that the question is finally one of the representativeness of the sample. If the sample can reasonably be considered to be representative of the population, it need not have been randomly selected. The thorny problem, of course, is that it can be difficult to convince a skeptic that a nonrandom sample *is* representative.

Regardless of how the sample for an experiment is selected, subjects within the sample *must* be randomly assigned to treatment groups within the experiment, or no valid causal inferences can be drawn from the results. Let us explain why this is so.

The Necessity for Random Assignment

We had occasion to point out in our earlier discussion of threats to internal validity (Chapter 5) that one such threat is *selection bias.* As it pertains to subject assignment in true experiments, selection bias is present whenever subjects have been assigned to treatment groups in such a way that initial differences between them, rather than a real experimental effect, may account for a post-treatment difference between groups. Given this potential problem, how should subjects be assigned to the groups of an experiment in order to assure internal validity of the experimenter's causal inferences while maintaining a satisfactorily low level of error variance?

Recall that random assignment refers to any procedure in which subjects are assigned to groups in such a manner that every subject in the research has an equal chance of being assigned to any of the experimental groups. Such a procedure reduces the likelihood that differences among the groups after treatment will be due to initial differences in the samples rather than to true experimental effects. Two general procedures can be used for subject selection: *free random assignment* and *matched random assignment.*

Free Random Assignment

In a two-group experiment, coin tossing could be the method of assignment. This is the simplest example of free random assignment, that is, random assignment without other restrictions.

When more complicated free randomization procedures are necessary (for example, when subjects must be assigned to more than two groups), it is often convenient to employ a *table of random numbers* (see p. 33). Such tables are constructed from the digits 0 through 9, so that each digit is approximately equally likely to occur in any spot on the table. The experimenter may then list the prospective subjects and assign them to the numbered conditions by consulting the table. A table of random numbers prevents errors and biases that might be introduced through experimenter-invented procedures for arbitrary assignment.

Consider an experiment employing four conditions. The experimenter wrongly assumes that randomness means that two subjects will not be successively assigned to the same group. Thus, with the groups numbered from one to four, an assignment order such as 1, 3, 2, 3, 4, 1, 4, 2, and so on, seems random, whereas an order such as 1, 2, 2, 3, 3, 1, 4, 4, appears less random. However, a bias *against* repetitions may destroy the most important feature of randomization—the assurance that each subject has an equal likelihood of being assigned to any one of the groups.

The importance of selecting a formal randomization procedure over an intuitive one is particularly great when one begins with a roster of subjects that may have been prepared according to systematic criteria unknown to the investigator. For example, any class roster (other than, perhaps, an alphabetized one) may be based on a variety of characteristics such as subjects' age, sex, academic average, or any combination of variables. If the investigator has no knowledge of how the roster was constructed, his or her best protection against bias is to use the formal randomization procedure. In the extreme case, certain rosters may lead to strong bias. If a public school class roster is based on seating positions and if the teacher has alternated relatively bright and less bright children, for example, using it could produce a systematic bias in the results. Random assignment of subjects to groups would effectively solve or eliminate the problem. If each subject had an equal chance of being included in each group, the likelihood that the two groups of subjects would differ from each other on such relevant variables as intelligence would be virtually eliminated.

Matched Random Assignment

In many areas of investigation, a researcher may know or suspect that certain preexisting characteristics of his or her subjects (such as their age, intelligence, degree of prior hospitalization, and so on) will be related to the dependent measure. It may be easier to detect an experimental effect if initial differences among the subjects on these dimensions are controlled. Some form of *matching* is typically used to accomplish this end.

Appropriate use of the matching technique involves three separate steps.

1. Rank order the subjects on the variable for which control is desired.
2. Segregate the subjects into matched pairs so that each pair member has approximately the same score on the variable to be matched[5] and
3. *Randomly assign pair members to the conditions of the experiment.*

The decision of whether or not to employ matched random procedures (as opposed to free random assignment) depends on a number of factors. Among these are the availability or cost of obtaining information on the variable to be matched (from existing records or through a pretest), the degree of relationship

[5]The principle may be extended to units larger than pairs. Three, four, or even more individuals may be matched and then randomly assigned to treatments.

that is likely to exist between the matching variable and the dependent measure, and whether or not obtaining information on the matching variable can influence the subject's later performance in the experiment. Thus, the decision of whether to use matched random assignment in experimental research is based on much the same considerations as those involved in deciding whether or not to choose a stratified random sample in descriptive research (see Chapter 2, p. 51).

In general, matching is most desirable when the influence of the matching variable is likely to be so strong as to mask the experimental effect. For example, if an investigator wishes to determine the effects of hypnotic suggestion on physical strength and has available only a small number of hypnotizable subjects, matching may be absolutely necessary to eliminate the marked variability in subjects' physical strength under normal conditions. On the other hand, it would be wasteful and costly to match for initial strength in an experimental study of learning perception.

EMPLOYING A CONTROL GROUP

A second aspect of experimental design involves the use of a control group. As we have mentioned previously, at least one control group is necessary in any true experiment. In many experiments, the control group is one that does *not* receive the experimental treatment. Thus, the control group provides a *baseline* against which the effects of the experimental treatment may be evaluated. For example, when a group of phobic patients is treated and found to be less fearful than before treatment, no firm conclusion can be advanced as to whether the treatment (rather than, say, history or maturation) is responsible for the change. (See Chapter 5.) Had an untreated control group of equally phobic patients been included, data would be available for evaluating this competing hypothesis. If competing processes such as history and maturation were operative, they would presumably be equally likely to cause improvement in the control group as in the treated experimental group. With a control group, we would have reasonable confidence that differences between the groups after treatment were, in fact, due to the treatment.

The major features of an experiment—manipulation of an independent variable, random assignment, and a control group—having been considered, we can turn our attention to some classic experimental designs that embody these principles.

PRETEST-POSTTEST CONTROL GROUP DESIGNS

In one form of the pretest-posttest control group design (type *A*), subjects are randomly assigned to one of two groups, and both groups are then pretested. In a second form (type *B*), subjects are first pretested and then matched and randomly assigned to groups. In either case, one group receives the treatment, and after an equal period of time, both groups are retested. A convenient notation for this procedure, adapted from Campbell and Stanley (1966), is presented below.

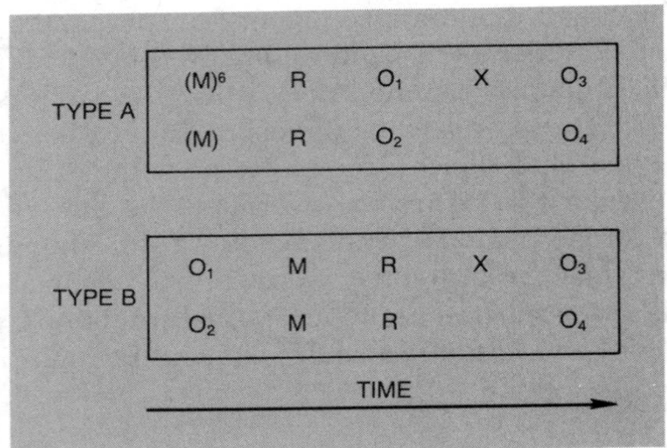

R in this notation indicates random assignment of subjects to groups. *M* signifies matching. *O* refers to the observation or measurement and *X* to the experimental treatment. Temporal order is indicated by the left-right progression, as seen by the arrow. Thus, symbols directly above or below each other indicate events that occur at the same time.

Let us further consider this design in an experiment on the effects of exposure to a social model upon children's willingness to engage in aggressive behavior. Suppose that seven-year-old children are assigned randomly to two groups and each member of each group is allowed a period of free play. During this time each child is observed (by two observers who are blind to the treatment the child will be in), and instances of aggressive play are noted, counted, and recorded. Then each child in the experimental group watches a film in which a model engages in aggressive play in a room similar to the one in which the child has previously played. After the film, the children are returned to the play room. In contrast, children in the control group watch a nonaggressive film and then are returned to the play room. The amount of aggressive behavior shown by the children in both groups is again systematically recorded. In such an experiment, the important comparisons will occur between the pretest level of aggression and the posttest level for each of the groups. Suppose that the following data were obtained:

	PRETEST	POSTTEST
Aggressive Film	4	12
Nonaggressive Film	6	5

Clearly, the children who observed the film of the aggressive model showed more aggression on the posttest than did the children who observed the nonaggressive

[6]The parentheses signify that the matching procedure may or may not occur.

film. Assuming that these results are statistically significant, can we assume that the difference is attributable to the treatment itself? Or could the difference between the two groups have been due to any of the sources of causal ambiguity that were discussed in Chapter 5?

Either of the pretest-posttest control group designs provides a control for each source of internal invalidity that we have discussed, and thus both are highly effective. The manner in which such designs succeed in controlling for each of the important competing causal explanations is considered below.

History and *maturation* are controlled inasmuch as effects due to either are equally likely to be present in the experimental and control groups. In our notation, factors that might produce an $O_1 - O_3$ difference would also produce an $O_2 - O_4$ difference. (Recall that the groups were formed randomly.) Likewise, the effects of *testing* are controlled adequately because both groups of children received both the pretest and the posttest. *Instrument decay* should not be a problem as long as the investigator ensured that observers did not know which children have received which of the treatments. *Regression effects* will be controlled, even if both the experimental and control groups were randomly selected from an extreme population. We would still expect that both groups would show equal regression toward the mean, though the effect might be large.[7] *Selection* is effectively ruled out as a source of internal invalidity because the groups were formed by random assignment. The data produced by such a design allows the hypothesis of *differential attrition* to be tested. If the experimental treatment led to more dropping out of children from the experimental group than from the control group, this would be apparent. Finally, *diffusion, compensatory equalization, compensatory rivalry,* and *resentful demoralization* can be ruled out as long as the children in each group did not know what sort of film the children in the other group had watched.

THE POSTTEST-ONLY CONTROL GROUP DESIGN

Following our previous scheme, the posttest-only control group design may be represented as follows:

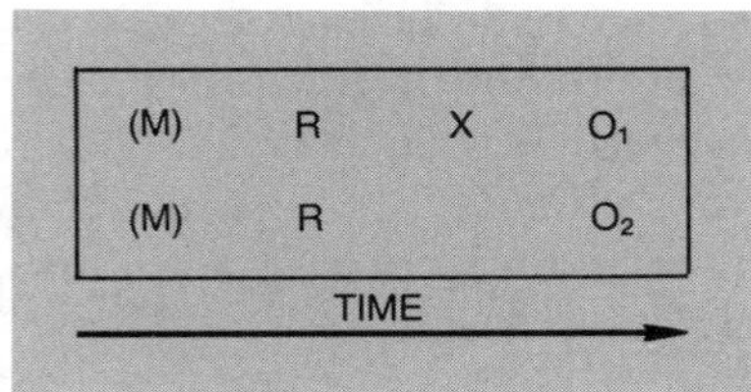

[7] In extreme cases such effects might be so large as to mask a treatment effect.

Like the previous design, the posttest-only control group design adequately controls for all eleven sources of internal invalidity. Specifically, as in the pretest-posttest design, *history, maturation,* and *regression* are all controlled in the sense that they will tend to affect both groups equally and thus cannot provide a rival explanation for observed group differences. *Selection* is controlled for directly, by proper random assignment. *Testing, differential attrition,* and *instrument decay* present little problem because there is only one test per subject. And, as in the pretest only design, as long as the groups remain ignorant of each others' treatment, *diffusion, compensatory equalization, compensatory rivalry,* and *resentful demoralization* will not be problems. However, the *effects* of several of these factors cannot be assessed. Going back to the previous design, we may note that the effects due to maturation, history, or testing may be assessed by the $O_2 - O_4$ comparison. In contrast, in the posttest-only design, such possible influences are controlled for but not assessable. The reason for this difference is that the posttest-only design permits only between-subjects comparisons, whereas the pretest-posttest design allows the experimenter to examine changes that occur within-subjects as well. The pretest-posttest comparison in the latter design allows the experimenter to discern the amount of change (if any) that occurs from one test to another in the absence of the treatment (for example, history, maturation, or testing effects). Such changes cannot be detected by between-subjects comparisons alone, although they are adequately controlled in the $O_1 - O_2$ comparison above.

To illustrate, suppose an experimenter randomly assigns college student subjects to either a special tutoring or a no-tutoring control group and then administers a series of questions from the Medical Aptitude Test (MAT) to both groups. Using the posttest-only control group design, the experimenter finds that the tutoring group has an average score of 40 on the MAT, whereas the control group has an average score of 27. If this difference is statistically significant, the experimenter can conclude that tutoring improves MAT performance; however, he or she does not know whether repeated testing alone would also have done so. In contrast, had the same experimenter used a pretest-posttest design and obtained the same mean posttest scores for the two groups, 40 and 27, it would be possible to discriminate between the alternatives in which repeated testing does or does not have an effect of its own. The difference can be seen graphically in Figure 7-3. The two cases shown, *A* and *B,* are indistinguishable in terms of posttest scores; in each case, the treatment group has a mean of 40 and the no-treatment control group has a mean of 27. On the other hand, the two cases differ clearly in that there is no change due to repeated testing in case *A,* whereas there is a marked change in case *B.* A difference such as this can be detected only by including a pretest and thus making within- as well as between-subjects comparisons possible.

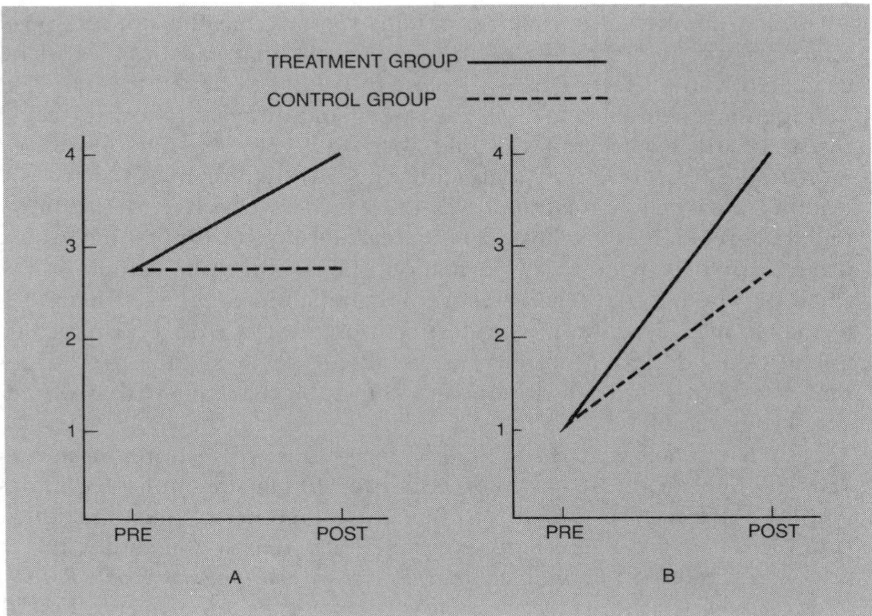

Figure 7-3 Two hypothetical patterns of results for a pretest-posttest experimental design. Subjects are randomly assigned to groups either given a special tutoring program (*treatment*) or not given such tutoring (*control*). Although the posttest scores for the treatment and control groups are identical in cases A and B (between-subjects), the amount of within-subjects change is dramatically different in the two cases.

CHOOSING BETWEEN DESIGNS WITH AND WITHOUT A PRETEST

In many research areas the posttest-only control group design is used much less frequently than the pretest-posttest control group design, most likely because of the advantages of a pretest. Specifically, whereas randomization is expected to ensure the equality of the two groups, a pretest allows a check on the adequacy of the randomization process. It must be recalled that randomization does not *guarantee* equality of the groups. Rather, with large samples, randomization assures us that initial differences between the groups on the variable of interest become increasingly less probable. But differences between randomized groups are sometimes found, and when they are, knowledge of the initial difference gained from a pretest assumes critical importance in the research. Further, if initial differences between the two groups are found on a pretest, procedures are available for "statistically correcting" them. No such correction could be accomplished with a posttest-only design.

A number of research problems require that the subjects possess some characteristic at the outset of the experiment that can only be identified and evaluated by a pretest. This is the case in studies designed to test the efficacy of therapeutic treatments such as the systematic desensitization of fears.[8] In such research, the experimenter would wish to treat only persons who were demonstrably fearful before treatment. The investigator might also wish to know whether a particular treatment was more or less effective, depending upon the initial degree of fear displayed among fearful subjects. Only some form of orderly pretest could provide this information. Thus, when the sample is likely to be small or when certain characteristics of the subjects *vis-à-vis* their original performance may be critical, a pretest-posttest design is to be preferred over the posttest-only design. Moreover, as we noted previously, the pretest-posttest design also allows an examination of within-subjects changes that would not otherwise be possible.

Nonetheless, if the sample is large, the posttest-only design has an advantage. Specifically, reactivity (see Chapter 6) may be implicated in designs that employ a pretest. To understand this phenomenon, we must introduce the concept of *interactions* as effects in experimental research. Generally, the concept of interaction refers to *the situation in which a particular outcome is obtained because of the unique joint action of two or more variables or processes on behavior.* As a first illustration of the concept of interaction, we shall describe the special interaction that may result between a pretest and a treatment and may thus confound the pretest-posttest design. Subsequently, we shall consider in detail the forms of interaction that may occur in experimental research.

Suppose that two groups of randomly selected subjects are given a paper and pencil questionnaire to assess the degree to which they are prejudiced against black persons. Thereafter, one group is exposed to a well-written and apparently compelling essay explaining the social disadvantages for both blacks and whites that result from such prejudicial attitudes. The control group is not given this essay. Subsequently, both groups of individuals are again given the questionnaire. The experimental group shows a marked reduction in the frequency with which they make prejudicial statements, but no such change is found for the control group. Although it is tempting to attribute this difference entirely to the essay, there is another possibility. Suppose the experimental group subjects, when they are tested for the first time, have no inclination as to the political and social orientations of the experimenter. When they read the essay that favors equality of opportunity for blacks and whites, they conclude *not* that the message is an important and sensible one, but that (1) the purpose of the test that they were given at the outset was to determine whether they were prejudiced and (2) the investigator must surely take a dim view of individuals who express such attitudes. It might well be this combination of having taken the questionnaire at the outset and the treatment that gives rise to the change in responses on the questionnaire.

[8] Systematic desensitization is a procedure for reducing fear and anxiety developed by the psychiatrist, Joseph Wolpe.

In other words, the change might not have occurred if a posttest-only design had been used.

Note that the possible effects of the peculiar combination (that is, interaction) of the pretest and the treatment do not reduce the internal validity of the causal inference that exposure to the essay was sufficient to produce a change in questionnaire responses *in this situation.* However, the possible interaction between treatment and repeated testing in the pretest-posttest design does cast doubt on whether the findings can be generalized beyond the immediate experimental situation. For example, in naturalistic situations we normally do not test individuals before trying to persuade them via pamphlets, television programs, or the like. Therefore, the results may well be different from those we would expect on the basis of the pretest-posttest design.

The Solomon Four-Group Design

One way of eliminating the pretest problem is to use some form of nonreactive measure (that is, one that would not call attention to the fact that the subject is being assessed). When this is not possible, it may be advisable to assure validity by dropping the pretest altogether and relying on random assignment of subjects into groups. This will ensure a reasonable degree of equivalency prior to the introduction of the treatment.

A complete but somewhat more cumbersome way to handle the pretest problem involves the *Solomon four-group design.* In this design, two groups receive the treatment, but only one of these two is pretested. One of the remaining two groups is pretested and then posttested, and the second control group is posttested only. Following our usual notation, the design has the following form.

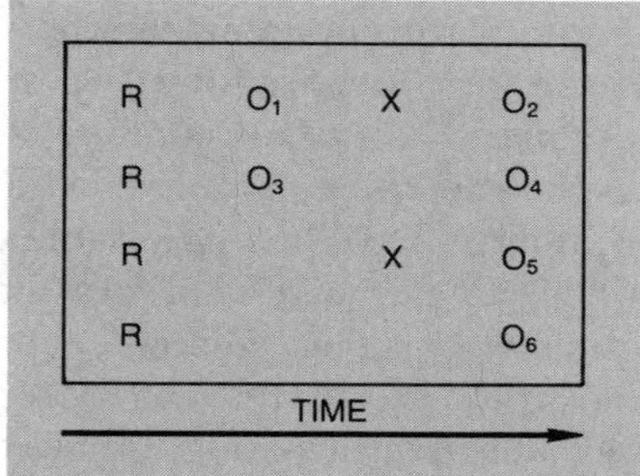

With this design the effects of the pretest and of the treatment can be separately determined. Solomon first implemented it in an early (1949) investigation in which elementary school children were given a spelling test (the pretest), then the treated groups were given a standard lesson on general rules of spelling, and then all four groups were given another spelling test. In this study the pretest *decreased* the effectiveness of the spelling lesson. Thus we can see that the effects of the pretest may interact with the particular experimental treatment and either increase *or* decrease the effect of the treatment.

FACTORS THAT INCREASE THE POWER OF AN EXPERIMENT

The *power* of an experiment is the degree to which it is able to detect the actual effects of the manipulated variables (see p. 62 for a discussion of power in correlational studies). Just as a powerful microscope provides a high degree of resolution and thus permits the scientist to see things that might be missed with a weaker instrument, so a powerful experiment permits the investigator to detect real effects that might be missed if a less powerful experiment were conducted. Broadly, there are two ways of increasing the power of an experiment: maximizing systematic variance and minimizing error variance.

Maximizing Systematic Variance

Systematic variance is the extent to which the presence or absence of the experimental manipulation leads the scores of the subjects in the groups to depart from the overall mean of the distribution of the combined scores. It is reflected in the obtained mean differences between or among the groups and contributes directly to our ability to detect an experimental effect. Thus, *an important principle of experimental design is to maximize the likelihood that the manipulation of the independent variable will change the distributions of scores such that they can be discriminated from the overall variability.*

This principle is especially important in the early phases of research. For example, an investigator may have generated the hypothesis that food reward would have a greater facilitating effect on learning if an animal had been deprived of food for a relatively long time. As an initial test of this hypothesis, she might compare learning in a group of animals who were nearly satiated with food with learning in a group for which no food had been provided for forty-eight hours. Clearly, the experimental conditions differ widely and, if the hypothesis is correct, the expected results should be obtained. With an initial test of a hypothesis such as this one, it would not have been desirable to compare nearly satiated animals with animals who had not eaten for one hour. The variation between these conditions might not be great enough to produce changes in the dependent variable, but one would hardly be willing to conclude that satiation-deprivation per se is unimportant in anticipating the effect of a food reward.

In more advanced stages of research, small variations in an independent variable may be appropriate and in fact desirable. Generally, this condition occurs when a researcher wishes to refine further an already discovered relationship. For example, after demonstrating that animals deprived of food for forty-eight hours learn more quickly with a food reward than do nearly satiated animals, an experimenter might want to refine or "map out" this relationship over increasingly smaller changes in the independent variable.

Minimizing Error Variance

Error variance refers to the variability in the dependent variable generated by unknown factors. Returning to our classroom participation examples, recall that error variance would be indexed by the variability within each of the two groups that is assumed to be due to processes of an unknown origin.

The importance of the interrelationship between systematic variance and error variance can also be seen through our two hypothetical experiments. Specifically, the magnitude of the systematic variance in the first experiment (indexed by the mean difference between the praise and no-praise groups) is greater than the corresponding difference in the second. However, and of particular importance to this discussion, the unaccounted-for spread (see Figures 7-1 and 7-2) or error variance in the former experiment is also greater than the error variance in the latter experiment. The larger error variance in the first experiment markedly reduces our ability to detect a difference between the groups for the praise factor, and it works against the relatively large mean difference. If the average difference between the two groups had remained the same and we had some way of reducing or controlling for the fluctuations that occurred within each group, the obtained mean differences would become much more impressive statistically. We turn next to the question of how error variance can be reduced.

There are five basic ways of minimizing error variance: applying stringent experimental control, employing reliable measurement, aggregating data, using homogeneous samples, and increasing sample size.

Minimizing Error Variance by Experimental Control. To the extent that the experimenter provides constant conditions for all subjects, many possible sources of error variance will be eliminated. Obviously, the first step in achieving this goal is to be assured that all subjects within a particular condition of an experiment are treated in exactly the same way. To the extent that subjects within the same group are treated differently (for example, if a teacher said words such as "right" more enthusiastically for some children than for others in the example we have given), we might expect that variations would occur within this group. The variability in the scores across subjects would be increased, with the resulting undesirable effect of increasing our within-group or error variance. The effect of permitting this to happen will be to reduce our ability to detect a difference *between* the groups that we could call significant.

Minimizing Error Variance by Reliable Measurement. The second major means of reducing error variance involves the notion of *reliability of measurement.* Any effort to measure a naturally occurring event, regardless of what that event is, is to some degree subject to error (see Chapter 2). For example, in measuring children's height or weight, some degrees of error is introduced because the rulers or weight scales we use are manufactured to imperfect specifications and thus differ (at least slightly) from each other. However, when we say a particular child is sixty inches tall and another child is fifty-four inches tall, it is reasonable to assume that most of the difference is a true difference in the relative heights of the two children. In the previous experimental examples, a greater degree of error will doubtless be present in measuring the frequency with which children participated in class. If a child asks an extremely simple question regarding a classroom assignment, it might be difficult to decide whether this event counts or does not count as "classroom participation." The contrast suggested here reflects the more general concepts of the *true score* and of *error variance in measurement* discussed in Chapter 2. That is, an obtained score may be thought of as having two parts: the true score (the score that would result if no error of measurement were present) and error.

The fact that there is error in all measurement does not mean that the degree of this error is uncontrollable, however. Reliable measures are those that contain relatively little measurement error; less reliable measures contain more such error. Unsystematic measurement error will serve to increase the overall degree of error variance in an experiment and reduce our ability to detect reliable systematic variance. Thus, it behooves the experimenter to make his or her measurement instruments and procedures as reliable as possible.

Minimizing Error Variance by Aggregation. Error is always present to some degree in any obtained score. The *principle of aggregation* has recently been suggested by Rushton, Brainerd, and Pressley (1983) as a means of minimizing the error associated with individual scores. The principle states that "the sum of a set of multiple measurements is a more stable and representative estimator than any single measurement" (p. 18). Simply put, the principle calls for obtaining numerous scores to represent each instance of the phenomenon of interest rather than just one. For example, in any study involving ratings by judges, random error can be reduced by employing several different independent judges and pooling or averaging their judgments about each subject or event being studied. Or, in an investigation of reaction times, one may obtain the subjects' reaction times to a particular stimulus on several, dozens, or even hundreds of occasions rather than just once; averaging over each subject's many scores will produce a better estimate of his or her true performance than would any single score. In all such cases error is reduced because random variations from one judge to another or one response to another will tend to cancel each other out.

Minimizing Error Variance by Using Homogeneous Groups of Subjects. In any study involving a group of subjects (either animal or human), one can expect individual differences among the organisms. Although such individual differences will contribute to the error variance of an experiment, they can be minimized by employing homogeneous groups. Much animal research is done with highly inbred strains of rats and much human research with samples who share many characteristics—for example, social class, race, and sex. But as we shall see later, this tactic may have the undesirable effect of limiting the degree to which findings can be generalized to other populations.

Minimizing Error Variance by Increasing Sample Size. In Chapter 2 we had occasion to point out that larger samples provide a better and more reliable description of the populations they represent than do smaller samples, everything else being equal. One reason for the superiority of larger sample sizes is that as sample size increases, the effects of chance factors on individual subjects tend to cancel out. Thus, a fifth way to protect oneself against large error variance is to increase sample size.

OPERATIONALIZING EXPERIMENTAL VARIABLES

We have seen already that one of the most challenging aspects of all behavioral science research is to come up with ways of procedurally defining or "operationalizing" the variables of interest so as to best get at the underlying processes while minimizing the reactivity of the measures taken. When using the experimental method, this means choosing both independent and dependent variables that reflect the phenomena of underlying interest while satisfying the demands of ethics and practicality.

Choosing an Independent Variable

When a particular experiment is embedded in a series of projects dealing with the same phenomenon, the choice of the independent variable is not difficult. An investigator interested in the area of motivation in animal learning would most likely select an independent variable from the extant literature (for example, depriving the animal of food or water). Similarly, the choice of an independent variable should present little problem when the investigator's interest lies in the variable itself (for example, the effects of different schedules of reinforcement on performance).

Often, however, an investigation begins with a *conceptual hypothesis* such as that of Freedman et al. (1967). When this is the case, the critical problem is choosing a specific independent variable that will correspond adequately to the conceptual variable. The conceptual independent variable of Freedman et al. was guilt—presumably produced by having subjects tell a lie. But how could the investigators be sure that after lying the subjects would feel guilty? There are no easy answers to such questions, but we shall return to them in Chapter 13.

Choosing a Dependent Variable

Many criteria must be taken into account in selecting an appropriate dependent variable for a given experiment. In addition to the obvious restraint that it must be a reasonable reflection of the phenomenon in which the investigator is interested and the previously mentioned requirement that it be reliable, the measure selected must also be (1) readily observable in the experimental situation, (2) economically feasible, and (3) capable of being collected with little distress to the subject and without violating his or her right to privacy or breaching accepted research ethics (see Chapter 1).

The dependent measure must also be a sufficiently sensitive measure to detect the experimental effects being sought. For example, a researcher who has hypothesized that a particular food supplement will make people stronger would be ill-advised to use the lifting of a thimble as a dependent measure (even the subjects in the presumably weaker control group will all be able to do that), nor would it be wise to select the lifting of a 500-pound weight, a feat beyond the capacities of even those who have benefited greatly from the experimental modification in diet.

A parallel, yet subtler, example may be drawn from an investigation of two methods of learning a list of nonsense syllables on retention a week later. A number of ways of assessing retention are available in such an investigation. Subjects might simply be asked to *recall* the list; they might be asked to relearn the list to provide a measure of *savings;* or they might be asked to *recognize* the initial items when presented in a larger list containing new items. The results obtained in such a study could be expected to depend heavily on which of the possible dependent variables was selected. It is known, for example, that recognition produces data indicating more retention than does recall. If recognition was the dependent variable, retention might be extremely high regardless of the method of learning being studied. With recall as the measure, on the other hand, retention might be greatly affected by the method.

These examples are extreme, but the investigator must be careful to avoid conceptually similar errors. After the fact, a faulty hypothesis and a faulty dependent measure cannot be distinguished.

FOR REVIEW AND DISCUSSION

1. Discuss the concept of variance overlap as it pertains to both experimental and nonexperimental data.
2. A school psychologist wishes to test his idea that friendly teachers cause students to be more attentive.
   (a) State the hypothesis involved.
   (b) Put the hypothesis into testable form; that is, select an independent variable and a dependent variable.
3. Many professional journals will not publish reports of experiments in which the results did not reach at least the .05 level of significance. If you were a journal editor, what defense could you give for this practice? What arguments might be made against it? Consider, for example, (a) whether it is possible for data reaching the .10 level to be more meaningful than data reaching .001, and (b) the difference between "meaningful" and "significant" findings. If the negative

results are correct (that is, there really is no difference between groups) what might be the advantages of publishing?

4. Design experiments to test the following proverbs:
   (a) Haste makes waste.
   (b) He who hesitates is lost.
   (c) Love is blind.
   (d) Too many cooks spoil the broth.
5. An investigator compares the number of cavities of children who have been advised to use either toothpaste *A* or toothpaste *B* for a year. At the end of the year, she finds group *A* has significantly fewer cavities (at the .05 level) than group *B*.
   (a) State H_0 and H_1
   (b) What would be the Type I and Type II errors?
   (c) What is the probability of a Type I error?
   (d) If the experimenter had used .01 as her required significance level, would the probability of a Type II error have changed? In what way?
6. A drug manufacturer wishes to test a drug she feels can cure cancer. She must consider the following before producing the drug for the public: (a) its high expense, (b) its side effects, and (c) its effectiveness. Discuss the sizes of Type I and Type II errors you would be willing to accept before allowing production of the drug.
7. In a social psychology experiment on racial attitudes, one group of subjects views a film showing both black and white actors, while a second group sees a film with only white actors. Following the film each subject enters a room in which two blacks and two whites (confederates of the experimenter) are seated. Observers in the room record the amount of interaction between the subject and the members of each race.
   (a) Discuss the use of the dependent variable according to the criteria presented in the text.
   (b) What effects might the observation procedure itself have on the subjects? How would this affect the results?
8. An experimenter reports that two groups differ significantly ($p < .05$). What does he mean?
9. An investigator wishes to determine whether the process of remembering and repeating a short story is influenced by different instructions to the subjects before they read it. Her subject population is college sophomores. How should they be assigned to groups? Suppose her subjects were preschoolers. Would she be more or less likely to use matched random assignment? Why?

8

Complex Experiments

FACTORIAL DESIGNS

MULTIPLE CAUSATION: ADDITIVITY AND INTERACTIONS

- Catalytic Interactions
- Terminative Interactions
- Antagonistic Interactions
- Effects of Treatment Strength on Interactions

ANALYSIS OF VARIANCE (ANOVA)

- Interpreting Anova Results

REPEATED MEASUREMENT (WITHIN-SUBJECTS COMPARISONS) IN THE FACTORIAL EXPERIMENT

- Carryover Effects and Counterbalancing

FOR REVIEW AND DISCUSSION

In the preceding chapter we discussed the essential features of a true basic experiment involving a treatment and control condition and a single posttest. Our discussion now turns to important elaborations and extensions of the true experiment, embodied in more complex designs.

FACTORIAL DESIGNS

It is a well-established observation in both the physical and social sciences that events are often multiply determined. Any phenomenon observed is likely to result from a variety of influences that have impinged upon it. An experiment in which a single treatment is employed (even with an appropriate control group) is unable to shine much light on such multiple determination. To understand better a particular event or outcome, it would appear desirable to identify and systematically manipulate various possible causes or factors that might operate within a particular piece of research. Such a strategy is the *factorial experiment.*

In a factorial experiment, two or more different treatments, events, or characteristics are independently varied in a single piece of research. The simplest possible arrangement for such a design is one in which only two treatments or factors are involved (customarily abbreviated A and B), and within each of the two factors, only two levels are manipulated (for example, the presence or absence of a particular treatment). Such an arrangement is referred to as a 2 × 2 factorial design. Suppose one is interested in nursery school children who are frustrating their teachers by spending a good deal of their time having tantrums and too little time with their peers. One possible way of attempting to modify the behavior of such children is to systematically punish them whenever they engage in tantrums. Another is to reward them whenever they engage in prosocial activities with other children. We are interested in the effects of either of these procedures and even more so in determining the consequences of using both of them or neither of them. Posing the question in this way immediately gives rise to a 2 × 2 factorial design, creating the groups shown in Table 8-1(a).

Note that this 2 × 2 factorial design produces an experiment containing four cells. We can readily determine the number of cells in any factorial experiment by multiplying the levels of each factor times the levels of every other

Table 8-1(a) 2 × 2 Factorial Design

CONSEQUENCE FOR PROSOCIAL BEHAVIOR	*CONSEQUENCE FOR DISRUPTIVE BEHAVIOR*	
	PUNISHMENT	*NO PUNISHMENT*
Reward		
No Reward		

factor in the experiment. If instead of using simply the presence or absence of reward and the presence or absence of punishment, we had high punishment, moderate punishment, and no punishment (as factor A) and high reward, moderate reward, and no reward (as factor B), we would have a 3 × 3 factorial design. As seen in Table 8-1(b), the resulting experiment produces 9, or 3 × 3, experimental cells. This rule is infinitely generalizable. In addition, the factors can have any number of levels, limited only by the constraints of practicality. Thus, one can use a 3 × 4 design or a 2 × 6 design. Finally, any number of factors can appear in such a design (for example, a 3 × 2 × 2 × 4), limited only by the practicality of generating all the cells within a reasonable sample. (There are 48 groups in a 3 × 2 × 2 × 4 design, and the difficulties involved in interpreting interactions that could involve all four factors are enormous.)

Since we have continually emphasized the importance of a control group, perhaps our first observation should be that *in any factorial design in which one of the levels of each of the factors being employed involves the absence of treatment* (for example, punishment versus no punishment), *a cell in which none of the treatments is present inevitably appears.* This is the familiar untreated control group of simple (nonfactorial) experiments.

A second feature of the factorial design is the degree to which it economically employs subjects. Suppose, for example, that 60 children were available for an experiment on the effects of reward and punishment on the elimination of tantrums. We might, using a nonfactorial design, divide these children randomly into three groups. One of the groups would receive reward for appropriate social activities, one would receive punishment for inappropriate activities, and one would receive no treatment. In this situation we would be able to determine the effects of reward for only 20 of the 60 children in the experiment. Likewise, the effects of punishment could be considered only for the 20 children who received that treatment, and we would get no information whatsoever as to the combined effects of reward and punishment. In contrast, the factorial design would allow us to expose 30 of the 60 children to reward, expose 30 of the 60

Table 8-1(b) 3 × 3 Factorial Design

CONSEQUENCE FOR PROSOCIAL BEHAVIOR	*CONSEQUENCE FOR DISRUPTIVE BEHAVIOR*		
	HIGH PUNISHMENT	*MODERATE PUNISHMENT*	*NO PUNISHMENT*
High Reward			
Moderate Reward			
No Reward			

children to punishment, and still provide 15 children who received both of the treatments.

An additional qualification must be added to these figures. Only for the overall or "main" effect of reward do we have 30 children in the treated group of the experiment. To the extent that the reward operates in very much the same way (presumably to increase the likelihood of prosocial behavior) regardless of whether punishment is present or not, we can reasonably speak of the main effect of reward upon the 30 children. There is, however, another possibility. The effects of reward (or punishment) may operate differently depending on whether the remaining treatment is present or absent. For example, any one of the following possibilities might obtain:

1. Reward and punishment are both effective in modifying the children's behavior, but the combination of these two treatments is no more effective than either would be alone.
2. Reward and punishment are each separately effective in modifying the children's behavior, but when they are combined their effects disappear entirely, so that the children's behavior is not changed any more than that found in the control group.
3. Reward and punishment are both effective in modifying the children's behavior, but their combination is even better than would be expected from the effects of either separately. This would be the case if the children in the control group produced the most tantrums, both the rewarded and the punished children had fewer, but those who received both treatments became virtual paragons of good behavior after the experimental treatments.
4. Finally, it is possible that neither reward nor punishment would have any detectable effect, but that the two together would produce a strong effect (in principle, in either direction) that would be totally unexpected from our knowledge of what either does separately. We discussed the possibility of such contributory causes in Chapter 1.

Among the enormous benefits of employing a factorial design is the ability to detect, in a straightforward, statistical way, the presence of any one of these types of unique combinations or interactions, as well as to rule out the possibility that they occur.

In the discussion that follows we shall suggest specific descriptive labels for the various forms of interaction and identify possible examples of each in social scientific research.

MULTIPLE CAUSATION: ADDITIVITY AND INTERACTIONS

Unless they are told otherwise, most people would probably assume that if two factors each had an effect when considered separately, then the combined effect of the two factors would be the sum of their separate effects, as if they had been literally "added up." Such *additive relationships* among factors are found quite often in the social and behavioral sciences. Figure 8-1 displays the data reported by Gates (1917) in an early experiment on the factors that contribute to successful academic test performance. Specifically, Gates's experiment was concerned with the relative effectiveness of self-recitation versus silent reading on students' recall of material they had studied. Recall was assessed both immediately after study and again four hours later. As may be seen, for both immediate recall and recall after four hours, the amount remembered increases as a function of the percentage of study time spent in self-recitation and decreases with the amount of delay before the test.

Of course, not all multiple causation occurs additively. Many variables *interact* when they combine, producing results that would not be anticipated from the effects of each factor considered separately. Somewhat more technically, *two factors (or variables) are said to interact whenever the effect of one factor is not the same at*

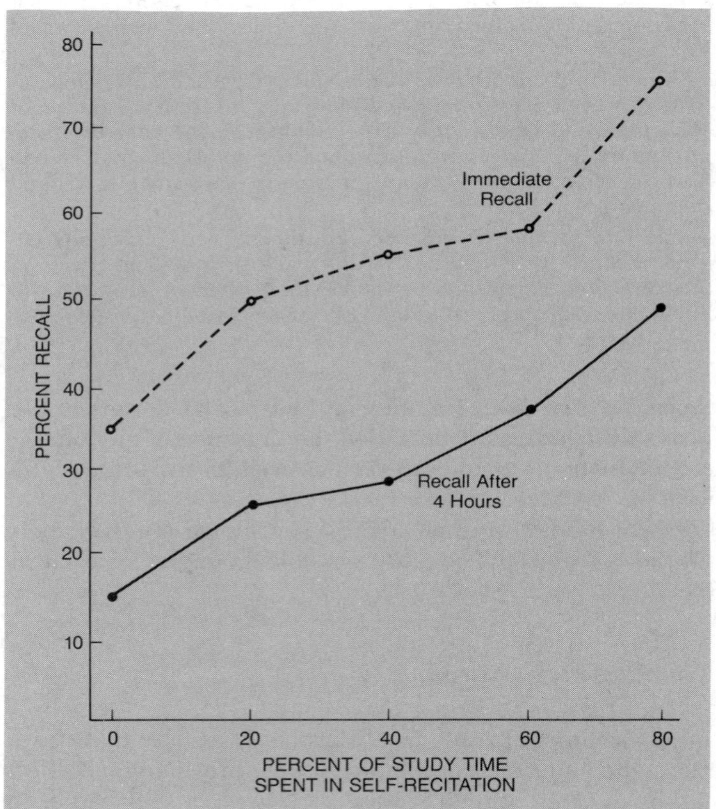

Figure 8-1 Recall performance in Gates's (1917) experiment, illustrating additivity of effects.

every level of every other factor. Interactions therefore indicate the presence of conditional (as opposed to general) causal relationships.

We will consider three frequently encountered patterns of interactions: catalytic, terminative, and antagonistic.

Catalytic Interactions

The novice student of chemistry may find in his or her laboratory two common reagents, potassium permanganate and glycerine. Either of these can be comfortably rubbed on the fingers, with no apparent unpleasant effect except for a purplish stain from the potassium permanganate. If, however, a student is unwise enough to place a bit of potassium permanganate on his thumb, a drop of glycerine on his forefinger, and touch the two together, he will almost immediately experience a severe and very painful burn. If larger quantities of potassium permanganate and glycerine are combined, they will sizzle, smoke voluminously, and give rise to an extremely hot flame. In this case, the novice chemist would, by simple observation of the separate effects of the two substances, be unable to detect that they would combine to catalyze a powerful oxidation reaction. *A catalytic interaction is one in which two or more treatments are effective only when they occur together.*

Consider a 2 × 2 factorial design for an experiment concerning attitudes toward energy consumption. We might begin with individuals known to be heavy consumers and expose half of them to a treatment (for example, a highly persuasive film) designed to modify their attitudes toward the energy crisis. Subsequently, members of both the treatment and no-treatment groups might be asked, either alone or in a group of their peers, to describe their attitudes toward energy consumption. The dependent variable might be the number of positive statements made about energy conservation. Presumably the number of positive statements made would be low for untreated subjects regardless of whether they spoke in a one-to-one or in a group situation. Likewise, it would not be surprising to find that heavy consumers are rather unlikely to forsake their previous attitudes, even after treatment, if other individuals who believe that the energy crisis is exaggerated are watching. But given the unique combination of a compelling treatment *and* a one-to-one test with a proconservation experimenter, it is possible that a fairly sympathetic attitude toward energy conservation will be displayed. Such an outcome, which is illustrated in Figure 8-2, may be called a catalytic interactive effect between the two factors we have considered here.

Terminative Interactions

A terminative interaction is one in which two or more variables are clearly effective in modifying behavior, but when combined their effect is not increased over what either alone would do. As an illustration of this phenomenon, consider an experiment con-

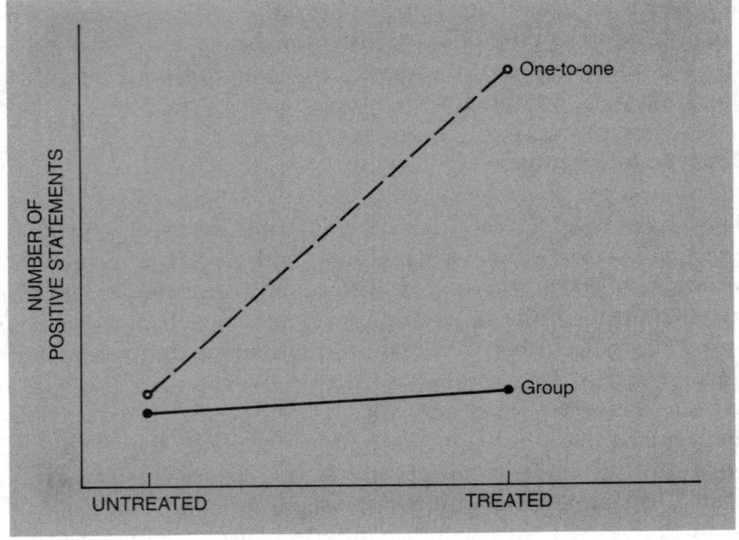

Figure 8-2 Hypothetical effects of individual and group situations on the expression of positive statements about energy conservation by individuals who have or have not seen a persuasive film. The pattern of results illustrates a *catalytic interaction.*

cerning the effects on how much children share when they (1) observe a sharing model and (2) are exhorted to share (Poulos & Liebert, 1972). These investigators found that both children who were exhorted by an adult to share with other children and those who observed an adult share were more likely to share, and shared a larger amount, than did children who received neither of these treatments. Nonetheless, the investigators obtained a reliable interaction between verbalization and modeling as modes of inducing sharing. When such an interaction occurs statistically, it is often helpful to graph the findings so as to get a direct picture of the form they take. Such an illustration, based on the Poulos and Liebert experiment, appears as Figure 8-3.

From the illustration it is clear that both verbalization and modeling had an effect on each of the measures of children's sharing. Nonetheless, the combination of the two variables was no more effective than either separately, despite the fact that the children might have shared more than they did. (Even in the most generous group the children shared less than half of their total earnings.) Viewed historically, this experiment carries a particularly important lesson about the importance of a factorial approach for detecting certain effects. Prior to this study, a great deal of evidence had been accumulated to suggest that observing another person share would markedly increase children's sharing. To determine whether verbal exhortations to share had some effect, a number of experimenters

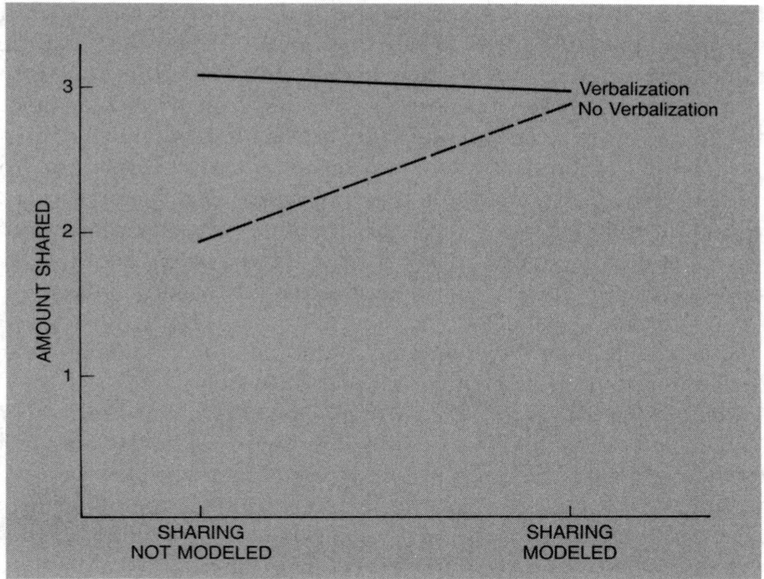

Figure 8-3 The effects of verbal exhortation and a sharing example on children's sharing. The pattern of results illustrates a *terminative interaction* (Poulos & Liebert, 1972).

simply added exhortative verbalizations to the sharing example provided in their experiments. In none of these studies did the verbalization increase the potency of modeling in sharing. In describing this earlier work, it was tempting to conclude that such verbalizations were ineffective as child-rearing practices for inducing donations. However, as Poulos and Liebert's results show, such a conclusion would have been unwarranted from the earlier data. Instead, it appears that the usual type of verbalization can be effective, just as modeling can, but that, since the two treatments are terminative in their effects, their relative, separate, and combined potency can only be understood and evaluated through a factorial experiment.

Antagonistic Interactions

By returning to the chemistry laboratory, we can illustrate the nature of antagonistic interactions. The following demonstration was used by one of us in an undergraduate laboratory. The experimenter pours a carefully measured quantity of hydrochloric acid into one beaker and a carefully measured quantity of sodium hydroxide into another. From the first beaker a small quantity of hydrochloric acid is poured into a shallow glass tray. A copper penny is dropped in the acid and great billows of smoke emerge as the penny is rapidly eroded. Soon the penny is completely gone. Then a small piece of beefsteak is dropped into a tray containing some of the sodium hydroxide. This fluid, too, proves to be highly destructive. The caustic sodium hydroxide appears to consume the meat completely in a short time. When observers are challenged to drink the remaining contents of either of the beakers, it is usual (and not surprising) to find no volunteers. Then the demonstrator may announce that he or she is "twice as brave" as any of the observers, pour the contents of both beakers into a larger third beaker, and immediately drink all the newly prepared fluid. Instead of destruction of the mouth and internal organs, the investigator suffers no ill effects save for a rather marked increase in thirst. Although both substances are, separately, highly dangerous, they combine in an antagonistic way so as to provide the relatively nonnoxious substance, simple salt water.[1]

Such antagonistic interactions may appear in behavioral research. Consider the possibility that a person's conformity to group norms may be increased when he or she performs in a public (as opposed to a private) situation. Likewise, an individual who is offered some monetary incentive for adhering to group norms may become more likely to do so. What, then, would be the effect of combining the incentive and group observation? The two treatments combined might not produce a higher level of conformity. Individuals might be very reticent to behave, in public, so as to make it apparent that they were permitting their own judgments to be modified for money. Thus the separate effects of an audience and a financial reward might be antagonistic when combined.

A perhaps even more striking example of an antagonistic interaction may be seen in an experiment by Kiesler and Baral (1969). Male college students were asked to participate in a one-hour study on intelligence testing. As a manipulation of "self-esteem," after a portion of the test had been completed the experimenter indicated to half the subjects that they had done extremely well (high self-esteem) and to the remaining subjects that they had done poorly (low self-esteem). Next, the experimenter suggested a coffee break and he and the subject were joined by a female confederate. The physical attractiveness of the girl was varied in two conditions. Thus, the design was a 2 (high versus low self-esteem) $\times$ 2 (attractive versus unattractive female confederate) factorial.

During the coffee break the experimenter excused himself to make a phone call, and the confederate engaged the subject in conversation. The dependent variable was the extent to which the subject displayed interest in the girl (for example, asking for her phone number or for a date). The results are shown in Figure 8-4. As may be seen, subjects whose self-esteem was enhanced displayed more romantic behavior to the girl when she appeared to be highly attractive. Conversely, subjects with *lowered* self-esteem displayed more romantic behavior to the unattractive female.

[1] $HCl + NaOH \rightarrow NaCl + H_2O$.

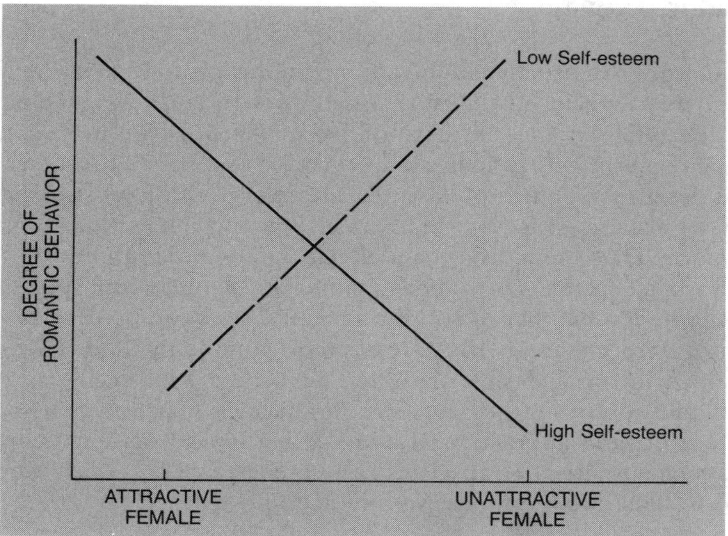

Figure 8-4 Data obtained by Kiesler and Baral (1969) illustrating an *antagonistic interaction.*

Effects of Treatment Strength on Interactions

Suppose an investigator obtains one of the types of interaction we have discussed. If the findings are successfully replicated and the design is free of the contaminations described in Chapter 5, we would accept the particular pattern as internally valid.

But a second question arises. Would the same pattern be obtained if treatments of very different strengths had been used? Often, they would not. For example, a monetary incentive and a persuasive communication might be additive in their effects upon reducing the number of cigarettes smokers consume while participating in a given experiment. But the pattern of results could be quickly turned into a terminative interaction if the incentive was raised to $100 per day for not smoking and the persuasive communication was that diseased tobacco plants, causing an immediate jeopardy to health, had been used in the manufacture of the cigarettes now on the market. Or consider the fact that verbalization and modeling did not act additively upon children's sharing (p. 166). A "stronger" verbalization than has been customarily used in these experiments (perhaps one bordering on threat) might produce additive results for the two treatments or a different type of interaction. Thus, more generally, *any description of a pattern of results as interactive or additive may be applicable only to the effects of the treatment variables at the strengths (and under the conditions) actually employed in the experiment.* This fact again raises the question of the generalizability of social science research, a problem to which we shall return in Chapter 12.

ANALYSIS OF VARIANCE (ANOVA)

Factorial designs are usually employed in conjunction with a statistical approach called analysis of variance (ANOVA). Analysis of variance is a statistical strategy in which the total variance in a set of scores (such as the dependent variable scores of an experiment) is analyzed into various sources. Each of the factors in a factorial design is a source of variance, as are each of the possible interactions. Variance not accounted for by the main effects and interactions is unexplained error variance. These sources—main effects, interactions, and error—add up to the total variance in the scores, both mathematically and conceptually.

Although a number of specific statistical tests can be used to analyze the variance in a factorial design, the *F*-test is most commonly used. Thus, the results obtained in a factorial design are often presented statistically in an ANOVA summary table reporting the statistical significance of *F* values associated with each main effect and interaction. Table 8-2 is a typical ANOVA summary table for a between-subjects design (Poulos & Liebert, 1972, which we previously presented to illustrate a terminative interaction).

Interpreting ANOVA Results

Interpreting the results of an ANOVA need not be difficult even if one is unfamiliar with the actual computational procedures involved in computing the various *F*s. Nonetheless, there are some important principles of interpretation, and unless they are understood all but the simplest ANOVAs will lead to unwarranted or inaccurate conclusions.

Table 8-2 is not a particularly simple ANOVA. The experiment giving rise to the ANOVA in Table 8-2 was designed to look at the effects of Modeling (whether or not the subjects saw a sharing model), Verbalization (whether or not the subjects heard an adult "preach" the virtues of sharing), and Surveillance

Table 8-2 Analysis of Variance of Mean Number of Tokens Shared in Poulos and Liebert's (1972) Experiment

SOURCE	*df*	*MS*	*F*
Modeling (*A*)	1	3.10	2.39
Verbalization (*B*)	1	8.36	6.43*
Surveillance (*C*)	1	4.03	3.10
$A \times B$	1	5.61	4.32*
$A \times C$	1	.75	.58
$B \times C$	1	5.78	4.45*
$A \times B \times C$	1	.16	.12
Error	72	1.30	—

*$p < .05$

(whether or not an experimenter was present during the test) on children sharing with other children. Of the main effects, only Verbalization (B) is statistically significant. However, the role of Verbalization does not end with a significant main effect. The Modeling X Verbalization and Verbalization X Surveillance interactions are also significant. Thus, every factor is involved in at least one significant effect. Despite the complexities, an examination of the results shows that they make good sense.

One firm principle involved whenever interpreting ANOVAs is that *no simple overall interpretation can be given to a significant main effect when the factor is also involved in a significant interaction.* Thus, in the Poulos and Liebert experiment it would *not* be correct to talk about the overall effect of verbalizing to a child without first considering the verbalization treatment's interaction with the other two variables.

And what of the interactions? As we indicated before, they can best be seen and understood through line graphs. Figure 8-3 (p. 167) shows the $A \times B$ interaction in the experiment. Recall that the interaction between Verbalization and Modeling is terminative. Both treatments succeeded in raising the level of children's generosity, but their combined effect produced no more sharing than did exposure to either influence by itself.

Figure 8-5 shows the interaction between Verbalization and Surveillance. This interaction is catalytic. Surveillance increased children's sharing only when they had first been exposed to an adult who exhorted them to be generous.

One further point (probably a familiar one by now) should be kept in mind when interpreting ANOVA results. Specifically, the fact that a main effect or interaction is statistically significant does not mean that it is important. F ratios can be statistically significant while reflecting weak effects of no practical significance. There are several ways of estimating the magnitude of the effects of factors in an ANOVA. Essentially, these statistical tests provide an index of the percentage of variance in the dependent variable accounted for by each main effect or interaction. Thus, just as r can be tested for statistical significance (for example, is this r significantly different from zero?) and scaled on magnitude (recall that r^2 is an estimate of variance accounted for), so the effects of factors in ANOVA can be evaluated for both statistical significance and strength. Discussions of how to perform these and other computational procedures regarding ANOVA can be found in most intermediate and advanced statistics texts.

The interested reader may also wish to note that although our examples in this chapter have dealt mostly with between-subjects comparisons in experimental designs, the same basic logic can be applied in factorial designs and ANOVA that involve within-subjects comparisons or a combination of within and between-subjects comparisons. Also, ANOVA can be used to deal with purely correlational designs (those with only classificatory variables) as well as with mixed designs having both classificatory and manipulated variables. The breadth and versatility of factorial designs and the analysis of variance have led many methodologists to conclude that this approach is one of the social scientist's most powerful tools.

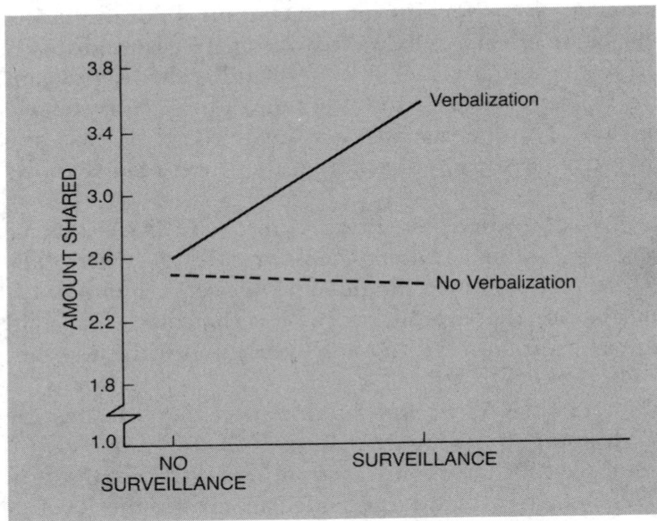

Figure 8-5 The $B \times C$ interaction in Poulos's experiment (see Table 8-2).

REPEATED MEASUREMENT (WITHIN-SUBJECTS COMPARISONS) IN THE FACTORIAL EXPERIMENT

As we saw when comparing pretest-posttest and posttest-only designs, experimenters may sometimes choose to make within-subjects as well as between-subjects comparisons. This can be accomplished only by obtaining more than one measure from each subject. Thus, all within-subjects comparisons involve *repeated measurement.* Repeated measurement may be woven into factorial experiments, in combination with between-subjects comparisons, to form one of a number of *repeated measures designs.*

Repeated measures designs are used in two major ways. First, the repeated measure is taken several times with *no* change in the independent variable. Second, the dependent variable may be repeatedly assessed in an investigation in which each subject successively receives several different treatments. Here we will discuss only the first usage of repeated measures, in which there is no change in the independent variable. The second case, in which the independent variable is changed between measurements, creates a quasi-experiment rather than a true experiment. Quasi-experiments are discussed in Chapter 10.

The nature of the phenomenon under study may logically require the use of repeated measurement. This would be the case, for example, in studies of learning where the repeated measure is performance across a series of trial blocks. In this instance, the experimenter is interested in the effects of earlier performance on later performance and hence employs the repeated measures design.

To illustrate, we shall consider portions of an experiment by Martens (1969), which dealt with the effects of the presence of an audience on learning. Briefly, earlier research (for example, Zajonc, 1965) had shown that the mere presence of another person may facilitate or impede performance depending respectively on whether the correct answers on the task were already dominant (well learned) or not. To test the generality of this pattern further, Martens had undergraduate male subjects perform a complex motor skill, involving "hitting" a moving target, either alone or while being observed by ten peers who were unknown to them. The expectation suggested by Zajonc's (1965) *social facilitation theory* is that the audience will have a debilitating effect on the performance of such an unfamiliar and complex motor skill, which will diminish as correct responses become more dominant through learning. Such a prediction can be tested only by obtaining successive or repeated performance measures on the same subjects. Employing this strategy, by analyzing his subjects' performance in three trial blocks (of five trials each), Martens obtained the data shown in Figure 8-6. They are clearly in line with predictions and can be understood by the author's own description-interpretation: "A significant Conditions of Learning × Blocks interaction was found. . . . As illustrated . . . the effect of an audience was greatest during the initial learning trials, with a significant, but decreasing, difference with continued practice."

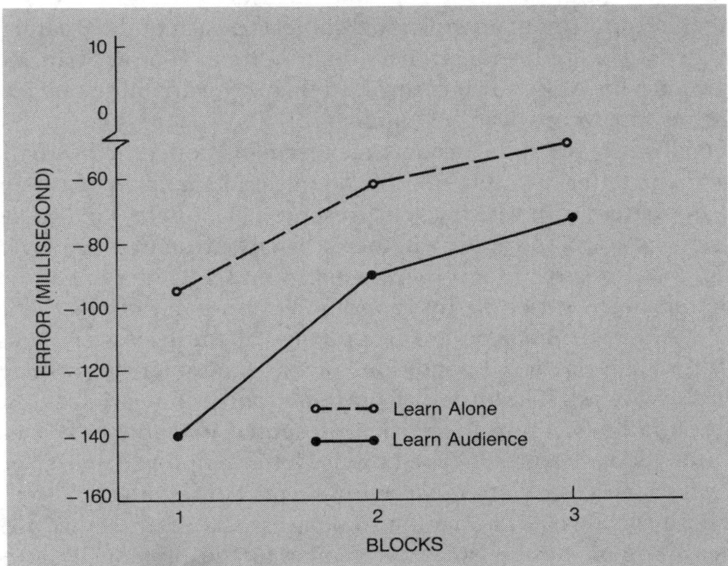

Figure 8-6 Effects of presence of an audience on performance of a motor skill, illustrating a *repeated-measures design*. The same subjects are tested repeatedly across blocks. Also note that the effect of the experimental manipulation decreases over time (Martens, 1969).

Table 8-3 Proportion of Correct Detections as a Function of Display Size and Noise Condition, Illustrating a Repeated Measures Design (McIntyre, Fox, & Neale, 1970). Every Subject Was Tested Under Both Display Sizes and All Five Noise Letter Conditions

	DISPLAY SIZE	
NOISE LETTER	*8*	*14*
Random	0.68	0.62
O	0.82	0.83
U	0.81	0.74
I	0.77	0.69
E	0.64	0.66

The second type of repeated measures design is used primarily as a control for individual differences among subjects. In many experiments, the responses of people to the same experimental treatment are quite variable. If this source of variability can be removed from experimental error, the sensitivity of the experiment may be markedly increased through minimizing error variance (see Chapter 7). Both types of repeated measures designs try to do this by measuring the responses of an individual subject to each of the treatments relative to the subject's average responsiveness to all of them. To put it another way, the subject becomes his or her own control. In this way, variability due to differences in average responsiveness can be eliminated.

To illustrate, we will consider an experiment concerned with the detection of an alphabetic letter as a function of the physical similarity between the target and the other letters with which it was presented (McIntyre, Fox, & Neale, 1970). The subject's task was to report whether a briefly presented display contained a *T* or an *F*. Two sizes of display were used: 8 and 14 letters. The nontarget or "noise" letters were varied in five conditions: random, all *O*'s, all *U*'s, all *I*'s, and all *E*'s. After an initial period of practice, all subjects were presented 200 trials—20 for each of the 10 conditions of the experiment (2 display sizes × 5 types of noise letters). The order of presentation of the various conditions was determined randomly. From the results presented in Table 8-3, it may be seen that detection did vary with the type of noise letter employed; better performance occurred when the target letters were unlike the noise letters.

There is, however, a major problem associated with this use of the repeated-measurement design, which is similar to the previously noted problem associated with pretests. This issue has been aptly described by Grice (1966):

> It is quite common to hear an experimenter say, with obvious pride, that in his experiment, each subject served as his own control. The reasons for the pride

> are obvious. After all, what more comparable control group can there be than the same group? Furthermore, the method is efficient and economical, and one had done something elegant. However, such an experiment may or may not be a proper source of pride, and one very simple point should be raised: a subject who has served as his own control may not be the same subject that he would have been if he had not. If the experience in the control condition in any way influences performance in the experimental condition, then a different result may be obtained than if a separate control group had been employed. Such an experiment may be good or bad, but if the experimenter thinks that he has merely done more efficiently the same investigation as the independent group experiment, he is mistaken (p. 488).

As support for his contention that the two classes of design may lead to different conclusions, Grice noted the different results that may be obtained in examining the effects of the intensity of the conditional stimulus (CS) in classical conditioning. He reported that the influence of intensity was five times as great in the repeated measures design as in the between-subjects design. Such a large difference in the magnitude of the effect produced by a variable may be of great importance in clarifying both the theoretical validity and the generalizability of experimental results. (Grice was led to modify an earlier stimulus-energy formulation of the effects of stimulus intensity and add such concepts as adaptation level and contrast.)

Carryover Effects and Counterbalancing

Whenever making within-subjects comparisons in which each subject is given more than one treatment, an important principle is that subjects must not all be given the same treatments in the same order. This principle recognizes the fact that exposure to one manipulation or test may produce persistent consequences, called *carryover effects,* that influence the subject's response to any subsequent manipulation.

Johnson and Liebert (1977) have provided the following example. Suppose an experimental psychologist wished to compare people's reaction times to two colored traffic signals, red and orange, to determine whether responses are quicker to one color than to the other. The psychologist would very likely choose a repeated measures design in this situation, because effects produced by the color of the light would be expected to be quite small relative to individual differences in reaction time. That is, people will vary in alertness, coordination, motivation, and a variety of other factors that could make them fast or slow. These variations might completely mask the effects of the lights if subjects were compared in a between-subject design. Also, an experimental psychologist working on a problem like this would probably present each subject with a number of trials on each light (say, thirty) and use the average of these trials under each color condition as the person's score in that condition. Averaging over many trials in this way helps to minimize the influence of chance factors (such as temporary distraction) on the scores and therefore further reduces error variance (see p. 156).

Suppose, now, that each subject in the study first received his or her thirty trials in the red light condition and then received thirty trials in the orange light condition. Would this procedure be acceptable? No. Very likely individuals would improve as they became more familiar with the procedure, more comfortable with the experimental setting, and more practiced in the task. A general improvement resulting from experience with a task or experimental procedure, usually called a *practice effect,* must not be confounded with the color conditions. All the subjects might be expected to respond a bit faster in the second thirty trials because they would be more practiced, but we would not want to attribute this improvement to a difference in the color of the light. The general problem is therefore to avoid confounding the order in which treatments are presented with the treatments themselves.

Table 8-4 illustrates three potential consequences of permitting the carryover effect to enter our hypothetical experiment. (To simplify the discussion, we have assumed that the practice effect would be the same for everybody and would decrease reaction time approximately 0.20 seconds.) Table 8-4(a) is a case in which the true difference between conditions is 0; that is, the color of the light does not affect reaction time. However, the practice effect makes it appear as though reaction time is faster to orange light than to red light (0.55 versus 0.75 seconds). In Table 8-4(b), a potential real difference, in which reaction times to the red light are faster, is actually masked by the practice effect. And finally, in Table 8-4(c), a potential real difference, in which reaction times to the orange light are faster, is magnified by the practice effect.

A very similar argument can be made for contamination of the data by a carryover effect referred to as the *fatigue effect.* People may get tired or bored during the course of a challenging or long experimental procedure, and if one condition always follows another, this fatigue effect will contribute more to our estimate of performance under one condition than to our estimate of performance under the other. In the colored light example, a fatigue effect would produce a systematic tendency to overestimate reaction time for the orange light condition.

Practice and fatigue are fairly common processes, but there are numerous other carryover effects that may also threaten particular types of within-subjects comparisons. When comparing two drugs, for example, one must be sure that the first drug administered is not still active when the second is given. In actual research situations, it is often very difficult to specify all the possible carryover effects, and it is virtually impossible to assess the relative contribution to scores of carryover effects (such as practice and fatigue) that exert their influence in opposite ways. Then, too, we do not usually know the true difference between conditions in advance of experimental research.

Carryover effects are very similar to testing effects, and they constitute a threat to the internal validity of all within-subjects comparisons. That is, *a repeated measures design can also confound differences in the test situation with the measures themselves.* This possibility is illustrated in experiments (for example, Bandura, 1965: Liebert & Fernandez, 1970) designed to show that observation of a social

Table 8-4 Some Potential Consequences of Confounding the Order of Conditions with the Conditions Themselves*

SUBJECT	*(FIRST) RED*	*(SECOND) ORANGE (REAL)*	*REAL ORANGE PLUS PRACTICE EFFECT*
		(a)	
1	0.50	0.50	0.30
2	0.75	0.75	0.55
3	1.00	1.00	0.80
M	*0.75*	*0.75*	*0.55*
		(b)	
1	0.50	0.70	0.50
2	0.75	0.95	0.75
3	1.00	1.20	1.00
M	*0.75*	*0.95*	*0.75*
		(c)	
1	0.70	0.50	0.30
2	0.95	0.75	0.55
3	1.20	1.00	0.80
M	*0.95*	*0.75*	*0.55*

* Data are reaction times in seconds, and we have supposed that practice decreases reaction time by 0.20 for every subject.

Source: Adapted from Johnson and Liebert (1977).

model will not always lead to as much imitative performance as has actually been learned. These studies endeavored to substantiate the learning-performance distinction by first exposing children to an exemplary model and then permitting them to perform imitative responses spontaneously. Thereafter, as a test of learning, all subjects were specifically asked to reproduce as many imitative responses as they could. Results showed, in both experiments, that the second test produced more matching imitative responses than the first. Do these studies unambiguously support the hypothesis? No. An alternative explanation is that performance became more imitative on the second test merely as a function of the subject's being exposed to the first (as, for example, by stimulating recall through exposure to the situation). In such instances the initial hypothesis may be correct; it simply cannot be demonstrated adequately by a repeated measures design. It has now been shown that imitative recall *does* exceed imitative performance in such situations when the more appropriate between-subjects design is used. In such a design half the subjects are immediately given a learning test ("Show me what the lady did"), and the remaining subjects are tested for spontaneous imitative performance (Liebert, Sobol, & Copemann, 1972).

To guard against potential erroneous conclusions which result from carryover effects in within-subjects comparisons, investigators commonly use a procedure called *counterbalancing.* The general purpose of counterbalancing is much like that of assigning subjects randomly to treatment conditions: Potential error resulting from carryover effects is distributed equally across all conditions of the study, thereby tending to cancel out these interferences. When subjects in a within-subjects experimental design are run in a counterbalanced way, an equal number receive the treatments in *A-B* order and in *B-A* order. All the problems illustrated in Table 8-4 would have been avoided if half the subjects had seen the lights in the order orange-red and the other half had seen them in the order red-orange.

A major limitation of counterbalancing is that it becomes quite complicated whenever more than two treatments are involved. For example, although there are only two possible orders of two treatments (*A-B* and *B-A*), there are *six* possible orders of three treatments (*A-B-C, B-C-A, C-A-B, C-B-A, B-A-C,* and *A-C-B*) and *twenty-four* possible orders of four treatments, too many to list here. One solution to this problem is to pick randomly a few of the possible orders and then, again randomly, assign subjects in equal numbers to each of the selected orders. Another alternative is to create a randomized order of treatments for each subject. In either case, by using the powerful tool of random assignment, one can control many carryover effects.

But a word of caution is also needed. *Counterbalancing the order of administration of treatments across subjects in a within-subjects experiment is an effective way to deal with carryover effects only when we are reasonably certain that the carryover effect from treatment A to treatment B is the same as the carryover effect from treatment B to treatment A.* For example, if one treatment is more fatiguing than the other, counterbalancing the order of presentation will not equally distribute the carryover effects to the two conditions. Thus the decision whether to use within-subjects experimental designs must be based on knowledge of the likely magnitude of possible carryover effects, and in many circumstances this knowledge will not be available to the experimenter.

FOR REVIEW AND DISCUSSION

1. Tests of statistical significance need not be limited to only two experimental conditions. In cases in which three or more conditions are used, the implications of the *F* statistic are identical with the two-group experiment. Suppose an experiment is performed in which different amounts of reinforcement are given to three groups of rats: Group *A* receives 15 pellets, group *B*, 10 pellets, nd group *C*, 5 pellets. The dependent measure is running time through an alley. The mean running time for rats in groups *A*, *B* and *C* are 5 seconds, 7 seconds, and 8 seconds respectively, and the *F* ratio is 1.05 (not significant).The experimenter concludes that, in general, amount of reinforcement does not affect behavior. Is this statement justified? Suggest design factors that may have resulted in a failure to find an experimental effect.

2. Matching of subjects in an experiment is often carried out indiscriminately, without consideration of the consequences. Under what conditions is it useful to match subjects? When might this procedure detract from the results of an experiment?
3. Discuss the advantages of the factorial design over other designs.
4. Draw graphs illustrating the results of the following experiments. What kinds of interaction, if any, are shown?
   (a) In an experiment intended to determine the effects of anxiety on performance, a 2×2 factorial design is used. Factor *A* is manipulated anxiety level (high or low) and Factor *B* is task difficulty (complex or simple). The results indicate that poor performance on the dependent measure results from both (a) high anxiety and complex tasks and (b) low anxiety and simple tasks; good performance is associated with (a) high anxiety and simple tasks and (b) low anxiety and complex tasks.
   (b) In a 2×2 factorial experiment the effects of drugs (400 or 800 mg. a day) and treatment (psychoanalysis or milieu therapy) on patient improvement are observed. Good improvement is associated with (a) high drug level and psychoanalysis, (b) low drug level and psychoanalysis, and (c) high drug level and milieu therapy. Poor improvement goes with low drug level and milieu therapy.

9

Mixed Designs

DEFINITION OF MIXED DESIGNS
USES OF MIXED DESIGNS
Demonstrating the Generality of Experimental Effects
Identifying Limitations of an Experimental Effect
Identifying Antagonistic Interactions Between Classificatory and Manipulated Variables
INTERPRETING MIXED DESIGNS: FALLACIES IN CAUSAL INFERENCE
FOCUSING ON THE CLASSIFICATORY VARIABLE IN A MIXED DESIGN
SELECTING GROUPS FOR A MIXED DESIGN
FOR REVIEW AND DISCUSSION

Throughout the previous chapters, we have seen how social science proceeds from observing events to detecting associations between events and finally to attempts at making causal inferences. Our intent has been to present an integrated view of various research strategies, emphasizing their commonalities as well as their differences. But in actual research practice, there appears to be a strong division between scientists who typically use the correlational method and those who favor the experimental method. Indeed, the separation of these two methods was strong enough for Cronbach (1957) to refer to them as "the two disciplines of scientific psychology."

As early as 1879, Wilhelm Wundt, the founder of modern psychology, argued that the experimental and correlational strategies are complementary for gathering complete information about a particular problem. The schism between the two approaches can be traced, in part, to the writings of John B. Watson, who eschewed the correlational technique by suggesting that the existing (or preexisting) characteristics of people, often focused on in correlational research, are less important as determinants of behavior than are environmental influences, which can be manipulated. Watson (1929), whose viewpoint often bordered on the extreme (see Chapter 1), wrote:

> Give me a dozen healthy infants, well-formed, and my own specified world to bring them up in and I'll guarantee to take any one at random and train him to become any type of specialist I might select—doctor, lawyer, artist, merchant-chief, and, yes, even beggar-man and thief, regardless of his talents, penchants, tendencies, abilities, vocations, and race of his ancestors (p. 104).

The experimental tradition that followed in Watson's wake has not focused on sampling subjects from the broadest possible backgrounds in order to demonstrate experimental effects. Instead, experimental research has typically focused on either very homogeneous groups (for example, highly inbred strains of laboratory rats, undergraduate college students enrolled in psychology courses, or children from one school with relatively similar socioeconomic backgrounds). When subjects sharing many characteristics are used in an experiment, potential differences that occur in the larger population, whether within a species or within a community, tend to be masked. Single-subject research (discussed in detail in Chapter 10), of course, is completely impervious to effects of individual differences.

In this chapter we will demonstrate that the correlational and experimental approaches, Cronbach's "two disciplines of scientific psychology," can indeed be fruitfully merged in the manner implied by Wundt, in what we call a *mixed design.*

DEFINITION OF MIXED DESIGNS

As was noted in Chapter 7, experimental design involves randomly assigning subjects from the same initial population to two (or more) groups and then providing different treatments for each group. Subsequently, if the groups differ, the differences can be attributed to the experimental treatment. In contrast, *a mixed design is one in which subjects from two or more discrete and typically nonoverlapping populations are assigned to each treatment.* Thus, a mixed design always includes at least one classificatory variable and one manipulated variable. Some mixed designs will yield only between-subjects comparisons; others can give rise to both between- and within-subjects comparisons.

For example, in the simplest possible between-subjects case (a 2 × 2 factorial design), subjects might first be divided by sex and then assigned randomly to a treatment or a no-treatment condition. Suppose that the researcher was interested primarily in the effects of special training on young children's motor skills. Recognizing the possibility of sex differences leads the investigator to use a mixed design rather than a simple two group (treatment-control) experiment in which the sexes are not distinguished. A sample of boys and girls is obtained, and then within each group half the participants are randomly assigned to the special training regimen and the remainder get no special treatment. Table 9-1 illustrates the design. The design is *mixed* because the first factor of the investigation (sex) is not an experimental or treatment variable but is rather a *classificatory variable.* The relationship between a classificatory variable and the dependent variable is best thought of as correlational. The second variable (exposure to the special training) is, however, a treatment. A mixed design may involve three, four, or more factors, and each of the factors may have more than two levels. Subjects might, for example, be divided on the basis of whether they show high, moderate, or low anxiety. Then, persons from each of the three groups could be assigned to three different levels of treatment, which vary in the degree to which they are stressful. Mixed designs can also use more than one classificatory variable. In a study of the effectiveness of different methods of teaching mathematics, children could be classified into groups based on both gender and age. Mixed designs can also use within-subjects comparisons. In the study of anxiety and stress mentioned previously, the stress variable could be used in a within-subjects manner. In this case, subjects with either high, moderate, or low levels of anxiety would *each* experience the three different stress treatments.

If the divisions among subjects on the classificatory variables are potentially of practical or theoretical significance, the mixed design has many features to commend it over simpler "straight" experimental designs. We consider some of these features next.

Table 9-1 Schematic of a Mixed Design with Two Factors, Sex and Training in Motor Skills. Sex Is the Classificatory Variable, Training the Experimental One.

	BOYS	*GIRLS*
Training		
No Training		

USES OF MIXED DESIGNS

All mixed designs permit the researcher to obtain correlational and experimental evidence simultaneously as two separable main sources of variability on a given measure. Such a design may be used primarily for this purpose, but it can also disclose the generality of experimental findings or point to their limitations. As we shall see, in either case the sensitivity of the significance test may be increased by reducing error variance.

Employing a mixed design so that correlational and experimental data may be simultaneously collected often turns out to be a straightforward procedure. For example, Mischel and Metzner (1962) investigated children's willingness to choose large, delayed rewards over smaller but immediately available gratifications as a function of both the length of the delay period (an experimentally manipulated variable in which the wait interval varied in five levels from one day to four weeks) and the age of the children (a classificatory variable involving children at each of six grade levels). Both their expectations, that willingness to delay gratifications would be greater for older than for younger children and would decrease with longer delay intervals, received support in this mixed design.

Demonstrating the Generality of Experimental Effects

Mixed designs can demonstrate the generality of an experimental effect across variables such as age, sex, or socioeconomic status. Suppose, for example, that two methods of teaching a foreign language are being compared, a traditional method and a newer one. The investigator might combine this experimental manipulation (type of language training) with four ages of students (5, 7, 9, and 11) in a 2×4 mixed design. One possible outcome of the research appears in Figure 9-1, which shows the new form of training to be better than the traditional one regardless of a pupil's age.

Certain perils are associated with attempting to show the generality of an experimental effect in this way, because the logic of concluding generality is conceptually equivalent to accepting the null hypothesis (see Chapter 5). The same language experiment could have been conducted with four subjects in each of the eight cells of the 2×4 design, yielding results such as those shown in Figure 9-2. Analysis of these data might show significant effects for treatments and for age but no significant interaction. Yet one would be reticent to conclude that the new treatment worked better than the older one for all ages—it clearly did *not* work for the five-year-olds in this particular experiment. In such an instance the investigator will have to proceed with common sense and knowledge about the variables involved. He or she may wish to devise new tests or use a more sensitive design to study the apparent anomaly. For example, five-year-olds might be specifically compared with eleven-year-olds in a 2×2 design.

Mixed designs may also increase the sensitivity of an experimental test. An investigator may fail to detect an experimental effect because of great within-group variability. Consider an investigation of the effects of witnessing a prosocial

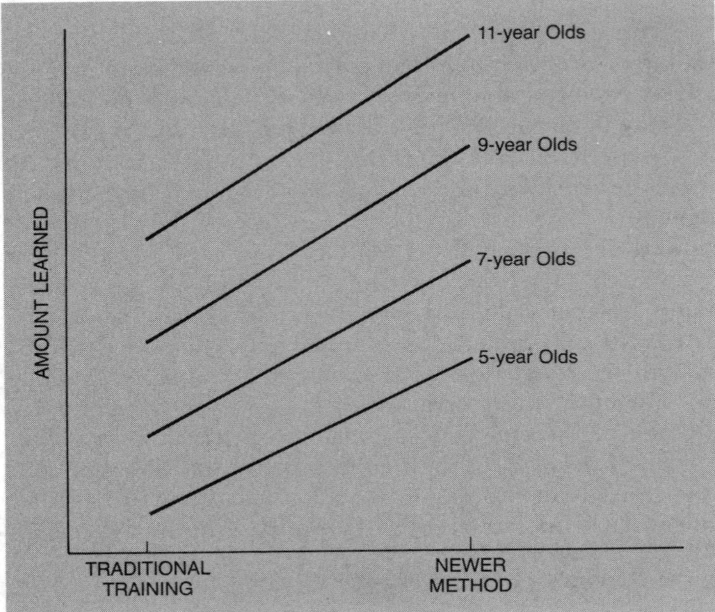

Figure 9-1 Effects of two methods of teaching on children of varying ages, illustrating the generality of an experimental effect. For all ages, the newer method is superior.

television program on subsequent prosocial behavior of first grade children. Both male and female children are randomly assigned to either a prosocial or neutral TV condition, and their prosocial behavior is subsequently assessed.

The data from this hypothetical study are presented in Table 9-2. Let us suppose that the investigator, thinking that sex will not be important, ignores sex and analyzes the data for an effect due to the treatment. A graphic representation of this analysis, shown in Figure 9-3, demonstrates considerable overlap between the two treatment groups (the shaded area in the figure) and little effect of the treatment.

Table 9-2 shows, though, that there is a considerable difference between the girls and boys. The data, plotted separately for each sex, are shown in Figure 9-4. The inclusion of the classificatory variable reduces the amount of overlap between groups. Comparing Figures 9-3 and 9-4, we see that the latter has a considerably smaller shaded area; therefore, the mixed design provides a more sensitive test of the hypothesis under consideration by reducing error variance (see Chapter 7).

Identifying Limitations of an Experimental Effect

One of the most valuable uses of mixed designs is to disclose the limitations of an experimental effect. Consider an investigation by Poulos and Davidson (1971). These investigators were interested in determining the effectiveness

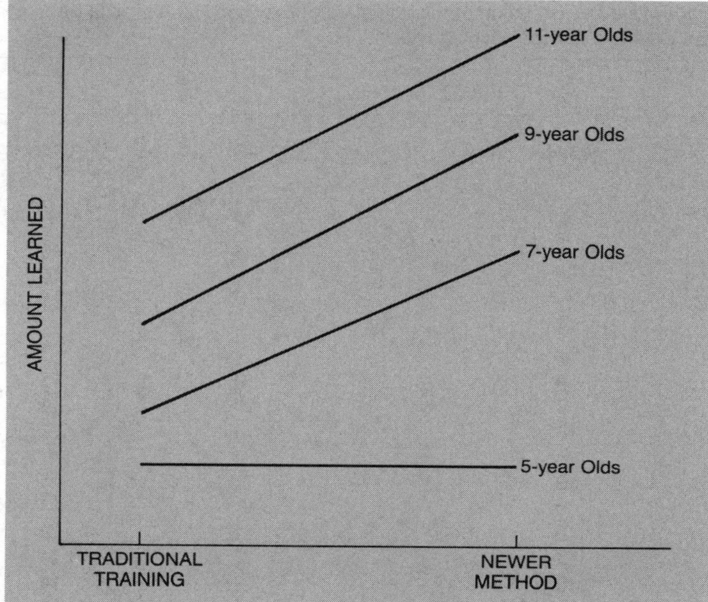

Figure 9-2 Effects of two methods of teaching foreign languages on children of varying ages, illustrating the presence of differential effects depending on age which were not statistically detected. The newer method seems to be superior for all ages except the 5-year-olds.

of a short film, "The Red Toothbrush," on children's attitudes toward the dentist. The film, which was designed primarily to create more positive reactions toward the dentist in fearful children, depicts two children visiting a dentist's office. One child, an eight-year-old boy, is fearless throughout. He enters the dentist's office, seats himself in the dental chair, and is the subject of a dental examination and cleaning, which includes the use of a dental mirror, probe, and belt-driven rotary polishing instrument. At the conclusion of the session, he receives a reward, a red toothbrush. The second child, a four-year-old girl depicted as initially fearful, is shown observing the behavior of the fearless child. This period of observation is seen to result in a gradual diminution of her own fears. Then, after watching the first child, she is seated in the dental chair and willingly goes through the dental procedure with the same instruments.

The fearful child in this film was expected to provide a model to whom the viewer, even if initially fearful, could relate. However, since both of the characters in the film were quite young, one possibility was that the film would be effective only for young children. To determine whether this was true, children in the Poulos and Davidson research were divided into two age groups: under and over seven years. Within these groupings, some of the children saw "The Red Toothbrush" and others did not. As seen from Figure 9-5, an interaction between film and age of the observer was obtained. The positive effect of the film was limited to children under seven.

Table 9-2 Results of a Hypothetical Investigation of the Influence of Exposure to Prosocial Behavior on Television on Children's Prosocial Behavior

	CONDITION				
	Neutral TV	*Prosocial TV*		*Neutral TV*	*Prosocial TV*
Females	3	5	*Males*	7	9
	4	6		8	10
	4	6		8	10
	5	7		9	11
	5	7		9	11
	5	7		9	11
	6	8		10	12
	6	8		10	12
	6	8		10	12
	6	8		10	12
	7	9		11	13
	7	9		11	13
	7	9		11	13
	8	10		12	14
	8	10		12	14
	9	11		13	15

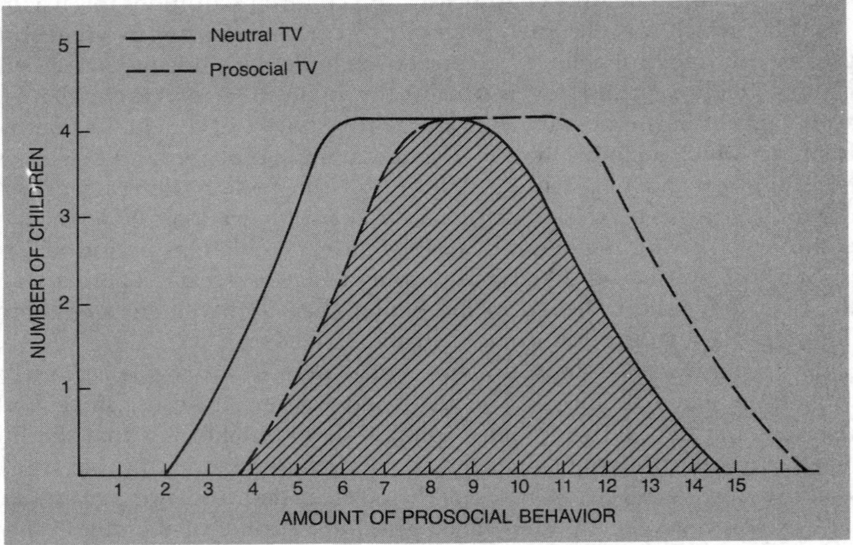

Figure 9-3 Effects of exposure to prosocial TV on children's prosocial behavior, illustrating a large amount of overlap between the two treatment groups.

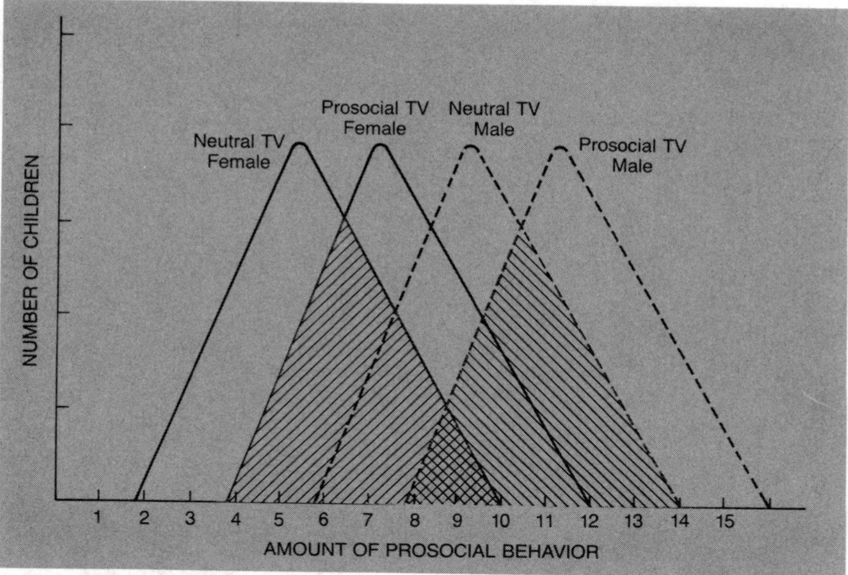

Figure 9-4 Effects of prosocial TV on behavior in male and female children, illustrating how the inclusion of a classificatory variable makes the study more sensitive by accounting for some of the overlap seen in Figure 9-3.

The advantage of using a mixed design in this way is particularly applicable to therapy studies in which it is important to identify the limitations of a particular treatment. Consider an investigation of the effectiveness of three types of treatment in psychiatric patients who have been divided into two groups on the basis of ratings of severity of symptoms. A hypothetical pattern of results from such a study is presented in Figure 9-6. Figure 9-6(A) shows that treatment 3 produces the greatest amount of improvement when patients with symptoms of low and high severity are not separated. Hence, in the absence of any information concerning differential characteristics of the patients, treatment 3 would be preferred. *But when the severity of the patients' difficulties is considered, treatment 3 would no longer be the therapeutic approach of choice for any of the patients.* As seen in Figure 9-6(B), for patients with symptoms of low severity, treatment 1 would be selected, and for patients with symptoms of high severity, treatment 2 would be selected.

Similar limitations as a function of the age, sex, socioeconomic background, and other preexisting characteristics of the subjects can be identified in other research areas.

Again, finding such a limitation can go hand in hand with increasing the sensitivity (that is, reducing error variance) of an experimental test. For example, it is possible that one would fail to obtain an "overall" effect in an investigation such as the one described above, but would obtain a significant and meaningful

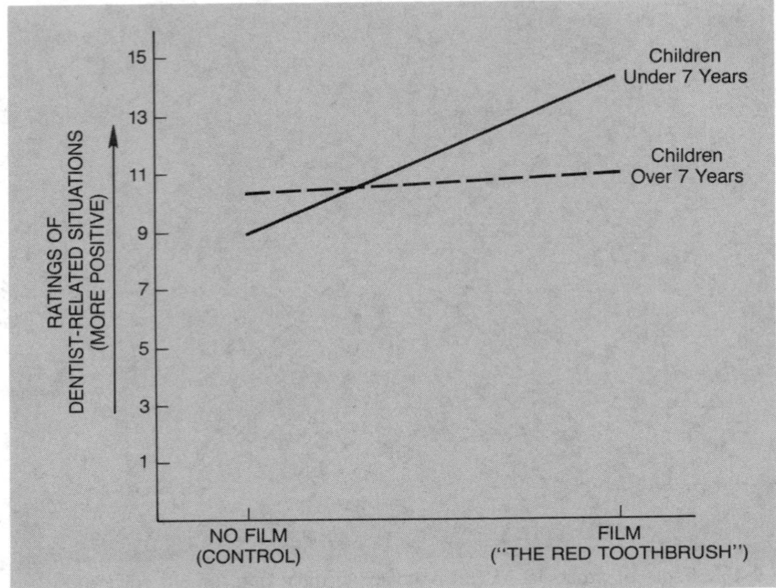

Figure 9-5 Data from Poulos and Davidson (1971), illustrating that the effects of a particular modeling film were limited to children under the age of seven.

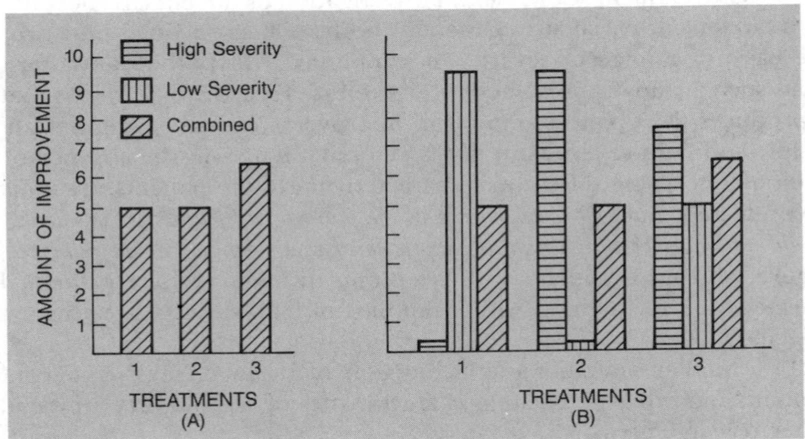

Figure 9-6 Effects of three treatments on patients whose symptoms are either high or low in severity, illustrating how different therapeutic approaches would be selected depending on absence (A) or presence (B) of information concerning severity.

interaction that identifies a subset of the population that will reliably experience some positive outcome from a given treatment. Of particular interest are certain antagonistic interactions.

Identifying Antagonistic Interactions Between Classificatory and Manipulated Variables

When a new psychological test is developed, a number of procedural decisions in standardizing its administration must be made. Critical in these determinations, and in the subsequent interpretation of test scores, is the effect of any incidental procedural detail on test performance. In addressing such questions mixed designs, by virtue of their ability to identify certain types of antagonistic interaction between classificatory and manipulated (experimental) variables, may be very valuable.

For example, if the timed and untimed subtest scores for the Wechsler Adult Intelligence Scale (WAIS) are compared for a randomly drawn sample, one would form the impression [see Figure 9-7(A)] that timing does not influence the examinee's performance. Nevertheless, Siegman (1956) has shown that timing can have a powerful effect on IQ scores, but the effect varies dramatically with the anxiety level of the examinee. The actual data from Siegman, shown again in Figure 9-7(B) according to whether subjects scored high or low on a measure of general anxiety, indicate that highly anxious persons suffer when an IQ test is timed, whereas persons with low anxiety actually benefit from the pressure that timing presumably induces. The critical point is that without the mixed design, timing would be (mistakenly) shunted aside as a variable irrelevant to IQ test performance.

INTERPRETING MIXED DESIGNS: FALLACIES IN CAUSAL INFERENCE

Most mixed designs are analyzed using the same statistical procedures (for example, analysis of variance) that are employed with pure experimental designs. Thus, it is tempting to interpret the results of a mixed design as if all the factors were manipulated variables.

The investigation that we previously discussed concerning the influence of different teaching methods on children of varying ages may be analyzed by a 2 (Teaching Method) × 4 (Age) analysis of variance, the usual "experimental" statistic. In such an instance, both the treatment and the age factors produced significant F ratios, but the interpretation of the two should be different. Specifically, although it is appropriate to speak of the different treatments as *causing* differences in amount learned, a similar interpretation of the age factor is inappropriate; age does not cause anything in the same sense that an experimental

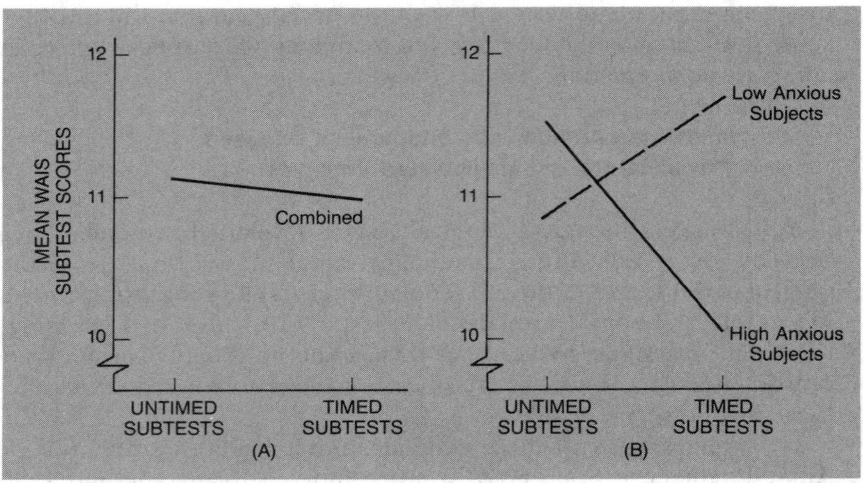

Figure 9-7 Effects of timing on WAIS subtest scores as a function of whether anxiety level of the examinee is considered.

Source: From data reported by Siegman (1956).

manipulation does. Thus, statements such as "Increasing age caused increases in the amount learned" are incorrect. It is not age per se but some underlying age-related process that produces the obtained result.

The investigator has two options in interpreting effects associated with nonmanipulated subject characteristics in mixed designs. First, he or she may be willing to describe the age factor in simple correlational terms, for example, by noting the presence of the association between age and the measure of interest. Second, the researcher may endeavor to explain, in causal terms, why the relationship is obtained. For example, it might be argued that the newer teaching method is not effective for younger children because they lack certain types of previous experience (for example, training in English grammar) on which the method is based. But any such interpretation is speculative, inasmuch as there are a number of additional ways in which age could operate. Younger children might simply learn more slowly than older ones, in which case extending the training period involved in each method would wipe out the interaction and show that the newer method can be more effective than the traditional one for both ages—when there are a sufficient number of trials. One partial solution to this dilemma is to translate interpretations of correlational results into an experimentally testable form.

An experiment could be devised in which younger children were trained using the methods as an experimental factor. The number of trials and the presence or absence of preparatory training in English grammar could also be varied. Then one, both, or neither of the hypothesized mechanisms underlying age differences might receive experimental support. Ultimately, age is merely a reflection of numerous age-related processes, virtually any of which might be manipulated experimentally.

FOCUSING ON THE CLASSIFICATORY VARIABLE IN A MIXED DESIGN

As we have noted, mixed designs may offer improved prediction when the manipulated variable affects groups of preselected subjects differentially. However, the purpose of a mixed design is not always simply to improve the prediction of behavior in a given situation. Instead, mixed designs have often been used in attempts to gather information that is more directly concerned with the correlational or classificatory variable itself. Rather than including subject variables, such as anxiety level, so that predictability may be increased, an investigator may have the *process* of anxiety as the primary interest of the study. Similarly, in many investigations involving naturally defined clinical groups (for example, schizophrenics, phobics, hysterics, and so on) both a classificatory variable (for example, schizophrenic-nonschizophrenic) and a manipulated variable are included. However, the focus of such research is not usually on the independent or manipulated variable but on differences between schizophrenic and nonschizophrenic subjects.

Consider, for example, the well-known finding that schizophrenics are slower than various contrast groups in reaction time. Such a finding may be interpreted as indicating that if one wishes to predict the reaction time of an individual, knowledge of whether he or she is schizophrenic would improve predictability. At this level, the interpretation of the finding produces little problem. However, most researchers who have dealt with clinical groups have been interested in drawing further inferences. Slow reaction time among schizophrenic patients has been interpreted as indicating that schizophrenics suffer from an inability to "maintain major sets." That is, the deficit in reaction time has been taken to implicate a particular process involved in schizophrenic pathology (Shakow, 1962).

In this example, slowed reaction time among schizophrenic patients has been interpreted as a *result* of schizophrenia. Such an inference is not logically justifiable, and, in fact, in the example, it would be hazardous because there are a number of plausible rival alternative hypotheses for the slowed reaction time of schizophrenics. For example, schizophrenic patients are likely to be on high doses of tranquilizing medication, whereas the other subjects are not. In many investigations, schizophrenics who have been institutionalized for long periods are compared with noninstitutionalized subjects. The slowed reaction time of schizophrenics could thus be due to either the medication or the apathy associated with long-term institutionalization. The crux of the problem, then, is that in addition to the presence or absence of the schizophrenic diagnosis, a schizophrenic group and a contrast group are likely to differ on a number of other, perhaps important, variables.

Investigators have often attempted to simulate an experimental design using either matching procedures (*ex post facto* analysis) or statistical control. As we will see in Chapter 10, both of these procedures are unable to solve completely the problems involved.[1] More practical issues also arise.

Consider the problem of trying to control for the fact that schizophrenics are apt to be heavily dosed with tranquilizers. Several solutions have been attempted. First, if cooperation of hospital authorities is available, the schizophrenic patients may be withdrawn from their drug regimen until the effects have worn off. Chapman (1963) has noted serious problems involved with this attempt, including the reactions of hospital staff to behavior of certain patients when medication is withdrawn. Patients who cause trouble may be put back on drugs, and the sample remaining at the end of the "drying out" period is thus a biased one, comprised of individuals with a schizophrenic diagnosis who did not react adversely to the termination of medication. Differential attrition (see Chapter 5) has occurred.

A second strategy could be to withhold medication from newly admitted patients until tests are performed, but it is not generally used. In addition to the possible ethical considerations raised by such a procedure, a large percentage of newly admitted patients are already taking medication. Further, many are in such a disorganized state that they cannot be tested.

A third attempt to gain some insight into the possible influence of drugs has been to investigate their effects in a normal population. Little gain can be expected from such a strategy. The effect of a single dose versus prolonged use by chronic patients is unknown,[2] and the same dose may produce different effects on a highly agitated acute schizophrenic than on a calm college sophomore.

Finally, some investigators have attempted to correlate level of drug dosage with the performance in question. But forming a scale of dosage level presents a problem. Rarely will all the patients in a sample be taking the same drug, and there is wide variation in the assumed equivalence of doses within different types of medication. Even if a correlation between level of drug dosage and performance were obtained, such a correlation would be difficult to interpret; the relationship could be produced by some third variable, for example, level of pathology. Patients who manifest the most severe pathology may also be those who are given the highest doses. In sum, when the focus is on the classificatory variable in mixed designs, many problems arise that are like those in purely correlational designs.

But the inclusion of a manipulated variable, particularly one with multiple levels, does offer some advantage to these investigators. Consider a study (Neale, 1971) in which schizophrenic and nonschizophrenic subjects were administered

[1] Both matching and statistical control may lead to problems such as unrepresentative subpopulations and cannot handle all possible variables.

[2] In fact, there is reason to suspect that they *would* be different; for example, under prolonged high dosage, adverse side effects have been reported in clinical populations (May, 1968).

an information-processing task of four different levels of complexity. The subjects were briefly presented with visual displays containing either 1, 4, 8, or 12 alphabetic characters. Their task was to search the display and tell the investigator whether it contained a *T* or an *F.* The results of this investigation, which are presented in Figure 9-8, illustrate an interaction between the designation schizophrenic-nonschizophrenic and the manipulated independent variable.[3] Such an interaction is referred to as a *differential deficit.* The schizophrenics' performance was poorer than the contrast subjects' in some but not all the conditions. A differential deficit is more informative than a simple deficit on a single task. Maher (1974) explains why:

> With the hypothesis that bulls are characterized by a desire to break Royal Worcester China, we stock a shop exclusively with that item, turn the bulls loose, and watch the ensuing destruction. Our hypothesis is duly confirmed—especially if our control group is composed of mice (p. 2).

Maher goes on to point out, "Just as bulls tend to break any kind of china, patient populations tend to do poorly at many tasks." In other words the demonstration of a simple deficit provides little specific information, because the poor performance could be caused by any number of factors. The presence of an interaction, however, allows certain plausible rival hypotheses for the effect to be ruled out. For example, the equality of performance between schizophrenics and control subjects when only a single letter was presented makes it unlikely that the schizophrenics' deficit could be attributed to a general failure to comprehend the task. If the schizophrenic subjects manifested a general inability to understand the task or failed to comply with the experimenter's instructions, they should have differed from the control subjects on each of the possible comparisons.

SELECTING GROUPS FOR A MIXED DESIGN

Mixed designs always entail selection of groups on the classificatory factor of the investigation. Sometimes the decision is only whether to include a particular variable, such as sex or race. Often, however, the investigator must divide the sample on the basis of some continuously distributed information, such as previous test scores or economic backgrounds of the subjects. For instance, a researcher might be interested in the effects of stress on college students' performance on some cognitive task and choose to include the classificatory variable of general anxiety level. In such an investigation, one is interested in both the

[3] Actually, several contrast groups (convicts, nonschizophrenic patients, and hospital aides) were employed, but no differences among them were obtained. The inclusion of the convicts and nonschizophrenic patients afforded some measure of control over influences of institutionalization and medication.

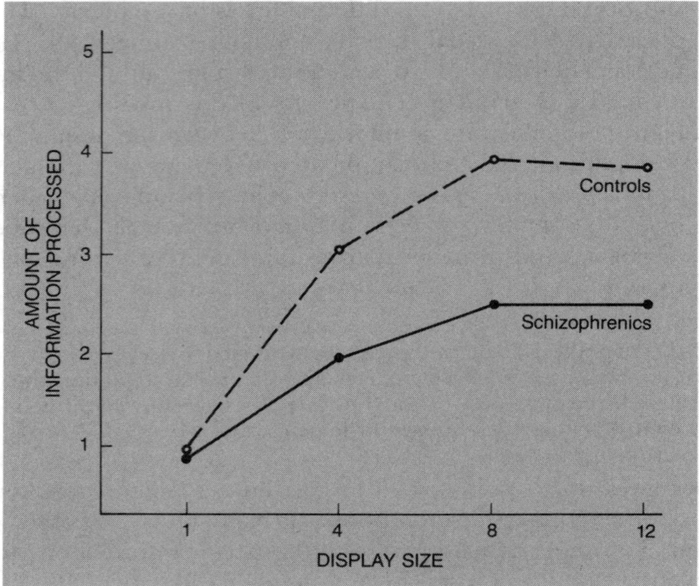

Figure 9-8 Performance of schizophrenic and control subjects on an information processing task, illustrating an interaction between the manipulated and the classificatory variable.

Source: Neale (1971).

experimental and the classificatory factors, as well as in the possible interaction between anxiety level and the stress conditions. The question arises: How should subjects be selected from the distribution of initial anxiety test scores so as to maximize the power and information value of the research?[4]

There are several ways a sample might be divided. In one strategy, the *median-split* technique, subjects are divided at the median into those with high and those with low anxiety scores. In this instance, the full range is used, either by employing all the available subjects or by selecting random samples from the above-the-median and below-the-median groups. Many studies use the *extreme groups* technique, employing subjects only from the ends of the distribution, perhaps the upper and lower 10 or 20 percent. McNemar (1960) has noted two problems involved in using extreme groups:

> Suppose each extreme group represents 10 percent of a possible supply of 170 cases—that is, 17 highs and 17 lows—and [a comparison] yields significance at the 5 percent level. Now it can be shown that the obtained difference between

[4] Instead of selecting subjects, the data may be analyzed using multiple regression. In this case, the classificatory variable does not need to be arbitrarily divided, and the relationships between the full range of scores on it and the dependent variable can be assessed.

> means corresponds to a correlation of only .20. Let us take another example: 10 percent of a supply of 440 permits 44 cases for each of the extreme groups: [yielding] significance at the .05 level. This time the exultation over a significant difference actually pertains to a piddling underlying correlation of .10. Of course, there are those who shout when an actually computed *r* of .10 reaches the .05 level, but others can see the trivial basis for the shouting. By the extreme groups method everybody is kept in a state of blissful ignorance. Furthermore, the extreme groups design is particularly fallacious in case the underlying relationship happens, unbeknownst, to be nonlinear (p. 298).

Thus, the use of extreme groups may lead to an overestimation of the importance of "significant results." In addition, as McNemar noted, fallacious interpretations may be made if the relationship between the classificatory and dependent variable is nonlinear (see Chapter 3). Let us return to our earlier example of the effects of anxiety on learning. Four groups of subjects are constructed by factorial combination of anxiety with the amount of stress induced during the learning task. The results of this hypothetical experiment are presented in Table 9-3. Note that high- and low-anxiety subjects differ only in the stressful learning task. From data such as these it might be concluded that on stressful learning tasks there is a general relationship between anxiety and learning (the higher the anxiety, the poorer the learning).

Suppose, however, that the high- and low-anxiety subjects were selected from the upper and lower 10 percent of a distribution of scores, whereas the relationship between anxiety and learning is curvilinear in the total population. A depiction of this possibility is illustrated in Figure 9-9. The figure shows that learning is optimal in subjects with moderate levels of anxiety. This discovery could not have been made from an extreme-groups study, because the most relevant subjects were thrown out before the investigation began! Hence, when extreme groups are employed, conclusions about the overall relationship between the classificatory and dependent variable cannot be drawn.

If the curvilinear relationship depicted in Figure 9-9 were an accurate description of the relationship between anxiety and learning, the results of extreme groups designs would often fail to replicate to the extent that different investigators used different selection procedures or different samples. If a subsequent investigator chose the upper and lower 30 percent of subjects and all other things were equal, the previous results would not be obtained. Broadening the selection of low-anxiety subjects would produce only a slight increment in

Table 9-3 Effects of Anxiety on Number of Items Learned in Stressful and Nonstressful Situations

	NO STRESS	*STRESS*
High anxiety (top 10 percent)	8.4	2.7
Low anxiety (bottom 10 percent)	8.3	8.8

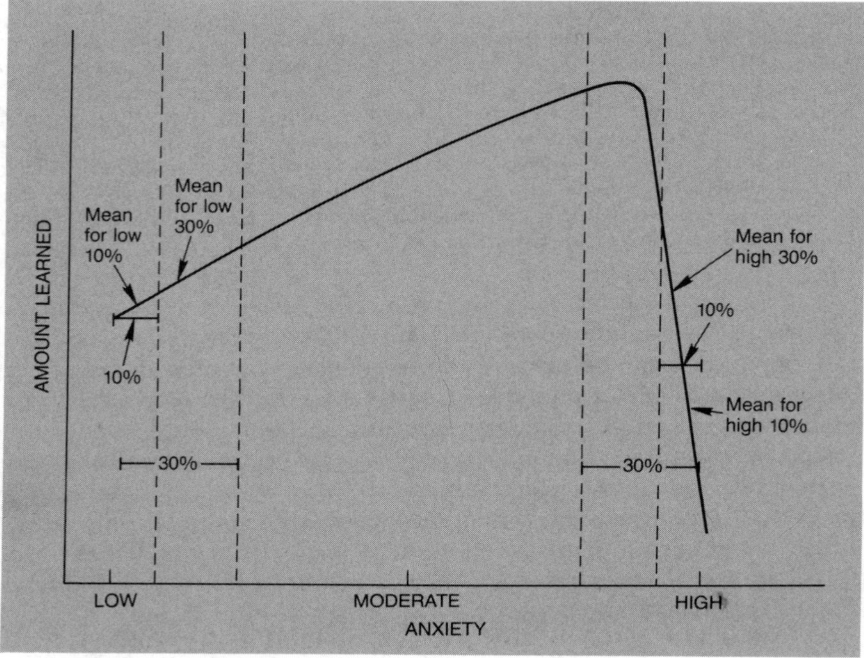

Figure 9-9 Effects of anxiety on learning, illustrating a curvilinear relationship in which differences are detected for the very extreme (10 Percent) but not for the less extreme (30 percent) comparisons.

their average score, but the scores of the high-anxiety group would markedly increase, perhaps enough so that no difference could be detected between the two groups.

One solution to the problem involves *multiple discrete leveling* of the classificatory factor. For example, in a study of the influence of anxiety on academic performance, the distribution of anxiety scores could be divided into quartiles. Such a design allows both nonlinear main effects and nonlinear interactions to be detected.

To illustrate this advantage we shall consider two alternative analyses of a study of the relationship between need achievement and persistence on a soluble versus an insoluble task. In the first analysis, subjects were split at the median (dichotomized) on the need achievement variable. As may be seen from Table 9-4(a) there were no differences for either the classificatory or the manipulated variable. However, in the second analysis, a quadripartite division of subjects was employed and an interaction between type of test and need achievement level obtained. As may be seen from Table 9-4(b), subjects who are very low or very high in need achievement persisted less than the remaining groups, but only on

Table 9-4 Dichotomized and Quadripartite Splits in a Hypothetical Experiment on Task Persistence, Illustrating the Advantages of a Multiple Discrete Leveling Procedure

(a)
DICHOTOMOUS BREAK

Soluble Task		*Insoluble Task*	
*High n Ach**	*Low n Ach*	*High n Ach*	*Low n Ach*
10	10	10	10

(b)
QUADRIPARTITE BREAK

	Soluble Task				*Insoluble Task*		
Very High	*High*	*Low*	*Very Low*	*Very High*	*High*	*Low*	*Very Low*
10	10	10	10	5	15	15	5

* n Ach, or need for achievement, is implicated in many interesting relationships. For an extensive review the reader is referred to McClelland, Atkinson, Clark, and Lowell (1953) and Birney (1968). A briefer summary can also be found in Liebert and Spiegler (1982).

the insoluble task. From a consideration of the a and b parts of the table it can be seen how the dichotomization masked the interaction.[5]

Mixed designs can clearly be used to serve many research purposes. Although they are subject to certain pitfalls of interpretation, they form one type of research strategy that can amplify the amount and type of knowledge gathered in a social scientific investigation. They also play a vital role in examining the external validity of research, as we will see in Chapter 12.

FOR REVIEW AND DISCUSSION

1. What is a mixed design? Under what circumstances is it used?
2. Suppose that an experimenter is investigating the effects of social deprivation on the power of social reinforcers such as praise. Children are placed in a small room with toys for fifteen minutes. In the social deprivation condition the subjects are left alone. In the control, or no social deprivation, condition subjects are joined by an adult female who plays with them for the entire fifteen minutes. Then a second adult female gives each subject a dull task, such as bead stringing, and praises the child for each sixty seconds of performance. The dependent variable is total time spent on the task. Subjects are six-year-old males and females, and ten-year-old males and females. Given the following sets of data, should the experimenter classify the subjects on

[5] Typically, the investigator should not try out various breaks in his or her data *post hoc*; instead, prudent *a priori* decisions should be made.

age, sex, or both? (Note: In practice, the experimenter should choose the variables on which to classify *before* collecting the data.)

(a)

	6-YEAR-OLD		10-YEAR-OLD	
	M	*F*	*M*	*F*
Social Deprivation	8	14	11	9
	5	9	8	13
	10	10	9	11
	12	12	10	13
	8	8	5	8
Control	12	6	10	9
	8	8	8	13
	10	11	12	8
	7	9	6	6
	9	10	9	10

(b)

	6-YEAR-OLD		10-YEAR-OLD	
	M	*F*	*M*	*F*
Social Deprivation	10	8	6	9
	13	7	8	11
	11	10	10	10
	8	11	11	13
	10	7	9	12
Control	10	12	11	9
	7	8	8	7
	6	13	11	11
	9	9	10	6
	11	11	13	10

3. Which of the following designs are mixed? If mixed, identify which variable is classificatory and which is manipulated experimentally.

   (a) Male subjects were given a Test of Sexual Preference, and separated into groups on the basis of their scores. One-third of the subjects in each group were then given one of three dosages of the male sex hormone testosterone. All subjects were then shown pictures of nude females. The dependent measure was degree of penile erection, as measured by a penile plethysmograph.

   Mixed (yes or no)____________________

   Classificatory variable(s)____________________

   Experimental variable(s)____________________

   Mixed (yes or no)____________________

   Classificatory variable(s)____________________

   Experimental variable(s)____________________

   (b) College sophomores were given a short course in speed reading. Three groups had courses lasting for five, fifteen, or twenty-five sessions. Then all subjects were asked to read a passage and given a test of comprehension. Within each group, one-third of the subjects were offered no money, one-third $1, and one-third $10, contingent on a certain level of performance. Dependent measures were time taken to read the passage and number of items correct on the comprehension test.

Mixed (yes or no)____

Classificatory variable(s)___________________________________

Experimental variable(s)____________________________________

(c) An investigator is interested in the effects of various treatments on reduction of fear in phobic subjects. He suspects that the type of phobia may interact with treatments, specifically that agorophobics (persons with fear of open spaces) may differ from subjects with more specific fears. He therefore divides the subjects into two groups on the basis of type of fear and then assigns members of each group to treatment groups: desensitization, insight, attention-placebo, and no-treatment control. The dependent measure is improvement in ability to approach the feared situation.

Mixed (yes or no)____

Classificatory variable(s)___________________________________

Experimental variable(s)____________________________________

4. An investigator is interested in the effects of various types of information on changing attitudes toward communist countries. She divides her subject pool into three groups based on socioeconomic status. Each group has the same original *mean* rating of the USSR. She then assigns subjects to one of four treatment groups: reading books about the USSR; exposure to panel discussions by members of the Russian embassy; viewing films about the USSR; and a no-treatment control. She finds significant differences between socioeconomic groups: high-status subjects showed the greatest increase in liking; low-status the least increase. She also finds significant differences between treatment conditions: The panel discussion produces the greatest change, no treatment the least; films produce more change than books but less than the panel discussion.

   (a) What conclusions can the investigator draw from these results?

   (b) How else could the investigator have classified her subjects? Devise a set of data to show significant effects for *both* the experimental and the classificatory variables. State the appropriate conclusions and give a plausible account of the process through which the classificatory variable might operate. Be sure your account would be testable.

5. Give a brief definition of each technique of selecting groups and give a general rule for when it should be used.

   (a) Median split (full range)

   (b) Extreme groups

   (c) Multiple discrete leveling

6. You wish to evaluate the effects of watching "Sesame Street" at age five on reading ability at age six (the end of first grade). You suspect that level of intelligence may influence the response to "Sesame Street," but you don't know the nature of the relationship. You give all your five-year-olds the WPPSI (Wechsler Preschool and Primary Scale of Intelligence), divide them into groups on the basis of their IQ scores, and assign them to experimental conditions.

   (a) What method do you use to select your groups on IQ score (remember, you don't know if the relationship is linear or curvilinear)? Why?

   (b) If the relationship is curvilinear, what effects would another method of selection (for example, extreme groups) have on your results? Graph a set of data that demonstrate the different results that might occur using two different methods of selection.

7. On TV you see the following commercial: the announcer shows a "before" picture of ten Saint Bernard puppies and ten beagle puppies all weighing approximately the same. He says that he has been feeding the Saint Bernards Grow Fast Puppy Chow and the Beagles Brand X. Next,

he shows a picture taken six months later in which the Saint Bernards clearly outweigh the Beagles. The announcer concludes that Grow Fast is superior to Brand X.

After receiving a barrage of letters from critical social scientists, the Grow Fast Company has become concerned over the quality of their research program. They come to you for consultation and advice. Point out the problem with their research and design a study that will adequately test their claim (use a mixed design).

10

Quasi-Experiments

NONEQUIVALENT CONTROL GROUP DESIGNS
- The Posttest Only Nonequivalent Peer Control Group Design
- The Pretest-Posttest Nonequivalent Peer Control Group Design
- The Simulated Posttest Only Design with a Cohort Control
- The Simulated Pretest-Posttest Control Group Design
- The Regression-Discontinuity Design

INTERRUPTED TIME SERIES DESIGNS
- Simple Interrupted Time Series Designs
  - the random interruption design
- Interrupted Time Series with Reversal (A-B-A and A-B-A-B Designs)
- Interrupted Time Series with Replication (the Multiple Baseline Design)
- The Changing Criterion Design
- Complex (Multiple Treatment) Interrupted Time Series Designs
  - the a-b-c-b design
  - decomposition interrupted time series designs
- Evaluating Single Subject Interrupted Time Series Designs
  - advantages: Sidman's arguments
- Limitations of the Single Subject Quasi-Experiment

FOR REVIEW AND DISCUSSION

In the last three chapters we have been discussing true experiments, in which treatment effects are examined between (or among) groups formed by random assignment. Now we turn to another broad class of designs, called *quasi-experiments.*

Quasi-experiments are like true experiments in that they employ the same units of analysis, i.e., they involve one or more manipulated independent variables (as treatments) compared by considering subjects' performance on one or more dependent variables (outcome measures). *The major difference between quasi-experiments and true experiments is that the scores compared in a quasi-experiment are not based on the performance of groups formed by random assignment.* As a result of lifting this requirement, quasi-experiments become more feasible than true experiments in many applied or field settings where random assignment of individuals to treatment groups is not possible. On the other hand, the lack of random assignment robs the quasi-experiment of the logical force of the true experiment and leaves it a much weaker tool for drawing solid causal inferences. In addition, whether any useful conclusion can be drawn from a quasi-experiment often depends on the specific pattern of outcomes obtained. With some patterns, interpretation is relatively straightforward; with other patterns using the same design, interpretation is uncertain or impossible. Well-designed true experiments, in contrast, are interpretable under a much wider range of possible outcomes.

There are two broad classes of quasi-experimental designs: nonequivalent control group designs and interrupted time series designs. Nonequivalent control group designs involve actual or simulated between-subjects comparisons, whereas interrupted time series designs involve within-subjects comparisons, i.e., successive observations of the same individuals as they are exposed to a succession of changes in the independent variable. Our discussion begins with nonequivalent control group designs.

NONEQUIVALENT CONTROL GROUP DESIGNS

In many practical situations people are aggregated into groups for social, educational, or economic purposes. For example, children in school are grouped into grades and classrooms, patients in hospitals are grouped into wards, and workers in many industries are grouped into shifts or work teams. These assignments are institutionally made, and ordinarily researchers cannot tamper with them simply in order to test an experimental hypothesis. Instead it is often necessary to compare preexisting or intact groups where some groups have received the treatment of interest while other groups have not.

Two new threats to internal validity exist with nonequivalent control group designs that we have not encountered before: selection-maturation and local history. *Selection-maturation* is a threat to internal validity whenever it is plausible that the groups being compared are developing at different rates on any dimension correlated with the dependent variable. *Local history* is a threat whenever some experience that might be related to the dependent variable has occurred for one of the groups but not for the other.

The internal validity of nonequivalent control group designs is also placed at considerable risk by *compensatory rivalry* and *resentful demoralization* whenever those in the control group are aware of the special or different treatment received by the experimental group. The problem is made worse by the fact that many pre-existing groups have traditional rivalries that may be brought out by giving special treatment to one group.

As with true experimental designs, quasi-experimental designs can take on different forms. We next consider the basic configurations and forms of nonequivalent control group designs and explain the advantages and limitations of each.

The Posttest Only Nonequivalent Peer Control Group Design

Suppose a computer manufacturer has two workshops in which computers are assembled and wants to see if a bonus system will increase productivity of work teams, with productivity defined as the number of computers a work team assembles in a week. The manufacturer flips a coin to decide which work team is to receive a bonus for increased productivity, institutes the bonus plan for that group, and uses the number of units produced by both the bonus and no-bonus groups for the next four weeks as the dependent measure. The design can be diagrammed as shown below, with the broken horizontal line indicating that the two groups were employed "intact," rather than being formed by randomly assigning individuals to the bonus and no-bonus conditions:

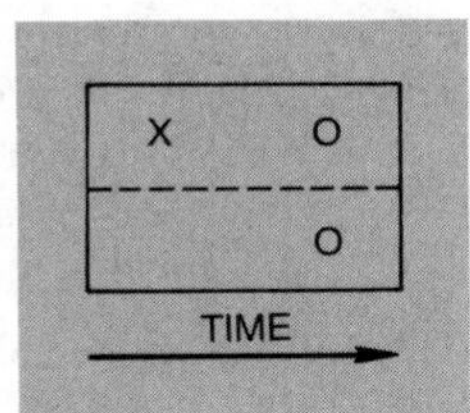

Suppose the bonus group produces twice as many units as the no-bonus group in the four weeks following the introduction of the bonus scheme, a difference which the manufacturer considers very impressive. Can we conclude that the bonus was effective in raising productivity? No. In the absence of a pretest it remains completely plausible that the bonus group had much higher productivity than the no-bonus group even before the bonus plan was introduced, so selection is a plausible rival hypothesis or alternative explanation for the observed posttest difference. In fact, selection always poses a serious threat to the posttest only nonequivalent control group design, rendering this design virtually uninterpretable in most instances.

The Pretest-Posttest Nonequivalent Peer Control Group Design

Suppose a fourth-grade math teacher has two math classes and wishes to determine if a new method for teaching mathematics to young children is more effective than the current conventional method. The teacher gives the children in both classes a mathematical achievement test at the beginning of the year and, by the flip of a coin, gives one of the classes the new math curriculum during the year while the other class receives the conventional curriculum. The mathematical achievement test is readministered to all the children at the end of the year. In this case the design would be a pretest-posttest nonequivalent peer control group design, as diagrammed below:

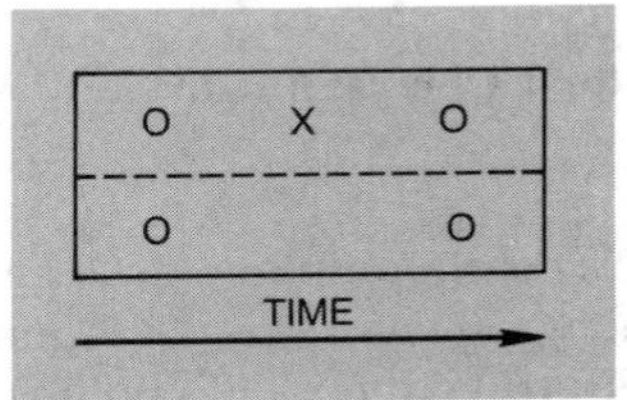

Whether this design is interpretable in a relatively unambiguous way depends on the pattern of results actually obtained. Figure 10-1 (A) shows a pattern of results in which the new treatment group was superior to the conventional group at posttest, but was also somewhat different from the conventional group at pretest. This outcome cannot be interpreted unambiguously because it is seriously threatened by the possibility of selection-maturation. That is, the children in the new curriculum group may have been progressing at a more rapid rate than those in the conventional curriculum group, in which case the difference at posttest might be explained by the difference in initial aptitude between the two groups rather than as a result of any superiority of the new curriculum. The outcome shown in Figure 10-1 (B) is somewhat more interpretable because the two groups began with virtually identical achievement scores, thus reducing the plausibility of the argument that the posttest differences occurred because of initial differences in aptitude or achievement. If the outcome obtained is like the one shown in Figure 10-1 (C), then the interpretation of the posttest difference as a real experimental effect is even stronger. Inasmuch as the new curriculum group began with lower achievement scores than the conventional group, it is quite unlikely that the new treatment group started out with an achievement advantage or were maturing at a faster rate than the conventional curriculum group.

A valuable elaboration of the pretest-posttest nonequivalent peer control group design is to employ multiple pretests, especially if the pretests are equally spaced among themselves and the same time interval also passes between the final pretest and the posttest. One possible version of the multiple pretest non-

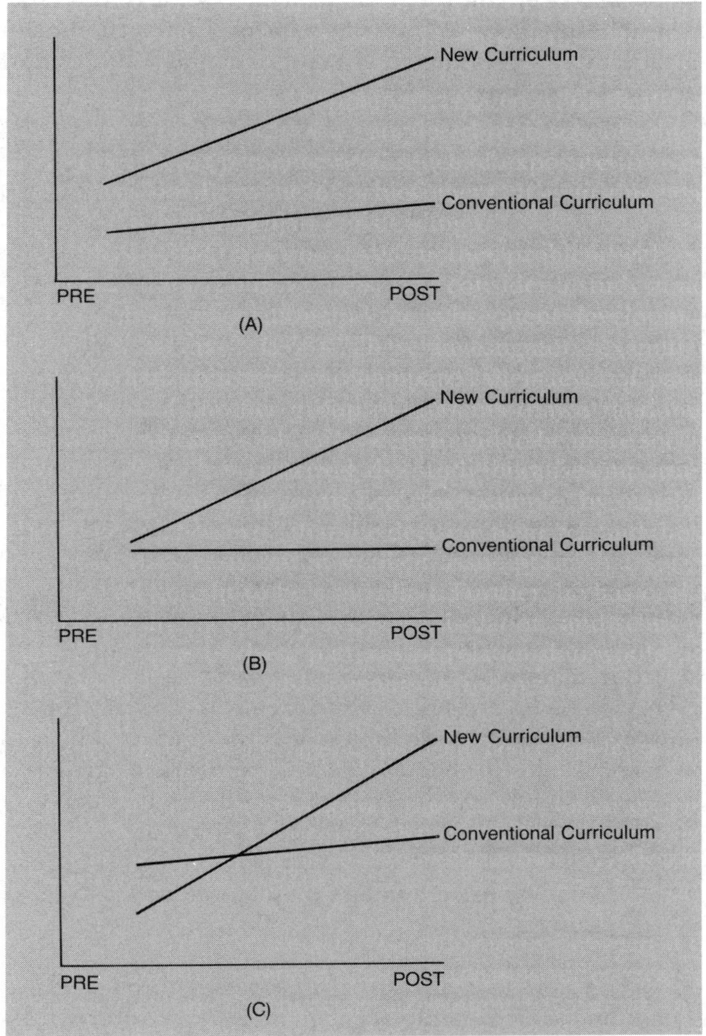

Figure 10-1 Three hypothetical outcomes of a quasi-experiment in which intact classrooms receive either a new or the conventional math curriculum. 10-1A is uninterpretable because the posttest difference may arise from selection-maturation. 10-1B is less likely to be an artifact of selection, and 10-1C is even more convincing as a real treatment effect. All three outcomes nonetheless may still be open to the threat of local history.

equivalent peer control group design, with three pretests, is diagrammed below. The multiple pretests provide a check on selection-maturation, because if the groups are progressing at different rates this would almost certainly be apparent across the pretests.

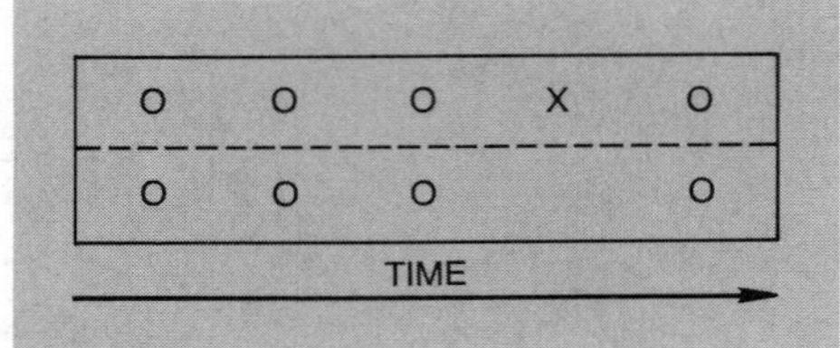

There is, however, one important threat to internal validity that cannot be ruled out by any pattern of results in a pretest-posttest nonequivalent peer control group design, and that is local history. Specifically, *local history refers to the possibility that some experience that might influence the dependent variable occurred between pretest and posttest for one of the groups but not for the other.* Whether local history is in fact a serious threat in any particular study will depend on its plausibility. Is there or might there reasonably have been some intervening experience for one group and not the other which might in fact be relevant to scores on the dependent measure? Answering this question in any real instance depends on an intimate knowledge of the situation and context in which the research occurred.

The designs we have considered so far are threatened by selection and selection-maturation because we ordinarily have no way of arguing that the groups being compared are sufficiently alike in all relevant respects except the treatment one of them has received. Simulated designs, to which we turn next, endeavor to increase the likelihood that the comparison groups are in fact sufficiently similar by simulating the kind of equivalence between groups that is guaranteed by random assignment in the true experiment.

The Simulated Posttest Only Design with a Cohort Control

A cohort is any group that passes through experiences together at the same time. For example, all the children who were in the first grade in 1974–75 form a cohort and all the children who were in the first grade in 1984–85 form another cohort. Contiguous cohorts are those which pass through an institution in immediately adjacent time periods. The class of 1984 and the class of 1985 in a college are contiguous cohorts. Contiguous cohorts are of interest in nonequivalent control group designs because they are generally highly similar to one another. In some cases it is possible to capitalize on this similarity by comparing contiguous cohorts that seem to differ only in that one of them has received a treatment of interest while the other has not. We will offer a hypothetical example loosely based on several efforts to determine the effects of the television series Sesame Street.

Suppose an investigator interested in the impact of a new educational program designed to promote reading skills in preschoolers can identify a reading test that is commonly administered in standardized form to first-grade children all over the country. If these reading scores can be obtained for a large random sample of first-graders who passed through the first grade in the year immediately before the new TV program was introduced and in the year after the program was introduced, any difference in reading scores favoring the younger cohort might be interpreted as an effect of the new TV series. Following Cook and Campbell (1979), the design can be diagrammed as shown below with the wavy line designating the use of presumably equivalent cohorts.

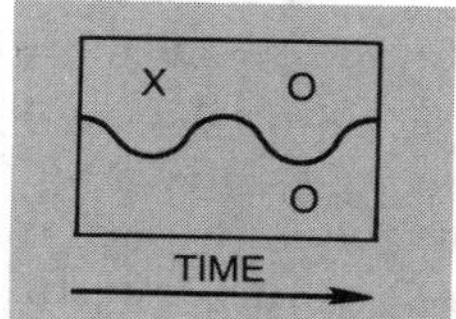

Selection-maturation is unlikely to contaminate a design involving contiguous cohorts selected on a random basis. However, the possibility of a local history effect cannot be ruled out logically (though it may be shown to be implausible under some circumstances).

The Simulated Pretest-Posttest Control Group Design

Suppose that a major public information campaign on energy conservation is about to be instituted in a particular community and a team of researchers sets out to determine the campaign's effectiveness (i.e., the degree to which it lowers energy consumption). Plainly, it will not be possible to use any of the true experimental designs; there is no practical way of controlling people's access to newspapers, radio, and television. Therefore random assignment to the campaign is not possible. However, *random selection* may be possible by identifying the relevant population—all the households in the community—and drawing two random samples. Using the simulated control group design, we would then determine the energy consumption of one group of households before the campaign is introduced with the energy consumption of the other group after the campaign has been completed. In this way we have simulated a comparison between two presumably equivalent groups (both were drawn randomly from the same population), who differ only on whether they have been exposed to the campaign at the time the measurement takes place. The design is quite sophisticated but, like all other quasi-experimental designs involving nonequivalent control groups, the possibility of local history masquerading as a treatment effect cannot be completely ruled out. For instance, in the foregoing example we cannot be sure that the two groups were completely comparable at the time their energy consumption was measured. In the interim between the time the "control" group was measured and the time the "experimental" group was measured experiences that might influence energy consumption other than being exposed to the campaign itself may have occurred.

The Regression-Discontinuity Design

In many applied settings a treatment may become available only for those who have a pretreatment status above or below some cut-off point. For example, it is common in many colleges and universities to put students who have reached or exceeded a particular grade point average for the semester on the "dean's list" at the end of the semester. Similarly, sales personnel who exceed a certain number of sales may be given an end-of-the-year bonus. We may wonder in such situations whether these special treatments improve recipients' performance in the following time period. That is, does being put on the dean's list for good grades during Semester 1 cause students to do better during Semester 2 than would otherwise have been predicted from their Semester 1 grades?

One approach to such questions is to generate a regression equation (as explained in Chapter 4) to predict Semester 2 grades from Semester 1 grades. If Semester 2 grades are higher than expected for those on the dean's list it may mean that being put on the dean's list contributes to motivation and thus to better grades. This would be true if the regression line was discontinuous, showing a "break" at the dean's list cutoff point. (See Figure 10-2.) Unfortunately, valid causal inferences can only be drawn from the regression-discontinuity design when the relationship between Semester 1 and Semester 2 grades follows a simple rectilinear (straight line) pattern across the entire distribution of Semester 1

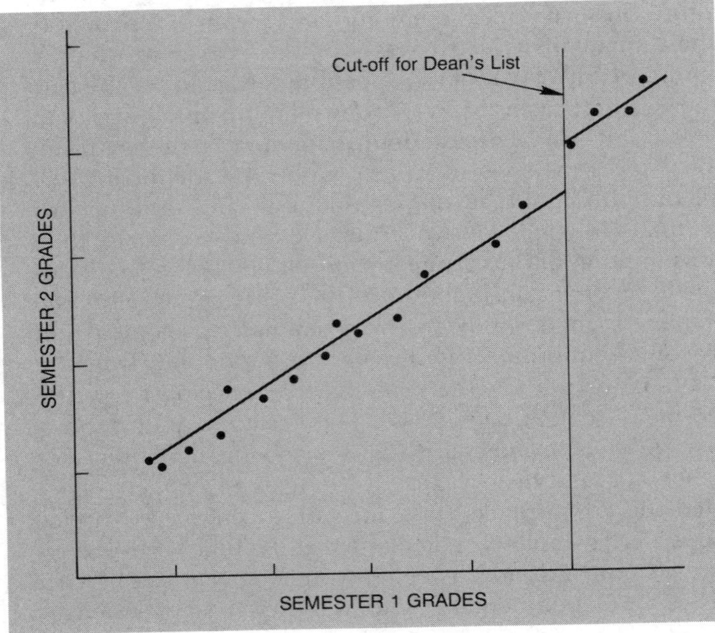

Figure 10-2 Regression of semester 2 grade point average on semester 1 grade point average for dean's list and non-dean's list groups.

Source: After Cook and Campbell (1979).

grades. In fact, however, it is plausible that the true underlying regression line is curvilinear. For example, students with higher grades during Semester 1 may be developing their study skills at a faster rate than those with lower grades, independent of whether there is a dean's list or not. In such a case the true regression line may be curvilinear, and fitting a rectilinear regression line to the data would give the impression that the dean's list award had contributed to Semester 2 grades when in fact it had not. This is yet another example of the problem of selection-maturation in quasi-experiments. The problem is further compounded by the fact that those selected for special awards, bonuses, or attention typically form only a small percentage of the total sample (i.e., only a few students make the dean's list), which makes it difficult to estimate the true shape of the distribution on the short (top) side of the cutting point.

INTERRUPTED TIME SERIES DESIGNS

We first encountered time series in Chapter 3, noting the many instances in which it is of interest to correlate the occurrence of events with time. *Interrupted time series designs are those in which the ongoing flow of events is interrupted by the introduction of a treatment at some specific point in time.* Then the question becomes whether the interruption causes the expected change in the time series.

As noted at the beginning of this chapter, interrupted time series designs involve within-subjects comparisons, that is, repeated measurement of the same subjects with changes in the independent variable occurring between successive measurements. Thus, interrupted time series designs are limited by the possibility of carry-over effects and history. That is, subjects' response to a second treatment or condition may be influenced by some residue of the first treatment (carry-over), or some experience irrelevant to the experiment (history) may have occurred between the successive treatments. In addition, maturation, statistical regression, testing, and instrument decay also pose serious threats to this class of designs under some circumstances. If any of these threats is plausible, then the internal validity of the interrupted time series design is seriously compromised.

Interrupted time series designs can be employed with either small or large groups of subjects, or they can be employed as single-subject designs. In general, the logic of these designs is the same, regardless of whether one or many individuals are involved, but using the designs with single subjects does have some unique disadvantages and advantages, as we shall see.

Simple Interrupted Time Series Designs

The simplest way to use interrupted time series is to take a measure of the dependent variable of interest, introduce a treatment hypothesized to cause a change in the dependent variable, and take a second measure of the dependent variable after the treatment has been introduced. This design is called an A-B design, in which the measurements taken under "A" occur before the treatment, whereas the measurements taken under "B" occur after the treatment. When employed with single subjects the simple interrupted time series design is often called a "clinical" trial. Many such studies have been reported in the literature of clinical psychology, psychiatry, and medicine.

To illustrate, we shall begin with a simple example. Let us assume that an investigator has designed a treatment to reduce the self-mutilative behavior of an autistic child. Using the terminology we have employed previously, the simplest experimental test of this treatment would be represented as follows:

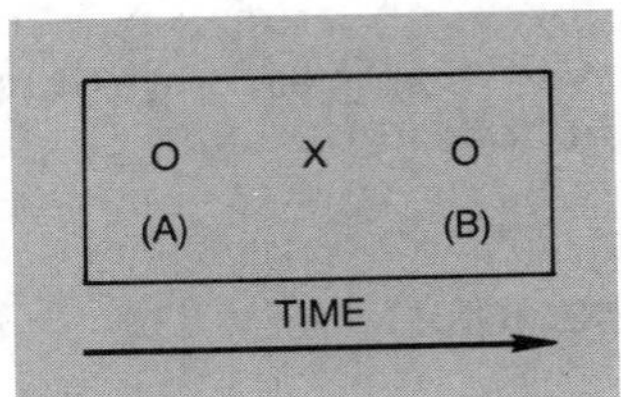

In this quasi-experiment an initial baseline period of observation O_1 was followed by the application of punishment (X) contingent on these behaviors. Subsequently, the frequency of self-mutilation was reassessed (O_2). If the frequency of self-mutilative behaviors declines from O_1 to O_2 is the investigator justified in concluding that the effect was due to the treatment? No. Such a result could also be due to any of the following sources of internal invalidity.

1. *History:* Other specific events between O_1 and O_2, for example, a change in ward personnel could have produced the effect.
2. *Maturation:* The self-mutilative behaviors could have decreased because of a "spontaneous remission" (although it should be noted that if the change produced by the treatment was rapid, maturation becomes less likely as an alternative hypothesis, since it is typically involved when the treatment is protracted and the change is gradual).
3. *Instrument decay:* The observer may have become less diligent in recording the behaviors on O_2 versus O_1 (this condition could clearly be removed by ensuring the reliability of measurement).
4. *Regression:* If the child being studied was selected for an extremely high base rate in O_1, the frequency of self-mutilative behavior can be expected to regress toward the mean, that is, to decrease on a second assessment (O_2).
5. *Testing:* Although unlikely in this particular case because of the nature of the test used, repeated testing could be especially important in similar therapy studies where a personality test was employed before and after treatment. (As discussed in Chapter 5, individuals tend to appear more "normal" when taking a personality test a second time.)
6. *Interactions among the aforementioned threats to internal validity.*

In the preceding example there was only one pretreatment measure and one posttreatment measure. However, with interrupted time series designs any number of observations can be made before or after the treatment. The simple interrupted time series design is strengthened considerably by taking multiple measures before and after introduction of the treatment.

Consider the hypothetical example in which a child who is a bedwetter is treated with a urine alarm.[1] Suppose, too, that a record is kept of the number of nights per week the child wets the bed for four weeks before the introduction of the treatment and four weeks in which the alarm is used. The design is represented in Campbell's notation as follows:

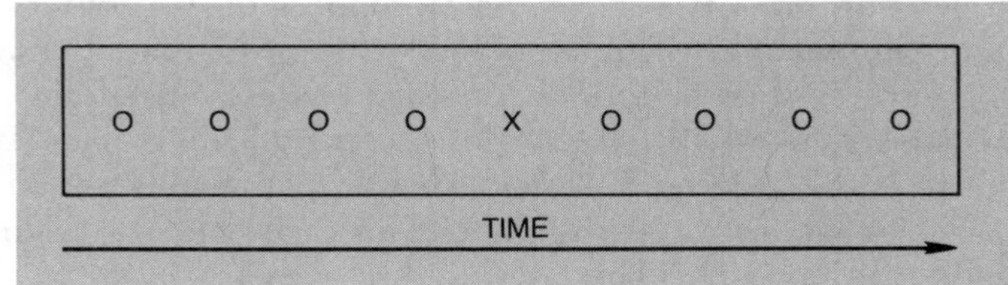

Figure 10-3 shows a fairly typical pattern of results. Supposing the child is ten years old and has never had three dry nights in a row before, the results become quite compelling.

Another way to strengthen the simple interrupted time series design is to select the point at which the treatment is introduced on a random basis.

The Random Interruption Design. Suppose that an investigator develops a treatment for a child's fear of the dark and wishes to evaluate its effectiveness with a single youngster. The investigator might assess the child's fearfulness,[2]

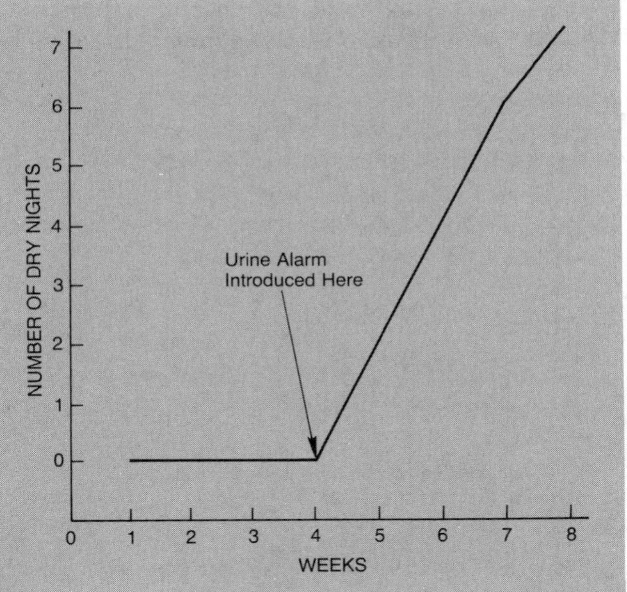

Figure 10-3 Hypothetical example of the effects of a urine alarm on the bedwetting of a ten-year-old illustrating an interrupted time series design with multiple pretreatment and posttreatment measures.

[1] The urine alarm has been successfully employed for simple bedwetting (primary nocturnal enuresis) since the late 1930s. See Houts and Liebert (1984) for a further discussion of types of bedwetting and their treatment.

[2] As, for example, by measuring how far the child is willing to be placed from an adult companion in a darkened room or by systematically darkening a room with a precision rheostat.

administer the new treatment, and then test the child again. But as we have seen, maturation, history, or testing might explain any improvement.

One possible solution can be found in a *random time series single-subject design.* If it were decided to test the child on seven separate occasions, the point at which the treatment is introduced could be selected randomly; for instance, by drawing one of the "internal" numbers (2–6) from a hat and administering the treatment after the interval drawn. Suppose that the number 4 were selected. There would then be four pretreatment assessments followed by three posttreatment assessments. If the procedure were effective, data such as those shown in Figure 10-4 would be expected. Should such results obtain, the likelihood of this particular pattern occurring by chance or by history, testing, or maturation operating in this particular way would be very low.

Thus far we have seen that the major issue in simple interrupted time series is how the time of introduction of the treatment is determined. If the decision to introduce the treatment is based on the dependent measure (for example, if patients seek treatment when their symptoms are most acute or businesses institute new practices when their sales or productivity is at its lowest ebb), then the design may allow seasonal trends or statistical regression to masquerade as a treatment effect. That is, an improvement might have occurred at about the same point in time even if no treatment at all had been introduced. On the other hand, if multiple pre- and post-measures are taken and the time at which the treatment is introduced can be decided randomly, and the effects of the treatment are dramatic and durable, then the results can be quite persuasive.

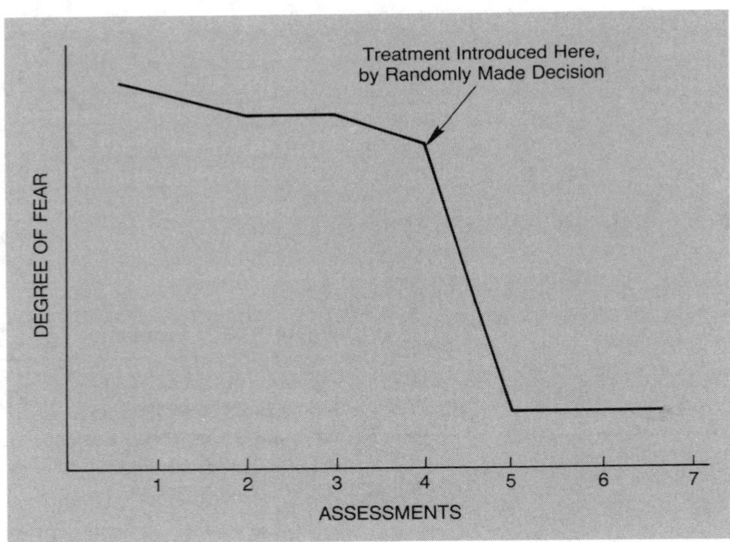

Figure 10-4 Hypothetical data from a fearful child, illustrating the random time series single-subject design.

In such circumstances we expect to see a sharp discontinuity in the dependent measure occurring immediately (or very shortly) after the treatment was introduced.

The rub of course is that not all problems are as consistent as our bedwetting and fear examples, and many treatments may have a real effect which is delayed rather than immediate or temporary rather than permanent. In such cases, more powerful designs are needed.

Interrupted Time Series with Reversal (A-B-A and A-B-A-B Designs)

Reversal designs involve careful measurement of some aspect of the subject's behavior during a given time period (as a *baseline* or control procedure), the introduction of some environmental modification or treatment during the next (*experimental*) time period, a return to the conditions that prevailed during the control period, and finally a second introduction of the experimental manipulation. The intent of this procedure, sometimes referred to as an *ABA* or *ABAB* design, is straightforward. If behavior changes from *A,* the control period, to *B,* the experimental period, reverses again when the experimentally manipulated conditions are reversed again (that is, returned to *A*), and "re-reverses" when *B* is again introduced, then there is little doubt that it is the manipulation, and not chance or uncontrolled factors, that have produced the change. And, logically, the design itself satisfies Mill's requirements (see Chapter 5).

The *ABAB* single-subject experimental design may be illustrated by a report of Tate and Baroff (1966), in which methods of reducing the self-injurious behavior of a nine-year-old boy, Sam, were investigated. The lad, who had been diagnosed as psychotic, engaged in self-injurious behavior, including ". . . banging his head forcefully against floors, walls, and other hard objects, slapping his face with his hands, punching his face and head with his fists, hitting his shoulder with his chin, and kicking himself." The investigator also reported that such acts were "a frequent form of behavior observed under a wide variety of situations" (p. 281).

Despite his self-injurious behavior, Sam was not entirely asocial. In fact, it was noted that ". . . he obviously enjoyed and sought bodily contact with others. He would cling to people and try to wrap their arms around him, climb into their laps and mold himself to their contours" (p. 282). It was this observation that gave rise to the experimental treatment. Specifically, the investigators decided to determine the effects of punishing Sam's self-injurious outbursts by the contingent withdrawal of physical contact. Their hope, of course, was that this "time-out" from human contact would reduce the frequency of the behaviors that produced it.

The study, run for twenty days, involved a daily walk around the campus for Sam. Two adult experimenters talked to him and held his hands continuously. During the control days, Sam was simply ignored when he engaged in self-injurious behavior. However, during the experimental days, the adults responded to any self-injurious actions by immediately jerking their hands away from Sam and maintaining this time-out until three seconds after the last self-injurious act. The results of the systematic reversal of these procedures, shown in Figure 10-5, illustrate the dramatic effects of contingent punishment for reducing undesirable behavior in this case. The bars show the relative frequency of self-injurious acts during each of the four periods of the experiment. It is clear that the major changes are due to the punishment rather than to chance or accident. Moreover, the side effects of the punishment procedure appear to be positive rather than negative. Tate and Baroff note:

> On control days Sam typically whined, cried, hesitated often in his walk, and seemed unresponsive to the environment in general. His behavior on experimental days was completely different—he appeared to attend more to environmental stimuli . . . there was no crying or whining, and he often smiled (1966, p. 283).

It should be apparent from the Tate and Baroff study that the single-subject design can serve as a well-controlled investigation and demonstrate convincing causal relationships. The investigators purposely reinstated the original

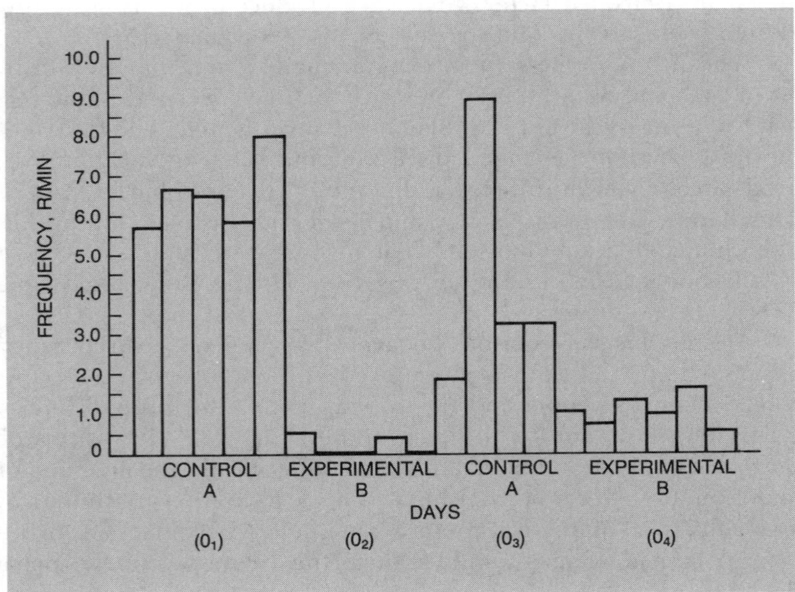

Figure 10-5 Effects of the contingent punishment procedure in Tate and Baroff's study, illustrating experimental effects within a single-subject design. (The individual bars are data for each day of the experiment).

Source: Adapted from Tate and Baroff (1966).

(premanipulative) circumstances to determine whether the subject's behavior would also return to its baseline under these conditions at time O_3. Employing this procedure, they demonstrated that the behavior under observation was indeed controlled by the systematic withdrawal and reintroduction of reward. If the change in frequency from O_1 to O_2 had been due to history, maturation, instrument decay, regression, or testing, the removal of the treatment would not have been expected to produce a difference between O_2 and O_3. The conclusion that the treatment was directly related to the decrease that occurred between O_1 and O_2 is yet further attested to by the difference that again appears between O_3 and O_4. Thus, the evidence is extremely convincing; the single-subject design clearly can lead to empirically valid causal inferences. Rather than illustrating the complexity of an individual case, the design can demonstrate a principle of behavior through the systematic treatment of one individual under controlled conditions.

Interrupted Time Series with Replication (The Multiple Baseline Design)

Sometimes use of the reversal technique is not possible. Subjects' initial state may not be recoverable, as, for example, in the study of learning. Or, as in psychotherapeutic studies, it might be possible to reinstate the initial condition of the subject or patient, but to do so would be unethical. Who, for example, would be willing to reinstate a severe depression to demonstrate the effectiveness of a treatment?

In such circumstances, a *multiple baseline* or replication is often employed. With this procedure, two or more behaviors are chosen for study. For example, a child who is having "learning problems" may be chosen and both mathematical and reading performance selected as the two areas for treatment. The investigator, after observing the child, notes that this subject is inattentive during lessons and proceeds to collect baseline data on the degree of inattentiveness during *both* mathematics and reading lessons. Subsequently, reward is introduced for attention in math lessons but not for reading. A second observation of both classes of behavior then occurs. Finally, in a third phase of the study, reward is introduced for reading as well as mathematics. A hypothetical pattern of results using this procedure is shown in Figure 10-6.

If such a pattern were obtained, it would provide convincing support for the inference that reward, and not other factors, modified the child's behavior. If one of the threats to internal validity were operative, it should affect inattention during both math and reading lessons; hence, rewarding the child's attention during math would not markedly change math *relative to reading* if some other factor were operating. Two baselines for the behavior to be modified made it possible to eliminate certain threats to internal validity without returning the subject to his or her initial state.

One important disadvantage of the multiple baseline procedure should be noted. The behaviors under study may not be independent; for example, the experimental treatment for math may also indirectly influence reading. In such

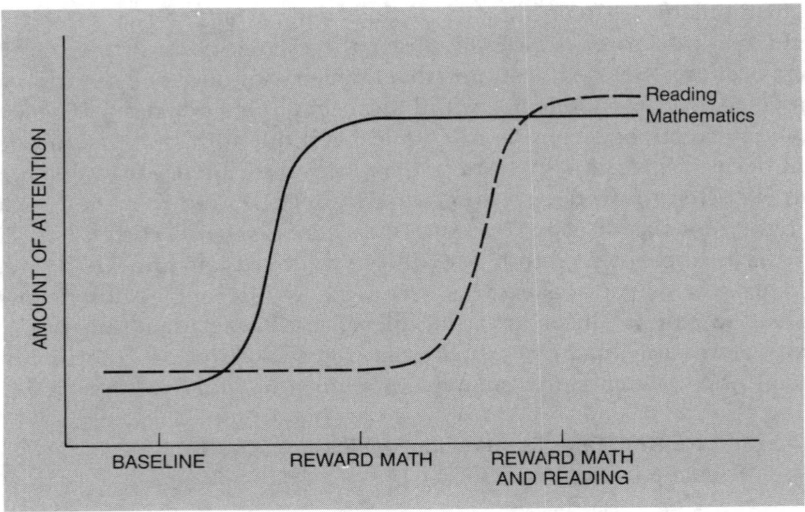

Figure 10-6 Effects of reward on attention during mathematics and reading lessons, illustrating the multiple baseline procedure.

an instance the investigator will be unable to distinguish between history, maturation, or testing and real experimental effects.

The concept of using a multiple baseline is by no means limited to single-subject designs. An analogous procedure can also be used in group studies. The difference is that, instead of employing a second dependent measure (e.g., math after reading), the group version of the design involves introducing the treatment for a second group (the "replication") after a longer baseline than was used for the first group. In group applications it is often possible to have not just one, but several replications, each with a baseline of different length.

An example of a group multiple baseline study is found in the work of Sulzer-Azaroff and Consuelo de Santamaria (1980). These investigators were interested in reducing the number of safety hazards in each of six departments of a large industrial organization. The treatment involved giving department supervisors a "feedback package" that included information as to the number and location of hazardous conditions in their departments, along with specific suggestions as to how each hazardous condition might be corrected. Before administration of the treatment a baseline measure of hazardous conditions was taken, but the duration of the baseline was 3 weeks for two of the departments, 6 weeks for two other departments, and 9 weeks for the remaining two departments. As expected, each department showed a relatively stable number of hazards for the baseline (regardless of whether it was 3, 6, or 9 weeks in length) and a marked decrease in hazardous conditions shortly after the treatment was administered. The design of this study is shown in Table 10-1.

Table 10-1 The Sulzer-Azaroff and Consuelo de Santamaria (1980) Multiple Baseline Group Design. (A is Baseline; B is Treatment.)

	O	O	O	O
First 2 Departments	A	B	B	B
Second 2 Departments	A	A	B	B
Final 2 Departments	A	A	A	B

The Changing Criterion Design

One rather interesting quasi-experimental design recently developed for single subject research is the changing criterion design. This design is a variant of the multiple baseline (replication) design but involves changing the criterion for reinforcement of a single target behavior over time rather than initiating reinforcement for two or more different behaviors at different points in time. This design thereby eliminates the possibility of carry-over effects that plague multiple baseline single subject designs.

The essence of the design is to begin by taking a baseline of the target behavior and then to introduce reinforcement for a level of the desired behavior higher than baseline. Once the new level of performance is reached, the reinforcement criterion is raised, so that a yet higher level of reinforcement is required. The reinforcement criterion is thus progressively stepped upward until some desired final criterion is reached. The unique strength of the design is that it effectively uses each step as a baseline for the next step.

As an illustration of the changing criterion design, consider a study by Hall and Fox (1977), in which a "behavior disordered" boy, Dennis, was permitted to play basketball (a favorite activity) at recess contingent on doing an ever-increasing number of arithmetic problems in his math sessions. As seen in Figure 10-7, Dennis' math accomplishments increased steadily to accommodate the increasing demands of each new criterion. The overall pattern of results leaves little doubt that it was the contingent reinforcement that was responsible for the lad's dramatically improved performance during math sessions.

Complex (Multiple Treatment) Interrupted Time Series Designs

There are many possible extensions and elaborations of the interrupted times series designs discussed so far. Each is applicable to a special set of hypotheses or circumstances, or helps to further reduce the threats to internal

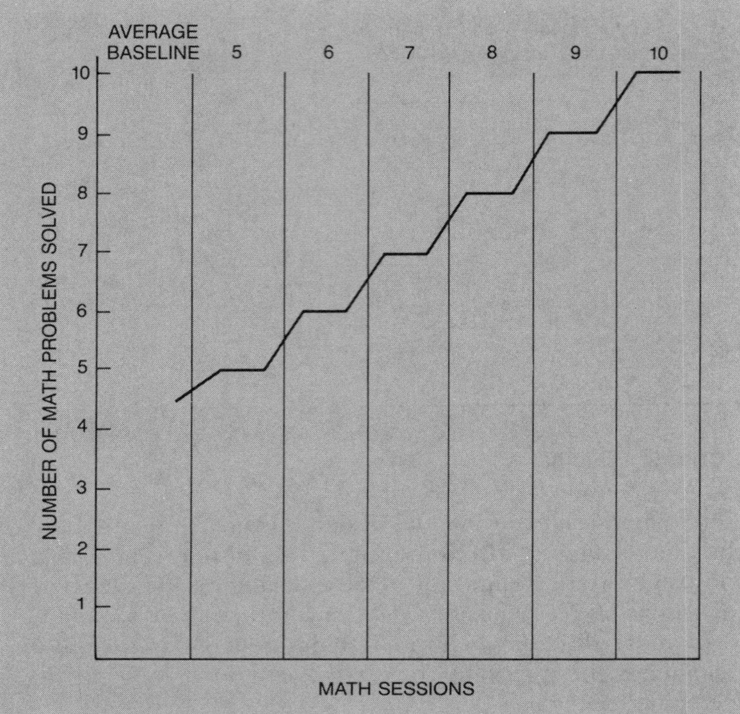

Figure 10-7 The number of math problems solved by Dennis in Hall and Fox's (1977) study, illustrating the changing criterion design.

Source: From data reported in Hall & Fox (1977).

validity that are faced by simpler interrupted time series designs. In this section we shall provide a few illustrative examples of these more complex designs. For a wider survey, the interested reader is referred to Barlow and Hersen (1984), Cook and Campbell (1979), and Kratochwill (1978).

The A-B-C-B Design. Single subject interrupted time series designs have been widely used by researchers interested in behavior modification, a family of therapy techniques that relies heavily on contingent reinforcement. One challenge that can be raised to the A-B-A-B reversal design as used in behavior modification studies is that the subjects' response to reinforcement does not necessarily demonstrate that contingent reinforcement is required for behavior change. The administration of noncontingent reinforcement might produce the same change (e.g., by diverting the subjects' attention). One way to handle this challenge is to employ the A-B-C-B design, in which A is the baseline period, B is contingent reinforcement, C is noncontingent reinforcement, and B is a return to contingent reinforcement. This design was used by Miller, Hersen, Eisler, and Watts (1974) with a 48-year-old skid row alcoholic. The dependent measure was the patient's blood-alcohol level (determined from breathalyzer samples). After eight biweekly baseline measures (A), reinforcement consisting of canteen booklets was administered contingent on a low blood-alcohol level (B), which resulted in a sharp drop in blood alcohol level. The same reinforcement was then given noncontingently (i.e., regardless of the results of the breathalyzer test), whereupon the patient's blood-alcohol level began to rise (C). Finally, contingent reinforcement was again introduced, whereupon the patient's blood alcohol soon dropped back to 0 again. The pattern of results, shown in Figure 10-8, shows convincingly that it is the reinforcement contingency and not the mere presentation of reinforcement which accounts for the change.

Decomposition Interrupted Time Series Designs. Investigators have also developed interrupted time series designs to analyze a complex treatment into component parts, to see which are the truly active or necessary ingredients. An example is a recent study of a classroom of hyperactive children in a university laboratory school (Rosén, O'Leary, Joyce, Conway, & Pfiffner, 1984). The dependent measure, recorded unobtrusively by highly trained observers, was the percentage of time which the children spent "on task," defined as "sitting and working quietly, listening to the teacher give group lessons, and working on any other task approved by the teacher" (p. 584).

The baseline here was not a no-treatment condition; rather it was taken under the teacher's usual behavior, which included both praise for on-task behavior (positive consequences) and reprimands for off-task behavior (negative consequences). After the initial baseline, negative consequences were withdrawn and the teacher simply ignored all inappropriate behavior, whereupon the per-

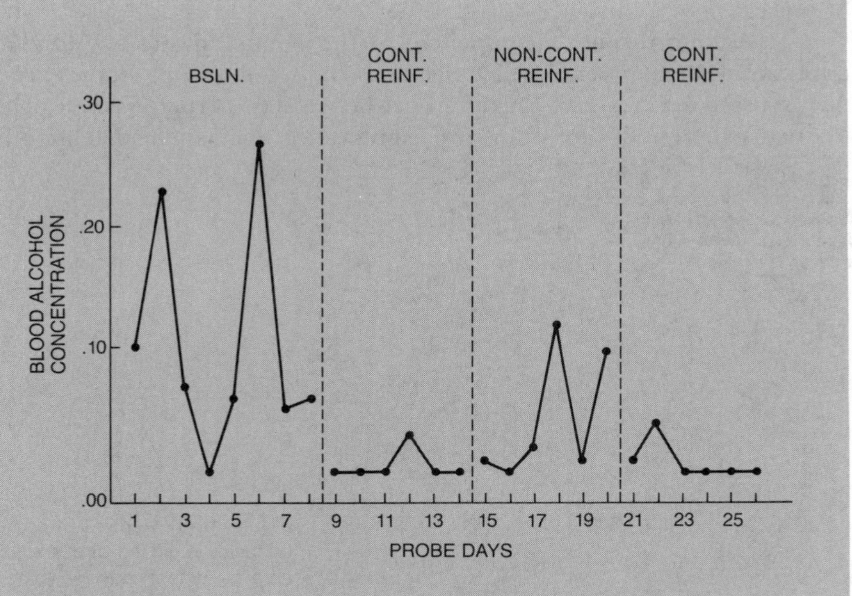

Figure 10-8 Biweekly blood alcohol concentrations of an alcoholic treated with contingent and noncontingent reinforcement for abstinence, illustrating the A-B-C-B design.

Source: From Barlow and Hersen, (1984, p. 171).

centage of time the youngsters spent on a task plummeted. The third phase was a return to baseline (i.e., reinstituting both positive and negative consequences); this quickly brought on-task behavior up again to its previous level. Next the positive consequences were removed while the negative consequences continued. In sharp contrast to what happened when the negative consequences were withdrawn, removing the positive consequences did not decrease on-task behavior. In the final phase the teacher's usual practice of both positive and negative consequences was restored. The overall pattern of results, shown in Figure 10-9, suggests that a willingness to reprimand off-task behavior is the critical ingredient in managing hyperactive children.

Evaluating Single Subject Interrupted Time Series Designs

For years a controversy has raged about the advantages and disadvantages of single subject interrupted time series designs. Our aim in this final section is to give the reader a reasonable sense of the issues involved.

Advantages: Sidman's Arguments. Murray Sidman (1960), a vigorous and outspoken proponent, has advanced several arguments that single-subject research is *preferable* to between-groups experimental study. We will consider some of these.

Among the most compelling of the points advanced by Sidman is his criticism of the manner in which data from between-groups studies are analyzed. As discussed in Chapter 7, the difference between two groups is typically evaluated in such experiments for statistical significance against the likelihood that the

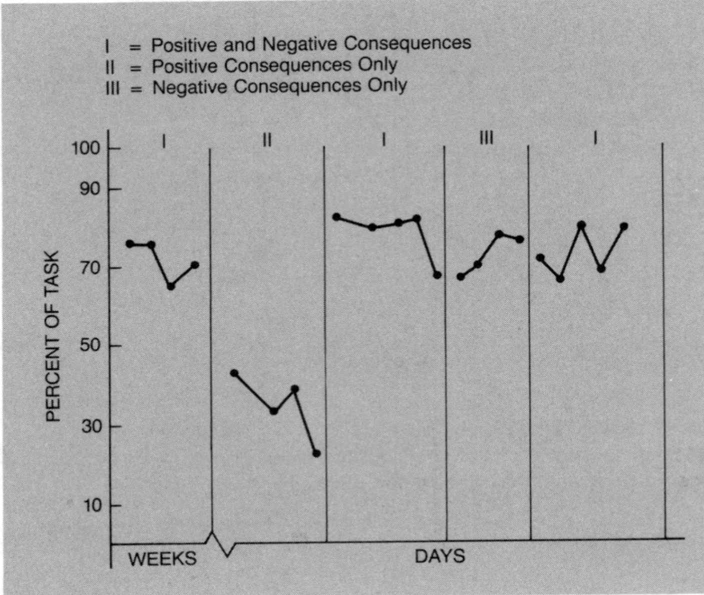

Figure 10-9 Percent of on-task behavior in Rosén et al's study as a function of positive and negative consequences, illustrating decomposition interrupted time series design.

Source: From Data Reported in Rosén et al (1984).

obtained finding would have occurred by chance. The inclusion of *chance* as a basis for evaluating experimental hypotheses forms the basis of Sidman's objection. He argues that chance, in essense, represents ignorance (that is, error variance, or that variation we are unable to successfully attribute to any specific factor). By evaluating results against "chance," we are passively accepting our ignorance.

As an example of a possible consequence of this tacit acceptance of ignorance, consider a between-groups investigation of the influence of observing appropriate social models on the development of language skills in retarded children. In one such study (Odom, Liebert, & Fernandez, 1969) children exposed to a short audio tape of an adult model producing, and being rewarded for, appropriate prepositional constructions later produced significantly more of these constructions in their own sentences than did children in an untreated control group. A follow-up approximately three weeks later demonstrated that the obtained modification in language behavior was durable even for these retarded children. From the point of view of a between-subjects experimental approach, the results proved to be entirely acceptable.

However, although a statistically significant difference between the two groups was obtained, the beneficial effects of the treatment were not uniform within the treated group. Some of the children who had been exposed to the audio tape failed to show improvement in their language skills while others showed considerable improvement. According to Sidman's argument, one might comment at this point that the between-group design may mask the weakness of a treatment. The between-groups investigator is satisfied at having produced a reliable difference between (or among) the means in his or her experiment and is thus unconcerned with the fact that variance may still be unaccounted for. From Sidman's vantage point, it would have been preferable to apply the treatment to individual children and examine the effects of the treatment on each child separately. Then if the treatment proved to be ineffective for some children, this fact would be readily apparent, and modified techniques would be sought to improve the language skills of every child.

A second major criticism that Sidman has made concerns the artificiality that may be produced by pooling data. Let us consider the question of the relationship between the number of times a response has been rewarded and the "resistance to extinction"[3] of that response. Most psychologists have assumed that one exposure to extinction (that is, a series of nonrewarded trials) will exert an irreversible influence on later exposures; therefore, a single subject could not be used to obtain the functional relationship between the two variables. In other words, it is presumed that successive introductions of the extinction procedure would be contaminated by previous ones, resulting in patterns of behavior that

[3] The term *resistance to extinction* refers to the number of nonrewarded trials, following a series of rewarded ones, in which a response continues to occur. At least for some purposes, the measure is considered an index of the strength of the response that has been established experimentally.

would not be a "pure" function of the number of rewards but rather a function of the preceding extinction experiences.

The usual solution to this kind of problem has been to conduct a between-groups experiment. Independent groups of subjects are exposed to varying numbers of rewards and then "put on extinction." The data points for the groups of subjects are then connected to represent the functional relationship between number of rewards and resistance to extinction. For example, in Figure 10-10, separate groups of subjects were given 10, 20, 30, or 40 rewarded trials for a particular response, and then reward was withheld for subsequent responses. The curve drawn connecting the data from each group is then taken as an expression of the functional relationship between the two variables.

Sidman has two related arguments against procedures such as the one just described. First, he argues that the function obtained does not represent the underlying behavioral process accurately; that is, the "uncontaminated" extinction data obtained from separate groups yields a functional relationship that *has no counterpart in the behavior of the individual subjects.* Since the "pure" relationship doesn't exist, we should stop trying to find it. Sidman's second argument is a mathematical variant of the first, showing explicitly that the behavior of individuals cannot be adequately deduced from a group curve.

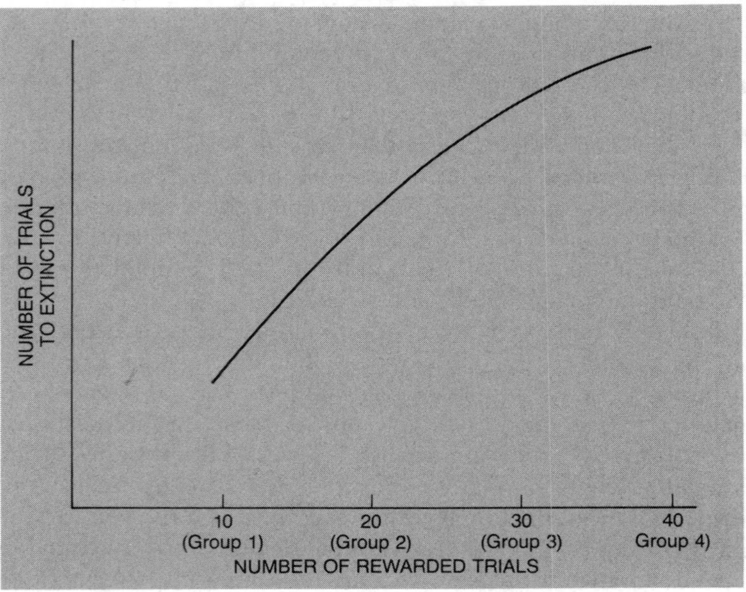

Figure 10-10 Resistance to extinction in four different groups of subjects who had received different numbers of rewarded trials. The data from each group are then connected to obtain the theoretical function relating number of rewarded trials to resistance to extinction.

Sidman's argument is an attack on the general practice of averaging results over a group of subjects. Consider, for example, a study in which children are asked to predict which of two lights will illuminate on a given trial. Five children are tested in five trial blocks of ten trials each in which the experimenter presents them with a double alternation pattern of lights (the left light illuminates twice, then the right light twice, and so on).

The results of this hypothetical study, averaged over all five children, are displayed in Figure 10-11. There is a smooth increase in the probability of correct responses from the first to the fifth block of trials. From data such as these, it might be concluded that learning is a gradual or *continuous* process. However, an examination of the data from individual subjects might not produce such a conclusion.

Such a pattern is shown in Figure 10-12, which plots the data for each individual child. When individual children are considered, the learning process appears to be *dis*continuous. For each child the probability of correct responding jumps from 0.50 (chance performance, since there are only two alternatives) to 1.00. Since the transition occurs at different times for different children, the averaged curve appears continuous and smooth. However, in this instance, if the behavior of the individual children had not been examined, an erroneous conclusion about the nature of the learning process could have been drawn.

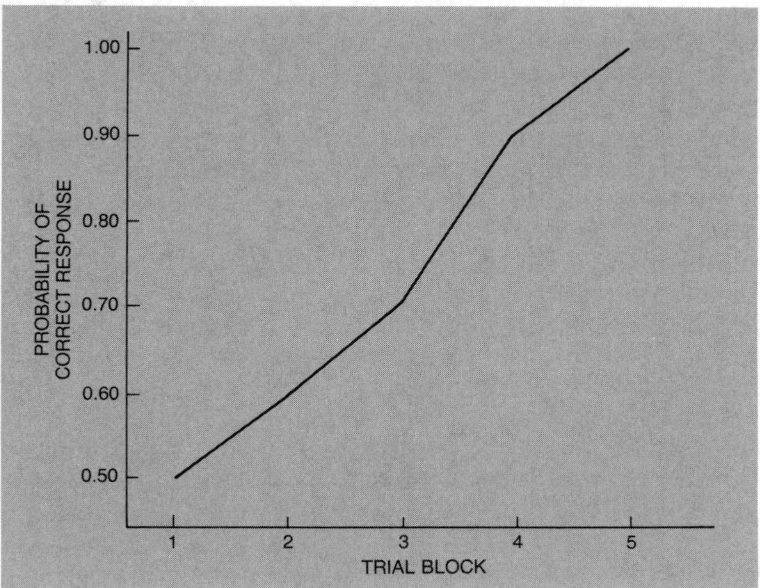

Figure 10-11 Results of hypothetical learning experiment with five children, illustrating a continuous increase in probability of correct response when the data are averaged over children. The smooth curve, though, may not tell us how individual subjects actually learn over trials.

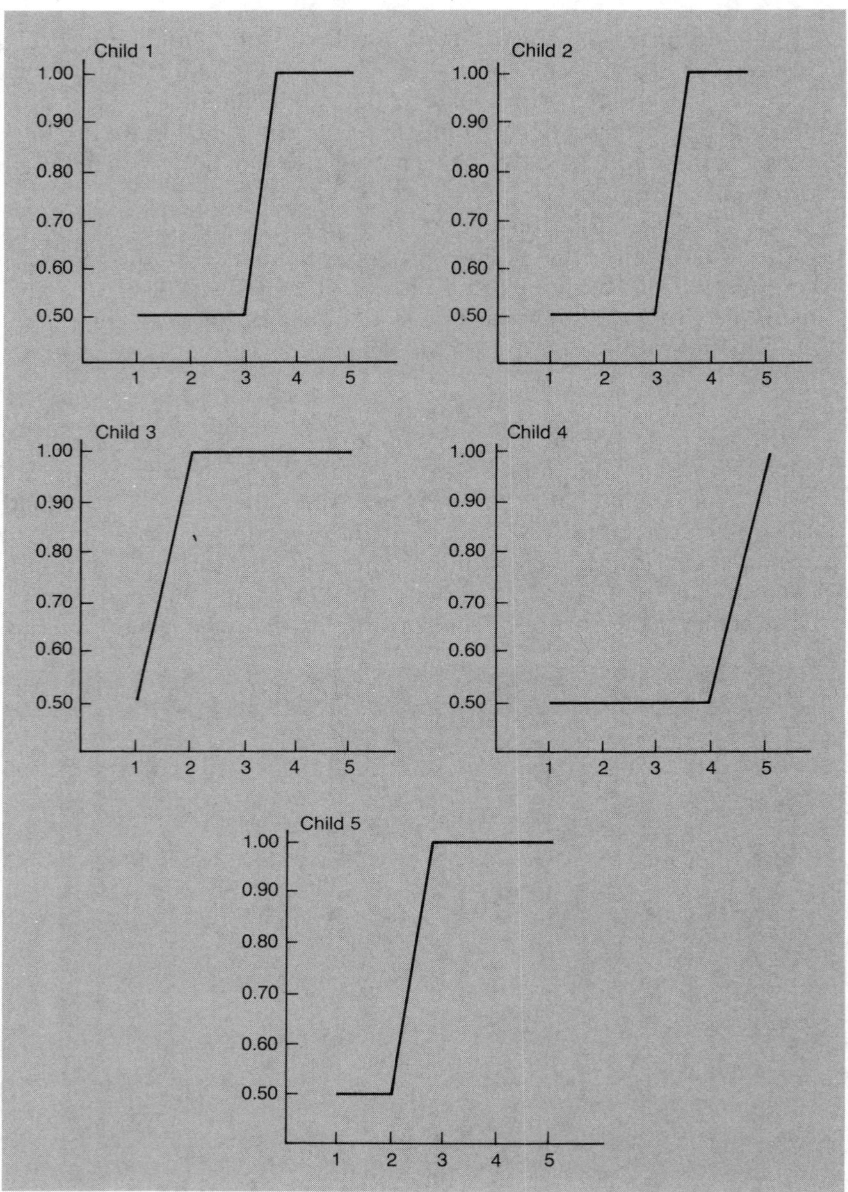

Figure 10-12 Results of the same hypothetical learning experiment as in Figure 10-11. These graphs reveal that learning was, in fact, discontinuous rather than smooth, as seen when we look at the data for each child individually.

But the practice of employing conditions that have no counterpart in nature has a long history of being fruitful in theory construction in many different branches of natural science. For example, Newton's laws of motion were based on a convenient fiction of a so-called "frictionless plane." Although Newton supposed a fictional universe that in fact did not (and could not) exist, by advancing these suppositions he was able to make great strides in understanding the universe around us. Similarly, in building a theory of the effects of reward on behavior, it may be advantageous to create a situation in which the "pure" relationship between the number of rewards and the resistance to extinction can be examined.

Part of Sidman's argument stems, no doubt, from his concerns about theorizing in general (at least for the behavioral sciences). The primary goal of many operantly oriented psychologists is the discovery of lawful relationships between environmental conditions or stimuli and responses produced by the organisms they are studying. Since theoretical terms do not often enter into the operant conditioner's account of behavior, it is not surprising that Sidman considers experiments having as their primary purpose the establishment of theoretical relationships to be misguided or at least premature.

Limitations of the Single-Subject Quasi-Experiment

One obvious drawback of single-subject quasi-experiments is that they are suitable only for evaluating treatments that are discrete or for responses that can be expected to reverse fairly rapidly.

Further, since single-subject quasi-experiments often do not include information on the within-periods variability of the measures employed, the magnitude of the mean differences is difficult to interpret—leaving only the *pattern* of directional changes. In turn, this means that a good *ABA* reversal shows only a change from A_1 to B and an opposite change from B to A_2. The probability of each of these directional changes is 0.50, so the likelihood of obtaining the expected pattern is 0.50×0.50 or 0.25. It would, therefore, occur by chance in one-quarter of all cases in the absence of a real experimental effect. If only two or three single-subject quasi-experiments out of ten show the expected *ABA* effect, it is easy to see why the result can be faulted as weak or even invalid. Such a problem is by no means inevitable, but it is one that single-subject experimenters and their critics must be on guard to avoid. A related problem appears if the investigator does not change the manipulation until the subject's behavior begins to shift in the "right" direction. Such a procedure, which may be common, maximizes the likelihood that naturally occurring cyclic changes will be mistakenly attributed to the experimental manipulation.

Finally, the single-subject experimental design, like the case study, may produce data of little generality. Even though such designs may often be internally valid, the results may not be generalizable to the population; hence, the results may have little *external validity.*

FOR REVIEW AND DISCUSSION

1. The sales manager of a large automobile dealership institutes a two week vacation bonus in Hawaii for sales people who sell at least 10 cars during the month of June. Only two of the 20 sales people who work at the dealership achieve this goal. The sales manager wants to examine the number of cars sold by each sales person during August to see if the bonus increased sales. What design(s) could be used? Supposing there is no apparent bonus effect, could compensatory rivalry have masked the possible effect of the bonus? How?
2. Devise a set of results for a hypothetical study in which the pretest-posttest nonequivalent peer control group design produced relatively unambiguous results. Using your hypothetical data, explain how each of the threats to internal validity can be ruled out by the pattern of data you have devised.
3. A number of drugs have been used in the treatment of schizophrenia. An investigator wishes to know which drug is most effective in reducing schizophrenic behavior. Each subject is given drug X for three days, drug Y for three days, and drug Z for three days. What kind of design is this? What are its advantages and disadvantages?
4. Suppose you are interested in teaching a retarded boy to dress and feed himself. Your treatment will involve both modeling and reinforcement of appropriate behavior. What kind of single-subject design would you use? Why?
5. Discuss Sidman's argument that analysis of group data causes one to accept one's own ignorance. Do you agree or disagree with this position? Why?
6. In what ways is the single-subject quasi-experiment an improvement over the simple case study approach? Include a discussion of how the *ABAB* design controls for sources of internal invalidity.
7. An investigator wishes to test the effectiveness of a treatment for hyperactivity with one subject. She uses an *ABA* design and obtains the results shown in the figure. How could these data be criticized? How much would you wish to generalize?

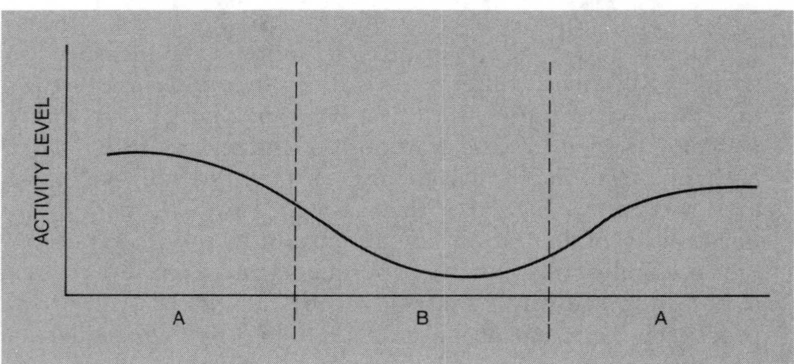

8. Discuss the possible ways in which contiguous cohorts might differ from one another. For what kinds of treatment effects are cohort controls most likely to be suitable? For what kinds are they likely to be unsuitable? Why?

11

Causal Analysis from Passive Observation

A WORD OF CLARIFICATION
FORECASTING VERSUS CAUSAL INFERENCE
CORRELATIONS WITHOUT CAUSAL ARROW AMBIGUITY: DIFFERENTIAL INCIDENCE
NATURALLY OCCURRING INTERRUPTED TIME SERIES DESIGNS
EX POST FACTO ANALYSIS
PARTIAL CORRELATION
Illusory Residual Correlations
A PARTIAL SOLUTION TO THE DIRECTIONALITY PROBLEM: TIME-LAGGED CORRELATIONS
ASSOCIATIVE NETWORK ANALYSIS
PATH ANALYSIS
FOR REVIEW AND DISCUSSION

Quasi-experiments are undertaken when true experiments are impractical or impossible, as is often the case when addressing applied problems. However, although quasi-experimental designs do not require random assignment to groups, they do require experimental control over the treatment of interest. Even this may be impossible to achieve in many settings. For example, investigators interested in the effects of completing high school on a person's later income will certainly not be able to decide when or to whom a high school education is available. Likewise, investigators interested in the effects of TV violence will not be able to decide which programs children will and will not watch in their own homes (not, at least, for very long). In fact, a complete lack of control characterizes our ability (or inability) to search for causal relationships when dealing with some of the most pressing social and economic problems of our time.

In the past forty years many social and behavioral scientists and statisticians have tackled the problem of causal analysis from passive observation, i.e., situations in which the investigator has no control over either "subjects" (i.e., the individuals of interest) or "treatments" (i.e., the experiences of interest). The principal belief behind all such efforts has been stated succinctly by Heise (1975).

> Causal explanations can be abstracted beyond manipulations or at least to the point at which manipulations are purely hypothetical; for example, it might be said that the sun's gravitational field causes certain peculiarities in the motions of the planets even though there is no possibility of experimental proof. With the concept generalized this way it is possible sometimes to examine causality nonexperimentally by using existing patterns of events (p. 3).

Unfortunately, most of these efforts have turned out to be flawed or unsatisfactory for one reason or another, but there have been some partial successes. Also, research methods and designs which cannot stand on their own for causal inference may nonetheless contribute to our confidence—or reduce our confidence—in causal inferences that have been drawn from experiments and quasi-experiments. Our purpose in this chapter is therefore to explain briefly the approaches that have been tried and to describe the logic and limitations of each.

A WORD OF CLARIFICATION

A word of clarification should be added at the outset. The present chapter deals almost entirely with correlations, and this fact alone may seem to be a sharp line of demarcation between experimental and nonexperimental studies. Any such presumption would be incorrect, however. In an important sense associations (i.e., correlations) are what we deal with in both experimental and nonexperimental studies. That is, we are interested in covariation regardless of whether any variable is manipulated. Moreover, correlational statistical techniques can in principle be used to analyze data from experiments and analyses of variance could be used with nonexperimental data. This is because both statistical procedures are derived from the same underlying statistical model. *The important difference between experimental and nonexperimental data is how the data are obtained, not how they are analyzed.*

FORECASTING VERSUS CAUSAL INFERENCE

Economists, stock market analysts, and applied statisticians have long used complex correlational techniques as a tool in forecasting. However, as Cook and Campbell (1979) point out, forecasting and causal inference are fundamentally different tasks. Even quite knowledgeable researchers have often confused the two, falling into the trap of drawing causal inferences that are misleading or just plain wrong.

To illustrate, consider how enrollment in a preschool Headstart program might relate to a child's later school performance. If Headstart enrollment is used simply to forecast (i.e., predict) how well a child will do in elementary school, a significant negative association will be found. This is because (1) Headstart is available only to children from disadvantaged homes, and (2) children from disadvantaged homes do considerably less well as a group in elementary school than do those from middle class homes. So, if you randomly select a first-grade child from the whole population of first-graders and ask whether the child was in a preschool Headstart program, the child who was in Headstart will probably be doing somewhat less well than one who was not in such a program. In this sense, Headstart enrollment figures in as a "negative predictor" for first-grade performance. But these results must not be interpreted as meaning that Headstart programs have an adverse effect. That determination can only be made by asking about causal influence, as opposed to predictive ability. The fair (and correct) comparison is to ask how children who were in Headstart did compared to how well we would have expected the same children to do had they not been in Headstart. Plainly this is a very different question. The answer, by the way, is that Headstart appears to have had a facilitating (positive) influence on later performance, albeit not one strong enough to completely overcome the disadvantages of a disadvantaged background.

CORRELATIONS WITHOUT CAUSAL ARROW AMBIGUITY: DIFFERENTIAL INCIDENCE

In early 1985 a decision was made to put a warning on all aspirin packages indicating that children and adolescents with flu, chicken pox, or other viral infections should not be given aspirin. The warning reflected a recent discovery: Combined with these infections, aspirin may cause a catalytic interaction that results in Reye's syndrome. (Reye's syndrome is a sickness that occurs in some children after a viral infection. It is characterized by sudden onset of vomiting and severe headaches, which progress rapidly toward convulsions, delirium and coma. It is fatal in about one-quarter of all cases.)

The determination of a causal link between aspirin and Reye's was made in the absence of any experimental or quasi-experimental tests, on the basis of a differential incidence of Reye's between children who had been given aspirin to relieve the symptoms of a viral infection and those who had not. The evidence was considered strong despite its nonexperimental nature because the magnitude of the difference in incidence between the two groups was too large to make other (rival) hypotheses plausible. The underlying study, conducted by the Center for Disease Control, traced 29 cases of Reye's syndrome in which the victim had taken aspirin and compared them with 143 "control" cases of children who had not taken aspirin. The difference was striking. Dr. Sidney Wolfe, of the Health Research Group, was quoted as saying "that the best statistical model indicated that aspirin raised the risk [of Reye's following a viral infection] by 25 times [and that] this extraordinarily high risk ratio was much higher than seen in any previous study [and was] one of the largest risk ratios found in any recent epidemiological study" (Quoted by Boffey, 1985).

It is rare to find such a clear-cut and convincing pattern in the social sciences, but the Reye's case does illustrate that differential incidence rates obtained without experimentation may, in principle, demonstrate a causal link. A similar way in which researchers may learn about causal relations from naturally occurring events is through naturally interrupted time series.

NATURALLY OCCURRING INTERRUPTED TIME SERIES DESIGNS

Our previous discussion of time series designs involved series that were interrupted purposely by the researcher, in order to probe for causal effects. Sometimes, however, a time series will be interrupted naturally (that is, by circumstances having nothing to do with the researcher's interests), such that information about causal relations can be adduced. In such cases, we speak of *naturally occurring interrupted time series designs.*

Naturally occurring interrupted time series designs may be used whenever some natural event occurs which is hypothesized to change the behavior of interest. These designs, like their quasi-experimental counterparts, rely on repeated measurement to improve the quality of inferences that can be drawn. The investigator looks for an association between sharp discontinuities or sudden changes in the behavior being measured and the occurrence of the event that is presumed to be the cause.

To illustrate, consider an investigation of a major social problem—violent crimes. In an attempt to demonstrate the specific instigating effect of violent behavior by a few individuals upon society, Berkowitz (1970) plotted the frequency of violent crimes before and after the assassination of John F. Kennedy. As can be seen in Figure 11-1, there is a sharp discontinuity in the curve; violence appears to have increased markedly immediately after (and apparently as a result of) the assassination. The results seem to suggest that "violence breeds violence." The major threat to the conclusion of a cause and effect relationship between the assassination and the subsequent increase in violent crime lies in the possibility that a third variable, operative at the same time as the Kennedy assassination, produced the observed increase. However, because the third variable would have had to occur at a specific point in time, the data are more convincing than if we were dealing only with a simple correlation in which a third variable could operate at any time.

Campbell and Ross (1968) have reported an intriguing example of how naturally occurring interrupted time series can be misleading. In 1955 the state of Connecticut began a severe crackdown on speeding with the intent of reducing traffic fatalities. No formal research plan was developed, but in 1956 the governor reported the data shown in Figure 11-2 and concluded that the program had saved forty lives and had therefore been highly successful.

The governor had made a strong causal inference, and Campbell and Ross wondered whether it was valid. As a test they used the naturally occurring interrupted time series design and plotted the number of traffic deaths for several years before and after 1955. These data are shown in Figure 11-3. This figure

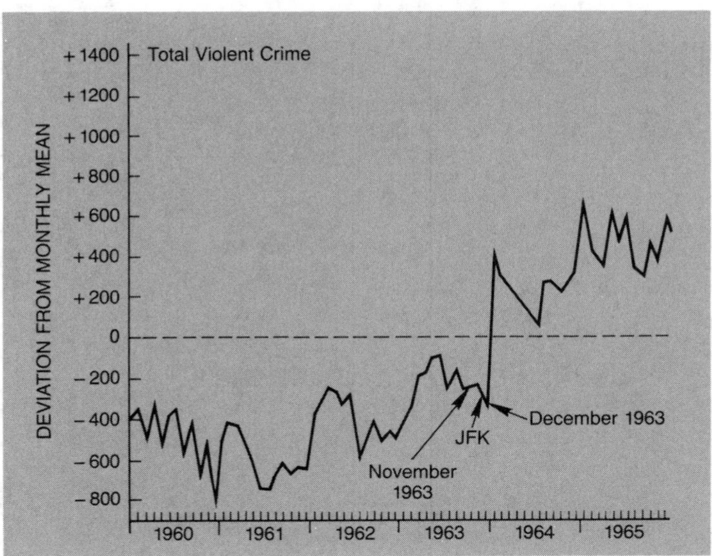

Figure 11-1 Deviations from monthly mean for sum of violent crimes, 1960–1966.

Source: Adapted from Berkowitz (1970).

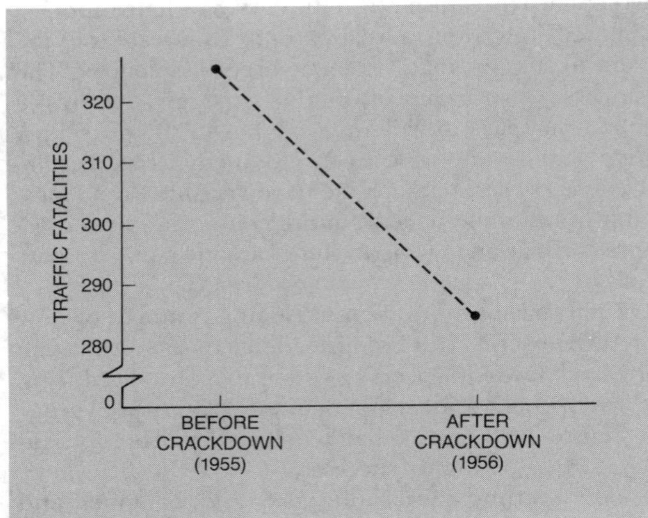

Figure 11-2 Connecticut traffic fatalities, 1955–1956.

Data from: Campbell and Ross (1968).

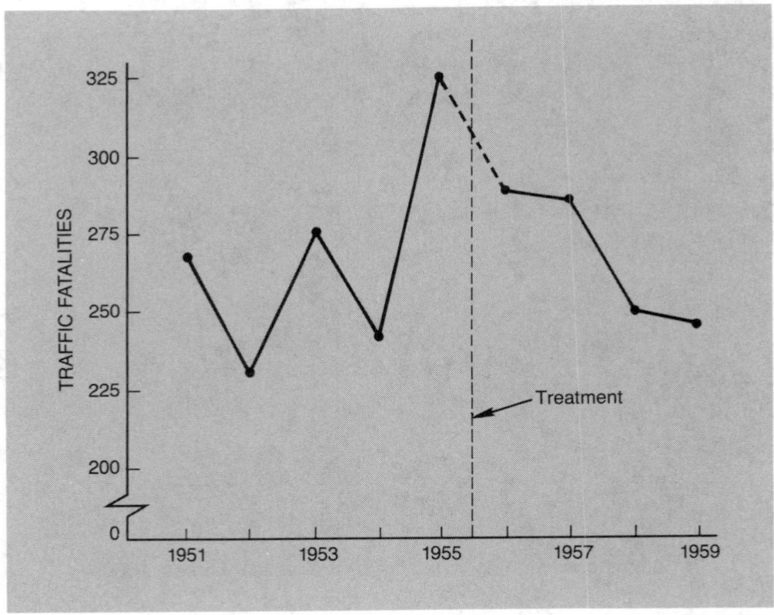

Figure 11-3 Connecticut traffic fatalities, 1951–1959.

Data from: Campbell and Ross (1968).

dramatically illustrates that the drop in fatalities from 1955 to 1956 is only part of wide year-to-year fluctuations in the number of traffic deaths. An even greater drop in the number of fatalities occurred in a year when there was no change from low to high enforcement of speeding laws (1957 to 1958). The drop from 1955 to 1956 could be simply a part of a larger (but unexplained) trend toward fewer fatalities over the years 1955 to 1958.

Another point that can be raised is the possible operation of regression. Notice in Figure 11-3 that the crackdown began when traffic deaths were at their highest. Thus, it might be expected that the next year's figure would be lower, simply because of regression. In sum, when more data are examined, the validity of the causal inference "reducing speeding causes fewer fatalities" is certainly not well substantiated. The drop in traffic deaths between 1955 and 1956 could be due to regression, to especially dry weather, to fewer cars on the road, to new safety devices, or to any of a large number of other uncontrolled factors.

To examine the possible operation of some of these other variables, Campbell and Ross compared the data from Connecticut with those of neighboring states that did not initiate a crackdown. The idea is that such variables as dry weather, improved safety features or the like *would* likely be operating in these states. Thus, the hypothesis that some variable other than the crackdown produced the drop would be supported if the other states' data showed a drop similar to Connecticut's. These data are shown in Figure 11-4. Notice that Rhode Island, Massachusetts, and New Jersey all showed declines in fatalities between

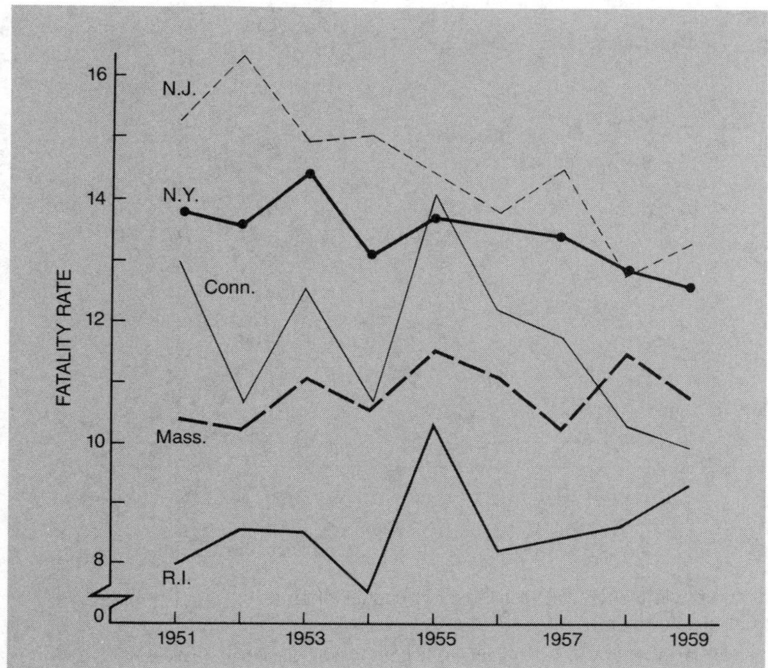

Figure 11-4 Traffic fatalities for Connecticut, New York, New Jersey, Rhode Island, and Massachusetts (per 100,000 persons).

Data from: Campbell and Ross (1968).

1955 and 1956. This information supports the notion that all of the Connecticut decline cannot be attributed to the crackdown. But Connecticut also shows a greater persisting decline over the years 1957, 1958, and 1959. These data suggest that the crackdown may have had a genuine effect. In sum, we are left with a somewhat ambiguous array of data. Some, but not all, of the decline of traffic deaths in Connecticut may have been due to the crackdown. The naturally occurring interrupted time series analysis has revealed the complexity involved in trying to draw causal inferences from correlational data.

Naturally interrupted time series, again like their quasi-experimental counterparts, are greatly strengthened when there is a replication of the treatment with a second group at a later period in time. Parker and his associates (cited in Cook & Campbell, 1979) employed this design to determine the effects of the introduction of television on reading. The investigators capitalized on the fact that there had been a two-year freeze on new TV stations in the United States in the early 1950s, which split Illinois communities into those where TV had been introduced before the freeze and those that did not get TV until after the freeze was lifted. The Parker group used archival data (see p. 123), namely, records of circulation from local libraries, as their dependent measure. Their

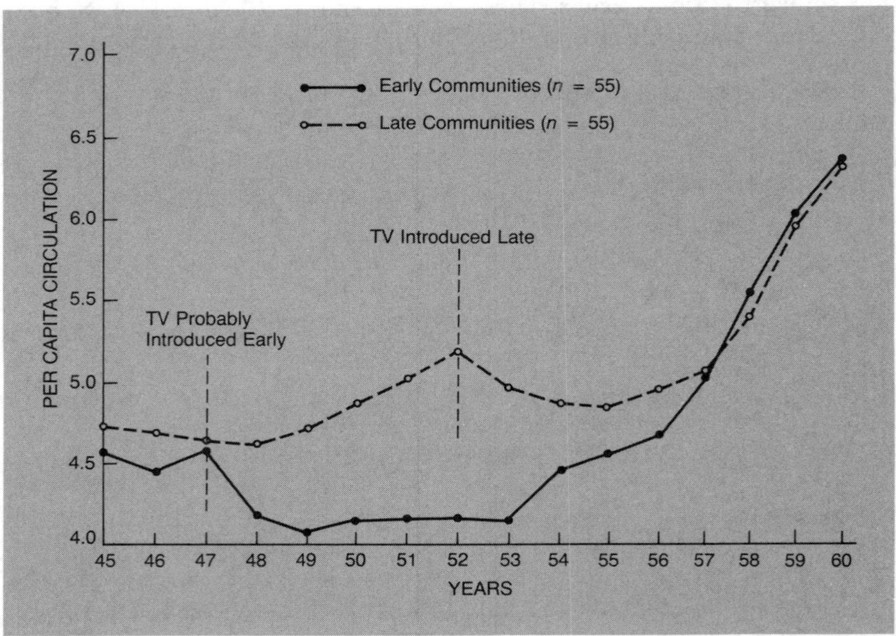

Figure 11-5 Per capita library circulation in two Illinois communities, as a function of the introduction of television.

Source: Adapted from Cook and Campbell (1979, p. 224), originally from Parker, Campbell, Cook and Katzman, unpublished paper, Northwestern University (1971).

results are shown in Figure 11-5, from which it can be seen that library circulation in both types of communities showed a clear drop in the years immediately following the introduction of television. The data are obviously more convincing because of the replication than they would be for either type of community alone.

We should note that there are several different statistical techniques that can be used for time series analysis, and determining which is appropriate depends on the nature of the data set involved and the assumptions that can be made about it. Most important, perhaps, is *temporal precedence*, that is, whether the investigator can assume "that change in one of the variables precedes that in another or in others" (Catalano, Dooley, & Jackson, 1983, p. 507). (The reader may recall that a cornerstone of all causal logic is that a cause must precede an effect in time.) As intuition suggests, time series analysis is considerably more straightforward when temporal precedence can be assumed. A detailed discussion of this and other issues may be found in Catalano et al.

EX POST FACTO ANALYSIS

Suppose that an investigator is interested in determining whether completing high school (potentially a treatment) increases the future earning power of young people. He or she realizes that a simple correlational design will not permit a causal inference about the impact of a high school education on later income. Even if there is a relationship in a large random sample between completing high school and higher incomes later, it may be mediated by a third variable. Brighter or more able individuals are both more likely to finish high school *and* more likely to have high incomes later than are duller students. Such a factor would clearly account for the relationship between completing high school and later economic success, but it would rival the suggestion that the high school education per se produces higher income. In other words, one would hardly be willing, from this sort of data, to urge individuals to complete high school on the grounds that if they do so their own incomes will be higher as a result. Although the purpose of the ex post facto design is to reduce just such problems, as we shall see, this widely used design is unable to do so.

The ex post facto design is an effort to simulate experimental procedures by matching subjects who have with those who have not received some "natural manipulation" on factors that might have been relevant before the time of the study. Thus, for example, an effort might be made to identify a large number of individuals, some of whom finished high school and some of whom did not, and obtain information about their later income. Then the investigator might return to subjects' grade school and junior high school academic records, intelligence test scores gathered at those times, information about family background, and the like, and find pairs of individuals (such that one member of each pair did finish high school and the second member did not) who are matched on these third variables. Presumably, if in the comparison of these two groups (matched *after the fact*, rather than at the outset, hence ex post facto) a difference is detected, then the investigator will wish to conclude that high school does have the effect of increasing income. At first blush, such a procedure does seem to compellingly eliminate a third variable and thus permit causal inferences. However, as Campbell and Stanley (1966) have noted, in practice the design has many pitfalls.

The first problem with the ex post facto matching procedures is that third variables that can be eliminated, in part, by matching will often be related to the dependent measure (in our example, income) in the original sample. At least some students drop out of high school because they do not have the intellectual ability to complete this level of schoolwork. These very dull individuals will not have any equally dull counterparts to be matched with in the completed high school group. As a result, the size of the then available sample will inevitably be smaller than the size of the original one. The restriction of the sample may markedly limit the generality of any differences obtained and thereby restrict the causal inference for the general proposition that a high school education will increase income.

The severity of this problem may be seen in a study by Chapin (1955), which employed the ex post facto design to explore the very problem we have been discussing. Chapin began with a sample of over 2,000 students. However, in seeking appropriately matchable pairs in terms of grades in grammar school, parental occupation, age, neighborhood in which the students grew up, and the like, he ended up with only 46 cases that he judged to be usable (23 pairs). This subsample is less than 4 percent of the sample with which he started and thus clearly restricts the generality of the study.

Second, and at least equally important, the ex post facto design, regardless of the number of variables on which matching occurs, can never guarantee that some other variable for which matching was not employed may be the important controlling factor in the differences in the incomes of the two groups in later life. As was pointed out earlier, the notion of "third variable" is partially a misnomer because it refers to *any* variable that might account for the effects we have observed in a way that has been masked by the research procedure employed.

The effects of matching on one variable may also have the ironic effect of "systematically unmatching" on another variable. Consider, for example, a case suggested by Meehl (1970). A relatively dull adolescent may finish high school because his parents place a great deal of emphasis on the importance of education, whereas a bright adolescent may drop out of high school because his parents do not place much value on education. Since parental values, which clearly can be very important in later achievement, are not likely to appear in any of the records available to an investigator after the fact, this would remain a potentially important but uncontrolled factor in an ex post facto design. But the problem does not end there. If the foregoing analysis is correct, a student with an IQ of 125 who has dropped out of school will, when matched with a student of like IQ who remains in school, produce a pair of individuals who (although alike on IQ) differ sharply from one another in motivation. Likewise, a student with an IQ of 90 who remains in school because he has been subjected to a strong achievement ethic by his family will likely differ on this second, and uncontrolled, variable from his matched 90 IQ counterpart who did not experience family pressure and thus dropped out. The problem is illustrated in Table 11-1.

In both cases, the effect of matching has been to further "unmatch" or confound the presence or absence of a completed high school education in the ex post facto design with the presence or absence of exposure to strong parental training and emphasis on the value of achievement. It is in this sense that the effect of matching may be particularly misleading.

Finally, Meehl (1971) has noted yet another problem with ex post facto designs. To understand this point we must first consider a study aimed at establishing a link between social isolation and the subsequent development of schizophrenia (Barthell & Holmes, 1968). These investigators examined the high school yearbooks of schizophrenics and compared their level of participation in social activities to that of another group of students drawn randomly from the yearbook pictures. The preschizophrenics were found to be more socially isolated. However, Schwarz (1970) has criticized the study because important variables such as social class had not been controlled (for example, by matching).

Meehl has noted, however, that the decision to match and thus to attempt to control for social class rests on an implicit assumption that social class is a "nuisance variable" and ought to be controlled. Further, he has outlined several possible relationships among social class, social isolation, and schizophrenia and pointed out that only some of these patterns of relationship would point toward controlling for social class. Two of his examples follow:

1. Lower-class students have less money to spend, hence join fewer activity groups, hence suffer more isolation . . .
2. The genes predisposing to schizophrenia [contribute] to anxiety-proneness, low dominance, low energy level, low persistence, etc. These genetic factors tend to produce lesser social competence in the preschizophrenics, reflected in their low participation (Meehl, 1971, p. 145).

Clearly, in the first case, social class differences between the preschizophrenic and control students might produce a spurious difference in social participation in the two groups. In this case an attempt to control for social class

Table 11-1 Results of Ex Post Facto IQ Matching of Youngsters Who Did and Did Not Finish High School, Showing How Matching on IQ Systematically Unmatched on Motivation. Differences in Later Income Between the *Finished* and *Didn't Finish* Groups Could Be Due to Differences in Schooling, Differences in Motivation, or an Unknown Combination of the Two Factors.

FINISHED HIGH SCHOOL	*DIDN'T FINISH*
Normal motivation, High IQ	Low motivation, High IQ
High motivation, Low IQ	Normal motivation, Low IQ

should be made. However, in the second case, if social class were controlled by matching, a *valid* association between social isolation and schizophrenia would be reduced. Thus, *the decision to attempt to control for a variable by matching after the fact must be made in conjunction with an explicit causal model of the way the variable operates.*

PARTIAL CORRELATION

Under some circumstances, it is possible to assess the degree to which the third variable problem is present in correlational research. To determine the degree to which a third variable is responsible for an obtained relationship, we would wish to "subtract out" the influence of this variable and determine the magnitude of the relationship that remains. A statistical procedure that is approximately analogous to such an outcome is available: *the partial correlation technique.*[1]

The logic is this: If we can identify a third variable that is suspected of accounting for an obtained relationship, the partial correlations technique may be used to eliminate its influence. Then the obtained correlation between the two variables is again inspected. Suppose we had observed a substantial correlation between two variables but suspected that the relationship might be due to a third variable. A partial correlation could then be computed that would be independent of (unrelated to) values of the third variable.

As a concrete illustration, consider an observed correlation between anxiety level and problem-solving. The investigator supposes that the relationship might be due to a third variable, intelligence. The partial correlation between anxiety and problem-solving is computed, holding constant the potential influence of intelligence. The mathematical procedures involved in computing such a partial correlation are analogous to computing the correlation between anxiety and problem solving with subjects *who all had exactly the same score on the intelligence test*.

If the relationship (which was previously strong in either the positive or negative direction) is now markedly reduced, then the third variable may be responsible for the obtained effect. In contrast, if the partial correlation reveals a relationship that is as strong, or nearly as strong, as the simple correlation with which we began, this third variable turns out to be a poor rival in terms of accounting for the obtained effect. Thus the partial correlational technique may be used to eliminate a possible third variable as a rival hypothesis.

A further point concerning the use of partial correlations is that the proper use of the technique depends on the investigator having an explicit model of the causal chain with which he or she is dealing. He or she must be willing to specify the exact means in which the third variable operates. Returning to our previous example, we may consider three different networks of relationship

[1] The computational procedures underlying this technique are beyond the scope of the present book. An excellent discussion of statistical procedures for partial correlations is to be found in Nunnally (1967).

among the three variables: anxiety, problem solving, and intelligence, as shown in Figure 11-6.

In case 1, intelligence is causally related to both anxiety and problem-solving, but the latter two variables do not depend on one another. In case 2, problem solving depends on both intelligence and anxiety, but the latter two variables are not causally related to each other. In case 3, problem solving depends on intelligence and on a causal chain from intelligence to anxiety to problem-solving. The procedures involved in a partial correlation are applicable only to the causal model presented in case 1. Other statistical procedures are available for dealing with cases 2 and 3. The important point is that the choice of which technique to use depends on having an explicit causal model of the relationships involved.

Illusory Residual Correlations

A major problem with partial correlation is that even in a complex regression equation with powerful covariates partialled out, an *illusory residual correlation* may be found for the hypothesized cause even when its true impact is nil. A mathematical demonstration of how this might occur is well beyond the scope of this book, but we will briefly present a simplified hypothetical example adapted from Cook and Campbell (1979).

The relevent correlations for our example are shown in Table 11-2. Assume that we are dealing with middle-level corporate managers and that the measure of interest is spending a year in a graduate school of management. Also assume that there is no real causal influence of graduate school on executive ability but that a *third variable,* "social advantage," produces a correlation of +.51 between a year of graduate education and executive ability. Assume further that social advantage can be tapped by father's income (C1), mother's educational level (C2), and the socioeconomic status of the neighborhood in which the subject grew up (C3). Because we are assuming that the year of graduate school had no real effect on those who received it, the likelihood of going to graduate school

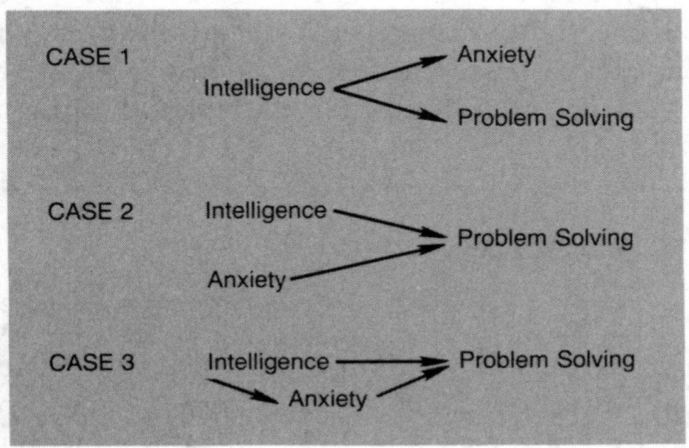

Figure 11-6 Possible causal paths among intelligence, anxiety, and problem solving.

Table 11-2 Hypothetical Intercorrelations Among Variables for Regression Adjustment Demonstration.

	(*Pr*)	*Po*	*T*	C_1	C_2	C_3
Po	(.800)					
T	(.505)	.505				
C_1	(.632)	.632	.399			
C_2	(.632)	.632	.399	.500		
C_3	(.632)	.632	.399	.500	.500	

Source: From Cook and Campbell (1979, p. 299)

(because of social advantage) is as highly correlated with executive ability as actually having gone to graduate school, with the education itself having no real effect! Thus, hypothetical pretest correlations (i.e., correlations before graduate school, which appear in parentheses under (*Pr*), are as high as the posttest correlations, listed under *Po*. Nonetheless, using standard techniques we would obtain a partial correlation of +.23, which would be significant ($p < .05$) with any reasonable size sample, even after all three measures of the latent variable have been partialled out. What this means, of course, is that an entirely different set of mathematical procedures is required, using so-called path analysis. (We will return to a discussion of path analysis at the end of this chapter.)

There are other limitations of the partial correlation technique, and often it is difficult to assess the importance of these limitations in actual research. Most important, perhaps, is that the statistical control on *Z* (the third variable) imposed by partial correlation cannot be equated with the actual control over *Z* obtained by random assignment in a true experiment.

For example, under some circumstances *X* and *Y*, *X* and *Z*, and *Y* and *Z* can all be positively related and yet the partial correlation between *X* and *Y* with *Z* removed is actually *larger* than the original *XY* correlation. Such an outcome results from using artificial statistical control but makes little sense intuitively. An additional limitation of the partial correlation technique is a practical one: There is a limit to the number of possible third variables an investigator is likely to be able to identify, measure, and partial out. Other unmeasured or overlooked third variables may still be responsible for the observed relationship. (Proper random assignment, in contrast, provides a blanket protection against all possible third variables.) In sum, the partial correlation technique is only a limited solution to the third variable problem.

A PARTIAL SOLUTION TO THE DIRECTIONALITY PROBLEM: TIME-LAGGED CORRELATIONS

The problem of interpeting the direction of a correlation can be partially solved by a repeated measurement strategy, in which the correlation between the two variables is first determined at time 1 and later at time 2. To illustrate how this procedure might be used to determine causality, let us consider a study of the relationship between "warmth" in a teacher's behavior and whether students respond to his or her requests. Assume that teachers can be judged as either warm or cold and students as either responsive or unresponsive. The hypothetical results of such a study are presented in Table 11-3 (Part I).

In the time 1 portion of the table the data show a positive relationship between the two variables. More students (60 percent) are judged as responsive than unresponsive (40 percent) if teachers are "warm," and more students are judged unresponsive (60 percent) if teachers are "cold."

However, we can also examine Table 11-3 *across* the rows. When we do, it appears that student responsiveness may influence teacher warmth, rather than vice versa. In the row for responsive students, more warm than cold teachers are found; the reverse is true for the row representing the nonresponsive students. Thus, although a relationship is evident, it cannot be determined whether (a) teacher warmth influences student responsiveness or (b) student responsivity influences teacher warmth. Suppose, however, the measurements were repeated on the same students and teachers at a later time and the results presented in the time 2 portion of Table 11-3 were obtained.

There is change in the measures when they are retaken. If the change were due to only one of two possible reasons, then it would be possible to determine which of these was the more likely by inspecting the data for individual students at both time periods. The reasoning is as follows.

If teacher warmth was influencing student responsiveness, we would expect that, over time, unresponsive students who had warm teachers would be likely to become more responsive. Conversely, responsive students who had cold teachers would become less responsive. If such were the case, the specific changes obtained might be like those shown in Table 11-3 (Part II[a]). In this situation, half of the students who were previously responsive have now become unresponsive, and half who were previously unresponsive have now become responsive. Clearly, the *changes* between time 1 and time 2 had to do with the coldness or warmth of the teacher. Alternately, if student responsiveness were influencing teacher warmth, then we would expect cold teachers with responsive students to become warmer and warm teachers with unresponsive students to become colder. Such a result is shown in Table 11-3 (Part II[b]). Thus, in this instance, an examination of Table 11-3 (that is, an examination of changes in correlational data over time) allows us to identify a causal relationship.

In this example, we were able to draw a causal inference by observing how people changed over time. The technique itself was originally proposed by Paul Lazarsfeld (1948). A limitation of the approach, however, is that we dealt with only two states: responsive versus unresponsive and warm versus cold. Frequently it is not possible to categorize a variable so neatly. Where, for example, do we draw the line to distinguish warm from cold teachers? In these cases we may implement a similar procedure, which involves examining the difference between two correlations: the correlation of an effect with a prior cause and the correlation of an effect with a cause that comes after it. Because logic requires

Table 11-3 Part I. The Data Show the Percentage of Students Who Are Responsive and Unresponsive as a Function of Teacher's Manner (Warm or Cold) at Time 1 and Again at Time 2. The Association between Teacher Warmth and Student Responsiveness Becomes Stronger Over Time, but It is Not Clear Whether the Students Influence the Teachers or Vice Versa.

PART I

Time 1

STUDENT'S BEHAVIOR	*TEACHER'S MANNER*	
	Cold	*Warm*
Responsive	40%	60%
Unresponsive	60	40

Time 2

	Cold	*Warm*
Responsive	20%	80%
Unresponsive	80	20

Part II. Essentially, This Is the Directionality Problem, and It Can Be Resolved by Examining the Path Through Which the Change from Time 1 to Time 2 Occurred. One Possibility, Shown in Part II(a), Is that Initially Responsive Students of Cold Teachers Became Less Responsive, while Initially Unresponsive Students of Warm Teachers Became More Responsive Over Time. A Second Possibility, Shown in Part II(b), Is that Initially Cold Teachers of Responsive Students Became Warmer Over Time, while Initially Warm Teachers of Unresponsive Students Became Colder. By Examining Both Teacher and Student Changes between Time 1 and Time 2, We Can Determine Through Which Path the Change Comes About.

PART II*

(a)

TEACHER WARMTH CAUSING STUDENT RESPONSIVENESS

STUDENTS	*TEACHERS*	
	Cold	*Warm*
Responsive	20% 20 ↙	60% ↗ 20
Unresponsive	60	20

(b)

STUDENT RESPONSIVENESS CAUSING TEACHER WARMTH

STUDENTS	*TEACHERS*	
	Cold	*Warm*
Responsive	20% 20 → (to Warm)	60% 20 → (to Cold)
Unresponsive	60	20

* The arrows summarize the direction of changes for students within the groups, but the actual data for individual students (on which the summary is based) are not shown here.

that the "cause" must precede the effect, the difference between the correlation of an effect with a prior, versus a subsequent, "cause" will necessarily shed light on the direction of the relationship. As was the case in the previous example, this requires the repeated measurement of the correlation and the introduction of a time lag in the measurement of the variables. The resulting procedure was devised by Campbell and Stanley (1966) and is called the *cross-lagged panel technique*.

A study by Lefkowitz, Eron, Walder, and Huesmann (1972), a correlational investigation of the relationship between watching violent television and aggressive behavior, used the cross-lagged panel design. In the Lefkowitz et al. study, all the children in a particular county were examined when they were in the third grade and followed up ten years later. Though many variables were investigated, for the present purpose only the measures relating to the viewing of violent television and rated aggressiveness need be considered. The measure of aggression in the classroom was a peer nomination technique, in which the children selected other children who fit descriptions such as: Who is always getting into trouble? Who starts a fight over nothing? The measure of the degree of violence in the TV programs watched by the child was obtained by having the parents provide a list of the child's favorite programs. Ratings of the violence contained in these programs was then made independently by two raters, so that the child's assumed TV diet could be assigned a violence rating.

Of the initial 875 subjects in the study, 427 were contacted 10 years later. The follow-up sample was composed of 211 boys and 216 girls who were interviewed by a member of the research team. During this interview, data were collected both on stated preferences for television programs and on ratings of aggression. As with the third grade sample, the subjects' preferred TV programs were independently rated for their violent content so that a score could be assigned reflecting the degree of violence in the preferred TV shows of each subject. To obtain a rating of degree of aggressiveness, subjects were presented with lists of names of other students and were asked which of them might fit into the various categories of aggressive responding. The categories represented a slightly modified version of the form used for the third graders. For the male subjects, the major outcome of the Lefkowitz et al. investigation is presented in Figure 11-7.

Within the cross-lagged technique, the critical correlations to be examined are those on the diagonals. Based on the assumption that a "cause" must precede an "effect," two rival hypotheses may be pitted against each other. If aggression during the third grade was causally related to the amount of TV violence preferred 10 years later, the correlation between these two variables should be high. Conversely, if the amount of TV violence preferred during the third grade were causally related to the level of aggressive behavior 10 years later, this correlation should be high. As may be seen from Figure 11-7, the Lefkowitz et al. cross-lagged data (on the diagonals) may be taken as support for the hypothesis that higher levels of violence on preferred TV programs in the third grade is causally related to the amount of aggressive responding 10 years later. The correlation between preference for violent TV programs in the third

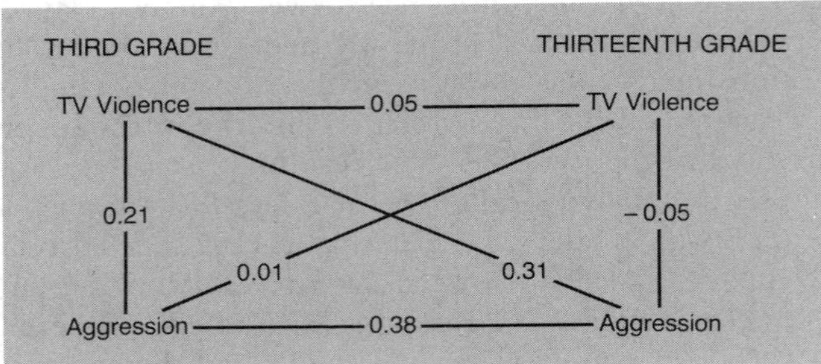

Figure 11-7 Correlations obtained in the Lefkowitz, Eron, Walder, and Huesmann study.

grade and peer-rated aggression 10 years later ($r = 0.31$) was significantly higher than the correlation between peer-rated aggression in the third grade and preference for violent TV fare in the thirteenth grade ($r = 0.01$).

A number of problems with the cross-lagged panel design limit its usefulness. First, the reliability of the measures should not change between the two measurement periods. It can be shown that a variable that increases in reliability relative to the others will appear as an "effect" rather than a "cause" (Campbell, 1963). Therefore, the cross-lagged panel technique should be used only with variables that have stable and satisfactory reliabilities. Second, for proper inferences the time period between the two measurements must be appropriate to the true causal effect being assessed. If the effects of the true cause were instantaneous, the correlation at the first measurement interval might be high but the time-lagged correlations could, in this instance, be low. Third, Rozelle and Campbell (1969) have noted that there are actually four possible relationships between the two variables being considered, not just the two we have presented thus far. To illustrate let us return to our example of TV violence viewing.

The two relationships we have considered were: (1) increases in TV violence viewing *increase* aggression and (2) increases in aggression *increase* TV violence viewing. But negative, or inverse, relationships are also logically possible. Specifically, (3) increases in TV violence viewing may *decrease* aggression and (4) increases in aggression may *decrease* TV violence viewing. The problem introduced by considering all four possibilities is that a simple comparison of correlations no longer leads to a unique conclusion. When the correlation between early TV violence viewing and later aggression is greater than the correlation between early aggression and later violence viewing, either alternative 1 or 4 could be operating. To take a hypothetical example, assume that the correlation between early TV violence viewing and later aggression is $+0.20$ and the correlation between early aggression and later TV violence viewing is -0.20. Similarly, when the correlation between early aggression and later violence viewing is higher than that between early violence viewing and later aggression, either alternative 2 or 3 could be correct. The point is that a simple comparison of the cross-lagged correlations may not allow an unambiguous causal inference to be made. To reach an internally valid conclusion requires what Rozelle and Campbell (1968) call the *no-cause baseline*, an estimate of the relationship between two variables if no causal relationship exists between them.[2] Then instead of comparing the cross-lagged correlations with one another, we compare them to the no-cause baseline.

Finally, there is a problem in interpreting the results of a panel design using the "raw" correlation coefficients. To understand this point, consider the results of the Lefkowitz et al. (1972) study (Figure 11-7). The higher lagged correlation, between viewing violent TV fare in the third grade and aggression in the thirteenth grade, was used as evidence for the presence of a direct causal path between these two variables. However, the correlation could have been produced by an indirect yet plausible path—specifically by (1) a high correlation between viewing TV violence and aggression in the third grade, together with (2) a high correlation between the measures of aggression in the third and thirteenth grades.

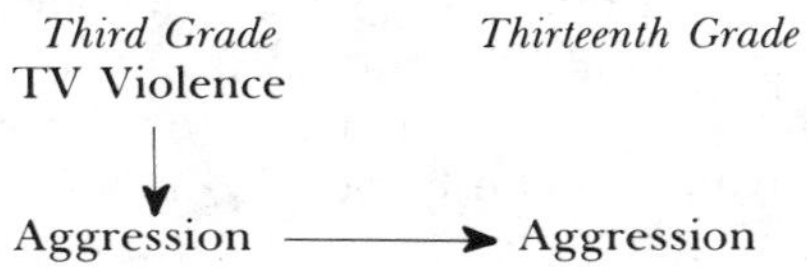

One way of handling this problem is to compute a partial correlation between early TV violence viewing and later aggression with aggression in the third grade as the partialled variable. Such an analysis was performed on the Lefkowitz et al. data (Neale, 1972), and it lent support to the initial conclusion concerning the causal influence of TV on boys' aggression.

In sum, the cross-lagged panel technique can, at times, allow meaningful statements to be made about causal relationships. But there are ever-present pitfalls, some of which are out of the researcher's control (for example, the reliability of a variable could change, or the time interval used may not be an ideal one).

ASSOCIATIVE NETWORK ANALYSIS

Thus far we have considered fairly specific ways of attacking the third variable and directionality problems. But there is a more general approach to attempting to shore up correlation designs: *causal analysis.* Theory and the measurement of a set of variables are the keystones of the approach. In the social sciences, it is rarely true that an explanation of some phenomenon postulates a single cause

[2] Recall that variables may be correlated for a variety of reasons other than one variable causing the other. The procedure for comparing a no-cause baseline can be found in Rozelle and Campbell (1969).

for it. More often, a theorist will propose that a phenomenon results from the simultaneous operation of a number of variables. In causal analysis, an explanatory model is proposed, several (or many) variables are measured, and the resulting network of associative relationships is then examined to determine whether the model has been supported. Because we are now evaluating a network of relationships, the operation of a single third variable and the possible bidirectionality of relationships become less problematic.

Let us first examine a rather nonformal example of the general logic of this approach. Chaffee and McLeod (1971) have presented an analysis to examine the regularly obtained correlation between viewing of televised violence and aggressive behavior among children and young adolescents (Dominick & Greenberg, 1972; Lefkowitz et al. 1972; McIntyre & Teevan, 1972; McLeod, Atkin & Chaffe, 1972).[3] As we had occasion to note in our earlier discussion of the Lefkowitz et al. cross-lagged analysis, the two major hypotheses for these findings are (H_1) that viewing violent TV leads to aggressive behavior and (H_2) that aggressiveness leads to viewing violent TV. But each of these explanations, in its turn, is based on certain underlying process accounts as to the manner in which the observed effect came about. These specific processes may be thought of as "subhypotheses," implicated by one, but not both, of the competing accounts. A process analysis of the type shown in Table 11-4 has been offered by Chaffee and McLeod (1971).

Note, in the table, that H_{1a} or the "learning hypothesis," is one of the intervening processes said to underlie H_1. Thus, further support for H_1 can be obtained by showing that youngsters learn aggressive behaviors from watching TV, and that they recognize the possibility of later using this knowledge. To determine whether such a process is operative, Chaffee and McLeod asked youngsters (for whom they also had independent information on violence viewing and aggressive behavior) whether it was "like them" to respond to television in the following ways:

> These programs show me how to get back at people who make me angry.
> Sometimes I copy the things I see people doing on these shows.
> Some programs give me ideas on how to get away with something without being caught.

As Chaffee and McLeod note, these questions are designed to probe a learning process that "can be thought of as an hypothetical 'path' through which viewing violence might lead to aggressive interpersonal behavior" (1971, p. 12). But what of the alternative? As Chaffee and McLeod indicate: "We would not

[3]No such synchronous relationship was obtained by Lefkowitz et al. (1972) for nineteen-year-olds, but as their data suggest, these young adults do appear to show the effects of earlier exposure.

Table 11-4 Two Hypotheses About Violence Viewing and Adolescent Aggressiveness, Showing Subhypothesis Involved in a Causal Analysis.

H_1: Viewing television violence increases the likelihood of an adolescent behaving aggressively.

H_{1a}: By viewing television violence, an adolescent learns aggressive forms of behavior; this increases the probability that he or she will behave in this fashion in subsequent social interaction.

H_2: Aggressiveness causes adolescents to watch violent television programs.

H_{2a}: Aggressiveness leads to a preference for violent programs, which in turn causes the aggressive adolescent to watch them.

Adapted from Chaffee and McLeod (1971).

want to infer that aggressiveness 'causes' violence viewing unless evidence indicates that this viewing is intentional and selective." This subhypothesis, H_{2a}, is tested in a manner analogous to H_{1a}, but the process measure is the youngster's list of his four "favorite" programs. The H_{2a} path requires that the violence preference measure be related to both antecedent aggressiveness and later viewing of violent programs.

Given the foregoing information, H_{1a} and H_{2a} can be compared. One such comparison, based on the data reported by Chaffee and McLeod, is shown in Figure 11-8. The learning hypothesis receives fairly clear support, whereas the violence preference hypothesis does not do very well. The better account is thus provided by H_1, and the causal inference with which it is associated therefore becomes somewhat more convincing.

Typically, more formal approaches to causal analysis do not rely on simple correlations between or among the variables that have been assessed. Although the mathematics of such approaches become somewhat complicated, we can illustrate many of the basic features by considering *flowgraphs* (Heise, 1975). Basically, a flowgraph is a stylized way of representing a theory. A basic convention is that two variables linked by an arrow indicates a direct causal connection (for example, $X \rightarrow Y$). When several variables are part of the theory, a flowgraph can appear more complicated, as Figure 11-9 shows. This flowgraph implies that W is a direct cause of Z and that X is an indirect cause of Z through its influence on Y. Notice that each causal path is given its own symbol (a, c, and d). These symbols, in turn, allow us to write what are termed *structural equations* for the variable in which we are interested. For example, for Figure 11-9, we can write the structural equation $Z = a \cdot W + c \cdot d\,X$. The actual values of a, c, and d, typically determined by a regression analysis, will either be simple or partial regression coefficients. There are two advantages to the approach. First, it forces the theorist to be quite specific about a network of relationships; because the entire network is evaluated it is unlikely that a single chance factor could account for the entire array. Second, the analytic procedures ensure that different causal paths are properly evaluated with either standard or partial regression coefficients.

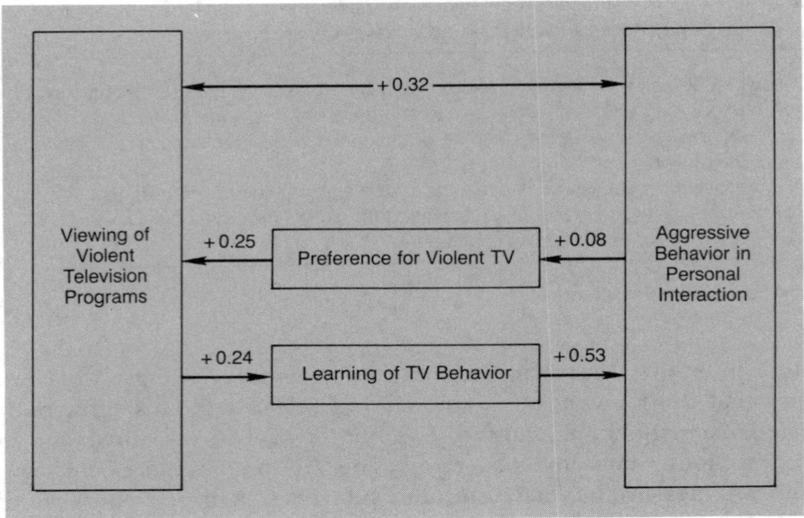

Figure 11-8 Correlations of violence viewing, aggressiveness, and two intervening processes. Entries indicate correlations between the two variables connected by each line ($N = 473$). Arrows indicate hypothesized time order. The overall relationship is clearly accounted for more adequately by the learning path (H_{1a}) than by the preference path (H_{2a}).

Source: Adapted from Chaffee and McLeod (1971).

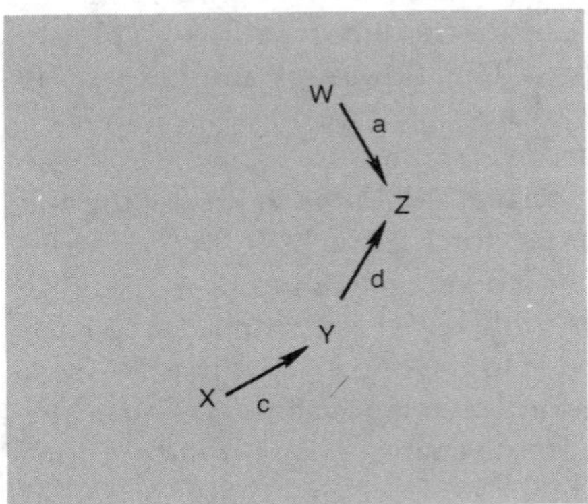

Figure 11-9 Flowgraph illustrating a causal model for *Z*. *W* is a direct cause of *Z* via path *A*; *X* is an indirect cause of *Z* through paths *C* and *D*.

PATH ANALYSIS

Path analysis may be thought of as a formal version of the associative network analysis discussed in the preceding section. True path analysis is a highly complex set of mathematical procedures, and we will make no attempt to explain the mathematics here. Our aim, instead, is to offer a rudimentary explanation of the underlying logic.

The essential requirement of path analysis is that the investigator generate linear equations ("models") to represent the relationships that are hypothesized to exist among the relevant variables, expressed in a path diagram. It is crucial to assume that all relevant variables have been specified; that is, the models must be complete. Each of the models that have been generated is then tested using observed correlation coefficients to estimate the causal path coefficients that would be expected in the presence and absence of a true direct causal relationship.

Path analysis, like other nonexperimental techniques that deal with large numbers of correlations (such as factor analysis, see Chapter 4), invariably involves some degree of subjective judgment. As Li observes:

> Two investigators, given the same data on the same variables, may very well come up with two different understandings of the variables and propose two different path diagrams for analysis. *Hence, path analysis is not a fixed and routine method of handling data that can be preprogrammed* [*like*] *traditional statistical procedures* (1975, p. 1, emphasis added).

To make these ideas concrete, we will offer two simplified examples. Suppose that *SA* is a measure of social advantage, *Ed* is a measure of education, and *In* is a measure of income. Let us hypothesize that social advantage is a direct cause both of receiving more education and of earning a higher income as an adult. We obtain the correlations shown in Figure 11-10(a), namely, a correlation of +.60 between social advantage and education and a correlation of +.60 between social advantage and income. We also obtain a correlation of +.36 between education and income. The question of underlying theoretical and practical interest to us is: Is there a direct causal relationship between education and income? If we assume the underlying relationships (i.e., true path coefficients) are as shown in Figure 11-10(b), then the answer to our question would be, No. This is because the causal relationships assumed to exist between *SA* and *In* and *Ed* and *In* would generate a correlation of +.36 even if there was no real causal path between *Ed* and *In,* but simply a "mediated path," through social advantage. (The mathematical rule, as expressed by Cook and Campbell, is that "mediated causal relations generate correlation components equal to the product of the path coefficients of the links that generate them" (1979, p. 302).

Figure 11-10 A simple hypothetical path analysis.

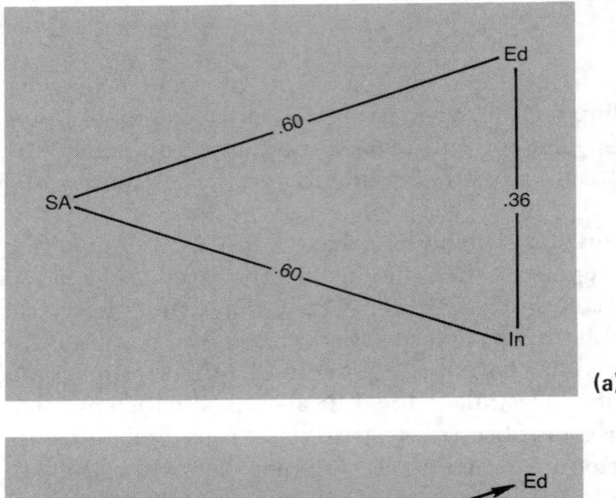

(a)

(b)

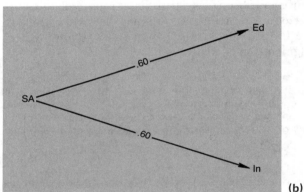

To see the same principle at work in a slightly more complicated situation, let us consider a model containing four variables instead of three. The variables of interest, depicted in Figure 11-11, are mathematical aptitude (*MA*), mathematical courses taken (*MC*), mathematical interest (*MI*) and computer interest (*CI*). The question we are trying to answer is, Does an interest in mathematics cause (directly lead to) an interest in computers? The (hypothetical) obtained correlation coefficients in Figure 11-11(a) might suggest that the answer is, Yes, inasmuch as there is a correlation of +.36 between *MI* and *CI*. However, if we assume that the true relationship is as shown in Figure 11-11(b), in which mathematical aptitude leads to taking math courses which in turn leads to both math interest and computer interest, then there would be no underlying causal link between interest in math and interest in computers. The correlation between these variables is exactly what would be expected from the other hypothesized path coefficients.

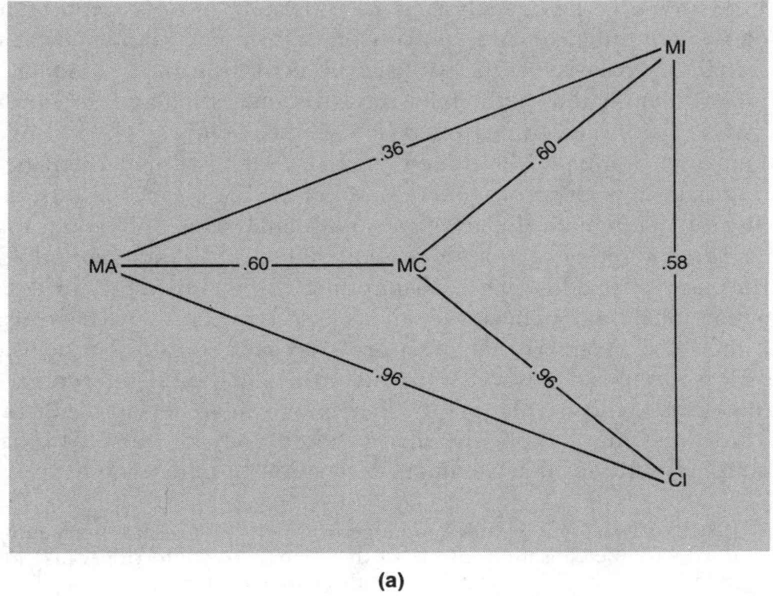

(a)

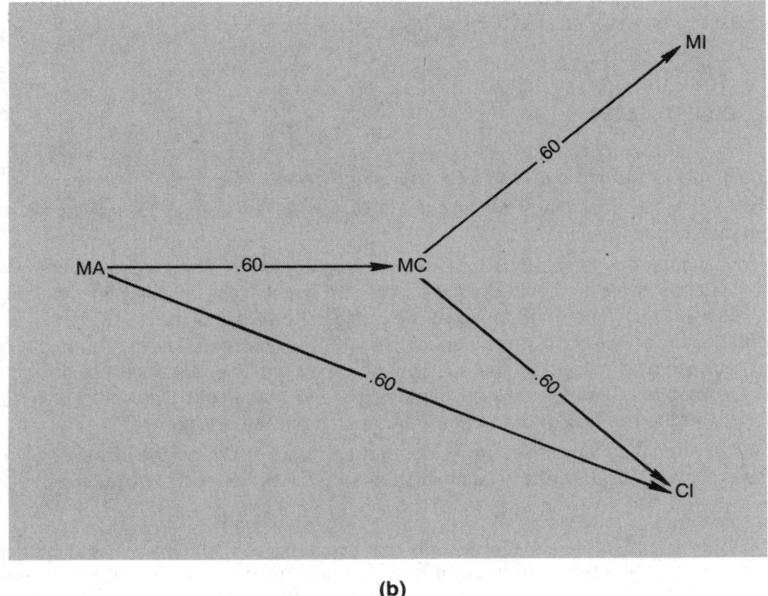

(b)

Figure 11-11 A more complex hypothetical path analysis.

In practice, path analysis is considerably more complicated than our examples might suggest[4] and, as with other complex mathematical techniques (such as factor analysis, see p. 80) it is subject to misunderstanding and abuse. A major problem is that path analysis has requirements and limitations that are easily overlooked, even by seasoned behavioral scientists. The reason is that the technique was originally developed (in the 1920s) as a mathematical tool for analyzing data in population genetics. Miller (1977, p. 331) points out that, like all statistical/mathematical procedures, path analysis is only applicable when "a rather stringent set of assumptions, both theoretical and methodological" are met. And, as Miller adds, these assumptions are in fact met "infrequently, if at all" in the social and behavioral sciences. Put in terms we have used before, causal inferences from path analysis probably lack statistical conclusion validity under most circumstances and thus invite invalid causal inferences. The most important use of path analysis may be in helping researchers in the theory-building stage to express more explicitly what a theory does, or must, assume. As Cook and Campbell note in their summary discussion of path analysis:

> [Path analysis] is a flexible language in which the precautionary messages about third-variable causation and the other dangers of inferring causation from correlation can be expressed. . . . [Path analytic] estimates of specific causal paths may occasionally be plausible and valid, but pressure to come up with a model permitting their estimation results in omissions which render most of these conclusions suspect (1979, p. 308).

FOR REVIEW AND DISCUSSION

1. Explain the difference between forecasting and causal inference.
2. Explain how the question of statistical conclusion validity applies to drawing causal inferences from passive observational data.
3. An investigator is interested in the cause of drug addiction. She takes a sample of drug addicts and matches them to nonaddicts on age, IQ, social class, stability in the home, race, and educational level. Then she looks at the subjects' past histories for evidence of emotional or mental disorder as measured by school records, police records, mental health clinic records, and retrospective reports by the subjects and their families. What kind of design is this? What are the problems associated with this design, and how might they affect this study? What is wrong with the method of data collection, apart from the design itself?
4. Consider the influence of two variables, diet and body build, on friendliness. Give the possible causal chains that describe relationships among these variables. (A number of theorists have

[4] We cannot emphasize too strongly that many practical, theoretical, and mathematical issues that must be taken into account in a real path analysis have been overlooked for the sake of achieving the simplest possible gist of the idea of path analysis. The interested reader is urged to consult Heise (1975), for an advanced discussion of the mathematical issues and Jöreskog and Sörbom (1978) for advanced computer applications.

suggested that body build is related to personality type.) In what case would examination of the partial correlation be appropriate?

5. Define the following terms:
   (a) causal analysis
   (b) no-cause baseline
   (c) time-series analysis
   (d) partial correlation
6. Given the many problems in interpreting a correlational study, why is the method used in social science research?
7. *Critically* consider the results of Berkowitz's study discussed on p. 230. Do the data permit an unambiguous causal inference? What further data might you want to evaluate?
8. In many studies, a strikingly high correlation has been found between social class and type of mental disorder: low social class is associated with psychosis. Two hypotheses can account for this relationship: H_1, the stress of being in a low social class produces psychosis; H_2, psychosis causes individuals to drift down to the lower social class. Design a time-lagged correlational study that would test these hypotheses. Make up two sets of data that would provide support for each of the hypotheses.
9. Explain the purpose and limitations of path analysis.

12

External Validity

THE PROBLEM OF INDUCTION
- Types of External Validity

POPULATION VALIDITY
- Random Assignment versus Random Selection
- Generalizing to versus Generalizing Across Populations
- Threats to Population Validity
  - cost-restricted sampling
  - self-selection and volunteer bias
  - misuse of clinical samples
  - animal research and generalizing across species

ECOLOGICAL VALIDITY
- Generalizing Across Geographic Areas
- Treatment by Setting Interactions
- Temporal Validity
- Generalizing Across Treatments
- Generalizing From Unique Contexts
- Generalizing Across Experimenters

HOW TO INCREASE EXTERNAL VALIDITY
- Field Experiments
- Broad Sampling
- Meta-Analysis

RELATIONSHIP AMONG TYPES OF VALIDITY
- Relationship Between Internal Validity and External Validity
- External Validity and Theoretical Validity

FOR REVIEW AND DISCUSSION

Suppose an experimenter, interested in the effects of reward on learning, demonstrates that laboratory rats will more quickly learn to turn right in a T-maze if they are rewarded for every such turn during training than if they are rewarded only occasionally. In addition to showing that there were no serious competing explanations (that is, that the research is internally valid), the investigator might want to know the degree to which these findings could be *generalized*. Do the results apply for learning situations other than the T-maze? Would similar findings occur if a situation were devised that employed human children or adults rather than laboratory rats? Would the same effect be obtained if another type of reward were used? All these questions involve *external validity*, or the generalizability of findings.

THE PROBLEM OF INDUCTION

External validity is related to the larger philosophical question of whether *induction*, or reasoning from particular facts to a general conclusion, should be admissible in scientific work. The issue may be traced to David Hume (1711–1776), the Scottish philosopher whose thoroughgoing epistemological skepticism led him to the conclusion that induction (and therefore any scientific generalizations based on it) is never logically justifiable.

The logical problem is that you can never be sure what form as yet unobserved data or situations may take. As an example of how induction may fail, suppose you were given the numbers 2, 4, 6, 8, 10, 12, told that they represented an orderly sequence, and asked to "predict" the next number. Understandably, most people would say 14 and feel quite confident in their answer. There are, however, an infinite number of other orderly sequences that could also have generated the six numbers you were given in which 14 is not the next number. For example: 2, 4, 6, 8, 10, 12, 27, 2, 4, 6, 8, 10, 12, 27, 2, 4, 6, 8, 10, 12, 27. . . .

Many contemporary philosophers, as well as most social scientists, regard the logical problem of induction as a technicality. Induction cannot be completely justified as a logical form, but modern science has been quite successful in using inductive generalizations fruitfully as a guide to further empirical knowledge, as in the application of Mendel's famous experiments on inheritance in peas to many plant and animal species. Nonetheless, real practical concerns remain as to when induction is safe and when it is risky, and several major threats to inductive generalizations have been recognized in recent years. Investigators have learned how to design research in such a way that generalization across experimenters, populations, treatments, and research settings is reasonable. Let us take a closer look at the specific issues.

Types of External Validity

Broadly speaking, there are two types of external validity: population validity and ecological validity. *Population validity* refers to the question of whether the responses or behavior of subjects in the actual research sample can be generalized to the target population, that is, the population of ultimate interest. *Ecological validity* refers to the question of whether the research findings can be generalized to all of the environmental contexts of interest. Environmental context, or ecology, includes a wide range of factors, including the time, place, and people that surround and interact with individuals as they go about the business of living their lives.

POPULATION VALIDITY

The A. C. Nielsen Company is famous for its "Nielsen ratings," which estimate the television viewing preferences of almost 200 million U. S. viewers with quite high accuracy from a sample of fewer than 2000 households. This sample is only about one-tenth of one percent of the population![1] Nielsen's sample data can be generalized because the population of interest can be specified clearly (all U. S. households with television sets) and a representative cross-national sample of households which closely matches population characteristics is employed. In most social and behavioral research the population of interest cannot be specified so clearly, nor can a truly random (or representative) sample be drawn. Rather, accidental samples or *samples of convenience* are the rule rather than the exception. For this reason, generalization in psychological research typically involves two steps. First, the investigator generalizes from the sample employed to the accessible population from which it was drawn. And then, second, the investigator generalizes from the accessible population to the target population of ultimate interest.

In order to understand the question of population validity more fully, it is important to appreciate two major distinctions. One is the distinction between *random selection* and *random assignment*, and the other is the distinction between generalizing *to* populations and generalizing *across* populations.

Random Assignment versus Random Selection

Random assignment involves assigning subjects to groups such that each subject has an equal chance of being assigned to any of the groups. Random selection is a different process and involves the selection of the individuals who will participate as subjects from the target population of interest. The distinction is an important one to keep in mind for two reasons. For one thing, whereas random assignment is fairly common in psychological research (especially in

[1]Tallying is done by Nielsen's Storage Instantaneous Audimeter. The Audimeter notes whether the set is ON or OFF: If it is ON the device records the minute-by-minute impulses of channel changes and stores them in an electronic memory. The unit is connected both to the family TV set and to a special telephone line, from which the stored information is relayed at least twice daily to a central office computer.

laboratory experiments) random selection is extremely rare in the social and behavioral sciences. And second, whereas the absence of random assignment is principally a threat to internal validity, the absence of random selection is principally a threat to external validity.

Generalizing to versus Generalizing Across Populations

Cook and Campbell (1979) stress the importance of the distinction between generalizing to a population and generalizing across subpopulations. The distinction can be illustrated with an example. Suppose our population of interest was the entire student body of a large university where two new food plans were being considered. Also assume we were able to draw two samples randomly from the population of all students and assigned the Eatwell food plan to one group and the Fryright meal plan to the other. After a one month trial, we ask the members of each group to rate the food plan they have been on and find that those on the Eatwell plan are more satisfied than those on the Fryright plan. Because our samples were drawn randomly from the entire student body we can safely generalize from the sample results to the population and infer that, in general, the Eatwell plan would be preferred by the student body as a whole. However, we could not safely generalize across all the subpopulations that comprise the student body. For example, despite our general results favoring the Eatwell plan, Fryright might be preferred by freshmen (or any other specific subpopulation). Thus, our generalization across all subpopulations (e.g., freshmen, sophomores, juniors, seniors, graduate students) would very possibly not hold up for all of them.

Threats to Population Validity

The major threats to population validity all involve the possibility of interactions between treatment and selection. Such interactions pose one of the most serious threats to external validity, especially because we can almost never obtain equal access and compliance from all members of the target population and thus can almost never have random selection. There are two major constraints that operate against ending up with a truly representative sample from the target population: cost and subject self-selection.

Cost-restricted Sampling. Most researchers have a very wide intended target population but are compelled by cost considerations to draw their subjects from only a narrow segment of the target population. For example, a team of investigators in San Francisco may be interested in adolescents all over the United States (or perhaps even all over the world) but will probably be forced to obtain their subjects entirely from California and perhaps entirely from one or two high schools in the San Francisco Bay area.

Self-selection and Volunteer Bias. The other constraint on subject selection is that, regardless of how extensive the subject recruitment effort is, participation is voluntary and thus we end up with an actual group of subjects who are different from the general population.

Although random assignment controls for the effects of selection as a threat to internal validity (see Chapter 7), without random selection the possibility remains that the effects validly demonstrated in a particular experiment hold only for the specific population from which the experimental and control groups have been selected. In studies in which it is necessary to seek volunteers who are apprised of, and agree to participate in, certain kinds of treatments, it is possible that the demonstrated effects of a particular manipulation or a simple association between variables will hold only for a sample possessing the special psychological characteristics of volunteers. In fact, *as a general rule, the possibility of drawing invalid generalizations because of selection bias tends to increase directly as a function of the difficulty involved in obtaining subjects for a study.*

The problem of volunteer bias is perhaps best exemplified through systematic analyses of the special characteristics of research volunteers, one of the few areas of selection bias in which information has been collected. Rosenthal and Rosnow (1969) found from their survey of the literature on the characteristics of voluntary subjects that these individuals tended to be (1) higher in educational level, (2) higher in occupational status, (3) higher in need for approval, (4) higher in IQ, and (5) lower in authoritarianism than the populations from which they came. Clearly, there would be ample opportunity for any of these characteristics to interact with an experimental treatment to produce results that cannot be generalized safely. Requiring subjects to participate in research does not solve the problem, as long as the subjects are still free to choose the experiments in which they will participate. Persons who are especially interested in some type of research may behave differently when exposed to the experimental treatments than would other randomly sampled individuals from the same population.

This problem is especially acute in research with college populations. The undergraduate shares with the laboratory rat the status of the most easily available and therefore the most favored subject for behavioral research. Consider a report by Smart (1966). He reviewed articles in the *Journal of Abnormal and Social Psychology* and articles in the *Journal of Experimental Psychology* from 1962 to 1964 and found that 73 percent of the articles in the former journal and 86 percent of those in the latter used college students as subjects. Furthermore, a disproportionate number of these subjects were male. Evidence is accumulating rapidly to suggest that many characteristics of college populations may interact with the treatments given them and thus sharply limit the generality of many conclusions.

The problem of limitations imposed by the sample on generalizability is by no means limited to college students. Consider an investigation that succeeds in teaching five-year-old children to recognize that pouring all the water from a tall thin beaker into a short squat beaker does not change the total volume of water. (The reader will recall that this is the Piagetian conservation of liquid volume problem.) The effects may be internally valid and generalizable to other five-year-old samples, but the investigator must be wary of advancing the more general proposition that this particular method will teach "conservation" to children regardless of age. The same methods might be totally ineffective with four-year-old children. Mixed designs using characteristics of subjects as the classificatory variable (see Chapter 9) may be used to assess this form of external validity directly.

Misuse of Clinical Samples. Detecting selection bias is not always obvious. For example, the widespread use of self-identified clinical populations (that is, people who present themselves to physicians or psychologists for treatment) also invites misleading conclusions about the tractability of their presenting problem. This possibility is clearly illustrated in a study by Schachter (1982). The origin of the study was the massive data on psychologists' attempts to help people quit smoking—attempts that have been notoriously unsuccessful. Schachter quotes numerous sources as concluding that the overwhelming majority of people treated for smoking, between 80 and 90 percent, relapse and return to their smoking habit within 12 months after treatment. (Many don't make it that long.) And yet, Schachter notes, "virtually everyone knows large numbers of people who have quit smoking, apparently permanently" (1982, p. 436). A similar contrast, he adds, holds for obesity.

Why does such a disparity exist between findings in the clinical literature and personal experience or the experience of friends and relatives? One answer is that people who cure themselves do not go to therapists. Thus:

> Our view of the intractability of the addictive states has been molded largely by that self-selected, hard-core group of people who, unable or unwilling to help themselves, go to therapists for help, thereby becoming the only easily available subjects for studies of recidivism and addiction (Schachter, 1982, p. 437).

To demonstrate his point, Schachter set out to study the "cure" rates for smoking and obesity in two nonselected populations, namely, all the people in the Psychology Department at Columbia University (including faculty, graduate students, secretaries, and technicians—a total of 84 people, 83 of whom agreed to be interviewed as part of the study) and all the people working in shops in the center of Amagansett, Long Island (a total of 48 people in 19 shops, of whom 47 consented to be interviewed).

The interviews, which were done with painstaking care to reduce the possibility of bias, revealed that almost 64 percent of those who once smoked and had tried to quit succeeded; likewise, almost the same percentage, 63 percent, of those who tried to lose weight and "keep it off" had done so. Thus,

> . . . . in nontherapeutic populations the rates of successful self-cure of cigarette smoking and of obesity are considerably higher than anything yet reported in the therapeutic literature. This conclusion is based on virtually 100% samples of

> two different populations—an urban university psychology department and a geographically defined portion of the entrepreneurial and working population of a very small town. The fact that the rates of self-cure are so similar in these two populations is taken as evidence that these findings are generalizable beyond any single demographic group. (Schachter, 1982, pp. 441–442)

Animal Research and Generalizing Across Species. The issue of population validity also arises in research with animals whenever investigators presume they can generalize across species.

The hazards involved in the assumption of interspecies generality can be illustrated by a discussion of avoidance learning. In a well-known investigation (Solomon & Wynne, 1953), dogs were placed into a compartment that was divided into two halves by a low barrier. The floor of the compartment was electrified so that a shock could be administered to the animals. On each trial a buzzer sounded for a ten-second period prior to the onset of the shock. If the dog jumped into the other half of the compartment before the buzzer went off it would not be shocked. If the dog did not jump during this period, the shock came on and remained on until the animals *escaped* to the other side. After an initial number of trials on which the dogs received shock, they learned to completely *avoid* shock by jumping when the buzzer came on. Once the avoidance response was established, it was found to be highly resistant to extinction; that is, the animals continued to jump for hundreds of trials even though they received no further shock.

Results such as those obtained by Solomon and Wynne were at first assumed to be widely general across populations and even formed the basis for accounts of the acquisition and maintenance of phobic behavior in humans. Later findings, though, called into question the generality of Solomon and Wynne's canine data. Bolles (1970) has shown that only the species' typical responses to fear can rapidly be acquired in this fashion. The rat's typical response to fear is flight. Thus:

> The frequently reported failures of rats to learn [avoidance responses], such as wheel turning . . . and bar pressing . . . should not be regarded as peculiar or exceptions . . . but rather as one end of a continuum of difficulty of learning (p. 34).

From the foregoing material it may be seen that *the generality of research findings across species should be assessed rather than presumed*. However, even when such assessments are made, a problem remains: An experimental situation may be created that artificially produces a close parallel between results obtained from animals and those from humans.

Suppose an investigator has noted that laboratory rats solve a particular problem in a trial-and-error fashion. The investigator now attempts to establish the generality of the original findings by creating a parallel situation for some human subjects and, in fact, finds a similar pattern of results. The problem with such a study is that the experimental arrangements could have effectively "decorticated" the human subjects. A situation may have been created that eliminates the major portion of the cerebral ability of humans from consideration. Although a parallel may be demonstrated between the two species, it may also be the case that humans in a nonlaboratory setting rarely learn in the way that was studied in the laboratory.

ECOLOGICAL VALIDITY

In addition to the limitations placed on generalization by the subject characteristics of the sample (i.e., the issue of population validity) there is also the question of the degree to which it is appropriate to generalize from one context to another, i.e., the question of ecological validity. In this regard we shall consider six specific issues.

Generalizing Across Geographic Areas

Presuming generality over geographic areas is one of the most common implicit assumptions made by psychologists and many other social scientists. However, populations tapped by a particular research method may vary from location to location geographically. For example, it is likely that public transportation systems serve very different segments of the population in Los Angeles than they do in New York City. Experiments conducted with samples drawn from public buses in Los Angeles might not produce the same effects had the research been conducted on the public buses running down Fifth Avenue or up to Harlem.

It is commonly assumed that generalizing across geographic areas is at least somewhat risky for applied or social research but considerably less risky when such basic processes as perception or memory are involved. It is not entirely clear that this asumption is correct, however. As we saw in Chapter 6, virtually all research involving contact between experimenters and subjects has a social component that may influence the nature, speed, or accuracy of responses. To this we would add that there is little doubt that there are substantial regional differences in such aspects of social behavior as how to deal with strangers, peers, and authority figures.

Treatment by Setting Interactions

Treatment by setting interactions occur when treatments have different effects because of type of setting (e.g., the same young men may react differently on a university campus than they do in a military camp). Such interactions also occur because volunteer organizations (like individual volunteers) may be atypical of the populations they are intended to represent. Volunteering organizations tend to be "the most progressive, proud, and institutionally exhibitionist" (Cook & Campbell, 1979, p. 74).

Consider, for example, a study of the effects of white and Hispanic teachers on Hispanic children in public elementary school systems. By virtue of the "socially sensitive" nature of such investigations, it is possible that a researcher will be turned down by several school systems or districts before finding an administration that will approve the research. In this case, it is entirely possible that the investigation will no longer have a representative sample of the population of Hispanic children and of Hispanic and white teachers. Inasmuch as a willingness to permit research of this type to be conducted in their schools might be related to classroom practices or to characteristics of the pupils, it is clear that a bias might occur and lead the researcher to generalize incorrectly from the results. Moreover, as long as the bias continues to exist, the problem cannot be solved by increasing sample size per se. If instead of making a request to five schools and obtaining one acceptance, the investigator made a similar request to fifty schools and received permission to work in five of them, the problem of selection bias would in no way be eliminated.

Temporal Validity

Social science research findings may be ungeneralizable to the extent that they are time bound. For example, a comparison of two types of teaching procedures, one of which is more likely to capture or focus a child's attention than another, might be very striking for groups of young children who participated in an experiment conducted at a nursery school in the late afternoon. However, the effects might not differ nearly so sharply if the experiment were conducted in the morning, when all children were better rested and more alert and attentive. Similarly, treatments designed to reduce cigarette smoking or energy consumption might be effective only because they are tried right after a cancer scare or an OPEC oil embargo. In these cases, temporal effects can interact catalytically with treatments to produce an effect of limited generality.

Likewise, many behaviors show seasonal or cyclical variations so that measures taken at one time may not be generalizable to other times (see Willson, 1981). College students, for example, appear to show considerably higher levels of anxiety and depression toward the end of the semester or quarter (when exams are imminent) than at other times during the academic year. Their performance in experiments during these times (which is also when voluntary participation for extra credit is most likely to occur) may not even generalize to what the very same students would have done at other times of the year! Similarly, laboratory animals demonstrate cyclical variations (e.g., circadian rhythms) in bodily functions that may make them respond to drug or environmental treatments very differently at one time than at another (Hunsicker & Mellgren, 1977).

Generalizing Across Treatments

When subjects are exposed to more than one treatment (see repeated measures designs, discussed in Chapter 8), the experimental effects may be limited to persons who in fact have experienced multiple treatments and may not be generalizable in terms of the effectiveness of the treatments when applied singly. Campbell and Stanley (1966) have called this problem *multiple treatment interference*.

In an early experiment (Jost, 1897), a comparison was made between "spaced" and "massed" practice in learning nonsense syllables. The investigator constructed twelve lists of nonsense syllables and had a single subject, Professor G. E. Muller, learn six lists under massed practice conditions and six under spaced practice conditions. Both lists were learned simultaneously over a period of seven days. The results suggested that spaced practice was superior to massed practice in learning.

However, in a much later experiment, Underwood and Richardson (1958) found that the superiority of spaced practice was limited to persons who were simultaneously learning several lists under the two conditions. No such differences appeared when a between-subjects design was used in which some persons learned with massed trials and others with spaced trials. (The limitation in the earlier finding probably stems from the fact that interference effects on the massed trials tend to be quite high when they are intertwined with the spaced trials.)

Generalizing from Unique Contexts

The ecological validity of generalizations is seriously threatened whenever data are collected on a special day (e.g., when a disaster such as a blackout, a severe storm, or the assassination of an important personage has taken place).

Consider, for example, a study by Zucker, Manosevitz, and Lanyon (1968) designed to demonstrate a relationship between birth order and anxiety reactions. These investigators capitalized on the massive power failure that encompassed the Eastern Seaboard of the United States on November 9 and 10, 1965. In New York City the blackout began at about 5:30 PM, at the height of the rush hour. As a result thousands of people on their way home from work were forced to spend the night in public places. During that evening Zucker and his associates went to a large bus terminal illuminated by emergency power and asked people to fill out a questionnaire requesting information regarding their birth order and their feelings about being stranded for the night. The investigators found that first born individuals expressed more anxiety about being stranded than did later borns, which certainly suggests that birth order is related to some anxiety reactions. Nonetheless, the context was so distinctive that it is impossible to know to which other contexts the results could be appropriately generalized.

Generalizing Across Experimenters

McGuigan (1963), in referring to the experimenter as a "neglected stimulus object," has noted:

> While we have traditionally recognized that the characteristics of an experimenter may indeed influence behavior, it is important to observe that we have not

> seriously attempted to study him as an independent variable. Rather, we have typically regarded the experimenter as necessary, but undesirable for the conduct of an experiment. Accordingly, in introductory textbooks on experimental psychology we provide prescriptions for controlling this extraneous variable; but seldom do we consider the experimenter variable further, and the extent to which we actually control it in our experimentation can be seriously questioned (p. 421).

Various investigator characteristics have been shown to have demonstrable effects on the behavior of subjects. Characteristics such as sex, race, and likability or "warmth," have all been documented as potential influences (Rosenthal, 1963). An example may be drawn from a sensory deprivation study reported by Walters, Shurley, and Parsons (1962). Following the isolation experience, male and female subjects were interviewed by either a male or a female. The way in which subjects responded to questions about sexual feelings differed as a function of whether the experimenter and subject were same or opposite in sex. (More sexual feelings were reported when subject and experimenter were of the same sex.)

Similarly, Kanfer (1958) reported a verbal conditioning experiment conducted by two experimenters. Subjects were requested to say words continuously and verbs were rewarded according to one of three reinforcement schedules. The results indicated a reinforcement schedule × experimenter interaction. There was more frequent reinforcement of words for one schedule than for others, the frequency varying for the experimenters. *The only means available for assessing the influence of the investigator is to employ more than one data collector in any piece of research.* Attempts to control for possible investigator effects generally take the form of making all research personnel as "neutral" as possible. For example, it is good practice to write out scripts and rehearse procedures to reduce unwanted variation.

HOW TO INCREASE EXTERNAL VALIDITY

There are many ways to try to increase the external validity of social and behavioral research. In this section we discuss four broad possibilities. In most cases where external validity is of concern at least one of these approaches, and perhaps more than one, can be considered.

Field Experiments

We have seen in previous chapters that whereas correlational investigations are often based on data obtained from naturally occurring events, experimental research has usually been collected in the laboratory. The basis and justification for this tradition has already been implied; Rosenthal has stated it this way:

> . . . In our discipline as in others, the laboratory experiment is a preferred mode for the observation of nature. It is so preferred because of the greater control it gives us over the inputs to the experimental subject. Unlike the usual situation in the field or in the "real world," when we observe the behavior of the subject of a psychological experiment we are in a position to attribute his behavior to the antecedent conditions that we have ourselves arranged (1967, p. 356).

The point appears to be well taken. We have already noted the many advantages of experimental over correlational research for adducing causal relationships. But on more careful consideration, arguments such as the foregoing mask two distinctions under the appearance of one. We must distinguish between the methods underlying an investigation (for example, experimental versus correlational) and the location in which the investigation takes place. The strength of the experimental method *vis-à-vis* internal validity should not seduce us into overlooking the weakness of the laboratory as a location regarding generalizability. A critic has argued:

> . . . Where an attempt is made to understand events in the natural world, which all theory must neccessarily do if it is to be more than an intellectual exercise, it is necessary to bridge the gap between the natural event and the experimental situation. . . . Because an event can be produced in the laboratory does not mean that the event is so produced in the natural world . . . [and the reverse is also true. An effect that does *not* appear in the laboratory may actually occur in the natural world].
>
> I can produce a light by pressing a button on a flashlight, but this does not prove that the sun is a giant flashlight, which someone turns on and off on a twelve-hour schedule (Epstein, 1962, p. 269).

One such bridge is the field experiment. *A field experiment is an investigation in which one or more of the events of interest are manipulated, as independent variables, in a manner and location that directly samples the naturally occurring situation that one wishes to explain or understand.* In the same vein, the dependent variable(s) employed in such an investigation are obtained as "spontaneously" occurring responses that the subject is not likely to perceive as produced or measured for the purposes of a scientific investigation. Thus, the field experiment may provide an excellent solution to the problem of uncertain generalizability.

The adequate field experiment must be internally valid or it is of no use whatever. Otherwise, though, no simple guidelines can be advanced for producing a wholly satisfactory field experiment. Some have been criticized for unfortunate contaminations in the service of preserving "naturalness." But others have embodied a flair for ingenuity and shrewd planning sufficient to identify both unambiguous experimental effects and to elucidate further some of the basic processes that underlie human social behavior. In the last category fall the well-designed experiments of helping behavior in the New York subways by Piliavin, Rodin, and Piliavin (1969), the highways of Los Angeles by Bryan and Test (1967), and in front of the supermarkets of Oklahoma by Wispé and Freshley (1971).

To illustrate, we shall briefly consider a carefully and neatly devised field experiment by Hornstein, Fisch, and Holmes (1968). These investigators began with the frequently obtained experimental laboratory finding that observation of a helping model can increase the probability that an observer will render assistance to a needy person. However, earlier studies provided relatively little information as to the mechanisms that underlie the modeling process in such situations. Hornstein et al. explored this issue, designing their field experiment to test the proposition that "an observer sees the model's experiences as a valid predictor of his own future experiences." In turn, this proposition leads to the prediction that when the observer perceives the model as *similar* to himself, he will see the model's experiences as a valid predictor of what his own experiences would be if he also engaged in the exemplary behavior. In such an instance, the observer would be expected to imitate the model if the helping experience had been positive for him but to avoid imitation if it had been negative. In contrast, should the observer see the model as *dissimilar* to himself he will not consider the model's experiences to be a valid predictor. In the latter case, the observer should be no more likely to imitate an exemplar who has had positive experiences than one who has had negative experiences. How can this sophisticated set of predictions, requiring a 3 × 2 factorial design, be tested outside of the laboratory?

Hornstein and his associates inconspicuously deposited addressed but unstamped envelopes containing a man's wallet and a letter on a sidewalk in midtown Manhattan's business district. The wallet contained an assortment of items designed to create the impression of an "average owner," Michael Erwin. Included were $2 in cash, an identification card, postage stamps, membership cards (for two fictitious organizations), a receipt for a rented tuxedo, the calling cards of a podiatrist and a florist, and some other nondescript items.

A typewritten letter, which provided the basis for the experience-of-the-model variable, gave the impression that the wallet had been lost not once but twice. The situation was designed to suggest that when the wallet was lost initially its first finder (the model) intended to return it and had placed it in an envelope, along with a letter describing his feelings. But this well-intentioned individual then lost both the wallet and the letter. The pedestrian who found the wallet the "second" time, and who thereby became an unwitting subject in the experiment, had to decide between returning the wallet (and thereby imitating his predecessor's helping behavior) or keeping it and the money for himself.

To manipulate the perceived similarity between the observer-subject and the model, the letter was written either in familiar English (*similar model* condition) or in ungrammatical broken English that created the impression of a foreign writer of ambiguous extraction (*dissimilar model* condition). Within each of these conditions, some of the letters described the writer's feeling of pleasure at returning the wallet (*positive letter* condition), some expressed distinct annoyance at having to be bothered (*negative letter* condition), and some did not reveal the feelings of the finder (*neutral letter* condition). The letters used are presented in Table 12-1.

The percentage of wallets actually returned intact for each group, the dependent measure, is presented in Figure 12-1, from which it can be seen that the Hornstein et al. predictions received clear and striking support. When the letter appeared to have been written by a similar model, positive and neutral experiences produced far more returns than negative experiences, whereas no such differences appeared for the dissimilar condition. In addition to being intrinsically interesting, the investigation demonstrates that adequate experimental control and ingenious probing of naturally occurring events can be obtained in the field. Although field experiments are often difficult to conduct, when they are well done they offer compelling evidence concerning the external validity of a causal relationship.

Table 12-1 The Letters Used by Hornstein et al. to Manipulate the Feelings of Its Original Finder (Model) and His Similarity to the Second Finder (Subject)

	MODEL CONDITION	
Letter Condition	*Similar*	*Dissimilar*
Neutral*	Dear Mr. Erwin: I found your wallet which I am returning. Everything is here just as I found it.	Dear Mr. Erwin: I am visit your country finding your ways not familiar and strange. But I find your wallet which I here return. Everything is here just as I find it.
Positive†	I must say that it has been a pleasure to be able to help somebody in the small things that make life nicer. It's really been no problem at all and I'm glad to be able to help.	It great pleasure to help somebody with tiny things which make life nicer. It is not problem at all and I glad to be able to help.
Negative†	I must say that taking responsibility for the wallet and having to return it has been a great inconvenience. I was quite annoyed at having to bother with the whole problem of returning it. I hope you appreciate the efforts that I have gone through.	To take responsibility for wallet and necessity to return it is great inconvenience. Is annoyance to bother with whole problem of return and hope you appreciate effort I went to.

* The neutral letter said no more than this.

† The positive and negative letters began with the neutral statement.

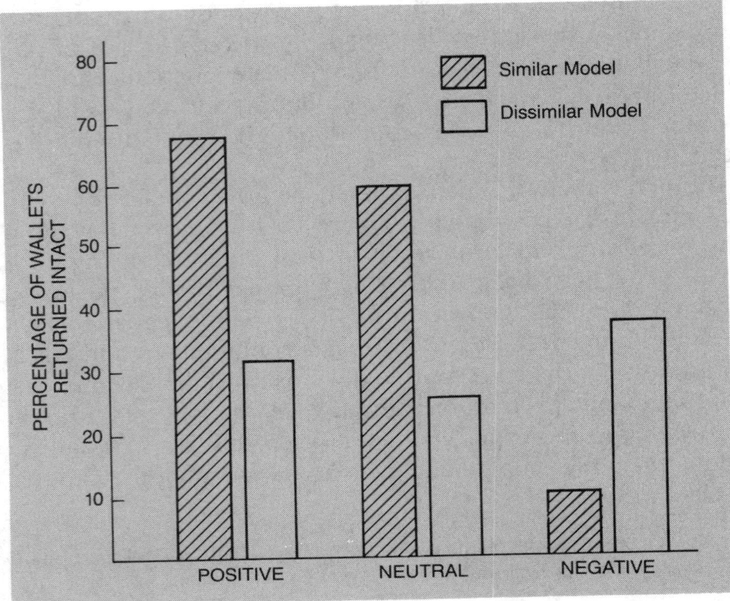

Figure 12-1 Percentage of wallets returned intact in the Hornstein et al. experiment as a function of the similarity to and feeling of the model. Only when the model was similar did his feelings influence the return rate.

Broad Sampling

Many investigations lack external validity because they suffer from narrow or inadequate sampling. In this section we discuss specific ways to increase the breadth of research samples.

In endeavoring to solve the problem of generalizing beyond a specific sample, the investigator should take two steps: (1) decide on an adequate definition of the population to which he or she is interested in generalizing and (2) determine the degree to which the particular sample in hand is sufficiently different from the population of interest in such a fashion as to render generalization hazardous.

Regarding the first point, it is clear that some investigators conducting research with child subjects may be interested in generalizing to the entire population of children. This would be the case, for example, in investigations that compare teaching techniques. Indeed, when such research is successful, the discussion of the results will typically include the implication that a discovery of wide generality has been found. Any such conclusions would be limited, however, if the research sample had been restricted, for example, to children from poor families. In contrast, the investigator who is particularly interested in educational programs for disadvantaged youngsters would have much less reason to be concerned about the generality problem if he or she used the same sample of children. As a general rule, *the best solution to the problem of population generalization is to define and randomly sample directly from the population of ultimate interest, employing mixed designs to include nonexperimental variables that may be of particular theoretical and practical importance.*

The second decision, involving the identification of plausible limits to generality, is somewhat more difficult. In most instances, a result in the social sciences is interpreted as "standing" (as an appropriate generalization) until compelling argument or antagonistic data explicitly suggest some limitation. For example, if an investigator wishes to test a particular hypothesis regarding the effects of a certain type of training on children's learning and arbitrarily selects seven-year-old youngsters as a research sample, the generality of the findings is likely to be accepted and presumed to be applicable to somewhat older and younger children until a serious failure to replicate (with a different age group) appears in the literature. Should the latter happen, then an appropriate investigation would involve a mixed design (see Chapter 9) including the two age groups in question and the presence or absence of the experimental treatment.

Suppose, however, that it is not possible to access the entire population of interest. In such cases the next best thing is to have the broadest possible sample within existing constraints. One way to do this involves increasing the range of persons who will volunteer to participate by making participation as convenient, inviting, and enjoyable as possible. Researchers who ask participants to complete lengthy and tedious questionnaires will end up with a less representative sample than those who have reduced their measures to simple, quick, attractive, and easy formats.

Another solution is to increase representativeness. Cook and Campbell (1979) suggest two novel ways to do this: *haphazard sampling* and *impressionistic modal sampling.*

Haphazard sampling involves purposely taking every opportunity to get the widest range of subjects, experimenters, treatments, and settings represented in one's research. Such a strategy will surely increase representativeness relative to using a single subpopulation in a single setting with a single experimenter because many selection biases will be reduced or canceled out by heterogeneity. The limitation of this strategy is that such heterogeneity serves external validity at the expense of statistical power by increasing the amount of random, unaccounted for variance ("error," see p. 155) in the measures of interest.

Impressionistic modal sampling is applicable to situations in which the population is comprised of institutional units and cost or other considerations limit the researcher's access to more than just a few of them. For example, the elementary schools in a large city are likely to be quite diverse and it would rarely be possible to randomly sample from all of them. One might, however, form an impression of what types of schools are "typical" (that is, modal) from examining the dimensions on which they vary and then selecting a few schools as modal cases. For example, if the schools vary in racial composition and in the economic groups on which they draw, we might select a middle-class, mostly white school, a lower-class school with many minority pupils, and a racially and economically mixed school as three modal cases that represent the range of elementary schools found in the city.

Finally, *constructive replication,* in which an experiment is repeated so as to preserve the presumed essential features of the original while varying details presumed to be irrelevant, is a powerful technique for increasing external validity by increasing representativeness.

Meta-analysis

So far in our discussion we have implicitly assumed that external validity is being sought for a "new" research question, that is, one which has not been raised before. Often, however, there is abundant literature related to a question of interest and the problem is one of summarizing the literature and tying it together. *Meta-analysis* is the name given to any set of systematic rules for combining and evaluating a collection of independent replications or partial replications.

Meta-analysis begins with a specification of the independent and dependent variables of interest. Then an exhaustive literature search is undertaken to identify all studies in the literature which fall within the specified domain. (Modern library computer searches, based on critical identifying words and phrases associated with the phenomena of interest, have led to enormous gains in the speed, efficiency, and thoroughness with which such searches can be conducted.)

Once all the relevant studies have been identified and gathered, meta-analytic statistical techniques are used to convert the outcome of each study to a common format and scale of measurement. There are several different ways to approach this task, but most involve computing a measure of statistical significance and a measure of the size of the effect found for each study. The converted data from each of the studies are then weighted and averaged to give a picture of the overall reliability and strength of the relationships with which the studies deal. We need not be concerned here with many of the actual statistical procedures involved. The interested reader is referred to Glass, McGaw, and Smith (1981), and Rosenthal and Rubin (1982) for detailed explanations of the meta-analytic approach and its several variations.

As an example of a recent meta-analysis, we will consider one reported by Findley and Cooper (1983), dealing with the relationship between locus of control and academic achievement. Briefly, locus of control refers to the degree to which individuals believe they themselves have control over the events in their lives. Locus of control is a continuous variable, but individuals who for the most part believe they control their own destinies are called internals, whereas those who believe that what happens to them is mostly determined by fate or luck are called externals. The question addressed by Findley and Cooper's meta-analysis was whether locus of control is related to academic achievement.

The initial literature search revealed that the question had been posed often. Findley and Cooper found 275 tests of the link between locus of control and academic achievement, reported in 98 different studies. The studies were extremely diverse; they involved the whole age range between first graders and adults, and represented both sexes and the entire gamut of backgrounds. In addition, 22 different measures of locus of control could be found among the studies, as well as 36 different measures of achievement. The problem in such situations becomes one of finding a common base on which the studies can be combined and compared. Findley and Cooper used the Z-scores (i.e., standard scores, see p. 70) associated with each study's reported *p* value. After the Z-scores were calculated they were combined to compute an overall or meta-analytic Z (Z_{ma}).[2] The meta-analytic Z obtained in this way was 11.08, which is highly significant. Indeed, the possibility of getting a Z_{ma} this large by chance is only about one in a million!

There is, however, a potential threat looming over any analysis that reviews and "averages" results reported in the literature; namely, the possibility that many investigators have conducted studies that looked for the effect in question but had not found it, in which case the studies probably would not have been reported at all. Rosenthal (1979) has called this the *file drawer problem,* because null findings are often simply filed away. The statistical check on such a possibility involves calculating the number of unreported studies that would be needed to reduce the obtained Z_{ma} to nonsignificance. In Findley and Cooper's meta-analysis 3,327 null studies would have to have been conducted but filed away to reduce their Z_{ma} to nonsignificance. It is obviously implausible to assume that that many null studies exist. We can therefore conclude with considerable confidence that there is a relationship between locus of control and academic achievement, such that internals tend to achieve more than externals.

Most meta-analyses do not stop here, however. Rather they go on to ask how strong the relationship is, both overall and for various subpopulations. The strength of these relationships, called *effect size,* can be indexed by *r* (see p. 61), and *r* can be computed easily from reported *F*s, *t*s, and chi-squares, which is how Findley and Cooper proceeded. The overall *r* averaging across all the studies was .18, which is highly significant because of the large N involved, but which means that locus of control accounts for barely more than 3% of the variance in academic achievement ($.18 \times .18 = .032$).

The other question that can be answered by meta-analysis is, Across which subpopulations is the relationship strongest and weakest? Table 12-2 presents the average *r*s found in Findley and Cooper's meta-analysis according to gender, age, race, and socioeconomic status. As can be seen from the table, the relationship between locus of control and academic achievement is stronger for males than for females, stronger for those from the lower class than those from the middle class, and stronger for young adolescents (i.e., those in junior high) than for any other age group.

[2] Details of the procedure are explained in Rosenthal (1978).

Table 12-2 Average Effect Size for Various Subgroups in Findley and Cooper's (1983) Meta-analysis of the Relationship between Locus of Control and Academic Achievement

CHARACTERISTICS	AVERAGE r
Gender	
Males	.20
Females	.11
Age	
College	.14
High school	.23
Junior high	.35
4th–6th grade	.24
1st–3rd grade	.04
Race	
Black	.25
White	.25
Socioeconomic status	
Middle class	.26
Lower class	.35

Source: From data reported in Findley and Cooper (1983)

Meta-analysis has also been used recently to demonstrate the external validity of the claim that psychotherapy is moderately effective (Smith, Glass, & Miller, 1980) and that modifying what people say to themselves about themselves ("self-statements") is an effective form of therapy for many psychological problems (Dush, Hirt, & Schroeder, 1983). A recent meta-analysis also confirmed the claim that males tend to be more aggressive than females, though the difference appears to be smaller than many people had supposed (Hyde, 1984).

RELATIONSHIP AMONG TYPES OF VALIDITY

It is time to say something about the relationship among the types of validity, in preparation for our discussion of theoretical validity in the next chapter.

Relationship between Internal Validity and External Validity

Some writers have suggested that in applied research it is prudent to sacrifice internal validity for external validity. We strongly agree with Cook and Campbell (1979) that such sacrifices are virtually always *un*wise. Internal validity must be the prime concern of both basic and applied research. Indeed, internal validity is the sine qua non for demonstrating cause and effect relationships, without which claiming external validity for any experiment or quasi-experiment is empty and meaningless.

External Validity and Theoretical Validity

It is well to point out, before closing this chapter, that many laboratory investigations do not require external validity in the conventional sense, nor do they have empirical generalizations as their aim. Rather, the truly important laboratory experiment is one that achieves theoretical validity. To make this point, Mook (1983) used the example of Harlow's classic work with baby rhesus monkeys who were brought up with terry cloth and wire mesh "mother monkeys" rather than their real mothers. Mook observes:

> Were Harlow's baby monkeys representative of the population of monkeys in general? Obviously not; they were born in captivity and then orphaned besides. Well, were they a representative sample of the population of lab-born, orphaned monkeys? There was no attempt at all to make them so. It must be concluded that Harlow's sampling procedures fell far short of the ideal. . . .
>
> Real monkeys do not live within walls. They do not encounter mother figures made of wire mesh, with rubber nipples; nor is the advent of a terry-cloth cylinder, warmed by a light bulb, a part of their natural life-style. What can this contrived situation possibly tell us about how monkeys with natural upbringing would behave in a natural setting?
>
> On the face of it, the verdict must be a flat flunk. On every criterion of EV [external validity] that applies at all, we find Harlow's experiment either manifestly deficient or simply unevaluable. And yet our tendency is to respond to this critique with a resounding "So what?" And I think we are quite right to so respond.
>
> Why? Because using the lab results to make generalizations about real-world behavior was no part of Harlow's intention. It was not what he was trying to do. That being the case, the concept of EV simply does not arise—except in an indirect remote sense. . . .
>
> Harlow did not conclude, "Wild monkeys in the jungle probably would choose terry-cloth over wire mothers, too, if offered the choice." First, it would be a moot conclusion, since that simply is not going to happen. Second, who cares whether they would or not? The generalization would be trivial even if true. What Harlow did conclude was that the hunger-reduction interpretation of mother love would not work. If anything about his experiment has external validity, it is this theoretical point, not the findings themselves. (Mook, 1983, p. 381.)

Berkowitz and Donnerstein (1982) make a similar point, using the example of filmed violence. They write:

> Consider what laboratory experiments on the effects of filmed violence can or cannot accomplish. [Most investigations in this area] do *not* tell us the likelihood that ordinary viewers will behave aggressively after they watch a violent TV program in their own homes—The settings, subjects, and stimulus materials employed in these experiments are hardly representative of naturalistic TV viewing. What the studies usually do indicate, however, is that observed aggression can influence people in the audience to display stronger aggression than they otherwise might have exhibited. Employing careful, systematic designs, the experiments have demonstrated such a causal effect far more clearly than great numbers of field surveys employing representative designs could (p. 248).

Thus, it is clear that many laboratory studies such as Harlow's are more concerned with theoretical validity than with the type of generalization usually thought of as external validity. It is to theoretical validity that we now turn.

FOR REVIEW AND DISCUSSION

1. How does the problem of external validity relate to the larger issue of whether induction is legitimate?
2. A repeated measures experiment was carried out with children to determine the effects of three levels of reinforcement on the performance of a simple motor task. The data indicate that moderate levels of reinforcement produced the best performance. How far can these results be generalized?
3. What is the value of field experiments in the behavioral sciences?
4. You are interested in determining the effects of a new drug on mood. Suppose you test rats first and then undergraduate males. What are the problems involved in generalizing from each of your samples to the general population? How can you solve some of these problems?
5. Discuss the role of subject selection and sampling alternatives in assuring and threatening external validity.
6. What is the relationship between internal validity and external validity?

13

Theoretical (Construct) Validity and Philosophical Issues

THE PROBLEM OF INTERPRETATION
- Operationism
- The Multimethod Approach
- The Manipulation Check
- Further Empirical Analysis

THE PLACEBO EFFECT
- Placebo Controls in Psychotherapy Research
  - analog versus true psychotherapy research
  - methodological problems with placebo controls
  - ethical problems with placebo controls
  - what are the alternatives?

INFORMED CONSENT AND THE INTERPRETATION OF EXPERIMENTAL FINDINGS
- "Old" and "New" Research on the Effects of Environmental Stress: A Case Study

RECENT TRENDS IN THE PHILOSOPHY OF SCIENCE
- Observation is "Theory-Laden"
- Explanation Revisited
- A Final Note on Science and Philosophy

THE SPECIAL POWER OF CONVERGING EVIDENCE

FOR REVIEW AND DISCUSSION

In Chapter 1 we mentioned the important role of theory in science and pointed out that theories are never directly proved or disproved by empirical research. We are now in a much better position to explain why this is so and to discuss the relationship between research and theory in social science.

When social scientists draw inferences from their empirical research that go beyond what has actually been observed, they must generalize from and interpret their data. Scientific interpretations involve a theoretical construction of the processes that underlie observed relationships (even well-documented causal relationships) between variables. Accurate interpretation absolutely depends on internally valid data—and, as we have seen repeatedly, there are many threats to the internal validity of causal inferences drawn from social science research. But even when internal validity is secure, the validity of an investigator's inferences can be challenged as wrongly interpreted. This type of validity can be referred to as *theoretical validity.*

THE PROBLEM OF INTERPRETATION

In the social sciences it is not uncommon to find individual scientists agreeing with one another on the data (for example, on the internal validity of some particular experiment) and then *dis*agreeing about how the data should be interpreted. Such disagreements are linked to the problem of generalizing across independent and dependent variables and occur for two main reasons. First, most experimental treatments are multidimensional. Each detail of the experimental treatment that is irrelevant to the investigator's theoretical argument is the source of a potential alternate hypothesis for explaining the obtained effects theoretically.

For example, suppose an investigator has examined the effects of telling subjects that they are failing on their subsequent intelligence test performance. In addition to wanting to conclude that the effects of this particular independent variable would be replicable, he or she also may want to advance some further generalizations concerning the effects of anxiety on performance (a large leap indeed from the particular operations in this study). The more elaborate and "process-oriented" the theory that gives rise to a particular experiment, the more likely are such difficulties.

Second, the problem arises because of the imperfect relationship between the dependent variable and the theoretical variable that the investigator is interested in. This problem is similar to the issue raised regarding treatment; that is, no one measure will be the theoretically "pure" representative of the dependent variable as conceptualized. For example, there are several possible ways of assessing a sensory threshold (the smallest amount of energy that a subject can detect). One technique, the method of limits, involves starting with stimulus intensities well below or well above the energy values required for detection and gradually increasing or decreasing the values until the subject reports either that he or she can now perceive the stimulus or that the previously detectable stimulus is no longer perceptible. Another technique, the forced-choice method, involves first selecting a number of stimulus intensities known to be fairly close to the sensory threshold. To understand the forced-choice aspect of the technique, consider the way in which the auditory threshold might be assessed. In such a study, trials would be arranged so that, on each, two observation intervals would be presented. One of these intervals would contain no signal, and the other would contain one of the values of stimulus intensity that had been previously chosen. On each trial, the subject is *forced* to choose which of the two observation intervals contained a signal. One obtains an estimate of the sensory threshold by examining the relationship between the probability of correct detections by the subject as a function of the energy of the stimuli.

It was known for many years that the forced-choice method generally produced lower estimates of the threshold than did the method of limits, but this fact did not present a great problem for researchers. As we have previously noted, small differences in main effects do not often seriously limit the generality of most social science research. More recently, however, it has been shown that the threshold measurement obtained by the two methods *interacts* with other variables. One such variable is the amount of reward offered for correct detections in sensory threshold experiments.

Thresholds obtained by using the method of limits can be radically altered by increasing the payoff to the subjects for correct detections. In contrast, thresholds obtained by the forced-choice technique appear to be relatively insensitive to the effects of rewards (Swets & Sewall, 1963). Thus, whether rewards have an influence on the sensory threshold depends heavily on the measurement technique that has been employed.

Operationism

One approach, *narrow operationism,* can solve the theoretical validity problem, but it also has some undesirable features. An *operational definition* completely specifies the meaning of a term by identifying the operations involved in its measurement. For example, we can define learning operationally in an experiment involving a rat in a T-maze as follows: the rat has learned if and only if it turns left when put in the maze after training. If the researcher asserts that the operations are the only events in which he or she is interested, it makes little sense to argue over different names for the same operation.

Although the notion of providing complete operational definitions once attracted much attention, it has a serious disadvantage. Because any operationally defined theoretical concept is synonymous with only one set of operations, only one isolated event falls under the purview of the theoretical term. The precision of the term is specious, and its value (generality) is entirely lost. If our operational definition of learning involves a rat's performance in a T-maze, the term "learning" could not be applied to changes in the academic performance of children unless the youngsters (after food deprivation) were put through the same maze and turned left. If we devise a different measure of learning for the children than the one employed for the rats, we no longer have a single set of operations for this theoretical term.

Operational definitions as such must be distinguished from the broader tradition of operationism, which has served behavioral and social research in extremely good stead and protected it from many of its earlier problems. This tradition softens the requirement of specified operations for theoretical terms so that a single set of operations need not uniquely and exclusively define one theoretical concept. Rather, a set of operations is viewed as providing only one possible operationalization or *partial definition* of the meaning of a theoretical term, and a term may thus apply to several different operations. For example, there are many possible referents for the term "anxiety." It may be measured variously: (1) by assessing the subjective report of an individual, (2) by monitoring psychophysiological changes, or (3) by observing a person's overt behavior (for example, amount of hand tremor). Each of these measurement techniques may be viewed as tapping a different aspect of anxiety.

But the partial definition also has some disadvantages. Because a partial definition specifies the meaning of a theoretical term under one test condition only, it leaves open the meaning of the term under other conditions. A judgment might be made about whether an individual is anxious or not (using other kinds of observations) even if no paper-and-pencil anxiety instrument were available. But by taking this tack we have given up the full, explicit definition of our theoretical term and instead made it an *open concept.* It is no longer completely defined by reference to an observable condition or set of conditions.

Moving away from operational definitions begins to erode the solidarity of meaning of a theoretical term and thus invites theoretical and conceptual invalidity. There are no simple rules or prescriptions to handle the problem of theoretical invalidity, because the problem resides in, and relates to, the theory in question. A careful and thoughtful analysis of possible alternative explanations of this sort should, of course, be undertaken by the investigator before beginning any study.

The Multimethod Approach

A *multimethod* approach, in which propositions are tested by using several manipulations or several different points on the dimension in which the treatment falls theoretically, will be necessary to adequately confirm a scientific proposition. This strategy is perhaps best effected by employing *constructive replications,* that is, a series of studies in which the conceptual basis of the investigation is maintained while details presumed to be irrelevant are systematically varied. If a sufficiently large number of variations is introduced, the possibility that irrelevant dimensions of the operations originally selected are producing the observed effect can be virtually eliminated. In one such series of experiments (Miller, 1957), the behavioral effects of various ways of reducing hunger in rats (for example, normal ingestion of milk, injection of milk directly into the stomach, and lesions of brain structures thought to control eating) were examined. The results of these studies and the different effects produced by the manipulations led to changes in our theoretical conceptualization of the phenomenon. For example, it appears that stomach contractions ("hunger pangs") may have little to do with hunger.

The Manipulation Check

Another approach to the question of the theoretical validity of an independent variable lies in collecting further data, usually after the experiment itself is over, that can clarify the interpretation of the study. When we first introduced the experimental method, we discussed Freedman et al.'s (1967) investigation, in which guilt was presumably induced by leading subjects to tell a lie. The independent variable (telling a lie) did have a statistically significant effect on the dependent variable (willingness to participate in a subsequent study). But is the theoretical interpretation of this effect valid? In Freedman et al.'s study it might have been possible to gather further data that would help in answering this question. For example, the study could have been described as an investigation of the relationship between mood and performance on the Remote Associates Test. In this context a questionnaire measuring mood, including guilt, could be administered and scored to determine whether the manipulation was having its intended effect.

A related approach to the issue of the theoretical validity of an independent variable is *pilot testing.* Here the investigator tries out the experiment on a few subjects.[1] These subjects can be interviewed in depth to determine whether the manipulation is having the desired effect.

Further Empirical Analysis

When competing theoretical explanations are raised, it is often possible to design shrewd experiments that will eliminate one of two alternatives. Consider, for example, an experiment by Rosenberg (1965) designed to reevaluate the literature on *cognitive dissonance* by employing his own construct—*evaluation apprehension.* To follow the argument, we must first consider a classic experiment by Cohen on cognitive dissonance (Brehm & Cohen, 1962). In Cohen's experiment, Yale University undergraduates were recruited to write essays supporting a position opposite to the one they actually held. Just before the study, a campus riot had led to the New Haven police being called onto the campus. Most students felt that the police had behaved badly. Cohen asked subjects to write an essay

[1] Pilot testing is a procedure that should be undertaken routinely. It allows "debugging" of many potential errors.

explaining "why the actions of the New Haven police were justified." They were randomly assigned to groups that varied in the monetary compensation offered for writing the essay: 50¢, $1.00, $5.00, or $10.00. After the essay was completed, the subjects filled out an attitude questionnaire concerning their reactions to the police incident.

According to dissonance theory, it would be expected that a person's beliefs and behaviors must be consistent; otherwise *dissonance,* an unpleasant psychological state, is presumed to occur. In the Cohen study, the prediction was that there would be an inverse relationship between the amount of money paid to the students for writing the essay and the extent of pro-police attitudes found on the attitude questionnaire. Students who wrote a pro-police essay for a remuneration of only 50¢ were considered to be in a state of dissonance—their "true beliefs" and their beliefs as given in the essay were in conflict, and the small financial reward was poor justification for this conflict. To reduce dissonance, these students were expected to *change* their beliefs in a direction increasingly favorable toward the police. In contrast, the students receiving $10.00 would presumably not experience much dissonance. Their writing of a pro-police essay was "justified" by the high rate of pay they were receiving. Hence, their attitudes were expected to remain antipolice.

The empirical predictions advanced in Cohen's study were confirmed. The 50¢ group had the most favorable attitudes toward the police, the $1.00 group the next most favorable attitudes, and so on through the $5.00 and $10.00 groups. The deductions from dissonance theory were supported.

Rosenberg, however, argued that the critical aspect of Cohen's treatment was not the production of dissonance but rather the arousal of *evaluation apprehension.* He suggested that the typical experimental subject expects to be evaluated in some way. If this initial expectation is confirmed when the subject interacts with the experimenter, a state of evaluation apprehension is created. Further, Rosenberg construes evaluation apprehension as a motivating force that leads subjects to attempt to present themselves in a good light.

Applying the evaluation apprehension notion to Cohen's experiment, Rosenberg (1965) suggested that

> . . . the low dissonance (high-reward) subjects would be more likely to suspect that the experimenter had some unrevealed purpose. The gross discrepancy between spending a few minutes writing an essay and the large sum offered, the fact that this sum had not yet been delivered by the time the subject was handed the attitude questionnaire, the fact that he was virtually invited to show that he had become more positive toward the New Haven police: all of these could have served to engender suspicion and thus to arouse evaluation apprehension and negative affect toward the experimenter. Either or both of these motivating states could possibly be most efficiently reduced by the subject refusing to show anything but fairly strong disapproval of the New Haven police; for the subject who had come to believe that his autonomy in the face of a monetary lure was being assessed, remaining anti-police would demonstrate that he *had* autonomy; for the subject who perceived an indirect and disingenuous attempt to change his attitude

> and felt some reactive anger, holding fast to his original attitudes could appear to be a relevant way to frustrate the experimenter (pp. 31–32).

Rosenberg's interpretation certainly qualifies as a rival and plausible *conceptual* hypothesis for certain findings in Cohen's study, but it does not challenge the internal validity of the findings themselves. His analysis also has empirical status inasmuch as he has performed experiments to try to disentangle the dissonance and evaluation apprehension interpretations. A brief review of one of these investigations will illustrate an attempt to resolve the issue of conceptual invalidity. Rosenberg (1965) argued that one way of separating the two competing explanations would be to lead the subjects to distinguish between the dissonance induction phase of the experiment and the attitude measurement phase by casting them as two different studies. In such a situation the effects of evaluation apprehension should be considerably reduced, whereas dissonance, if the process occurs, should remain strong. With a separation between the dissonance and attitude measurement phases, Rosenberg expected that effects such as those found in the Cohen study would no longer be present.

The experiment concerned the ban on further participation of the Ohio State football team in Rose Bowl games. The response of the student body to the ban had been quite unfavorable and had included a variety of demonstrations. The ban was later rescinded, and Rosenberg's experimental subjects wrote essays favoring restoration of the ban for 50¢, $1.00 or $5.00. However, Rosenberg's experiment was disguised to produce the belief that subjects were participating in two separate experiments. One was supposedly an experiment on essay writing and the other on attitudes about Rose Bowl participation. In contrast to Cohen, Rosenberg found that the $5.00 group expressed significantly *more favorable* attitudes toward the Rose Bowl ban than did either of the other groups.

The two experiments described above and Rosenberg's analysis of them illustrate the fact that the same manipulation may be construed in different ways. Equally important is the corollary that *different interpretations must be amenable to separation in experimental designs.* The competing accounts must, in some circumstances, lead to differential predictions that can be put to empirical test. Otherwise, a theoretical stalemate has been reached.

It is also important to note that theoretical debates, such as that between the evaluation apprehension and cognitive dissonance accounts of certain phenomena, are not often resolved by a single experiment. Thus, in some ways, the example we have provided is oversimplified. Rather than wrapping up the point at issue, Rosenberg's experiment stimulated further research and debate (see Aronson, 1966; Brehm, 1965). This pattern is not unusual. Interpretations of scientific data seem invariably to undergo change in the history of any science (see Kuhn, 1970). In fact, theories in any science are better thought of as more and more useful interpretations or constructions of events than as final truths. *Thus, the theoretical validity of any social science claim is being tested and challenged every time another, related investigation is done.*

Although many threats to theoretical validity apply to only one specific theoretical issue, a few have wide applicability. Perhaps the clearest example of a threat to interpretation that arises in many contexts is the so-called placebo effect.

THE PLACEBO EFFECT

Pilgrimages to Lourdes, religious conversion experiences, ingesting magical potions, and the like can all apparently produce therapeutic effects. Similarly, pharmacologically inert substances such as sugar pills or injections of saline solution can lead to improvement in conditions such as ulcers, headaches, warts, and psychiatric illness (Frank, 1961). These therapeutic effects are genuine but the changes are due not to any real healing power in the intervention (e.g., the sugar pill) but rather to the *placebo effect.* In medicine a placebo is defined as a pharmacologically inert substance and the placebo effect refers to the therapeutic gains which the ingestion of a placebo produces. The therapeutic effect is thought to result from the mobilization of the patient's expectation that the treatment will yield improvement. Placebo effects are so pervasive and powerful that proof of the effectiveness of new medicines is now expected to involve a true *double blind experiment* in which neither the patient nor the physician knows who is getting the placebo and who is getting the "real" medication. The placebo medication is made to look, taste, and "feel" like the real medication, although it is either an inert substance or one that produces irrelevant side effects to convince patients in the placebo control condition that they have gotten real medicine. (In the latter case we speak of *active placebos.*)

Placebo Controls in Psychotherapy Research

By the 1950s psychological therapy researchers had picked up on the importance of including placebo controls in their research (Rosenthal & Frank, 1956). By the 1960s placebo controls in psychotherapy research had become commonplace, and often led to significant improvement relative to no-treatment controls in true experiments. Paul (1966), for example, gave speech-anxious college students what was purported to be a "fast-acting tranquilizer" but which was in fact a two-gram capsule of sodium bicarbonate with no anxiety-related drug properties. This group showed significantly more improvement than a no-treatment control group, both in terms of their self-reported feelings and on independent measures of apparent anxiety reported by observers.

The widespread use of placebo controls in the late 1960s and early 1970s led to several important critiques which cast doubt on both the methodological and ethical appropriateness of this practice. The most cogent analysis was offered by O'Leary and Borkovec (1978).

Analog versus True Psychotherapy Research. O'Leary and Borkovec began their analysis with the observation that efforts to test and contrast types of psychotherapy fall on a continuum depending on the nature and severity of the subject's problem and the length of the treatment offered. At one extreme the treatment is only an analog to therapy, involving one or a very few sessions and a "target problem" of no real consequence to the subject. Numerous methods for treating minor or inconsequential phobias, such as snake phobias, in one or two group sessions fall into this category. At the other extreme are those studies in which the participants must be thought of as clients or patients with life debilitating or life-threatening problems such as severe depression; these problems often require substantial and lengthy treatment. O'Leary and Borkovec note that analog studies are basically laboratory experiments involving analysis of behavior change processes for theory development; in such studies placebo controls are ethically appropriate and may be quite useful from a methodological point of view. On the other hand, in true therapy studies such treatments may be methodologically unsound and ethically dubious.

Methodological Problems with Placebo Controls. The methodological problem can be understood by asking what, exactly, placebo controls are supposed to control for. Presumably, they are supposed to control for several of the rival hypotheses we have discussed in previous chapters, such as subject and experimenter expectancies and demand factors in the situation (see Chapter 6). In practice with real psychotherapy research, placebo treatments do not effectively control for these threats. For one thing, double blind studies, though quite feasible in drug research, are virtually impossible in psychotherapy research where therapists must know what they are giving and clients or patients must know (at least up to a point) what they are getting. Therapists can hardly have the same expectations for treatments they believe to be useful and those they believe or know to be irrelevant or inert.

Ethical Problems with Placebo Controls. Ethically, too, the placebo control is problematic in psychotherapy research because it inevitably involves serious deception and also serves as a deterrent to seeking alternative treatment by suffering individuals. An ineffective placebo may also be frustrating or demoralizing to those who receive it and thus actually worsen patients' conditions in some circumstances.

What are the Alternatives? O'Leary and Borkovec (1978) discuss several. One is to employ *best possible comparisons.* For example, new and promising therapies may be compared with the prevailing established alternatives. Thus, cognitive therapy for depression, a relatively new approach, has recently been compared with commonly used pharmaceutical antidepressants (Rosenhan & Seligman, 1984).

Second, there are *component control comparisons.* For example, many psychotherapy treatments consist of several components, and it is often possible to dismantle them to identify which ingredients are most effective. Houts and Peterson (1985), for example, recently analyzed Houts and Liebert's (1984) Full Spectrum Home Training for bedwetting (which consists of a urine alarm, practice in urine retention, and an "overlearning" procedure) by comparing the relapse rates of children who received only the urine alarm, the urine alarm and retention control training, and the full treatment. (Results showed the full package provided the best protection against relapse.)

Third, there is the possibility of using a *counterdemand manipulation* in which the therapist tells the subject not to expect any improvement for a specified period of time, when in fact treatment effects are expected to show up sooner than that. Counterdemand procedures have been shown to reduce the effects of placebos. Unlike standard placebo controls, they involve a relatively acceptable deception.

INFORMED CONSENT AND THE INTERPRETATION OF EXPERIMENTAL FINDINGS

In Chapter 1 we described the need for guarding the rights of human subjects in research and pointed out that new ethical guidelines and regulations appeared in the early 1970s in response to very dubious practices in some earlier medical and psychological research. Unsurprisingly, the new guidelines have greatly influenced the type of research being done in the social and behavioral sciences today.

Government grants provide the mainstay for most such research in most countries (including the United States). Thus, the effect of a government requiring that human subjects guidelines be met as a condition of funding is that research not in compliance with guidelines will rarely be conducted or published. Under such circumstances it behooves methodologists to raise questions about whether following human subjects requirements alters the impact of experimental manipulations.

"Old" and "New" Research on the Effects of Environmental Stress: A Case Study

Gardner (1978) fortuitously had the opportunity to notice the effects of implementing human subjects regulations in his continuing research dealing with the influence of environmental stress on performance. Gardner's report stands as a unique case study of the enormous and occasionally surprising impact the new regulations have had on the behavioral science enterprise.

To explain Gardner's research we must first describe the work on which it was based, a series of experiments published by David Glass and Jerome Singer in 1972 in their award-winning monograph *Urban Stress: Experiments in Noise and Social Stressors.* Among their many studies, Glass and Singer performed a series of experiments in which subjects worked for a period on simple tasks (such as adding columns of one- and two-digit numbers) either in a quiet room or in one where the silence was broken at unpredictable, random intervals with a very loud environmental noise, such as the sound of a jackhammer. Then, during the test phase of the experiments, all subjects were given the job of proofreading a seven-page passage from Jane Jacob's *The Death and Life of Great American Cities.* (The passage had been purposely typed with an average of ten errors per page. These included such things as obvious misspellings and grammatical errors.) Simply, Glass and Singer found clear evidence that exposure to loud environmental noise debilitated subjects' later performance. Those who had just been exposed to unpredictable loud noise performed significantly less well in their proofreading assignment than did those who had spent the previous few minutes working in silence.

Gardner's own work had attempted to replicate and extend the Glass and Singer experiments, and by the summer of 1974 Gardner had performed three experiments. In each case, exposure to unpredictable noise was found to have an adverse effect on later performance, thus replicating the findings of Glass and Singer. Then, in the fall of 1974, Gardner's experimental procedures had to be altered to comply with the newly instituted policies of the U.S. Department of Health, Education and Welfare designed to protect the rights of human subjects (as published by DHEW, 1975). Gardner recounted the nature of the changes that resulted:

> A Human Subjects Review Committee operating according to the above DHEW guidelines was established at the University of Michigan-Dearborn in the Spring of 1974, somewhat later than the corresponding board on the main campus in Ann Arbor. One of the first research projects it reviewed—the topic of this article—involved exposing students in the Introductory Psychology Subject Pool to 24 minutes of intermittent noise at approximately 100 db. . . . The procedure was similar to that of Glass and Singer (1972, Chapter 4), with subjects working on simple mental tasks during the noise exposure period and tested for cognitive aftereffects during a period following exposure. The committee decided that subjects in this research were not at risk, since total noise duration and intensity would not damage their hearing (Kryter, 1970) and since they were routinely exposed to noises of this type in their everyday life, for example, from the juke box in the campus cafeteria. However, since the subjects were performing valuable service to the department to fulfill a course requirement, it behooved the university to be especially zealous in the protection of their rights and welfare. As a result, the committee decided that this research project and subsequent ones using the subject pool should fulfill . . . [several] conditions of the federal guidelines outlined above, including informed consent, even though subjects were *not* at risk.
>
> In order to implement the guidelines as directed by the committee, the Introductory Psychology Subject Pool subsequently operated as follows: In the first

> week of classes, the subject pool coordinator visited class sections and distributed to each student a 1-page summary of pool operations. This summary described the participation requirement, its value to the department, the review of all experiments by the Human Subjects Review Committee, the absence of experiments involving deception, drugs, or shock, and the freedom of subjects to discontinue participation in any experiment without penalty. When actual experiments were run later in the semester, students signed up for those they wanted to on sign-up folders which bore short descriptions of the experiment and which were distributed in class. Lastly, subjects signed a specific consent form immediately before serving in *each* experiment. This form repeated a portion of the information from the written summary of pool operations and asked the student to acknowledge his/her understanding of that summary, as well as his/her consent to serve in the particular experiment. Note that the above format differed considerably from the previously used subject pool procedure. The old procedure involved only a short written statement, passed out the first week of class, explaining participation as a class requirement, its value to the department, and the absence of deception, drugs, and shock (1978, p. 629).

The new procedures were implemented in two further experiments, which were conducted in the fall of 1974 and the summer of 1975. In neither experiment was there evidence that environmental noise had any negative aftereffects whatsoever! Of course what had happened, as Gardner quickly suspected, was that the subjects' newly introduced and emphasized opportunity to drop out of the experiment at any time without penalty had removed the uncontrollable nature of the noise. In a subsequent experiment (done with the permission of the Human Subjects Committee at the University of Michigan-Dearborn) Gardner (1978) randomly assigned college student subjects to either the old human subjects procedures or to the new ones. The second factor in Gardner's (1978) between-subjects factorial design was whether subjects were exposed to the silent or the noise treatments. The results, portions of which are shown in Figure 13-1, confirmed experimentally what Gardner had suspected; the elaborate procedure designed to protect the rights of the subjects had the additional effect of masking the deleterious influence of environmental noise on performance, leading to a Type II error.

Findings such as those reported by Gardner raise the thorny question of how to conduct research that is ethically responsible regarding the rights of individual subjects without distorting the research enterprise so that the public is misled about the dangers of possible psychological and health threats. What Gardner's research does make very clear is that research into the adverse effects of such threats can be methodologically distorted in the name of ethical responsibility. Obviously, scientists *must* be concerned with both types of ethical concerns. The critical issue, according to many researchers including Gardner, is to carefully assess the matter of individual and collective risk under both the old and new procedures. Gardner concludes:

> In contrast to the new procedures, the old subject procedures used at the University of Michigan-Dearborn appeared not to interfere with the results of stressor

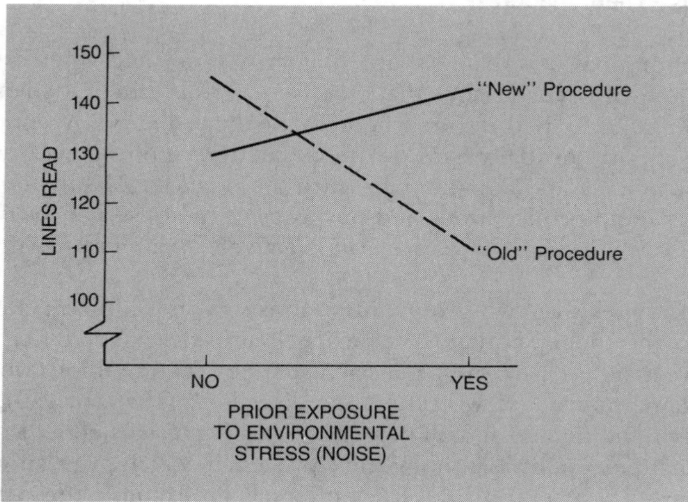

Figure 13-1 Partial results of Gardner's (1978) experiment, contrasting the effects of prior exposure to environmental stress (noise) under the "old" and "new" ethical guidelines. The new guidelines apparently provide subjects an unusual sense of control (by emphasizing that they may terminate the experiment at any time) and thus wipe out the adverse effects of stress that appear when the invitation to terminate the experiment at any time has not been extended repeatedly.

Source: From data reported in Gardner (1978).

experiments. Note further that these procedures are legal under current DHEW guidelines *if* the experimental subjects are judged *not* at risk by the institutional review board. The implication of the foregoing discussion seems clear: Department administrations should not apply uniform subjects procedures to all experiments regardless of their nature, but instead should use old-type procedures for experiments lacking risk, as determined by the institutional review board, and new procedures incorporating all the elements of informed consent when experimental risk is present. If the judgments of the University of Michigan-Dearborn Human Subjects Review Committee are representative, then most existing research on noise and crowding would fall in the no-risk category. This two-alternative approach is more complicated than the uniform procedures and bookkeeping systems used at the departments mentioned above and may at first seem contradictory to a spirit of zealous enforcement. On the other hand, the approach appears to follow both the letter and the spirit of federal law, and it may prevent invalidation of significant research (1978, p. 634).

RECENT TRENDS IN THE PHILOSOPHY OF SCIENCE

In Chapter 1 we briefly mentioned the traditional (Baconian) view of science, in which data ("facts") are assumed to be accessible through scientific research, thereby providing an objective foundation on which theories can be formulated, tested, and modified. In the past few decades this empiricist epistemology has come under increasing attack from philosophers of science. Manicas and Secord (1983) have summarized these developments as they apply to the social and behavioral sciences and Heelan (1983) has argued that the new view has vast implications for all science, from physics to psychology. Here we briefly describe some of the major issues and points made.

Observation is "Theory-laden"

Against the traditional view that facts are "theory-neutral" and objectively true, the new philosophy of science claims that all observation is "theory-laden." The heart of this claim is that all perception, whether it be the ordinary perception of lay persons going about their daily lives or the perception of physicists while using specialized instruments and apparatus to track the behavior of subatomic particles, is shaped by the preconceptions and purposes of the observer. In this so-called *hermeneutic view*[2] our perceptions are always actively created rather than passively received.

Kuhn (1970) argues that two groups of scientists taking different theoretical viewpoints (he calls them paradigms) "practice their trades in two different worlds" and therefore that "the two groups of scientists see different things when they look from the same point of view in the same direction" (1970, p. 150). A similar conclusion about all people and all perception has been reached by Rock (1983), who claims that perception is a thoughtlike process in which prior knowledge and expectancies play a central role. Rock offers as an example the visual stimulus shown in Figure 13-2. (The reader should look at this Figure now, before reading further, and try to answer the question, What is it?) To most people it appears to be no more than an unidentifiable pattern of white and black regions. Now, let us tell you that it is a man on horseback wearing a gaucho hat. If you look at the Figure now it will seem so, and you will never again be able to see it as the meaningless pattern it first appeared to be. In other words, for scientists (and ordinary lay people) *what we see depends upon more than what we are looking at.*

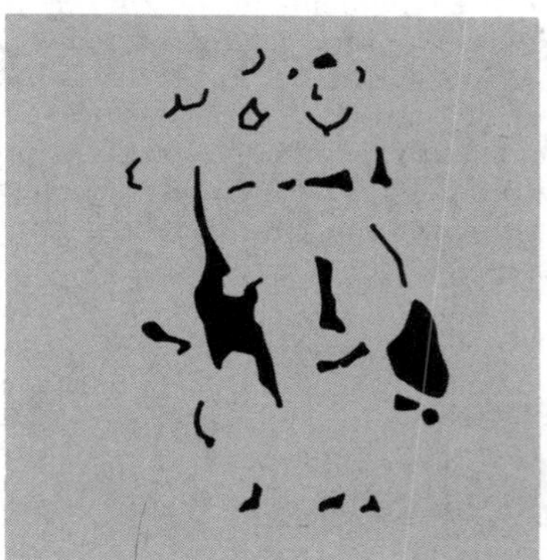

Figure 13-2 A figure that at first looks like a meaningless array of fragments but looks entirely different when interpreted.

Source: From Rock (1983, p. 12).

As Manicas and Secord (1983) point out, the significance of the writings of Kuhn and others is in showing that "scientific meanings could not be found

[2] Hermeneutics (a term derived from Hermes, the messenger god of Greek mythology) is the art of explaining or interpreting; the hermeneutic view states that all perception is interpretive. The hermeneutic approach to knowledge states that we see what we expect to see or intend to see; perception is the interpretation (or "reading") of sensation and is therefore always fallible.

in observations alone, as the logical empiricists had maintained. [Therefore] the idea that there could be unambiguous logical connections between theory and observation was overthrown" (p. 401).

But this conclusion brings with it a thorny question: If there is no theory-neutral base of facts available to scientific observers, can there be any criteria for truth? The answer recently offered by Heelan (1983), Manicas and Secord (1983) and others is that the essence of science must be redefined. The business of science, all these philosophers of science claim, is to invent theories rather than to discover facts. Theories, therefore, must rest on rational as well as empirical criteria. Theories are in fact judged by their goodness-of-fit with the understood or perceived world (which is not the same as *the* world).

Explanation Revisited

One implication of this new view is that the ability to explain does not always (or even usually) imply the ability to predict. That is, science can more readily explain what *has* occurred than what *will* occur, except in the laboratory. Or, as Manicas and Secord put it: "A good experiment confirms theory precisely because if it establishes the right conditions and eliminates interfering causal mechanisms, the experiment yields what would not have been observed without the experiment" (pp. 402–403). Put another way, prediction is only possible in the laboratory!

Truly, this is a radical departure from the traditional view. In the new philosophy of science theoretical validation within the established understandings of the scientific community becomes the paramount goal of research, while external validity (as outlined in the last chapter) is deemed to be largely irrelevant and often impossible to achieve with pure science. This is because, unlike the "closed" world of the controlled laboratory experiment, the real world is an "open" system in which individuals have so many immediate and long-term forces impinging on them that correct prediction or control of a single action or person is always uncertain.

A Final Note on Science and Philosophy

Here at the end we have taken a sharp turn in our discussion in order to point out issues in the underpinnings of all our previous discussion of scientific methods. Ordinary social and behavioral science is, however, quite able to proceed as usual without waiting for the ancient philosophical debate between empiricist and rationalist views to be resolved. Perhaps they never will be. As Manicas and Secord (1983) note in concluding their far-reaching analysis:

> Philosophy of science has most commonly been the work of philosophers, not scientists. . . . A few philosophically oriented scientists may perhaps be partly influenced in their choice of criteria by philosophical writings, but more commonly, scientists contrast with philosophers in generating their own criteria out of their daily practices in scientific research (p. 412).

THE SPECIAL POWER OF CONVERGING EVIDENCE

By now it should be clear that no one study, however shrewdly designed and carefully executed, can provide convincing support for a causal hypothesis or theoretical statement in the social sciences. Indeed, even the more advanced material sciences, such as physics and chemistry, have come to abandon the seductive notion that one crucial experiment can ever adequately establish a theoretical point by itself. Too many possible (if not plausible) confounds, limitations on generality, and alternative interpretations can be offered for any one observation. Moreover, each of the basic methods of research (experimental, correlational, and case study) and techniques of comparison (within- or between-subjects) has intrinsic limitations.

How, then, does social science theory advance through research? The answer is, by collecting a diverse body of evidence about any major theoretical proposition. When the evidence converges from many sources that a particular relationship holds or a particular process controls some aspect of behavior, then (but only then) can reasonable, scientifically admissible conclusions be reached about the relative worth of different theoretical accounts of behavior.

Social scientists are profoundly aware that human behavior is a natural phenomenon. They are also deeply committed to the belief that despite its myriad of complexities, the human condition can be understood in significant measure by objective scrutiny. But the task that lies ahead, enormous in scope, is rendered even more difficult by many pitfalls along the road. Belief is easily confused with evidence, evidence is easily misunderstood, and misunderstanding is easily perpetuated. Only when the systematic study of behavior is undertaken with a keen sense of the strengths and weaknesses of many different methods is the way opened to maximizing and confirming our knowledge of the processes that underlie it. Only when such knowledge is carefully sifted from the widest possible spectrum of research enterprises can an adequate and comprehensive theory of human behavior be developed. We hope to have made a small contribution to this goal here . . . and to have inspired some of our readers to do more.

FOR REVIEW AND DISCUSSION

1. Explain how an internally valid causal inference can be subject to more than one explanation.
2. Discuss at least two ways in which the multimethod approach can be helpful in assessing theoretical validity.
3. Discuss the role of deception in threatening and protecting theoretical validity.
4. It is often hypothesized that crowding (or overcrowding) has an adverse influence on human social relationships. Describe a research plan including experiments, correlational studies, and case histories that might yield converging evidence bearing on this hypothesis.
5. What is the hermeneutic view of science? How does it contrast with the traditional view?

Appendix A: The Computer as a Tool

In 1960 computers were almost unknown in behavioral science laboratories; the few that were available were big "mainframes" that had to be shared with others and were "down" for repair with annoying frequency. Today computers can be found in virtually every researcher's lab or office. As Galanter (1984) observed:

> Microcomputers have become the experimental psychologist's microscope, centrifuge, and telescope. By 1980 the microcomputer had established itself as a major tool of experimentation. . . . These machines have altered dramatically the way experiments are done. . . . Not only can the computer control the presentation of displays, and capture responses (both discrete and analog) and response time, but it can also make on-line, real-time calculations of the statistics of the experimental data. . . . On the inferential side, we no longer need statistical tables. Microcomputers can use high-resolution algorithms to calculate the *p* values of Type I and Type II errors. In addition, these machines can create graphs and other summaries of the data very quickly, and these displays can be transferred directly to paper by an inexpensive plotter or printer (pp. 559–560).

Here we briefly describe the modern computer and its uses in social and behavioral research.

WHAT IS A COMPUTER?

A computer is an information-processing machine. Three classes of computers are generally distinguished. *Mainframe* computers are large, general-purpose computers that can handle the needs of many users at once; they typically serve large businesses or institutions. *Minicomputers* are also able to serve more than one user, but have smaller memories and are slower at complex processing than mainframes. *Microcomputers,* also called personal computers, are designed for a single user and have become the most popular type for use in the behavioral sciences.

Every computer has two components, a central processing unit (CPU) and a memory. In turn, the memory is of two types. Random access memory (RAM) is available for information put in by the user and is stored temporarily. (When a microcomputer is turned off everything in RAM will be lost unless it has been stored on a disk or tape.) Read only memory (ROM), on the other hand, is built into the computer permanently and contains programs that are always available to the user.

Bits and Bytes

Computers operate on a binary system, i.e., one involving a vast number of two-state, on-off switches. Even the most complex information can be represented by a sufficiently elaborate set of zeros and ones, and it is this logic that makes computer technology possible. Each on-off switch in a computer is a binary digit, or *bit. Bytes* are sets of bits: Most microcomputers employ bytes containing 8 bits, which means that one byte can represent any of 256 binary combinations ($2\times2\times2\times2\times2\times2\times2\times2 = 256$). The measure of memory is usually expressed in K; one K is 1024 bytes. A 64 K memory therefore contains 65,536 bytes, which is sufficient to store about 30 pages of text.

Auxiliary Memory

Once information has been processed in a computer, the results are usually stored as permanent memory, using a peripheral storage device. The most common type of storage device for microcomputers is the disk drive, which saves information on inexpensive diskettes. Information can also be sent from a diskette back into the computer's RAM, by loading it from the diskette in the disk drive.

Hardware and Software

The CPU, RAM, and ROM make up the so-called "hardware" of the computer. Computers are able to serve many functions because of the numerous programs or "software" that have been written for them. Creating sophisticated programming is one of the most challenging jobs in the computer industry.

Computer Languages

All programs are written in a language that allows the programmer to tell the computer what to do. The "language" implicit in the computer's electronic circuitry is called *machine language* and directly employs the computer's binary code. The most sophisticated programs are typically written in machine language, but this language is extremely complex and is only mastered by professional programmers and very dedicated amateurs. Assembly language is easier to master than machine language because it employs letter codes. *Assembly language,* though easier than machine language, is still too difficult for most people whose ultimate interest is in research rather than in computer programming per se. The overwhelming majority of behavioral scientists who do their own programming sacrifice some sophistication and use one of the "higher level" languages, such as BASIC (Beginner's All-purpose Symbolic Instruction Code). Other commonly used languages that are somewhat more difficult (and more powerful) than BASIC are Pascal, Fortran, and C.

Software for Behavioral Research

You do not need to know any computer language in order to take advantage of the computer's capability as a research tool, because many commercially available programs are quite suitable for research applications.

Statistical Packages. Programs for statistical analysis are available both for campus mainframe computers and for direct use on personal computers. Those for personal computers are suitable for many commonly used analyses (such as ANOVA, correlation and regression, and multiple regression), but are generally unable to do factor analyses, multifactor ANOVAs with unequal cell frequencies, or unusual statistics. Many recent statistics textbooks simply assume that all but the most basic computations will be performed by computer. Programs for the Apple, IBM, and some other personal computers are advertised in the American Psychological Association's newspaper, the *APA Monitor,* and are also available through many computer stores.

The most widely used mainframe statistical packages are SPSS (Statistical Packages for the Social Sciences), SAS (Statistical Analysis System), BMDP (BioMeDical Computer Programs), and Minitab (Cozby, 1984). These packages all perform a wide variety of analyses, and also generate tabular and graphic presentations of summary data.

Each package has its own set of instructions and rules, which must be learned to a reasonable level of proficiency before the package can be used.

On-line Data Collection. Computers have proven to be very useful in data collection, both in the laboratory and in the field. Appropriate software enables researchers to use microcomputers to gather data by direct input. The data can be transmitted through almost any means that will allow a circuit to be closed. By learning to do their own programming, or collaborating with a programmer, many researchers have been able to harness the power of the computer to their own specialized needs.

Computer-generated Stimulus Presentations. Many areas of basic research, such as perception or memory research, involve well-controlled presentations of words, phrases, shapes and forms, or other visual stimuli. With appropriate programs, computers can be used to present such material with a higher degree of precision than with hand-drawn stimuli or the types of apparatus available in the past.

Computerized Literature Searches

A major issue for all behavioral researchers is to be able to gather together the relevant previous studies and writings that pertain to their own work. Until a few years ago, this involved long hours at the library, going through *Psychological Abstracts* or other volumes containing research summaries issue by issue. Today most articles are keyed into a computer search process as soon as they are published. This means that authors are asked to suggest the key identifying words or phrases that apply to the topic of their research (e.g., treatment of schizophrenics, memory span, visual perception) as well as the age, gender, and species of their subjects.

Later, other researchers can go to any major university library and search for the number of articles that have been abstracted on any intersect of terms (e.g., stereoptic viewing in children, memory studies involving gender comparisons) and determine the number of articles that have been stored in the data bank under each set of terms. Broad searches may pick up hundreds of previous articles this way, whereas narrow searches will pick up only a few. Such searches can also be defined by the year of publication of the work being sought; for example, one can look for all articles published on bedwetting before 1980. After determining the number of articles "caught" by their search specifications, researchers can decide to have the actual abstracts of the articles (ranging between 50 and 150 words per article) printed out directly along with specific references. This process allows researchers to limit their actual physical work at the library to articles that are directly pertinent to their needs. At the same time, there is greatly increased confidence that no important work will be overlooked. Nor does the process of searching the literature have to be done in the library. Home and office microcomputers can tie directly into a computer search service through their own telephone lines, using a so-called "modem" which adapts the computer to telephone signals sent over the line by larger computer service facilities. All these possibilities continue to amaze those who tediously worked by hand only a decade or two ago.

Word Processing

Not the least of the ways in which computers can be used is as tools to facilitate the writing task itself. Word processing programs allow for efficient typing of drafts which can later be edited, extended, checked, or modified without having to retype a document. Word processing makes storage easy on disk or tape, and permits a host of special verification procedures such as checking of spelling and identifying the location of all instances in which a term is used or a work cited. These latter capacities are especially useful when dealing with book-length or other long manuscripts. In fact, the current edition of this book would have taken considerably longer to prepare had it not been done on a word processor.

Appendix B: Scientific Report Writing*

Many readers of this book will have occasion to prepare a formal scientific report, either as a course assignment or perhaps with the actual aim of submitting the report to a scientific or professional journal. The American Psychological Association (APA) publishes a manual containing introductory statements on the content and organization of manuscripts and on writing style. Both statements are clearly and simply written. We have reprinted portions of them here. Readers contemplating submission of an article to an APA journal should consult the full 208 page manual, available directly from the American Psychological Association.

* The sections "Parts of a Manuscript," "Quality of Presentation," and "Writing Style" are reprinted by permission from *Publication Manual of the American Psychological Association, Third Edition.* American Psychological Association: Washington, D.C., pp. 22–29, and 32–36.

PARTS OF A MANUSCRIPT

1.06 Title Page

Title. A title should summarize the main idea of the paper simply and, if possible, with style. It should be a concise statement of the main topic and should identify the actual variables or theoretical issues under investigation and the relation between them. An example of a good title is "Effect of Transformed Letters on Reading Speed."

A title should be fully explanatory when standing alone. Although its principal function is to inform readers about the study, a title is also used as a statement of article content for abstracting and information services, such as APA's *Psychological Abstracts* and PsycINFO Database. A good title easily compresses to the short title used for editorial purposes and to the running head used with the published article.

Titles are commonly indexed and compiled in numerous reference works. Therefore, avoid words that serve no useful purpose: They increase length and can mislead indexers. For example, the words *method* and *results* do not normally appear in a title, nor should such redundancies as "A Study of" or "An Experimental Investigation of" begin a title. Do not use abbreviations in a title: Spelling out all terms will help ensure accurate, complete indexing of the article. The recommended length for a title is 12 to 15 words.

Author's Name and Affiliation. Every manuscript has a by-line consisting of two parts: the name of the author and the institution where the investigation was conducted (without the words *by* or *from the*).

Author's Name. The preferred form of an author's name is first name, middle initial, and last name. This designation reduces the likelihood of mistaken identity. Use the same by-line designation on all manuscripts; that is, do not use initials on one manuscript and the full name on a later one. Omit all titles (e.g., Dr., Professor) and degrees (e.g., PhD, MD).

Affiliation. The affiliation identifies where the author or authors conducted the investigation and is usually an institution. Include a dual affiliation only if two institutions contributed substantial financial support to the study. Add the author's department in the by-line only if it is other than a department of psychology. When an author has no institutional affiliation, list the city and state of residence below the author's name. If the institutional affiliation has changed since the work was completed, give the current affiliation in the author identification notes.

Running Head. The running head is an abbreviated title that is printed at the top of the pages of a published article to identify the article for readers.

The head should be a maximum of 50 characters, counting letters, punctuation, and spaces between words.

1.07 Abstract

An abstract is a brief, comprehensive summary of the contents of the article; it allows readers to survey the contents of an article quickly and, like a title, is used by abstracting and information services to index and retrieve articles. All APA journals except *Contemporary Psychology* require an abstract.

A well-prepared abstract can be the single most important paragraph in the article. An abstract (a) is read first, (b) may be the only part of an article that is actually read (readers frequently decide, on the basis of the abstract, whether to read the entire article), and (c) is an important means of access in locating and retrieving the article. A good abstract is

- accurate: Ensure that an abstract correctly reflects the purpose and content of the manuscript. Do not include in an abstract information that does not appear in the body of the paper. Comparing an abstract with an outline of the paper's headings is a useful way to verify the accuracy of an abstract.
- self-contained: Define all abbreviations and acronyms. Spell out names of tests and drugs (use generic names for drugs). Define unique terms. Paraphrase rather than quote. Include names of authors and dates of publication in citations of other publications (and give a full bibliographic citation in the article's reference list). Include key words for indexing purposes.
- concise and specific: Make each sentence maximally informative, especially the lead sentence. Be as brief as possible. Only abstracts of the longest and most complex papers require as many as 150 words.
- nonevaluative: Report rather than evaluate; do not add to or comment on what is in the body of the manuscript.
- coherent and readable: Write in clear and vigorous prose. Use verbs rather than the noun equivalents and the active rather than the passive voice. Use the present tense to describe results with continuing applicability or conclusions drawn; use the past tense to describe specific variables manipulated or tests applied.

An abstract of a *report of an empirical study* should describe in 100 to 150 words

- the problem under investigation, in one sentence if possible;
- the subjects, specifying pertinent characteristics, such as number, type, age, sex, and species;
- the experimental method, including the apparatus, data-gathering procedures, and complete test names or generic names and the dosage of any drugs, particularly if the drugs are novel or important to the study;
- the findings, including statistical significance levels; and
- the conclusions and the implications or applications.

An abstract for a *review or theoretical article* should describe in 75 to 100 words

- the topic, in one sentence if possible;
- the purpose, thesis, or organizing construct and the scope (comprehensive or selective) of the article;
- the sources used (e.g., personal observation, published literature); and
- the conclusions and the implications or applications.

An abstract that is accurate, succinct, quickly comprehensible, and informative will increase the audience and the future retrievability of your article. For information on how abstracts are used to retrieve articles, consult the *PsycINFO Psychological Abstracts Information Services Users Reference Manual* (1981).

1.08 Introduction

Introduce the Problem. The body of a paper opens with an introduction that presents the specific problem under study and describes the research strategy. Because the introduction is clearly identified by its position in the article, it is not labeled. Before writing the introduction, consider

- What is the point of the study?
- How do the hypothesis and the experimental design relate to the problem?
- What are the theoretical implications of the study, and how does the study relate to previous work in the area? What are the theoretical propositions tested, and how were they derived?

A good introduction answers these questions in a paragraph or two and, by summarizing the relevant arguments and the data, gives the reader a firm sense of what was done and why.

Develop the Background. Discuss the literature but do not include an exhaustive historical review. Assume that the reader has knowledge in the field for which you are writing and does not require a complete digest. Although you should acknowledge the contributions of others to the study of the problem, cite only that research pertinent to the specific issue and avoid references with only tangential or general significance. If you summarize earlier works, avoid nonessential details; instead, emphasize pertinent findings, relevant methodological issues, and major conclusions. Refer the reader to general surveys or reviews of the topic if they are available.

Demonstrate the logical continuity between previous and present work. Develop the problem with enough breadth and clarity to make it generally understood by as wide a professional audience as possible. Do not let the goal of brevity mislead you into writing a statement intelligible only to the specialist.

Controversial issues, when relevant, should be treated fairly. A simple statement that certain studies support one conclusion and others support another conclusion is better than an extensive and inconclusive discussion. Whatever your personal opinion, avoid animosity and *ad hominem* arguments in presenting the controversy. Do not support your position or justify your research by citing established authorities out of context.

State the Purpose and Rationale. After you have introduced the problem and developed the background material, you are in a position to tell what you did. Make this statement in the closing paragraphs of the introduction. At this point, a definition of the variables and a formal statement of your hypotheses give clarity to the paper. Questions to bear in mind in closing the introduction are, What variables did I plan to manipulate? What results did I expect and why did I expect them? The logic behind "Why did I expect them?" should be made explicit. Clearly develop the rationale for each hypothesis.

1.09 Method

The Method section describes in detail how the study was conducted. Such a description enables the reader to evaluate the appropriateness of your methods and the reliability and the validity of your results. It also permits experienced investigators to replicate the study if they so desire.

If you refer the reader to another source for details of the method, give a brief synopsis of the method in this section. (See section 1.12 for treatment of multiple experiments.)

Identify Subsections. It is both conventional and expedient to divide the Method section into labeled subsections. These usually include descriptions of the *subjects*, the *apparatus* (or *materials*), and the *procedure.* If the design of the experiment is complex or the stimuli require detailed description, additional subsections or subheadings to divide the subsections may be warranted to help readers find specific information. Your own judgment is the best guide on what number and type of subheadings to use.

Include in these subsections only the information essential to comprehend and replicate the study. Given insufficient detail, the reader is left with questions; given too much detail, the reader is burdened with irrelevant information.

Subjects. The subsection on subjects answers three questions: Who participated in the study? How many participants were there? How were they selected? Give the total number of participants and the number assigned to each experimental condition. If any participants did not complete the experiment, give the number of participants and the reasons they did not continue.

When humans are the participants, report the procedures for selecting and assigning subjects and the agreements and payments made. Give major demographic characteristics such as general geographic location, type of institutional affiliation, sex, and age. When a demographic characteristic is an experimental variable, describe the group specifically; for example, "The second group comprised 40 men between the ages of 20 and 30 years, all of whom had emigrated from Scandinavia, were permanent residents of the United States for at least 15 years, and lived in a major city in Minnesota."

When animals are the participants, report the genus, species, and strain number or other specific identification, such as the name of the supplier. Give the number of animals and the animals' sex, age, weight, and physiological condition. In addition, specify all essential details of their treatment and handling so that the investigation can be successfully replicated.

When you submit your manuscript, indicate to the journal editor that the treatment of participants (human or animal) was in accordance with the ethical standards of the APA (see Principle 9, Research With Human Participants, and Principle 10, Care and Use of Animals, in the "Ethical Principles of Psychologists," APA, 1981).

Apparatus. The subsection on apparatus briefly describes the apparatus or materials used and their function in the experiment. Standard laboratory equipment, such as furniture, stopwatches, or screens, can usually be mentioned without detail. Identify specialized equipment obtained from a commercial establishment by the firm's name and the model number of the equipment. Complex or custom-made equipment may be illustrated by a drawing or photograph, although such figures do add to manuscript preparation and printing costs. A detailed description of complex equipment may be included in an appendix.

Procedure. The subsection on procedure summarizes each step in the execution of the research. Include the instructions to the participants, the formation of the groups, and the specific experimental manipulations. Describe randomization, counterbalancing, and other control features in the design. Summarize or paraphrase instructions, unless they are unusual or compose an experimental manipulation, in which cases they may be presented verbatim. Most readers are familiar with standard testing procedures; unless new or unique procedures are used, do not describe them in detail.

Remember that the Method section should tell the reader *what* you did and *how* you did it.

1.10 Results

The Results section summarizes the data collected and the statistical treatment of them. First, briefly state the main results or findings. Then report the data in sufficient detail to justify the conclusions. Discussing the implications of the results is not appropriate here. Mention all relevant results, including those that run counter to the hypothesis. Do not include individual scores or raw data, with the exception, for example, of single-subject designs or illustrative samples.

Tables and Figures. To report the data, choose the medium that presents them clearly and economically. Tables provide exact values and can efficiently illustrate main effects; they are less expensive than figures to reproduce. Figures of professional quality attract the reader's eye and best illustrate interactions and general comparisons, but they are imprecise and are expensive to reproduce.

Although summarizing the results and the analysis in tables or figures may be helpful, avoid repeating the same data in several places and using tables for data that can be easily presented in a few sentences in the text. If you do use tables or figures, use as few as possible and be certain to mention all of them in text. Refer to all tables as *tables* and to all graphs, pictures, or drawings as *figures.* Tables and figures supplement the text; they cannot do the entire job of communication. Always tell the reader what to look for in tables and figures and provide sufficient explanation to make them readily intelligible.

Statistical Presentation. When reporting inferential statistics (e.g., t tests, F tests, chi-square), include information about the obtained magnitude or value of the test, the degrees of freedom, the probability level, and the direction of the effect. Be sure to include descriptive statistics (e.g., means or standard deviations). Assume that your reader has professional knowledge of statistics. Basic assumptions, such as rejecting the null hypothesis, should not be reviewed. If there is a question about the appropriateness of a particular test, however, be sure to justify the use of that test.

1.11 Discussion

After presenting the results, you are in a position to evaluate and interpret their implications, especially with respect to your original hypothesis. In the Discussion section, you are free to examine, interpret, and qualify the results, as well as to draw inferences from them. Emphasize any theoretical consequences of the results and the validity of your conclusions. (When the discussion is relatively brief and straightforward, some authors prefer to combine it with the previous Results section, yielding *Results and Conclusions* or *Results and Discussion.*)

Open the discussion with a clear statement of the support or nonsupport for your original hypothesis. Similarities and differences between your results and the work of others should clarify and confirm your conclusions. Do not, however, simply reformulate and repeat points already made; each new statement should contribute to your position and to the readers' understanding of the problem. You may remark on certain shortcomings of the study, but do not dwell compulsively on every flaw. Negative results should be accepted as such without an undue attempt to explain them away.

Avoid polemics, triviality, and weak theoretical comparisons in your discussion. Speculation is in order only if it is (a) identified as such, (b) related closely and logically to empirical data or theory, and (c) expressed concisely. Identifying the practical and theoretical implications of your study, suggesting improvements on your research, or proposing new research may be appropriate, but keep these comments brief. In general, be guided by these questions:

- What have I contributed here?
- How has my study helped to resolve the original problem?
- What conclusions and theoretical implications can I draw from my study?

The responses to these questions are the core of your contribution, and readers have a right to clear, unambiguous, and direct answers.

1.12 Multiple Experiments

If you are integrating several experiments in one paper, describe the method and results of each experiment separately. If appropriate, include for each experiment a short discussion of the results or combine the discussion with the description of results (e.g., *Results and Discussion*). Always make the logic and rationale of each new experiment clear to the reader. Always include a comprehensive general discussion of all the work after the last experiment.

The arrangement of sections reflects the structure described above. Label the experiments Experiment 1, Experiment 2, and so forth. These labels are centered main headings. They organize the subsections and make referring to a specific experiment convenient for the reader. The Method and Results sections (and the Discussion section, if a short discussion accompanies each experiment) appear under each experimental heading.

1.13 References

Just as data in the paper support interpretations and conclusions, so reference citations document statements made about the literature. All citations in the manuscript must appear in the reference list, and all references must be cited in text. Choose references judiciously and cite them accurately. The standard procedures for citation ensure that references are accurate, complete, and useful to investigators and readers.

1.14 Appendix

An appendix, although seldom used, is helpful if the detailed description of certain material is distracting in, or inappropriate to, the body of the paper. Some examples of material suitable for an appendix are (a) a new computer program specifically designed for your research and unavailable elsewhere, (b) an unpublished test and its validation, (c) a complicated mathematical proof, (d) a list of stimulus materials (e.g., those used in psycholinguistic research), or (e) a detailed description of a complex piece of equipment. Include an appendix only if it helps readers to understand, evaluate, or replicate the study.

QUALITY OF PRESENTATION

A manuscript that is important enough to write deserves thoughtful preparation. You should evaluate the content and organization of the manuscript just as you evaluated the investigation itself. The following questions (based on Bartol, 1981) may help you assess the quality of your presentation.

- Is the topic appropriate for the journal to which the manuscript is submitted?
- Is the introduction clear and complete?
- Does the statement of purpose adequately and logically orient the reader?
- Is the literature adequately reviewed?
- Are the citations appropriate and complete?
- Is the research question clearly identified, and is the hypothesis explicit?
- Are the conceptualization and rationale perfectly clear?
- Is the method clearly and adequately described? That is, can the study be replicated from the description provided in the paper?
- If observers were used to assess variables, is the interobserver reliability reported?
- Are the techniques of data analysis appropriate, and is the analysis clear? Are the assumptions underlying the statistical procedures clearly met by the data to which they are applied?
- Are the results and conclusions unambiguous, valid, and meaningful?
- Is the discussion thorough? Does it stick to the point and confine itself to what can be concluded from the significant findings of the study?
- Is the paper concise?

WRITING STYLE

The style requirements in the *Publication Manual* are intended to facilitate clear communication. The requirements are explicit, but alternatives to prescribed forms are permissible if they ensure clearer communication. In all cases, the use of rules should be balanced with good judgment.

2.01 Orderly Presentation of Ideas

Thought units—whether single words, a sentence or paragraph, or longer sequences—must be orderly. So that readers will understand what you are presenting, you must aim for continuity in words, concepts, and thematic development from the opening statement to the conclusion. Readers will be confused if you misplace words or phrases in sentences, abandon familiar syntax, shift the criterion for items in a series, or clutter the sequence of ideas with wordiness or irrelevancies.

Continuity can be achieved in several ways. For instance, punctuation marks contribute to continuity by showing relationships between ideas. They cue the reader to the pauses, inflections, subordination, and pacing normally heard in speech. Use the full range of punctuation aids available: Neither overuse nor underuse one type of punctuation, such as commas or dashes. Overuse may annoy the reader; underuse may confuse. Instead, use punctuation to support meaning.

Another way to achieve continuity is through the use of transition words. These words help maintain the flow of thought, especially when the material is complex or abstract. A pronoun that refers to a noun in the preceding sentence not only serves as a transition but also avoids repetition. Be sure the referent is obvious. Other transition devices are time links (*then, next, after, while, since*), cause-effect links (*therefore, consequently, as a result*), addition links (*in addition, moreover, furthermore, similarly*), or contrast links (*however, but, conversely, nevertheless, although, whereas*).

A few transition words (e.g., *while, since*) create confusion because they have been adopted in informal writing style and in conversation for transitions other than time links. For example, *since* is often used when *because* is meant. Scientific writing, however, must be precise; therefore, only the original meaning of these transition words is acceptable.

2.02 Smoothness of Expression

Scientific prose serves a different purpose than creative writing does. Devices that are often found in creative writing, for example, setting up ambiguity, inserting the unexpected, omitting the expected, and suddenly shifting the topic, tense, or person, can confuse or disturb readers of scientific prose. Therefore, these devices should be avoided in writing that aims for clear and logical communication.

Because you have spent so much time close to your material and have thus lost some objectivity, you may not immediately see certain problems, especially inferred contradictions. A reading by a colleague may uncover such problems. You can usually catch omissions, irrelevancies, and abruptness by putting the manuscript aside and rereading it later. If you also read the paper aloud, you have an even better chance of finding problems of abruptness.

If, on later reading, you do find that your writing is abrupt, more transition from one topic to another may be needed. Possibly you have abandoned an argument or theme prematurely; if so, you need to amplify the discussion.

Abruptness is often the result of sudden shifts in verb tense and the capricious use of different tenses within the same paragraph or in adjacent paragraphs. By being consistent in the use of verb tenses, you can help ensure smooth expression. Past tense (e.g., *Smith showed*) or present perfect tense (e.g., *researchers have shown*) is appropriate for the literature review and the description of the procedure if the discussion is of past events. Stay within the chosen tense. Use past tense (e.g., *the subjects performed*) to describe the results. Use the present tense (e.g., *the data indicate*) to discuss the results and to present the conclusions. By reporting conclusions in the present tense, you allow readers to join you in deliberating the matter at hand.

Many writers strive to achieve smooth expression by using synonyms or near synonyms to avoid repeating a term. The intention is commendable, but by using synonyms you may unintentionally suggest a subtle difference. Therefore, choose synonyms with care. The discreet use of pronouns can often relieve the monotonous repetition of a term without introducing ambiguity.

2.03 Economy of Expression

Say only what needs to be said. The author who is frugal with words not only writes a more readable manuscript but also increases the chances that the manuscript will be accepted. Editors work with limited numbers of printed pages and therefore often request authors to shorten submitted papers. You can tighten overly long papers by eliminating redundancy, wordiness, jargon, evasiveness, circumlocution, and clumsiness. Weed out overly detailed descriptions of apparatus, subjects, or procedure; gratuitous embellishments; elaborations of the obvious; and irrelevant observations or asides.

Short words and short sentences are easier to comprehend than long ones. A long technical term, however, may be more precise than several short words, and technical terms are inseparable from scientific reporting. Yet the technical terminology in a paper should be understood by psychologists throughout the discipline. An article that depends upon terminology familiar to only a few specialists does not sufficiently contribute to the literature.

The main causes of uneconomical writing are jargon and wordiness. Jargon is the continuous use of a technical vocabularly even in places where that vocabulary is not relevant. Jargon is also the substitution of a euphemistic phrase for a familiar term (e.g., *monetary felt scarcity* for *poverty*), and, as such, it should be scrupulously avoided. Federal bureaucratic jargon has had the greatest publicity, but scientific jargon also grates on the reader, encumbers the communication of information, and often takes up space unnecessarily.

Wordiness is every bit as irritating and uneconomical as jargon and can impede the ready grasp of ideas. Change *based on the fact that* to *because, at the present time* to *now,* and *for the purpose of* to a simple *for* or *to.* Change *there were several students who completed* to *several students completed. Reason* and *because* often appear in the same sentence; however, they have the same meaning, and therefore they should not be used together. Unconstrained wordiness lapses into embellishment and literary elegance, which are clearly inappropriate in scientific style. Mullins (1977) comprehensively discusses examples of wordiness found in the social science literature.

Writers often become redundant in a mistaken effort to be emphatic. Use no more words than are necessary to convey the meaning. In the following examples, the italicized words are redundant and should be omitted:

They were *both* alike
a total of 68 subjects
Four *different* groups saw
instructions, which were *exactly* the same as those used
absolutely essential
has been *previously* found
small *in size*
one and the same
in *close* proximity
completely unanimous
just exactly
very close to significance
period of time
summarize *briefly*
the reason is *because*

Although writing only in short, simple sentences produces choppy and boring prose, writing exclusively in long, involved sentences creates difficult, sometimes incomprehensible material. Varied sentence length helps readers maintain interest and comprehension. When involved concepts do require long sentences, the components should march along like people in a parade, not dodge about like broken-field runners. Direct, declarative sentences with simple, common words are usually best.

Similar cautions apply to paragraph length. Single-sentence paragraphs may be abrupt. Paragraphs that are too long, a more typical fault in manuscripts, are likely to lose the reader's attention. New paragraphs provide a pause for the reader—a chance to store one step in the conceptual development before beginning another. If your paragraphs run longer than a page in typescript, you are probably straining the reader's thought span. Look for a logical place to make a break or reorganize the material. Unity, cohesiveness, and continuity should characterize all paragraphs.

2.04 Precision and Clarity in Word Choice

Make certain that every word means exactly what you intend it to mean. Sooner or later most authors discover a discrepancy between their accepted meaning of a term and its dictionary definition. In informal style, for example, *feel* broadly substitutes for *think* or *believe,* but such latitude is not acceptable in scientific style.

Likewise, avoid colloquial expressions (e.g., *write up* for *report*), which diffuse meaning. Approximations of quantity (e.g., *quite a large part, practically all,* or *very few*) are interpreted differently by different readers or in different contexts. They weaken statements, especially those describing empirical observations.

Pronouns confuse readers unless the referent for each pronoun is obvious; readers should not have to search previous text to determine the meaning of the term. Simple pronouns are the most troublesome, especially *this, that, these,* and *those* when they refer to a previous sentence. Eliminate ambiguity by writing, for example, *this test, that trial, these subjects,* and *those reports.*

Omission of key verbs is another cause of ambiguity, as in the sentence, "Ten-year-olds were more likely to play with age peers than 8-year-olds." Does this sentence mean that 10-year-olds were more likely than 8-year-olds to play with age peers? Or does it mean that 10-year-olds were more likely to play with age peers and less likely to play with 8-year-olds? Thoughtful attention to good sentence structure and word choice reduces the chance of this kind of ambiguity.

Inappropriately or illogically attributing action in the name of objectivity can be misleading. For example, writing "The experimenter instructed the subjects" when "the experimenter" refers to yourself is at best ambiguous and may even give the impression that you disavow your own study. (For a study of editorial preferences for first- or third-person writing style, see Polyson, Levinson, & Miller, 1982.) In addition, do not attribute human functions to nonhuman sources (e.g., "The community program was persuaded to allow five of the observers to become tutors"). An experiment cannot *attempt to demonstrate, control unwanted variables,* or *interpret findings.* Use *I* or *we,* that is, the author or authors, as the subject of these verbs (but never use *we* in the editorial sense).

2.05 Strategies to Improve Writing Style

Authors use a variety of strategies in putting their thoughts on paper, and there is little basis for selecting one over another. Very likely the fit between author and strategy is more important than the particular strategy used. Three approaches to achieving professional and effective communication are (a) writing from an outline; (b) putting aside the first draft, then rereading it after a delay; and (c) asking a colleague to criticize the draft for you.

Writing from an outline helps preserve the logic of the research itself. It identifies main ideas, defines subordinate ideas, disciplines your writing, maintains the continuity and pacing, discourages tangential excursions, and points out omissions.

Rereading your own copy after setting it aside for a few days permits a fresh approach. Reading the paper aloud enables you not only to see faults that "were never there" on the previous reading but to hear them as well. When these problems are corrected, give a polished copy to a colleague—preferably a person who has published but who has not been close to your own work—for a critical review. Even better, get critiques from two colleagues, and you have a trial run of a journal's review process.

These strategies, particularly the latter, may require you to invest more time in a manuscript than you had anticipated. The results of these strategies, however, may be greater accuracy and thoroughness and clearer communication.

Glossary of Terms

Active Placebo. In an experiment, a substance or procedure not expected to have any effect on the dependent variable of interest, but which has irrelevant side effects that make it seem to be a real drug or legitimate treatment.

Analysis of Variance (ANOVA). A statistical procedure that divides the total variance of a set of scores into their component parts.

Antagonistic Interaction. A situation in which the direction of the effect of one treatment depends on the level of one or more other treatments.

Archives. The ongoing and continuing records of an institution or society.

Baseline. Data from an untreated group or condition used as a reference point for assessing treatment effects.

Behavioroid Measure. A measure that requires subjects to commit themselves to a course of action, without ever having to perform it later. The procedure requires that subjects believe they will have to follow through on their commitment at the time they make it.

Blind. As in blind experimenters; kept ignorant of.

Carryover Effects. Persisting consequences, resulting from a treatment, that affect subjects' responses to one or more subsequent treatments; practice and fatigue are common carryover effects.

Case Study. Intensive study of a single individual; also called case history.

Catalytic Interaction. A situation in which two or more treatments are effective only when they occur together.

Central Tendency. A number calculated to represent the most "typical" score in a set of scores.

Cohort. Any group that passes through a set of experiences or institutions at the same time.

Compensatory Equalization. A situation in which untreated individuals or groups obtain something "equally good" for themselves.

Compensatory Rivalry. The situation in which an untreated group works extra hard to see to it that the expected superiority of the treatment is not demonstrated.

Constructive Replication. Replicating an experiment so as to preserve the theoretically essential features while varying features presumed to be irrelevant.

Control. (1) The ability to influence or bring about change in a particular phenomenon or to know what the controlling factors are in a particular situation. (2) Holding theoretically irrelevant factors constant in order to observe a predicted cause and effect relationship.

Convergent Validity. The correlation between (or among) two or more measures of the same theoretical construct.

Correlation. The co- or joint relationship between (or among) two or more variables.

Correlation Coefficient. A numerical index of the magnitude and direction of a correlation; it can range from $+1.00$ to -1.00.

Correlation Matrix. A table of correlations in which the rows and columns list the variables and the entries display the correlation between each possible pair of variables.

Counterbalancing. The practice of running subjects in a repeated measures design so as to balance the order in which treatments are experienced, e.g., order A-B and order B-A.

Criterion. The variable to be predicted.

Cross-Lagged Panel Technique. A statistical procedure designed to facilitate drawing causal inferences from time-lagged correlational data.

Cross-Sectional Studies. Studies which look at individuals of several different ages at approximately the same point in calendar time.

Cross-Sequential Designs. Designs that employ several different cohorts (as in cross-sectional studies) but follow them longitudinally rather than relying on "one-shot" observations.

Curvilinear Relationship. A relationship that when plotted resembles a curved rather than a straight line.

Demand Characteristics. Hints and cues in a research situation that influence subjects' perceptions of what is expected of them.

Dependent Variable. In an experiment, aspects of subjects' behavior measured after manipulation of the independent variable.

Developmental Trends. Consistent, age-related changes in behavior.

Differential Attrition. Differences in the number or characteristics of subjects who drop out of a study that are related to the treatment they received.

Diffusion. The spread of treatment effects from treated to untreated groups.

Discriminant Validity. The correlation between (or among) two or more different constructs measured by the same method.

Double Blind Experiment. In medicine, an experiment in which neither the physician nor the patients know who is getting the "real medication" and who is getting the placebo.

Ecological Validity. The degree to which research results can be generalized to all the environmental contexts of interest.

Effect Size. An index of the magnitude (as opposed to the statistical significance) of any given effect.

Empirical Approach. The belief that direct observation and experience provide the only firm basis for understanding nature.

Error Variance. Variability generated by unknown or uncontrolled factors.

Experimenter Role. Roles involving contact with subjects, including making observations, giving tests, and administering treatments.

External Validity. The degree to which conclusions can be generalized.

Factor Analysis. A procedure for reducing a correlation matrix into a set of mathematical entities ("factors") which will account for the matrix.

Fatigue Effect. Any deterioration in performance due merely to becoming tired, bored, or the like.

File Drawer Problem. The possibility that null results are simply filed away, thereby biasing the published literature toward Type I errors.

Forecasting. Any procedure employing a time series analysis to predict future behavior by analyzing the patterns that seem to underlie previously observed behavior.

Haphazard Sampling. Taking every opportunity to include the largest and broadest possible range and variety of subjects and contexts in one's research, with the aim of increasing sample representativeness.

Hawthorne Effect. Increased productivity simply as a response to any new treatment.

Hermeneutics. In philosophy, the art of explaining or interpreting, or the view that all perception is interpretive.

History. Any environmental event other than the treatment of interest that occurs between successive measurements or tests.

Idiographic Approach. Belief that each individual must be studied and understood as a unique person.

Illusory Residual Correlation. When using the partial correlation technique, a significant correlation between X and Y that remains after partialing, despite the fact that there is no true causal relationship between X and Y.

Impressionistic Modal Sampling. Selecting several different samples judged to be typical of the various population subgroups of interest.

Independent Variable. The condition or stimulus manipulated in an experiment.

Induction. Reasoning from particular facts to a general conclusion.

Informed Consent. The ethical requirement that subjects have sufficient information about a research project to make an informed decision as to whether they choose to participate.

Instrument Decay. Any change in the characteristics of a measurement procedure over time. (Also called instrumentation.)

Interaction. An outcome in a factorial design in which the effect of one factor is not the same at every level of one or more other factors.

Internal Validity. Validity of empirical statements dealing with the question of whether X (as manipulated) causes a change in Y (as measured).

Interval Scale. A scale of measurement in which the numbers represent equal intervals, e.g., on such a scale going from 2 to 3 has the same meaning as going from 9 to 10.

Introspection. A method by which trained observers are asked to describe the contents of their own minds.

Investigator Role. The role of designing, analyzing, interpreting, and reporting research results.

"John Henry Effect." See compensatory rivalry.

Local History. Any environmental event other than the treatment of interest that has occurred for only some groups.

Longitudinal Studies. Studies which follow a group of individuals over time to observe age-related changes.

Maturation. Any changes in behavior over time due to the subject simply becoming older, wiser, stronger, or the like.

Measurement Error. That portion of any score due to random or irrelevant factors.

Median Split. Dividing a set of scores at the median to create a classificatory variable for a mixed design.

Meta-Analysis. Name given to any set of systematic rules for combining and evaluating a collection of independent replications or partial replications.

Mixed Design. A factorial design with both classificatory and manipulated variables.

Multimethod Approach. Testing a theoretical proposition by employing several different manipulations.

Multiple Correlation. A correlation between two or more predictor variables and a criterion variable.

Multiple Discrete Leveling. Dividing a set of scores into three or more levels to create a classificatory variable for a mixed design.

Multiple Regression. A technique for weighting, combining, and ordering two or more predictor variables nonredundantly into a mathematical equation.

Multiple Treatment Interference. Any situation in which observed results may be due to any of a combination of treatments which subjects have received.

Multitrait-Multimethod Matrix. A table of correlations between (or among) two or more entities ("traits") and two or more measurement methods.

Narrow Operationism. The view that every variable of interest should be operationally defined.

No-Cause Baseline. In time-lagged designs, an estimate of the expected relationship between two variables if no casual relationship existed between them.

Nominal Scale. A scale of measurement with no underlying quantitative metric; numbers in such scales merely serve as labels rather than as quantities which can be compared.

Nomological Net. A network of empirical relationships used to validate or support the existence of a theoretical construct.

Nomothetic Approach. Belief that behavioral science should aim to formulate general laws that apply to populations; often contrasted with the idiographic approach.

Null Hypothesis. The hypothesis of "no difference," created as a means of logically testing actual research hypotheses.

Oblique. Statistically related.

Open Concept. A theoretical term that is not fully defined by any given set of operations.

Operational Definition. A unique specification of the meaning of a term as equivalent to a single set of operations.

Operationalization. Choosing or creating concrete procedures to represent a theoretical construct or concept.

Ordinal Scale. A scale of measurement in which the numbers represent a rank ordering.

Orthogonal. Statistically independent.

Partial Correlation. The correlation between X and Y after the effects of Z have been removed statistically.

Partial Definition. A set of operations that provides only one of the possible sets of operations implied by a theoretical term.

Path Analysis. Any of a number of complex

mathemetical procedures for explicating and assessing the pattern of causal relationships that underlie a set of correlational data.

Period. The frequency with which any behavior repeats itself.

Physical Traces. The durable residue of any behavior, including erosion (visible wear and tear) and accretion (the laying down or accumulating of any observable residue).

Pilot Testing. A "trial run" of research procedures or hypotheses, usually undertaken to determine the feasibility of undertaking a larger or more formal study.

Placebo Effect. A change produced by an inert substance.

Plausible Rival Hypotheses. Rival hypotheses that have a more than remote chance of being correct; see Rival Hypotheses.

Population. Any well-defined set of individuals or events, identified by rules of membership.

Population Validity. The degree to which research results can be generalized to the populations of ultimate interest.

Power. Sensitivity of a statistical procedure or research design in detecting differences or effects when they are in fact present.

Practice Effect. Any improvement resulting merely from experience with a task or procedure.

Prediction. Accurate anticipation of future or as yet unobserved events.

Principle of Aggregation. The principle which states that the sum or average of a set of multiple measurements has less random error than a single measurement.

Prospective Study. A type of longitudinal study in which subjects are followed forward in time, so that each important event or circumstance can be noted and recorded as it occurs.

Quasi-Experiment. Any study which employs experimental units of analysis and manipulated treatments but without comparing groups formed by random assignment.

Random Assignment. Assigning subjects to treatments or groups such that each subject has an equal likelihood of being assigned to any treatment or group and the assignment of any one individual does not influence the assignment of any other individual.

Random Sample. A sample drawn in such a way that (1) every member of the population has an equal chance of being selected for the sample, and (2) the selection of any one member of the population does not influence the chances of any other member being selected.

Random Selection. Selecting a sample randomly from the population of ultimate interest.

Ratio Scale. A scale of measurement in which the numbers represent equal intervals and the scale has a meaningful zero point. In such scales ratios can be compared, e.g., a ratio of 2 to 1 has the same meaning as a ratio of 16 to 8.

Reactivity. Changes occurring in subjects' behavior merely as a reaction to being observed.

Regression. (1) A numerical measure of association between (or among) variables in which predictor and criterion variables are specified. (2) A tendency for individuals with unusually high or low scores to go back toward the mean on subsequent testing; also called statistical regression.

Reliability. Repeatability or consistency.

Resentful Demoralization. The situation in which individuals in an untreated or control group become less efficient, productive, or motivated because of feelings of resentment toward those in the treated group(s) or toward the experimenters.

Response Sets. A priori tendencies to respond in particular ways to test questions or items, including response acquiescence ("yea-saying"), response deviation (giving unusual responses) and social desirability (answering in the most socially accepted or approved direction).

Retrospective Study. A type of study in which subjects or those who knew them in earlier times are asked to "look back" and recall what was said or done at various times in the past.

Rival Hypotheses. Alternative explanations of an unobserved relationship.

Sample. A subset of a population, usually selected with the aim of generalizing to one or more populations.

Sample of Convenience. A sample chosen because it was easily accessible.

Selection Bias. Any systematic difference between comparison groups other than experiencing the treatment of interest.

Selection-Maturation. Any changes in the

amount of difference between groups over time, due to the groups developing at different rates.

Self-Fulfilling Prophecy. A type of bias in which observers or experimenters act so as to bring about the outcome or results they expect to obtain.

Self-Selection. Any situation in which subjects decide for themselves whether they will participate in research or decide for themselves which of several groups they will be in.

Solomon Four Group Design. An experimental design that factorially combines the presence or absence of a pretest with the presence or absence of a treatment.

Spontaneous Remission. Improvement due simply to the passage of time.

Standard Deviation. A measure of the variability in a set of scores; the square root of the variance.

Standard(ized) Scores. Mathematically transformed scores forming a distribution with a mean of 0 and a standard deviation of 1.00.

Statistical Conclusion Validity. The validity of a conclusion about whether two or more numerical values (e. g., group means) are statistically different; see statistical significance.

Statistical Regression. The tendency for extreme scores in a distribution to move (i.e., regress) toward the mean on subsequent testing due to shifts in the distribution of measurement error.

Statistical Significance. A numerical index of the probability that a particular difference occurred by chance; sometimes is expressed as or called a "p value."

Systematic Variance. Extent to which the presence or absence of an experimental manipulation causes the scores in the groups to depart from the overall mean of the distribution of the combined scores; a measure of treatment effect.

Temporal Precedence. The situation in which changes in one variable are known to precede changes in one or more other variables.

Temporal Validity. The degree to which research results can be generalized across time.

Terminative Interaction. A situation in which two or more treatments are each effective, but their effectiveness is not increased or enhanced when they are combined.

Test. Any systematic procedure for making and scoring observations.

Testing. The effect of having taken a test already upon one's performance when taking it again.

Theoretical Construct. Any entity posited to be meaningful by a theory; often simply called a construct (CON-struct).

Theoretical (Construct) Validity. The degree to which a research result is correctly interpreted or the degree to which the formulation of a construct is "true."

Third Variable. Any variable that might serve to explain an observed association between X and Y.

Time Series. Any procedure that examines behavior over time.

Total Design Method. An approach to surveying in which close attention is given to every factor that might influence responses to a survey.

True Score. That portion of any score due to the real characteristics of the thing being measured (as opposed to measurement error).

Truncated Range. Characterization of a set of sample scores indicating that the sample does not reflect the full range of scores in the population of interest.

Type I Error. Rejecting the null hypothesis when it is in fact true.

Type II Error. Failing to reject the null hypothesis when it is in fact false.

Unobtrusive Observation. Observing without being seen, heard, or interfering in any way with the ongoing flow of behavior.

Validity. Correctness or truth; measuring what one wants to or purports to measure.

Variability. The degree of spread in a set of scores.

Variance. A numerical index of the variability or "scatter" in a set of scores.

Volunteer Bias. The tendency of volunteers to be different from the general population of ultimate interest.

References

ALLEN, V. L., & LEVINE, J. M. (1969). Consensus and conformity. *Journal of Experimental Social Psychology, 55,* 389–399.

ALLPORT, G. W. (1961). *Pattern and growth in personality.* New York: Holt, Rinehart & Winston.

AMERICAN PSYCHOLOGICAL ASSOCIATION. (1954). Technical recommendations for psychological tests and diagnostic techniques. Published as a supplement to the *Psychological Bulletin, 51,* No. 2, Part 2, 1–38.

AMERICAN PSYCHOLOGICAL ASSOCIATION. (1982). *Ethical principles in the conduct of research with human participants.* Washington, D.C.: Author.

ANASTASI, A. (1968). *Psychological testing* (3d ed.). New York: Macmillan.

ARONSON, E., & CARLSMITH, J. M. (1968) Experimentation in social psychology. In G. Lindzey and E. Aronson (Eds.), *Handbook of social psychology* (Vol. II). Reading, MA.: Addison-Wesley.

ASCH, S. (1951). Effects of group pressure upon the modification and distortion of judgment. In H. Guetzkow (Ed.), *Groups, leadership and men* (pp. 177–190). Pittsburgh: Carnegie Press.

AX, A. F. (1953). The physiological difference between fear and anger in humans. *Psychosomatic Medicine, 15,* 433–442.

BALTES, P. B., & REINERT, G. (1969). Cohort effects in cognitive development of children as revealed by cross-sectional sequences. *Development Psychology, 1,* 169–177.

BANDURA, A. (1965). Influence of models' reinforcement contingencies on the acquisition of imitative responses. *Journal of Personality and Social Psychology, 1,* 589–595.

BARBER, T. X., & SILVER, M. J. (1968). Fact, fiction, and the experimenter bias effect. *Psychological Bulletin Monograph Supplement, 70,* 1–29.

BARLOW, D. H. & HERSEN, M. (1984). *Single case experimental designs.* Elmsford, NY: Pergamon Press.

BARTHELL, C. N., & HOLMES, D. S. (1968). High school yearbooks: A nonreactive measure of social isolation in graduates who later became schizophrenic. *Journal of Abnormal Psychology, 73,* 313–316.

BECHTEL, R. B., ACHELPOHL, C., & AKERS, R. (1972). Correlates between observed behavior and questionnaire responses on television viewing. In E. A. Rubinstein, G. A. Comstock & J. P. Murray (Eds.), *Television and social behavior,* (Vol. IV: *Television in day-to-day life: Patterns of use.*) Washington, D.C.: United States Government Printing Office.

BECHTOLDT, H. (1959). Construct validity: A critique. *American Psychologist, 14,* 619–629.

BEECHER, H. K. (1966). Ethics and clinical research. *New England Journal of Medicine, 274,* 1354–1360.

BERKOWITZ, L. (1970). The contagion of violence: An S-R mediational analysis of some effects of observed aggression. In W. J. Arnold and M. M. Page (Eds.), *Nebraska Symposium on Motivation.* Lincoln: Univ. of Nebraska Press.

BERKOWITZ, L., & DONNERSTEIN, E. (1982). External validity is more than skin deep: some answers to criticism of laboratory experiments. *American Psychologist, 37,* 245–257.

BIRNEY, R. C. (1968). Research on the achievement motive. In E. F. Borgatta and W. W. Lambert (Eds.), *Handbook of personality theory and research* (pp. 857–889). Chicago: Rand McNally.

BOFFEY, P. M. (1985, January 8). Study reported to tighten link of asprin and Reyés Syndrome, *New York Times.*

BOGATZ, G. A., & BALL, S. (1972). *The second year of Sesame Street: A continuing evaluation.* Princeton, N.J.: Educational Testing Service.

BOLLES, R. C. (1970). Species-specific defense reactions and avoidance learning. *Psychological Review, 77,* 32–49.

BORING, E. G. (1950). *A history of experimental psychology* (2nd ed.). New York: Appleton-Century-Crofts.

BRAMEL, D., & FRIEND, R. (1978). *Human relations in industry: The famous Hawthorne experiments.* Unpublished manuscript, State University of New York at Stony Brook.

BREHM, J. W., & COHEN, A. R. (1962). *Explorations in cognitive dissonance.* New York: John Wiley.

BRYAN, J. H. & TEST, M. A. (1967). Models and helping: Naturalistic studies in aiding behavior. *Journal of Personality and Social Psychology, 6,* 400–407.

CAMPBELL, D. T. (1963). From description to experimentation: Interpreting trends as quasi-experiments. In C. Harris (Ed.), *Problems in measuring change.* Madison: Univ. of Wisconsin Press.

CAMPBELL, D. T., & FISKE, D. W. (1959). Convergent and discriminant validation by the multitrait-multimethod matrix. *Psychological Bulletin, 56,* 81–105.

CAMPBELL, D. T., & ROSS, H. L. (1968). The Connecticut crackdown on speeding: Time-series data in quasi-experimental analysis. *Law and Society Review, 3,* 33–53.

CAMPBELL, D. T., & STANLEY, J. C. (1966). *Experimental and quasi-experimental designs for research.* Chicago: Rand McNally.

CAREY, A. (1967). The Hawthorne studies: A radical criticism. *American Sociological Review, 32,* 403–416.

CATALANO, R. A., DOOLEY, D., & JACKSON, R. (1983). Selecting a time-series strategy. *Psychological Bulletin, 94,* 506–523.

CHAFFEE, S. H., & MCLEOD, J. M. (1971). Adolescents, parents, and television violence. Paper presented at symposium "The early window: The role of television in childhood," American Psychological Association Convention, Washington, D.C.

CHAPIN, F. S. (1955). *Experimental designs in sociological research.* New York: Harper & Row.

CHAPMAN, L. J. (1963). The problem of selecting drug-free schizophrenics for research. *Journal of Consulting Psychology, 27,* 540–542.

COHEN, J., & COHEN, P. (1975). *Applied multiple regression/correlation analysis for the behavioral sciences.* Hillsdale, NJ: Erlbaum.

COHEN, J. A. (1960). Coefficient of agreement for nominal scales. *Educational and Psychological Measurement, 20,* 37–46.

COOK, T. D., APPLETON, H., CONNER, R. F., SHAFFER, A., TOMKIN, G., & WEBER, S. J. (1975). *Sesame Street Revisited.* New York: Russell Sage Foundation.

COOK, T. D., & CAMPBELL, D. T. (1979). *Quasi-experimentation.* Chicago: Rand McNally.

COOK, T. D., GRUDER, C. L., HENNIGAN, K. M., & FLAY, B. R. (1978). *The history of the sleeper effect: Some logical pitfalls in accepting the null hypothesis.* Unpublished manuscript, Northwestern University, Evanston, IL.

COZBY, P. C. (1984). *Using computers in the behavioral sciences.* Palo Alto, CA: Mayfield.

CRONBACH, L. J. (1957). The two disciplines of scientific psychology. *American Psychologist, 12,* 671–684.

CRONBACH, L. J., & MEEHL, P. E. (1955). Construct validity in psychological tests. *Psychological Bulletin, 52,* 281–302.

DARLEY, J. M., & FAZIO, R. H. (1980). Expectancy confirmation processes arising in the social interaction sequence. *American Psychologist, 35,* 867–881.

DAVISON, G. C., & STUART, R. B. (1975). Behavior therapy and civil liberties. *American Psychologist, 30,* 755–763. Material reprinted by permission.

DILLMAN, D. A. (1978). *Mail and telephone surveys: The total design method.* New York: John Wiley.

DOMINICK, J. R., & GREENBERG, B. S. (1972). Attitudes toward violence: The interaction of television exposure, family attitudes, and social class. In G. A. Comstock & E. A. Rubinstein (Eds.), *Television and social behavior* (Vol. III: *Television and adolescent aggressiveness*). Washington, D.C.: United States Government Printing Office.

DURANT, W. (1954). *The story of philosophy.* New York: Pocket Library.

DUSH, D. M., HIRT, M. L., & SCHROEDER, H. (1983). Self-statement modification with adults: a meta-analysis. *Psychological Bulletin, 94,* 408–422.

EDWARDS, A. L. (1953). The relationship between the judged desirability of a trait and the probability that the trait will be endorsed. *Journal of Applied Psychology, 37,* 90–93.

EDWARDS, A. L. (1957). *The social desirability variable in personality research.* New York: Dryden Press.

ELKIND, D. (1961). Children's discovery of the conservation of mass, weight, and volume: Piaget replication study II. *Journal of Genetic Psychology, 98,* 219–227.

EPSTEIN, S. (1962). [Comments on Dr. Bandura's paper]. In M. R. Jones (Ed.), *Nebraska symposium on motivation.* (pp. 269–272) Lincoln: Univ. of Nebraska Press.

FINDLEY, M. J., & COOPER, H. M. (1983). Locus of control and academic achievement: A literature review. *Journal of Personality and Social Psychology, 44,* 419–427.

FLAVELL, J. H. (1963). *The developmental psychology of Jean Piaget.* New York: Van Nostrand Reinhold.

FRANK, J. D. (1961). *Persuasion and healing.* New York: Schocken Books.

FRANK, J. D. (1977). Nature and functions of belief systems: Humanism and transcendental religion. *American Psychologist, 32,* 555–559.

FRANZBLAU, S., SPRAFKIN, J. N., & RUBINSTEIN, E. A. (1977). Sex on TV: A content analysis. *Journal of Communication, 27,* 164–170.

FREEDMAN, J. L., WALLINGTON, S. A., & BLESS, E. (1967). Compliance without pressure: The effect of guilt. *Journal of Personality and Social Psychology, 7,* 117–124.

GALANTER, E. (1984). Nostalgia in experimental psychology. [Review of F. J. McGuigan's *Experimental psychology* (4th ed.)]. *Contemporary Psychology, 29,* 559–560.

GALTON, F. (1872). Statistical inquiries into the efficacy of prayer. *Fortnightly Review, 12,* 125–135.

GALTON, F. (1908). *Memories of my life.* London: Mathews, 1908.

GARDNER, G. T. (1978). Effects of Federal human subjects regulations on data obtained in environmental stressor research. *Journal of Personality and Social Psychology, 36,* 628–634.

GATES, A. I. (1917). Recitation as a factor in memorizing. *Archives of Psychology, 6,* 40.

GLASS, D. C. & SINGER, J. E. (1972). *Urban stress: Experiments on noise and social stressors.* New York: Academic Press.

GLASS, G. V., MCGAW, B., & SMITH, R. (1981). *Meta-analysis in social research.* Beverly Hills, CA: Sage Publications, Inc.

GOTTMAN, J. M. (1981). *Time-series analysis.* Cambridge: Cambridge University Press.

GRANBERG, D., & BRENT, E. (1983). When prophecy bends: The preference-expectation link in U. S. Presidential elections, 1952–1980. *Journal of Personality and Social Psychology, 45,* 477–491.

GREENBERG, B. (1971). Personal communication.

GREENWALD, A. (1975). Consequences of prejudice against the null hypothesis. *Psychological Bulletin, 82,* 1–20.

GRICE, G. R. (1966). Dependence of empirical laws upon the source of experimental variation. *Psychological Bulletin, 66,* 488–499.

HALL, R. V., & FOX, R. G. (1977). Changing criterion designs: An alternate applied behavior analysis procedure. In C. C. Etzel, G. M. LeBlanc, & D. M. Baer (Eds.), *New developments in behavior research.* Hillsdale, NJ: Erlbaum.

HAMILTON, D. L., THOMPSON, J. L., & WHITE, A. M. (1970). Role of awareness and intentions in observational learning. *Journal of Personality and Social Psychology, 16,* 689–694.

HAYS, W. L. (1963). *Statistics for psychologists.* New York: Holt, Rinehart, & Winston.

HEELAN, P. A. (1983). *Space-perception and the philosophy of science.* Berkeley, CA: University of California Press.

HEINEMANN, E. G. (1961). Photographic measurement of the retinal image. *American Journal of Psychology, 74,* 440–445.

HEISE, D. R. (1975). *Causal analysis.* New York: John Wiley.

HEISENBERG, W. (1958). *Physics and philosophy.* New York: Harper & Row.

HERRNSTEIN, R. J., & BORING, E. G. (1966). *A source book in the history of psychology.* Cambridge, MA: Harvard Univ. Press.

HOOKE, R. (1972). Statistics, sports, and some other things. In J. M. Tanur et al. (Eds.), *Statistics: A guide to the unknown.* San Francisco: Holden-Day.

HONZIK, M. P. (1957). Developmental studies of parent-child resemblance in intelligence. *Child Development, 28,* 215–289.

HORNSTEIN, H. A., FISCH, E., & HOLMES, M. (1968). Influence of a model's feeling about his behavior and his relevance as a comparison on other observers' helping behavior. *Journal of Personality and Social Psychology, 10,* 222–226.

HOUTS, A. C., & LIEBERT, R. M. (1984). *Bedwetting: A Guide for Parents and Children.* Springfield, IL: Charles C Thomas.

HOUTS, A. C., & PETERSON, J. K. (1985). *Prevention of relapse in full-spectrum home training for primary enuresis: A components analysis.* Unpublished manuscript. Memphis State University, Memphis, TN.

HUNSICKER, J. O., & MELLGREN, R. L. (1977). Multiple deficits in the retention of an appetitively motivated behavior across a 24-hr period in rats. *Animal Learning and Behavior, 5,* 14–16.

HYDE, J. S. (1984). How large are gender differences in aggression? A developmental meta-analysis. *Developmental Psychology, 20,* 722–736.

HYMAN, R. (1964). *The nature of psychological inquiry.* Englewood Cliffs, N.J.: Prentice-Hall.

JOHNSON, M. K., & LIEBERT, R. M. (1977). *Statistics: Tool of the behavioral sciences.* Englewood Cliffs, N.J.: Prentice-Hall.

JÖRESKOG, K. G., and SÖRBOM, D. (1978). *LISREL IV: Analysis of linear structural relationships by maximum likelihood methods.* Chicago: International Educational Services.

JOST, A. (1897). Die assoziations festigkeit in Ihrer abhängigkeit von der vertellung der wiederholungen. *Z. Psychol. Physiol. Sinnesorgune, 14,* 436–472.

KANFER, F. H. (1958). Verbal conditioning: Reinforcement schedules and experimenter influence. *Psychological Reports, 4,* 443–452.

KELMAN, H. C. (1967). Human use of human subjects: The problem of deception in social psychological experiments. *Psychological Bulletin, 67,* 1–11.

KENT, R. N., O'LEARY, K. D., DIAMENT, C., & DIETZ, A. (1974). Expectation biases in observational evaluation of therapeutic change. *Journal of Consulting and Clinical Psychology, 42,* 774–780.

KIESLER, S. B., & BARAL, R. A. (1969). The search for a romantic partner: The effects of self-esteem and physical attractiveness on romantic behavior. In K. J. Gergen & D. Marlowe (Eds.), *Personality and social behavior.* Reading, MA: Addison-Wesley.

KLUCKHOHN, F., & STRODTBECK, F. (1961). *Variations in value orientation.* Evanston, IL: Row, Peterson.

KRATOCHWILL, T. R. (1978). *Single subject research: Strategies for evaluating change.* New York: Academic Press.

KUHN, T. S. (1970). *The structure of scientific revolutions.* Chicago: Univ. of Chicago Press.

LAZARSFELD, P. F. (1948). The mutual effect of statistical variables. Mimeographed report.

LAZARUS, A. A., & DAVISON, G. C. (1971). Clinical innovation in research and practice. In A. E. Bergin & S. Garfield (Eds.), *Handbook of psychotherapy and behavior change.* New York: John Wiley.

LEFKOWITZ, M. M., ERON, L. D., WALDER, L. O., & HUESMANN, L. R. (1972). Television violence and child aggression: A follow-up study. In G. A. Comstock & E. A. Rubinstein (Eds.), *Television and social behavior* (Vol. III: *Television and adolescent aggressiveness*). Washington, D.C.: United States Government Printing Office.

LENNEBERG, E. H. (1962). Understanding language without the ability to speak: A case report. *Journal of Abnormal and Social Psychology, 65,* 419–425.

LI, C. C. (1975). *Path analysis—a primer.* Pacific Grove, CA: The Boxwood Press.

LIEBERT, R. M. (1976). Sesame Street around the world: Evaluating the evaluators. *Journal of Communication, 26,* 165–171.

LIEBERT, R. M., & FERNANDEZ, L. E. (1970). Effects of vicarious consequences on imitative performance. *Child Development, 41,* 847–852.

LIEBERT, R. M., & MORRIS, L. W. (1967). Cognitive and emotional components of test anxiety: A distinction and some initial data. *Psychological Reports, 20,* 975–978.

LIEBERT, R. M., POULOS, R. W., & MARMOR, G. S. (1977). *Developmental psychology* (2nd ed.). Englewood Cliffs, N.J.: Prentice-Hall, Inc.

LIEBERT, R. M., SOBOL, M. P., & COPEMANN, C. D. (1972). Effects of vicarious consequences and race of model upon imitative performance by black children. *Developmental Psychology, 6,* 453–456.

LIEBERT, R. M., & SPIEGLER, M. D. (1978). *Personality: Strategies and issues.* Homewood, IL: The Dorsey Press.

LIEBERT, R. M., & WICKS-NELSON, R. (1981). *Developmental Psychology (3rd ed.).* Englewood Cliffs, NJ: Prentice-Hall.

LOSCIUTO, L. A. (1972). A national inventory of television viewing behavior. In E. A. Rubinstein, G. A. Comstock, & J. P. Murray (Eds.), *Television and social behavior* (Vol. IV: *Television in day-to-day life: Patterns of use*). Washington, D.C.: United States Government Printing Office.

MAHER, B. A. (1974). EDITORIAL. *Journal of Consulting and Clinical Psychology, 42,* 1–3.

MALMO, R. B. (1959). Activation: A neurophysiological dimension. *Psychological Review, 66,* 367–386.

MANICAS, P. T., & SECORD, P. F. (1983). Implications for psychology of the new philosophy of science. *American Psychologist,* April, 399–413.

MARLOWE, D., FRAGER, R., & NUTTALL, R. L. (1965). Commitment to action taking as a function of cognitive dissonance. *Journal of Personality and Social Psychology, 2,* 864–868.

MARTENS, R. (1969). Effects of an audience on learning and performance of a complex motor skill. *Journal of Personality and Social Psychology, 12,* 252–260.

MAY, P. R. A. (1968). *Treatment of schizophrenia.* New York: Science House.

MCCLELLAND, D. C. (1961). *The achieving society.* New York: Van Nostrand Reinhold.

MCCLELLAND, D. C., ATKINSON, J. W., CLARK, R. A., & LOWELL, E. L. (1953). *The achievement motive.* New York: Appleton-Century-Crofts.

MCGUIGAN, F. J. (1963). The experimenter: A neglected stimulus object. *Psychological Bulletin, 60,* 421–428.

MCINTYRE, C. W., FOX, R., & NEALE, J. M. (1970). Effects of noise similarity and redundancy on the information processed from brief visual displays. *Perception and Psychophysics, 7,* 328–332.

MCINTYRE, J. J., & TEEVAN, J. J. (1972). Televison violence and deviant behavior. In G. A. Comstock & E. A. Rubinstein (Eds.), *Television and social behavior* (Vol. III: *Television and adolescent aggressiveness*). Washington, D.C.: United States Government Printing Office.

MCLEOD, J. M., ATKIN, C. K., & CHAFFEE, S. H. (1972). Adolescents, parents, and television use: Self-report and other-report measures from the Wisconsin sample. In G. A. Comstock & E. A. Rubinstein (Eds.), *Television and social behavior* (Vol. III: *Television and adolescent aggressiveness*). Washington, D.C.: United States Government Printing Office.

MCNEMAR, Q. (1960). At random: Sense and nonsense. *American Psychologist, 15,* 295–300.

MEEHL, P. E. (1967). Theory testing in psychology and physics: A methodological paradox. *Philosophy of Science, 34,* 103–115.

MEEHL, P. E. (1970). Nuisance variables and the ex post facto design. In M. Radner and S. Winokur (Eds.), *Minnesota studies in philosophy of science.* Minneapolis: Univ. of Minnesota Press.

MEEHL, P. E. (1971). High school yearbooks: A reply to Schwarz. *Journal of Abnormal Psychology, 77,* 143–144.

MILLER, M. K. (1977). Potentials and pitfalls of path analysis: A tutorial summary. *Quality and Quantity, 11,* 329–346.

MILLER, N. E. (1957). Experiments on motivation. *Science, 126,* 1271–1278.

MILLER, P. M., HERSEN, M., EISLER, R. M., & WATTS, J. G. (1974). Contingent reinforcement of lowered blood/alcohol levels in an outpatient chronic alcoholic. *Behavior Research and Therapy, 12,* 261–263.

MISCHEL, W., & METZNER, R. (1962). Preference for delayed reward as a function of age, intelligence, and length of delay interval. *Journal of Abnormal and Social Psychology, 64,* 425–431.

MOOK, D. G. (1983). In defense of external invalidity. *American Psychologist,* April, 379–387.

NEALE, J. M. (1971). Perceptual span in schizophrenia. *Journal of Abnormal Psychology, 77,* 196–204.

NEALE, J. M. (1972). [Comment on "Television violence and child aggression: A follow-up study."] In G. A. Comstock & E. A. Rubinstein (Eds.), *Television and social behavior* (Vol. III: *Television and adolescent aggressiveness*). Washington, D.C.: United States Government Printing Office.

NEALE, J. M., & LIEBERT, R. M. (1969). Reinforcement therapy using aides and patients as behavioral technicians: A case report of a mute psychotic. *Perceptual and Motor Skills, 28,* 835–839.

NEALE, J. M., & LIEBERT, R. M. (1973). *Science and behavior: An introduction to methods of research.* Englewood Cliffs, N.J.: Prentice-Hall.

NEWMAN, H. H., FREEMAN, F. N., & HOLZINGER, K. J. (1937). *Twins: A study of heredity and environment.* Chicago: University of Chicago Press.

NUNNALLY, J. C. (1967). *Psychometric theory.* New York: McGraw-Hill.

ODOM, R. D., LIEBERT, R. M., & FERNANDEZ, L. E. (1969). Effects of symbolic modeling on the syntactical productions of retardates. *Psychonomic Science, 17,* 104–105.

O'LEARY, K. D., & BORKOVEC, T. D. (1978). Conceptual, methodological, and ethical problems of placebo groups in psychotherapy research. *American Psychologist, 33,* 821–830.

O'LEARY, K. D., KENT, R. N., & JENOWITZ, J. (1975). Shaping data collection congruent with experimental hypotheses. *Journal of Applied Behavior Analysis, 8,* 43–51.

ORNE, M. T. (1962). On the social psychology of the psychological experiment: With particular reference to demand characteristics and their implications. *American Psychologist, 17,* 776–783.

ORNE, M. T. (1969). Demand characteristics and the concept of quasi-controls. In R. Rosenthal & R. Rosnow (Eds.), *Artifact in behavioral research.* New York: Academic Press.

ORNE, M. T., & EVANS, F. J. (1965). Social control in the psychological experiment: Antisocial behavior and hypnosis. *Journal of Personality and Social Psychology, 1,* 189–200.

ORNE, M. T., & SCHEIBE, K. E. (1964). The contribution of nondeprivation factors in the production of sensory deprivation effects: The psychology of the panic-button. *Journal of Abnormal and Social Psychology, 68,* 3–12.

OVERALL, J. E. (1964). Note on the scientific status of factors. *Psychological Bulletin, 61,* 270–276.

PAUL, G. L. (1966). *Insight vs. desensitization in psychotherapy.* Stanford: Stanford University Press.

PILIAVIN, I. M., RODIN, J., & PILIAVIN, J. A. (1969). Good samaritanism: An underground phenomenon? *Journal of Personality and Social Psychology, 4,* 289–299.

POLITZ MEDIA STUDIES. (1958). *The readers of the "Saturday Evening Post."* Philadelphia: Curtis.

POULOS, R. W., & DAVIDSON, E. S. (1971). Effects of a short modeling film on fearful children's attitudes toward the dental situation. Unpublished manuscript, State University of New York at Stony Brook.

POULOS, R. W., & LIEBERT, R. M. (1972). The influence of modeling, exhortative verbalization, and surveillance on children's sharing. *Developmental Psychology, 6,* 402–408.

REID, J. B. (1970). Reliability assessment of observation data: A possible methodological problem. *Child Development, 41,* 1143–1150.

ROCK, I. (1983). *The logic of perception.* Cambridge: MIT Press.

ROGERS, C. R., & DYMOND, R. F. (1954). (Eds.), *Psychotherapy and personality change.* Chicago: Univ. of Chicago Press.

ROMANCZYK, R., KENT, R. N., DIAMENT, C., & O'LEARY, K. D. (1973). Measuring the reliability of observational data: A reactive process. *Journal of Applied Behavior Analysis, 6,* 175–184.

ROSÉN, L. A., O'LEARY, S. G., JOYCE, S. A., CONWAY, G., & PFIFFNER, L. J. (1984). The importance of prudent negative consequences for maintaining the appropriate behavior of hyperactive students. *Journal of Abnormal Child Psychology, 12,* 581–604.

ROSENBERG, M. J. (1965). When dissonance fails: On eliminating evaluation apprehension from attitude measurement. *Journal of Personality and Social Psychology, 1,* 18–42.

ROSENHAN, D., & SELIGMAN, M. E. P. (1984). *Abnormal psychology.* New York: W. W. Norton & Co., Inc.

ROSENTHAL, D., & FRANK, J. D. (1956). Psychotherapy and the placebo effect. *Psychological Bulletin, 53,* 294–302.

ROSENTHAL, R. (1978). Combining results of independent studies. *Psychological Bulletin, 85,* 185–193.

ROSENTHAL, R. (1967). Covert communication in the psychological experiment. *Psychological Bulletin, 67,* 356–367.

ROSENTHAL, R. (1963). Experimenter attributes as determinants of subjects' responses. *Journal of Projective Techniques and Personality Assessment, 27,* 324–331.

ROSENTHAL, R. (1966). *Experimenter bias in behavioral research.* New York: Appleton-Century-Crofts.

ROSENTHAL, R. (1978). How often are our numbers wrong? *American Psychologist,* November, 1005–1008.

ROSENTHAL, R. (1979). The "file drawer problem" and tolerance for null results. *Psychological Bulletin, 86,* 638–641.

ROSENTHAL, R., & FODE, K. L. (1963). The effect of experimenter bias on the performance of the albino rat. *Behavioral Science, 8,* 183–189.(a)

ROSENTHAL, R., & FODE, K. L. (1963). Three experiments in experimenter bias. *Psychological Reports, 12,* 491–511.(b)

ROSENTHAL, R., & GAITO, J. (1963). The interpretation of levels of significance by psychologists. *Journal of Psychology, 55,* 33–38.

ROSENTHAL, R., & ROSNOW, R. L. (1969). The volunteer subject. In R. Rosenthal & R. Rosnow (Eds.), *Artifact in behavioral research.* New York: Academic Press.

ROSENTHAL, R., & ROSNOW, R. L. (1984). *Essentials of behavioral research.* New York: McGraw-Hill.

ROSENTHAL, R., & RUBIN, D. B. (1982). Comparing effect sizes of independent studies. *Psychological Bulletin, 92,* 500–504.

ROZELLE, R., & CAMPBELL, D. T. (1969). More plausible rival hypotheses in the cross-lagged panel correlation technique. *Psychological Bulletin, 71,* 74–80.

RUSHTON, J. P., BRAINERD, C. J., & PRESSLEY, M. (1983). Behavioral development and construct validity: The principle of aggregation. *Psychological Bulletin, 94,* 18–38.

SARETSKY, G. (1972). The OEO P.C. experiment and the John Henry effect. *Phi Delta Kappan, 53,* 579–581.

SAWYER, H. G. (1961). The meaning of numbers. Speech before the American Association of Advertising Agencies.

SCHACHTER, S. (1982, April). Recidivism and self-cure of smoking and obesity. *American Psychologist,* pp. 436–444.

SCHUMAN, H., & DUNCAN, O. D. (1974). Questions about attitude survey questions. In H. L. Costner (Ed.). *Sociological methodology, 1973–1974.* San Francisco: Jossey-Bass.

SCHWARZ, J. C. (1970). [Comment on "High school yearbooks: A nonreactive measure of social isolation in graduates who later became schizophrenic"] *Journal of Abnormal Psychology, 75,* 317–318.

SELLTIZ, C., JAHODA, M., DEUTSCH, M., & COOK, S. W. (1959). *Research methods in social relations* (rev. ed.). New York: Holt, Rinehart & Winston.

SHAKOW, D. (1962). Segmental set. *Archives of General Psychiatry, 6,* 1–17.

SHIELDS, J. (1962). *Monozygotic twins brought up apart and brought up together.* London: Oxford Univ. Press.

SHONTZ, F. C. (1965). *Research methods in personality.* New York: Appleton-Century-Crofts.

SIDMAN, M. (1960). *Tactics of scientific research.* New York: Basic Books.

SIEGMAN, A. W. (1956). The effect of manifest anxiety on a concept formation task, and on timed and untimed intelligence tests. *Journal of Consulting Psychology, 20,* 176–178.

SIZEMORE, C. C., & PITTILLO, E. S. (1977). *I'm Eve.* Garden City, N.Y.: Doubleday.

SMART, R. (1966). Subject selection bias in psychological research. *Canadian Psychologist, 7,* 115–121.

SMITH, M. L., GLASS, G. V., & MILLER, T. I. (1980). *The benefits of psychotherapy.* Baltimore: Johns Hopkins University Press.

SOLOMON, R. L., & WYNNE, L. C. (1953). Traumatic avoidance learning: Acquisition in normal dogs. *Psychological Monographs, 67,* Whole No. 354.

STEVENS, S. S. (1968). Measurement, statistics and the schemapiric view. *Science, 161,* 849–856.

SULZER-AZAROFF, B., & CONSUELO DE SANTAMARIA, M. (1980). Industrial safety hazards reduction through performance feedback. *Journal of Applied Behavior Analysis, 13,* 287–295.

SWETS, J. A., & SEWALL, S. T. (1963). Invariance of signal detectability over stages of practice and levels of motivation. *Journal of Experimental Psychology, 66,* 120–126.

SYKES, A. J. M. (1965). Economic interest and the Hawthorne researches. *Human Relations, 18,* 253–263.

TATE, B. G., & BAROFF, G. S. (1966). Aversive control of self-injurious behavior in a psychotic boy. *Behavior Research and Therapy, 4,* 281–287.

THIGPEN, C. H., & CLECKLEY, H. (1954). *The three faces of Eve.* Kingsport, TN: Kingsport Press.

UNDERWOOD, B. J., & RICHARDSON, J. (1958). Studies of distributed practice XVIII. The influence of meaningfulness and intralist similarity of serial nonsense lists. *Journal of Experimental Psychology, 56,* 213–219.

WALTERS, C., SHURLEY, J. T., & PARSONS, O. A. (1962). Difference in male and female responses to underwater sensory deprivation: An exploratory study. *Journal of Nervous and Mental Disease, 135,* 302–310.

WATSON, J. B. (1913). Psychology as the behaviorist views it. *Pyschological Review, 20,* 158–177.

WATSON, J. B. (1929). *Psychology from the standpoint of a behaviorist* (3rd ed. rev.). Philadelphia: J. B. Lippincott.

WEBB, E. J., CAMPBELL, D. T., SCHWARTZ, R. D., & SECHREST, L. (1966). *Unobtrusive measures: Nonreactive research in the social sciences.* Chicago: Rand McNally.

WEIZMANN, F. (1971, February 12). Correlational statistics and the nature-nurture problem. *Science,* p. 589.

WELKOWITZ, J., EWEN, R. B., & COHEN, J. (1971). *Introductory statistics for the behavioral sciences.* New York: Academic Press.

WILLSON, V. L. (1981). Time and the external validity of experiments. *Evaluation and Program Planning, 4,* 229–238.

WINER, B. J. (1962). *Statistical principles in experimental design.* New York: McGraw-Hill.

WISPE, L. G., & FRESHLEY, H. B. (1971). Race, sex, and sympathetic helping behavior. *Journal of Personality and Social Psychology, 17,* 59–65.

ZAJONC, R. B. (1965). Social facilitation. *Science, 149,* 269–274.

ZUCKER, R. A., MANOSEVITZ, M., & LANYON, R. I. (1968). Birth order, anxiety, and affiliation during a crisis. *Journal of Personality and Social Psychology, 8,* 354–359.

Index

NAME INDEX

Achelpohl, C., 54
Akers, R., 54
Allen, V. L., 12
Allport, G. W., 25
Anastasi, A., 103
Aronson, E. 121, 181
Asch, S. 11
Atkin, C. K., 246
Ax, A. F., 117

Bacon, F., 3, 11
Ball, S., 104
Bandura, A., 176
Baral, R. A., 168
Barber, T. X., 126-27
Barlow, D. H., 218
Baroff, G. S., 213-14
Barthell, C. N., 237
Bechtel, R. B., 54
Bechtoldt, H., 48
Beecher, H. K., 17
Berkowitz, L., 230, 273
Binet, A., 38
Bless, E., 134
Boffey, P. M., 230
Bogatz, G. A., 104
Bolles, R.C., 260
Boring, E. G., 4
Borkovec, T. D., 282-83
Brainerd,C. J., 156
Bramel,D., 116n
Brehm, J. W., 279, 281
Bryan, J. H., 266

Campbell, D. T., 85, 98, 100n, 102, 121, 148, 208, 218, 229, 231, 234, 236, 239, 243, 244, 245, 245n, 249, 252, 257, 261, 263, 269, 272
Carey, A., 116n
Carlsmith, J. M., 121
Catalano, R. A., 235
Chaffee, S. H., 246
Chapin, F. S., 236
Chapman, L. J., 192
Cleckley, H., 26
Cohen, A. R., 279
Consuelo de Santamaria, M., 216
Conway, G., 219
Cook, S. W., 54
Cook, T. D., 96, 98, 105, 208, 218, 229, 234, 239, 249, 252, 257, 261, 269, 272
Cooper, H. M., 270-71
Copemann, C. D., 177
Cozby, P. C., 193
Cronbach, L. J., 47, 181

Darley, J. M., 125
Davidson, E. S., 184
Davison, G. C., 21, 27
Deutsch, M., 54
Diament, C., 127, 129
Dietz, A., 127
Dillman, D. A., 53
Dominick, J. R., 246
Donnerstein, E., 273
Dooley, D., 235
Duncan, O. D., 53
Durant, W., 3
Dush, D. M., 272
Dymond, R. F., 111

Eisler, R. M., 218
Elkind, D., 28
Epstein, S., 265
Eron, L. D., 243

Fazio, R. H., 125
Fernandez, L. E., 176, 221
Findley, M. J., 270-71
Fisch, E., 266
Fisher, R., 92
Fiske, D. W., 85
Flavell, J., 28
Flay, B. R., 96
Fode, K. L., 125, 127
Fox, R., 174
Fox, R. G., 217
Frager, R., 121
Frank, J. D., 9, 282
Franzblau, S., 44
Freedman, J. L., 134
Freeman, F. N., 66, 157, 279
Freshley, H. B., 266
Friend, R., 116n

Gaito, J., 96
Galantger, E., 291
Galton, F., 58, 123
Gardner, G. T., 284-87
Gates, A. I., 164

Glass, D. C., 284
Glass, G. V., 277
Gottman, J. M., 71-72
Greenberg, B. S., 53, 246
Greenwald, A., 96
Grice, G. R., 174-75
Gruder, C. L., 96

Hall, R. V., 217
Hamilton, D. L., 117
Heelan, P. A., 287, 289
Heinemann, E. G., 30
Heise, D. R., 228, 247, 252n
Heisenberg, W., 114
Hennigan, K. M., 96
Herrnstein, R. J., 4
Hersen, M., 218
Hirt, M. L., 272
Holmes, D. S., 237
Holmes, M., 266
Holzinger, K. J., 66
Honzik, M. P., 66
Hooke, R., 7
Hornstein, H. A., 266
Houts, A. C., 211n, 284
Huesmann, L. R., 243
Hume, D., 255
Hunsicker, J. O., 262
Hyde, J. S., 272
Hyman, R., 5

Jackson, R., 235
Jahoda, M., 54
Jenowitz, J., 127
Johnson, M. K., 32, 70, 175
Jöreskog, K. G., 252n
Jost, A., 263
Joyce, S. A., 219

Kanfer, F. H., 264
Kelman, H. C., 117
Kent, R. N., 127, 129
Kiesler, S. B., 168
Kluckhohn, F., 2
Kratochwill, T. R., 218
Kuhn, T. S., 281, 288

Lanyon, R. I., 263
Lazarus, A. A., 27
Lefkowitz, M. M., 243, 245-46
Lenneberg, E. H., 29
Levine, J. M., 12
Li, C. C., 249
Liebert, R. M., 21, 27, 32, 48, 70, 105, 166, 170, 175, 176, 177, 211n, 221, 284
LoSciuto, L. A., 54

McClelland, D. C., 123
McGaw, B., 270
McGuigan, F. J., 263
McIntyre, C. W., 174
McIntyre, J. J., 246
McLeod, J. M., 246
McNemar, Q., 194

Maher, B. A., 193
Malmo, R. B., 65
Manicas, P. T., 287-89
Manosevitz, M., 263
Marlowe, D., 121
Martens, R., 173
May, M. P. R., 192n
Meehl, P. E., 47, 96-97, 236-37
Mellgren, R. L., 262
Metzner, R., 183
Mill, J. S., 91-92
Miller, M. K., 252
Miller, N. E., 278
Miller, P. M., 218
Mischel, W., 183
Mook, D. G., 273
Morris, L. W., 21

Neale, J. M., 26, 174, 192, 245
Newman, H. H., 66
Nunnally, J. C., 65, 83n, 238n
Nuttall, R. L., 121

Odom, R. D., 221
O'Leary, K. D., 127, 129, 282-83
O'Leary, S. G., 219
Orne, M. T., 116, 118
Overall, J. E., 84

Parsons, O. A., 264
Paul, G. L., 282
Pavlov, I., 5
Pearson, K., 58
Peterson, J. K., 284
Pfiffner, L. J., 219
Piliavin, I. M., 266
Piliavin, J. A., 266
Pittillo, E. S., 26n
Politz, 122
Poulos, R. W., 166, 170, 184
Pressley, M., 156

Reid, J. B., 128
Richardson, J., 263
Rock, I., 288
Rodin, J., 266
Rogers, C. R., 111
Romanczyk, R., 129
Rosén, L. A., 219
Rosenberg, M. J., 279-81
Rosenhan, D., 283
Rosenthal, D., 282
Rosenthal, R., 96, 125, 127, 258, 264, 265, 270, 271, 271n
Rosnow, R. L., 125, 258
Ross, H. L., 231
Rozelle, R., 244-45, 245n
Rubin, D. B., 270
Rushton, J. P., 156

Saretsky, G., 107
Sawyer, H. G., 122
Schachter, S., 259-60
Scheibe, K. E., 116
Schroeder, H., 272
Schuman, H., 53
Schwartz, R. D., 121
Schwarz, J. C., 237
Sechrest, L., 121
Secord, P. F., 287-89
Seligman, M. E. P., 283
Selltiz, C., 54
Sewall, S. T., 277
Shakow, D., 191
Shields, J., 66
Shontz, F. C., 30
Shurley, J. T., 264
Sidman, M., 220
Siegman, A. W., 189-90
Silver, M. J., 126-27
Singer, J. ER., 284
Sizemore, C. C., 26n
Smart, R., 258
Smith, R., 270
Sobol, M. P., 177
Solomon, R. L., 152, 260
Sörbom, D., 252n
Stanley, J. C., 100n, 102, 148, 236, 243, 263
Strodtbeck, F., 2
Stuart, R. B., 21
Sulzer-Azaroff, B., 216
Swets, J. A., 277
Sykes, A. J. M., 116n

Tate, B. G., 213-14
Teevan, J. J., 246

Test, M. A., 266
Thigpen, C. H., 26
Thompson, J. L., 117

Underwood, B. J., 263

Walder, L. O., 243
Wallington, S. A., 134
Walters, C., 264
Watson, J. B., 5, 181
Watts, J. G., 218
Webb, E. J., 121-24
Weizmann, F., 63
White, A. M., 117
Wicks-Nelson, R., 48
Willson, V. L., 262
Winer, B. J., 144
Wispe, L. G., 266
Wundt, W., 4, 181
Wynne, L. C., 260

Zajonc, R. B., 173
Zucker, R. A., 263

SUBJECT INDEX

Note: Italicized items also appear in the Glossary of Terms

ABA design, 213
ABAB design, 213-15
ABCB design, 218-19
Active Placebo, 282
Additivity, 163-69
Age-related changes,
  identification of, 108-10
Analog research, 283
Analysis of variance (ANOVA), 170-71
Antagonistic interactions, 167-69
  in mixed designs, 189
Applied research, 16
Archives, 121, 123-24
Assembly language, 293
Associative network analysis, 245-48
Auxiliary memory, 292

Base-rate problems, 43-44
Basic research, 16
Baseline, 147
Behavioroid Measures, 121
Best possible comparisons:
  in clinical research, 283
Between-subjects comparisons, 101-2, 105-8, 137-43
Biased samples, 32
Bimodal distributions:
  and the experimenter bias effect, 130-31
Bits, 292
Blind, 127, 137n
Bytes, 292

Carryover effects, 175-78
Case study, 25, 28-31
Catalytic interactions, 165
Causal analysis, 11-12, 245-48
Causal arrow ambiguity, 229-30
Causal inference:
  from mixed designs, 189-91
  vs. forecasting, 229
Causal relationship(s), 10, 12, 89-92
Central tendency, 36-37
Changing criterion design, 217
Classificatory variables, 14-15, 182, 191
Clinical samples:
  misuse of, 259-60
Cognitive dissonance, 279-82
Cohort(s), 109
Cohort differences, 109
Compensatory equalization, 107, 119, 149-50
Compensatory rivalry, 107, 119, 149-50, 203
Component control comparisons, 284
Computers, 291-95
Construct validity, 46-48
Constructive replication, 270, 278
Content validity, 46
Control, 12
Control group(s), 147
Controlled accretion, 122-23
Controlled erosion, 122
Convergent validity, 85-86
Correlation(s), 58
  as rank order relationships, 65-67
Correlation coefficient, 58
Correlation matrix, 79
Correlational method, 14
Correlational research, 58-67
Cost-restricted sampling, 257
Counterbalancing 175-78
Counterdemand manipulation, 284
Covert assessment, 128
Criterion, 67
Criterion validity, 46
Cross-lagged panel technique, 243-44
Cross-sectional studies, 108-9
Cross-sequential designs, 110
Curvilinear relationship(s), 64-65

Debriefing, 20
"Debugging," 279n
Decomposition interrupted time series designs, 219-20
Demand characteristics, 116-19
Dependent variable, 136
  choice of, 157
Developmental trends, 108
Differential attrition, 106-7, 149-50
Differential deficit, 193
Differential incidence, 229-30
Diffusion, 107, 119, 149-50
Directionality problem, 89-90
Discriminant validity, 85-86
Distributed questionnaires, 52

Ecological validity, 256, 261-64
Effect size, 271
Empirical approach, 2
Empirical research, 7
Erosion, 121
Error variance, 51, 96, 138, 143, 155-57
Ethics:
  in social science research, 17-23
Evaluation apprehension, 279-82
Experimental control, 155
Experimental design, 142-44
Experimental method, 12
Experimenter bias, 121-31
Experimenter role, 114
Ex post facto analysis, 192, 235-38
External validity, 25, 254-74
Extreme groups technique, 194-95

Factor analysis, 80-85
Factor loadings, 81
Factorial designs, 161-63
Fatigue effect, 176
Feedback loop, 13
Field experiment(s), 264-67
File drawer problem, 271

"Fishing," 99
Flowgraphs, 247
Forced choice inventory, 120
Forecasting, 71, 229
Free random assignment, 145-46
Free random sampling, 51
F-test, 139

Haphazard sampling, 269
Hardware, 292
Hawthorne effect, 115-16
Hermeneutic view, 288
Hermeneutics, 288n
Hierarchical regression, 78
History:
as a threat to internal validity 105, 149-50, 210

Idiographic approach, 16-17, 25
Illusory residual correlation, 239-40
Impressionistic modal sampling, 269-70
Independent variable, 136
choice of, 157
Individual differences, 16-17
Induction, 255-56
Informed consent, 20
Instrument decay, 103, 149-50, 210
Interaction(s), 152, 163-69, 171, 261-62
Interitem reliability, 42
Internal validity, 100-111, 150
and external validity, 272
Interrater reliability, 42-43, 129-31
Interrupted time series designs, 209-25
Interval scale, 35
Introspection, 4
Investigator role, 114

"John Henry effect," 107, *see also Compensatory rivalry*

Loadings, *see* factor loadings
Local history, as a threat to internal validity, 206
Longitudinal studies, 109

Machine language, 293
Main effect(s), 171
Mainframe computers, 292
Manipulation check, 279
Matched random assignment, 145-47
Maturation, as a threat to internal validity, 102, 149-50, 210
Measurement error, 37, 40
Median split, 194
Meta-analysis, 270-72
Method variance, 86
Microcomputers, 292
Minicomputers, 292
Mixed design(s), 181-97
Multimethod approach, 278-79
Multiple baseline design, 215-16
Multiple causation, 163-69
Multiple correlation, 75-76
Multiple discrete leveling, 196
Multiple regression, 76-78
Multiple treatment interference, 263
Multitrait-multimethod matrix, 85-87
Multivariate research, 78-87

Narrow operationism, 277-78
Natural accretion, 122
Naturally occurring interrupted time series designs, 230-35
No-cause baseline, 245
Nominal scale, 35
Nomological net, 47
Nomothetic approach, 16, 25
Nonequivalent control group designs, 202-9
Nonprobability sampling, 49-50
Null hypothesis, 92-98
Null hypothesis testing, 92-98

Oblique, 83n
On-line data collection, 293-94
Open concept, 278
Operational definition, 277-78
Operationalization, 157-58
Operationism, 277-78
Ordinal scale, 35
Orthogonal, 83

Partial correlation, 238-40
Partial definition, 278
Partial regression coefficient, 76
Partialing, 78
Path analysis, 249-52
Period, in time series analysis, 71
Personal Preference Scale (Edwards'), 120-21
Phone surveys, 52-53
Physical traces, 121-23
Pilot testing, 279
Placebo controls, 282
Placebo effect, 97, 282-84
Plausible rival hypotheses, 101
Population(s), 31-34
Population validity, 255-61
Posttest-only control group design, 149-51
Posttest-only nonequivalent control group design, 203
Power, 98-99
Practice effect, 176
Prediction, 11
Predictive efficiency, 11
Predictor, in regression analysis, 67
Predictor variables, 75-76
Pretest-posttest control group design(s), 147-51
Pretest-posttest nonequivalent peer control group design, 204-6
Principle of aggregation, 156
Probability sampling, 49-50
Prospective study, 110
Psychophysics, 4

Quasi-experiment(s), 172, 202-25

Random assignment, 145, 207, 256
Random interruption design, 211-13
Random number table, 3
Random sample(s), 32-33
Random selection, 207, 256
Random time series single-subject design, 212
Random variance, 39
Ratio scale, 35-36
Rational approach, 2
Reactivity, 114-15, 121-24
Rectilinear relationship, 58
Regression, 67-71
as a threat to internal validity, 149-50, 210
Regression coefficient, 68, 70
Regression constant, 68
Regression-discontinuity design, 208-9
Reliable measurement, 155-56
Reliability, 8-9, 37-45
Repeated measures, 172-78
Representativeness, of samples, 32-33
Resentful demoralization, 108, 119, 149-50, 203
Response acquiescence, 119
Response deviation, 119

Response sets, 119-21
Retrospective study, 110
Rival hypotheses, 101
Role behavior, 116
Rules of membership, in defining populations, 31

Sample(s), 31-34, 45
Sample of convenience, 256
Sample range, and correlation, 63
Sample size, 51, 96
Sampling, of items, 44-45
Scales of measurement, 34-36
Scatter diagram, 59
Science, defined, 5
Scientific report writing, 296-308
Selection, as a threat to internal validity, 150
Selection bias, 106, 145
Selection-maturation, as a threat to internal validity, 202
Self-fulfilling prophecy, 125-31
Self-selection, 258-59
Shared variance, 59-61
Significant difference, 140 (*See also* Statistical significance)
Simulated posttest-only design with a cohort control, 206
Simulated pretest-posttest control group design, 207
Single-subject quasi-experiments, 225
Situational tests, 38
Social desirability, 119
Social facilitation theory, 173
Software, 292
Solomon four group design, 153
Spectral decomposition, in time series analysis, 71
Spontaneous remission, 111
Standard deviation, 37
Standard(ized) scores, 70, 105
Statistical conclusion validity, 98-100
Statistical power, See *power*
Statistical regression, as a threat to internal validity, 104-5
Statistical significance, 62-63
Stratification, 51-52
Stratified random sampling, 51
Structural equations, in causal analysis, 247
Subject role, 114
Survey research, 49-54
Systematic interviews, 53-54
Systematic variance, 39, 138, 140, 143, 154

Table of random numbers, 145
Temporal precedence, 235
Temporal validity, 262
Terminantive interaction(s), 165-67
Test-retest reliability, 40-42
Testing, as a threat to internal validity, 103, 149-50, 210
Theoretical validity, 46, 273, 276-90, (*see also* Construct validity)
Third variable, 239-40
Third variable problem, 90-91
Time lagged correlations, 240-45
Time series, 71-72
Total design method, 53
Treatment strength, 160, (*see also* *Effect size*)
"True experiment," 130-43
True score, 37, 156
Truncated range, 63
Type I error, 92-98
Type II error, 92-98

Unobtrusive measures, 121-24
Unobtrusive observation, 121, 124

Validity, 37, 45-48, 54
Variable, defined, 10
Variability, 33-34, 37
Variance, 37
overlap in, 141
Venn diagrams, 76
Volunteer bias, 258-59

Within-subjects comparisons, 101-5
Word processing, 294-95